The Ponzi Class:

Ponzi Economics, Globalization and

Class Oppression in the 21st Century

Michael William

Copyright © 2015 Michael William
All rights reserved.
ISBN:
ISBN-13: 978-1519670366
ISBN -10: 1519670362

PREFACE

In writing this book I am aware of its development and that it was originally intended to be two separate books; one dealing with Keynesianism, and one dealing with free trade.

I commenced the book on Keynesianism and as it progressed it became increasingly clear that to properly understand the true influence of Keynes and the economic difficulties of the 1920s and 1930s then an account of the struggle between those adhering to free trade and those advocating tariff reform had to be given. The economic history of the 1920s and 1930s is one dominated by disinformation and myth. I aim to set the record straight. That is why I decided to combine the two intended books. Out of this combination emerges a synergy and a third book that has become this book's title.

I am conscious that I have included a large number of quotes, some of which are quite lengthy. This particularly applies to the chapters on List and Joseph Chamberlain. Personally, I prefer to read what someone actually said rather than to read what someone else claims they said, or to read a paraphrase of what was said in which the thrust of the argument is lost. Sometimes to read the original is a pleasure due to its eloquence. With List, there is a sense of anger and frustration in his writing that is hopefully conveyed in the quotes given. He also develops his case well. With Chamberlain, it is a joy to read his speeches and to appreciate that he was a gifted orator. Chamberlain lived in an era before television and when people would attend public meetings to engage with politicians and hear what they had to say. I have tried to transmit the excitement of those meetings by quoting from his speeches at length; the quotes convey his conviction, his patriotism and are very entertaining.

My own cynicism with and contempt for contemporary politicians is demonstrated by the final chapters. This should be contrasted with my respect for Joseph Chamberlain, who was one of those rare politicians who genuinely wished to do the best for his country and its people. He was not a vote-catching career politician. He won elections by the brilliance of his campaigning. He was a man of principle and was prepared to sacrifice his career for his country.

I am aware that the chapters dealing with economic theory, especially Keynesianism, can be heavy going. I have tried to keep these parts short and to relate the theories as closely as possible to historic events. The chapter on Keynes' *General Theory* is a useful interlude before the account of the struggle between the Free Traders and the Tariff Reformers is recommenced.

Winston Churchill does not emerge well in this book. I did not set out to tarnish his reputation at all, and was surprised at where the historical evidence led. He was undoubtedly a great war leader. Regarding the economy, however, he was a menace.

The case set out in the closing chapters draws upon the history previously set out, including the examination of the development of economic theories, and is supported by the setting out of a large amount of facts of Britain's contemporary predicament. The other EU countries and the USA share Britain's problems. Furthermore, the USA is not in a dissimilar position to the declining Britain of the early 20th century.

If this book does set the record straight, if readers enjoy my account of the Tariff Reform Campaign as much as I enjoyed writing it, and if in consequence there is a more open debate about issues currently dominated by dogma, then this book will have been worth the effort.

Michael William
December 2015

Also by Michael William

Brexit Means Brexit: How the British Ponzi Class Survived the EU Referendum
The Genesis of Political Correctness: The Basis of a False Morality
Multiculturalist Ideology (Part One): A Rationale For Race War Politics
Multiculturalist Ideology (Part Two): The Rising Tide of Race War Politics

Table of Contents

1 INTRODUCTION 1
2 THE CLASSICAL SCHOOL AND THE GLUT THEORISTS . . 7
3 LIST AND THE CLASSICAL SCHOOL 15
4 JOSEPH CHAMBERLAIN AND THE TARIFF REFORM CAMPAIGN 33
5 THE GENERAL THEORY 87
6 THE INTER-WAR YEARS 113
7 POST 1945 BOOM AND COLLAPSE 147
8 THE MONETARIST EXPERIMENT 185
9 ASPECTS OF THE 2008/13 SLUMP 201
10 INFLATIONISM 227
11 TRADE POLICY AND THE TRADE DEFICIT 239
12 PONZI ECONOMICS 285
13 CONCLUSION 349

1 INTRODUCTION

'Ricardo conquered England as completely as the Holy Inquisition conquered Spain.' – John Maynard Keynes

'The ideas of economists and political philosophers, both when they are right and when they are wrong, are more powerful than is commonly understood. Indeed the world is ruled by little else. Practical men, who believe themselves to be quite exempt from any intellectual influences, are usually the slaves of some defunct economist. Madmen in authority, who hear voices in the air, are distilling their frenzy from some academic scribbler of a few years back.'[1]
– John Maynard Keynes

'The same people who would never touch deficit spending are now tossing around billions. The switch from decades of supply-side politics all the way to a crass Keynesianism is breathtaking. When I ask about the origins of the crisis, economists I respect tell me it is the credit-financed growth of recent years and decades. Isn't this the same mistake everyone is suddenly making again, under all the public pressure?' – Peer Steinbrück, The SPD German Finance Minister, speaking in December 2008

The credit crunch and the slump of early 21st century had the effect of resurrecting the early 20th century economic ideology developed by Keynes (1883-1946). In saying this one needs to be careful, as Keynes died in 1946 and he did not live to witness the implementation of what became known as Keynesianism and there is evidence that shortly before his death he was growing increasingly alarmed at what was being advocated in his name and the manner in which his ideas were being presented.

Keynes' writing was prolific. He not only had articles published in the press and academic journals but also wrote a number of books and essays. His two most prominent books were *Treatise on Money* (*Treatise*) and *The General Theory of Employment Interest and Money* (*General Theory*). The *General Theory* was his key work and it is from this book that Keynesianism was derived. The *General Theory* was the end result of Keynes' thinking at that time and he had not yet had the opportunity to change his mind on what he had written, as he had already done with *Treatise*. The *General Theory* is inconsistent with *Treatise* in many respects.

Nevertheless, the *General Theory* was the basis of the launch of Keynesianism after World War II (WWII) and has been declared by many as the reason for the low unemployment and high growth rate that the West in general enjoyed up until the 1970s when, in Britain, the hegemony of the prevailing economic theory collapsed amidst a decade of economic crises, industrial unrest ultimately culminating in the Winter of Discontent, stagflation (where inflation is combined with a stagnant growth rate and increasing unemployment), and the rise of monetarism.

In the 1980s Keynesian diehards continued to advocate favoured economic policies, and delivered a Keynesian critique of the monetarist experiment. But it was not until the credit crunch of 2008 and the banking crisis, that Keynesianism staged a determined come back. The Germans rejected this resurrection as 'crass Keynesianism' and were unpersuaded in the calls to adopt an expansionist economic policy. The banking crisis managed to drag down the wider economies of many Western countries, especially Britain and the USA, and the plight of Europe has been dangerously compounded by the euro and the falling output of several Eurozone countries, notably Greece.

To what extent is the post-credit crunch lurch towards Keynesiansm consistent with what the *General Theory* actually said? What is the *General Theory's* relevance? This book will begin by examining the prevailing economic ideologies of the classical school of economists and their critics, dubbed 'inflationists' or glut theorists, and their arguments, before examining the thinking of the German economist Friedrich List (1789-1846). Next will be an examination of the impact of Joseph Chamberlain (1836-1914) and the Tariff Reform Campaign – the historical importance of which is too easily understated if not completely ignored; at the start of the 20th century there was a bitterly fought and titanic power struggle that, by comparison, makes Britain's divisions regarding the EU a century later look like a teenage lovers' tiff. This will be followed by the setting out of the thrust of Keynesian ideology, what it advocated and why. It will then resume the historical narrative and examine the context in which Keynes advanced his theory (and it is important to remember that it was only an abstract theory and not a policy based on experience); this will involve an examination of the slump of the inter-war years and its causes and the resolution. It will be clear from this examination which economic ideology was responsible for the inter-war slump and which was responsible for the recovery.

This book will then give an account of the implementation of Keynesianism post World War II and of its crisis in the 1970s, before looking at the advent of monetarist experiment. Then there will be an examination of the aspects of the slump beginning in 2008 – with the emergence not of Keynesianism, but of Ponzi economics and the rise of the Ponzi class. This will also involve an analysis of the current trading policies of the leading economies today and the impact of the policy of globalization.

Globalization is presented as something new, beneficial and inevitable. We are told that Britain, as a trading country, must embrace globalization. Nevertheless, it should not be forgotten that Britain has been an international trading country for centuries without the trappings of what we now call globalization. The exploration of Africa, the opening up of trade routes to the Far East, and the colonization of North America were all a form of globalization at the time. The construction of railways and the merchant fleet for shipping were all a means of facilitating international trade. Today, globalization is something different. It does not reflect the power of Britain's economic might, but its weakness. Instead of exporting goods, services and emigrants, Britain now imports goods, services and immigrants. Globalization involves not development of undeveloped territories, but the deindustrialization of Britain. Foreigners now buy up Britain's assets and businesses; Britain's borders are, in practice, controlled by people smugglers including organised crime rackets, Al Qaeda and IS (IS is estimated to have pocketed as much as $323million from its people smuggling operations). Britain no longer colonizes but is being colonized. Globalization might be new, but it is neither benevolent nor inevitable.

This is not an economics book. It is not aimed at economists. It is a political book and is written for the ordinary person who is interested in finding out more about the basic differences in economic philosophy and how they are relevant to the present economic situation – which is far from over despite all the bold talk hailing Britain's return to growth. The banks continue to horde money, banking scandals continue to emerge, and the Eurozone remains an experiment the outcome of which is uncertain; the prospects for many countries are dire. The British government continues to promise austerity – and hence the attendant falling living standards – into the future.

This book will conclude that the economic policy being served up is neither Keynesianism, nor crass Keynesianism, but Ponzi economics. The policy is one of Ponzi economics for the benefit of the Ponzi class. The British economy is being run as a Ponzi scheme and faces the ultimate outcome of any Ponzi scheme: financial ruin amidst a pile of debt and unpaid bills. The policy of Ponzi economics is part and parcel of the current manifestation of free trade – globalization; and the rise of the Ponzi class – a class, despite some internal differences, who are politically correct with a belief that they are entitled to spend public monies on themselves and encompass most of the three main political parties, the banks, multinationals, the corporate sector, the unions, most charities, the media, senior civil servants and an array of quangos. They are the ruling class.

Oppression in the 21st century is not, contrary to clapped-out Marxist ideology from the mid-19th century, perpetuated by the bourgeoisie but by the Ponzi class, who grab and waste public monies on themselves and their own pet projects, leaving ordinary people poorer.

There is an alternative, and that is to learn the *real* lessons of the inter-war years and adopt proven, practical, common-sense policies to steer Britain back to prosperity, growth and a better quality of life, with higher standards of living for ordinary people.

While this book is written from a British perspective, with some references to the USA, the issues raised apply to many countries across the West and those from other countries can reflect on how they likewise are affected.

For ease of understanding, the book refers to the Unionist Party, the Conservative Party and the Tory Party. The Unionist Party was an alliance between the Conservatives and the Liberal Unionists, who had split from the Liberal Party over home rule for Ireland (the Liberal Party becoming fragmented into various groups). Eventually the Conservatives and the Liberal Unionists merged to form the Conservative and Unionist Party (to give it its full and formal name). The term Tory has been informally used as an alternative to Conservative in Britain for a very long time. The Tories and the Conservatives are seen as one and the same. This book will prefer the term Tory, as the Conservative Party ceased to be Conservative politically some time in the 1980s. Margaret Thatcher could be more accurately described as a classical liberal (with a philosophy focused on free trade and free markets) rather than a Conservative. Post-WWII, the Tories have absorbed free trade liberals with the demise of the Liberal Party as a party of government (in 2015 there remains a rump Liberal Party, having no MPs, and the Liberal Democrats who have a handful of MPs and who were recently in coalition government with the Tories). By 2015, the Tories have forcefully adopted the ideology of political correctness, which is totally incompatible with Conservative philosophy. However, historically, Tory and Conservative are interchangeable terms.

2 THE CLASSICAL SCHOOL AND THE GLUT THEORISTS

An economy has been defined as a community amongst whom resources are shared. It had been traditionally believed that this was best achieved by allowing market forces and free enterprise to operate with the minimum of interference and regulation from government.[2] The dominant economic theory in Britain in the 19th century, advanced by the classical economists, was, put simply: laissez-faire economics involving a minimal role for the state; that free markets were the best way of allocating resources; that the market would ensure that supply equalled demand; and a commitment to free trade.

Jean Baptiste Say, the originator of what became known as Say's Law, was a Frenchman born in 1767 in Lyons. Say was the opposite to Keynes as he held that: 'The encouragement of mere consumption is no benefit to commerce,' and he further asserted that: 'It is the aim of good government to stimulate production, of bad government to encourage consumption'.[3] JS Mill, a classical economist, set out Say's Law in *Principles of Political Economy* thus:

> 'What constitutes the means of payment for commodities is simply commodities. Each person's means of paying for the productions of other people consist of those which he himself possesses. All sellers are inevitably, and by the meaning of the word, buyers. Could we suddenly double the productive powers of the country, we should double the supply of commodities in every market; but we should, by the same stroke, double the purchasing power. Everybody would bring a double demand as well as supply; everybody would be able to buy twice as much, because every one would have twice as much to offer in exchange.'[4]

Say's Law, that supply creates its own demand, has been controversial since its formulation. It has caused heated debate amongst economists in the early 19th century and did so again one hundred years later with the advent of Keynesianism. The controversies lasted decades in each case, involved all leading economists at the time and were central to economic understanding. The difference between the 19th and 20th century debates is that in the 19th century those who supported Say's Law prevailed, whilst in the 20th century the Keynesians prevailed.

Both Thomas Malthus, a British cleric and scholar (1766-1834) and the Genevan writer Sismondi (1773-1842) disputed Say's Law (Karl Marx obviously rejected it, describing Say as 'inane', 'miserable', 'thoughtless', 'dull', 'comical', and a 'humbug'. He dismissed Say's Law as 'preposterous', 'a paltry evasion', 'childish babble', and 'pitiful claptrap'. Marx denied that supply would equal demand on the basis that such would involve a prediction of relative prices.[5]). Malthus was of the opinion that there could be a 'general glut' of excessive production.[6] The glut theorists, Sismondi and Malthus in particular, were also concerned at the prospect of over-investment. Sismondi advanced a theory of equilibrium income in 1819 and both his theory and Malthus's own attracted attacks from those who adhered to Say's Law. John Stuart Mill's *Principles* in 1848 ended the general glut controversy[7] and those who still advocated the general glut theory were no longer taken seriously. It was only the advent of Keynes and his various articles and books that the attack on Say's Law was once again treated as valid.

Adam Smith's *The Wealth of Nations* put forward three key aspects of Say's Law. Firstly, money was merely a means to enable the barter of goods. It did not alter the real economy. Money was neutral. Smith believed that although money constitutes a demand for products, products also constitute a demand for money. Smith repeatedly asserted that products purchase money. Secondly, Smith believed that savings are always invested: 'The consumption is the same, but the consumers are different'. Thirdly, saving and not consumption promotes growth.[8]

Say endorsed Smith and in his *Traite d'economie politique*, Say asserted that savings are always invested, that money's role is to facilitate barter and that the volume of money had no effect on the volume of real transactions. The volume of transactions created the demand for money and not vice versa: 'This shows, I hope, that it is certainly not so much the abundance of money which makes outlets easy, but the abundance of other products in general. This is one of the most important truths in political economy'.[9]

Say's Law therefore holds that real purchasing power is determined by the level of production. People can buy more things as they have themselves more to sell to pay for those things. Supply creates its own demand. Say's Law further held that there could be no general overproduction and that if there were an oversupply of one type of good then there would also be a corresponding under-supply of other goods. Say said: 'a glut can take place only when there are too many means of production applied to one kind of product and not enough to another'.[10]

Both Say and Mill acknowledged that there could only be a disequilibrium internally within an economy but that there could not be a general disequilibrium of aggregate supply. The economist David Ricardo, 1772-1823, in his *Principles of Political Economy* attempted to reconcile the theory of Say's Law with the experiences of economic downturns and unemployment. Ricardo believed that such were caused by changes in consumer demand, transition from a wartime economy to peacetime, and bad economic legislation. During these transitional phases of the economy, 'much fixed capital is unemployed, perhaps wholly lost, and labourers are without full employment'. Although Ricardo thought that the transitional period should be short, he remarked that the post-Napoleonic depression lasted longer than he expected due to the resistance of people to move to new employment in the belief that if they just hung on long enough then there would be a change for the better. On this concept, Ricardo wrote: 'it is at all times the bad adaptation of the commodities produced to the wants of mankind which is the specific evil, and not the abundance of commodities'. It was this lack of adaptation that was 'the only cause of the stagnation which commerce at different times experiences'.[11] Ricardo was however more fixated on the long run as he conceded regarding his dispute with Malthus:

> 'It appears to me that one great cause of our difference in opinion, on the subjects which we have so often discussed, is that you have always in your mind the immediate and temporary effects of particular changes – whereas I put these immediate and temporary effects quite aside, and fix my whole attention on the permanent state of things which will result from them.'[12]

Sismondi feared that government intervention would lead not only to over-investment and overproduction in particular sectors by reallocating resources from other sectors of the economy, but would also lead to an above equilibrium level of aggregate investment and output, ultimately causing a higher than equilibrium level of population, via higher wages, which could only be subsequently reduced by poverty and starvation.[13]

Malthus argued that even if the markets had an ability to rebalance, this did not prove that there was still something wrong in the first place and that the delay before the markets could correct constituted 'serious spaces' in peoples' lives.[14] The classical economists were adamant in their denial of the possibility of a general glut as, to them, if some goods were sold at less than the cost of production then other goods were being sold at above their cost of production. Malthus believed that a monetary analysis was necessary to properly understand the economy – i.e. money does matter.[15]

Those who supported Say's Law rejected that there was a need to promote consumption and that money invested and spent on capital goods was demand and that there was therefore nothing to be gained from changing the type of demand as the overall position would remain unchanged; they further believed that as the desire for consumption was 'insatiable' there was no need to encourage it and that whatever was produced would be consumed; they believed that there was no 'indisposition to consume' but only an indisposition to produce; and that international trade would only reduce the cost of production (by buying cheaper raw materials for production) or by allowing a different mix of goods to be consumed.[16]

While Sismondi and Malthus agreed with the proponents of Say's Law that desires were basically insatiable, they believed that those desires were tempered by a willingness to work for or pay to achieve them; in which case those desires were not insatiable if people were not prepared to make the 'sacrifices' to realise them.[17]

Say himself acknowledged that some goods might be sold at less than the cost of production. However, he reconciled his theory by excluding such goods 'made inconsiderately' from his definition of production, which only included those goods which were sold at prices sufficient to cover production costs. Having adopted this mental manoeuvre, Say could then claim that the theory was true.[18] The problem therefore becomes that although supply may always find a market, but it may not do so at a profitable price – and hence the production is unsustainable.

Of these influential figures on Keynes, Thomas Sowell, an American economist and political philosopher, wrote:

> 'One of the striking similarities among the major pre-Keynesian critics of Say's Law is that most of them were *not* primarily economists. Sismondi achieved fame as an historian, Lauderdale was a politician, Malthus a population theorist, Chalmers a moral and social philosopher, and Marx a revolutionary and theorist of history. Hobson could better be described as a crank whose prolific writings often dealt with economics than as an economist with unorthodox views. By contrast, Say, Ricardo, and McCulloch were primarily and almost exclusively economists, as were of course all the leading figures in the neoclassical tradition.'[19]

Keynes took particular exception to Ricardo, who he held responsible for dominating economic thought in Britain. Ricardo was an influential economist, who was involved in the debate about gluts and Says Law, and he was further responsible for the concept of comparative advantage, which is the received wisdom on the issue of free trade to this day.

Ricardo's writing is coloured by the nature of the economy at the time, and its reliance on agriculture. In dealing with rent, for example, he deals solely with agricultural rent and ignores rents in urban society.[20] He deals with the problems of rent relating to the different quality of land. Ricardo assumed that there was only one quality of labour.[21]

Ricardo, in one of a number of letters, wrote to Malthus: 'I can see no soundness in the reasons you give for the usefulness of demand on the part of unproductive consumers. How their consuming, without reproduction, can be beneficial to a country, in any possible state of it, I confess I cannot discover'.[22] With his tongue in cheek he wrote about 'Mr Malthus' peculiar theory is that supplies may be so abundant that they may not find a market' and suggested that we: 'petition the King to dismiss his present economical (*sic*) ministers, and replace them by others who would more effectually promote the best interests of the country by promoting public extravagance and expenditure. We are, it seems, a nation of producers, and have few consumers amongst us, and the evil has at last become of that magnitude that we shall be irretrievably miserable if the parliament or the ministers do not immediately adopt an efficient plan of expenditure'.[23] Ricardo further wrote: 'A body of unproductive labourers are just as necessary and as useful, with a view to future production, as a fire which would consume in the manufacturer's warehouse the goods which those unproductive labourers would otherwise consume'. Ricardo further wrote: 'If the people will not expend enough themselves, what can be more expedient than to call upon the state to spend it for them? What could be more wise, if Mr Malthus' doctrine be true, than to increase the army and double the salaries of all the officers of the government?'[24]

For Ricardo, demand and supply must always balance as a producer does so in order either to consume the goods himself or else to exchange them so that he can consume the other goods bought by the exchange. If he produces with neither intention, then they are not proper goods. Say held that this was so and defined goods as being created as 'to give a thing a recognised value susceptible of procuring in exchange another thing of equal value'.[25] For Ricardo the law of demand and supply also applied to the value of money. Ricardo wrote: 'An alteration in the value of money has no effect on the relative value of commodities, for it raises or sinks their price in the same proportion'.[26] To Ricardo: 'Productions are always bought by productions or by services; money is only the medium by which exchange is effected'.[27] Money, then, is said not to change the underlying working of the economy. (However, a nuclear power station would be unlikely to be built or operated in a barter economy.)

Ricardo tended to blame the labourers for their poverty as they had made no attempt, were such possible, to restrict the supply of labour to the demand for labour. He did make an exception for war when the eventual peace would lead to a switch back to a wartime economy, the redundancy of the former soldiers and other employed in the war economy, and the inevitable competition for jobs making peacetime goods.[28] Malthus agreed with this when he wrote:

> 'From the harvest of 1815 to the harvest of 1816, there cannot be a doubt that the funds for the maintenance of labour in this country were unusually abundant. Corn was particularly plentiful, and no other necessaries were deficient; yet it is an acknowledged fact that great numbers were thrown out of employment.'[29]

Malthus concluded from this: 'The failure of home demand filled the warehouses of the manufacturers with unsold goods, which urged them to export more largely at all risks. But this excessive exportation glutted all the foreign markets, and prevented the merchants from receiving adequate returns'.[30] The economic difficulties after the outbreak of peace following the Napoleonic wars led to Malthus complaining at the amount of unsold goods.

Ricardo tended to regard money as gold, the British gold sovereign, and this is reflected in his writing. On the value of money, Ricardo wrote: 'To say that commodities are raised in price is the same thing as to say that money is lowered in relative value; for it is by commodities that the relative value of gold is estimated'. He repeats this again: 'The advance in the value of money is the same thing as a decline in the price of commodities'. And again: 'When gold is cheap, commodities are dear; and when gold is dear, commodities are cheap'.[31]

To remedy the rise in the price of gold, Ricardo advocated a change in the value of the paper currency: 'The remedy which I propose for all the evils in our currency, is that the Bank should gradually decrease the amount of their notes in circulation until they shall have rendered the remainder of equal value with the coins which they represent, or in other words, till the prices of gold and silver bullion shall be brought down to their mint price'. And: 'That commodities would rise or fall in price in proportion to the increase or diminution of money, I assume, as a fact which is incontrovertible'.[32] This is of course entirely consistent with Monetarist thought 150 years later.

As the debate raged on to the point of exhaustion, and given the adjustments to each side's position, Say was able to write to Malthus in 1827 and state: 'Our discussion on markets begins to be no more than a dispute over words'.[33] Even so, the debate continued between economists regarding the general glut theory and despite the mutual understanding achieved, John Stuart Mill delivered his own riposte in his *Principles of Political Economy* in 1848. Mill's blast was forceful and, arguably, his book became the leading work on economics until Keynes's *General Theory*.

SUMMARY

The dominant economic reasoning in 19th century Britain was put forward by the classical economists. This reasoning involved a commitment to free markets, free trade and a government policy of laissez-faire. There was a protracted argument about the role of money and the possibility of gluts – or conversely a shortage of money and consumption.

The classical economists rejected the concept of gluts and underconsumption and relied upon what became known as Say's Law: that supply creates its own demand; that producers increase their production in order to sell more goods to buy more goods. Society becomes wealthier as people produce more to trade more and hence consume more. The glut theorists held that money did matter and that there could be a shortage of money and of consumption; and that a market was not necessarily self-correcting. They believed that a lack of consumption could cause an economic recession.

A key period was that following the Napoleonic Wars, when there was an economic downturn and unemployment as the economy switched back to peacetime production. Such a major economic shock had a serious impact that even the classical school acknowledged was a difficulty and that a longer period of time was necessary before the market was ultimately able to correct itself. The classical school remained unconvinced that there could ever be a general glut or that there could ever be a lack of consumption. The classical school triumphed in the debate with their critics and held sway until the advent of Keynes, who, like the glut theorists, was concerned that a lack of consumption could cause an economic downturn.

3 LIST AND THE CLASSICAL SCHOOL

Ricardo theorized that countries should specialise in those goods in which they had a comparative advantage. Even if a country could produce all goods better than another it would still be in the interests of both countries for the more advanced country to concentrate on producing that which offered the greatest advantage, and import other items from the less efficient country; likewise, the less efficient country should concentrate on producing those items in which it had the least cost disadvantage.[34] Each country would concentrate on producing those goods which it could do best and not produce those goods which it could buy from other countries even if, had it wanted to, it could in fact produce such goods better itself. In this way resources would be allocated to maximum efficiency and world output would be maximised. Free trade was a cornerstone of the theory of comparative advantage.

The theory does not take account of the need to develop manufacturing industry, nor does it take account of the need to achieve growth. The theory justifies the case for free trade and rationalises the case for free markets to allocate resources and output most efficiently; it assumes that workers and resources can easily move from one occupation or location to another when such changes may not always be easy, especially if a fall in incomes is involved as well. There will be a resistance to change. Ricardo's theory assumed that there was no change in the levels of technology, which might be true in the short term but not in the long term.[35] Today, the removal of capital controls and the policy of globalization means that capital can move across borders and may not therefore be available for internal investment for local industry – irrespective of the theory of comparative advantage.

Adam Smith's *Wealth of Nations*, which advocated free markets and free trade, was published in 1776, but it was not until the middle of the next century that Britain adopted a policy of *unilateral* free trade. Ricardo's theory of comparative advantage helped this move. The repeal of the Corn Laws, the Navigation Acts (which required all trade with Britain had to be transported using British ships[36]) and other tariffs in the 1840s were the decisive moment when Britain embraced *unilateral* free trade.

Other countries rejected Smith and Ricardo and preferred the arguments of Friedrich List. They did not adopt either the free trade or comparative advantage theories and learned from the way in which British manufacturing had been established and developed in its infancy.

Britain had been a relatively backward economy until the reign of the Tudors, paying for imports by exporting raw wool, especially to the Low Countries which had a well developed and highly profitable cloth production industry. Henry VII recruited skilled workers from the Low Countries to work in England, and increased the export tax on raw wool, aiming to increase the home production of wool products. In 1489, the export of unfinished cloth was banned, except for some cheap course items, and this policy was continued by Henry VIII. Nearly a century later, Elizabeth I banned all export of wool in 1578 to make it harder for the Dutch to compete with British clothmaking. By this time the production of cloth in Britain was advanced and the loss of raw materials dealt a serious blow to competitors in the Low Countries. Britain had developed from being an exporter of raw wool into a wool manufacturer. The export of wool manufactures became Britain's most important industry, accounting for 70% of all English exports in 1700 and still more than 50% of exports as late as 1770, and funded the import of raw materials and food which enabled the industrial revolution.[37]

A similar experience was achieved with the cotton industry, whose initial progress was slow until the government banned cotton imports, including fine cloths from the East India Company; once the industry was established, it was supported by an export bounty introduced in 1780, when the annual cotton exports were £370,000. By 1812, cotton exports had grown to £16,000,000.[38]

The same principle applied to the development of Britain's colonies, trade with which was reserved for Britain. In return, they received a variety of subsidies and preferences with strong positive results. For example, the North American Colonies in 1704 could only afford £500,000 a year worth of British goods; yet by 1772 this figure had grown to £5,000,000. Edmund Burke (1729-1797) described the colonial system as a 'hotbed' of growth well beyond what would have been achieved by 'the slow, languid operations of unassisted nature. Nothing in the history of mankind is like their progress'.[39]

Robert Walpole, the first British prime minister, stated: 'It is evident that nothing so much contributes to promote the public well-being as the exportation of manufactured goods and the importation of foreign raw material'.[40] In 1721, Walpole raised the tariffs in imported manufactures significantly and either abolished or reduced the tariffs on raw materials used for manufactures. Export subsidies for manufactures were introduced, as were quality control regulations to protect the quality and hence reputation of British goods. These measures remained in place for the next century. In 1820, the average tariff on imported manufactured goods was 45-55%, compared to 6-8% in the Low Countries, 8-12% in Germany and Switzerland, and around 20% in France.[41] Britain banned the development of rolling and slitting steel mills in America and cotton textile imports from India.

In 1699, the Wool Act banned the export of woollen cloth from colonies to other countries and hence competing with British goods.[42] In 1770, on being informed that the American colonies were creating new industries, Pitt the Elder declared that '[The New England] colonies should not be permitted to manufacture so much as a horseshoe nail'.[43]

In the period from 1700 to 1850 Britain had used protectionist measures to protect its industry and promote economic growth, with manufacturing tariffs of up to 55%. From 1738 onwards, the tariffs used to protect the development of the iron industry varied from 40 to several hundred per cent.[44] Ja Joon Chang wrote in *Bad Samaritans*:

> 'Tariffs on imported manufactured goods were significantly raised, while tariffs on raw materials used for manufacture were lowered or even dropped altogether. These policies are strikingly similar to those used with such success by the "miracle" economies of East Asia such as Japan, Korea, and Taiwan, after the Second World War.'[45]

The USA likewise used protectionist measures to industrialize and, like Britain, only embraced free trade once it considered its economic power to be supreme; meanwhile the British commitment to free trade assumed almost a religious fervour unlike any other country. In the late 19th century British manufactures were steadily priced out of US and European markets and eventually even out of the British market itself due to cheaper imports. In 1880, Britain's share of manufacturing output was 23%; in 1913 it was only 10%. Britain's share of world trade likewise fell from 23% to 14%.[46]

All four parts of List's work, *The History, The Theory, The Systems,* and *The Politics of National Economy* were written before 1844 and before the repeal of the Corn Laws, the Navigation Laws and other British tariffs; German industry was still in its infancy. List was therefore writing about matters which would soon change. List's ideas influenced both Germany and the USA. The basic idea advocated by List is that there should be the free import of raw materials and agricultural produce, combined with protection of home manufacturing by means of a modest tariff.[47] List was a keen advocate of a national policy and not the 'universal trade' policy adopted by Britain alone. List's view was that the liberty of individual citizens required the freedom to trade internally, that was not the case when dealing with foreign countries:

> 'Freedom of trade is spoken of in the same terms as religious freedom and municipal freedom. Hence the friends and advocates of freedom feel themselves especially bound to defend freedom in all its forms. And thus the term "free trade" has become popular without drawing the necessary distinction between freedom of internal trade within the State and freedom of trade between separate nations, notwithstanding that these two in their nature and operation are as distinct as the heaven is from the earth.'[48]

List highlighted that nations, 'so long as they remain in a state of barbarism', favour unrestricted trade as it enables them to trade 'raw products of every kind' for better clothing, materials, machines and equipment that they cannot produce for themselves; 'but experience also shows that those very nations, the farther advances that they make for themselves in culture and in industry, regard such a system of trade with a less favourable eye, and that at last they come to regard it as injurious and as a hindrance to their further progress'.[49] List wrote:

'[England's] merchant shipping and her foreign commerce rested on the solid basis of her native agriculture and native industry; her internal trade developed itself in just proportion to her foreign trade, and individual freedom grew up without prejudice to national unity or to national power; in her case the interests of the Crown, the aristocracy, and the people became consolidated and united in the happiest manner.'[50]

Regarding the demise of the Hanseatic League (a commercial and defensive confederation of merchant guilds and towns along the north European coast), List wrote:

'How, therefore, and for what reason could such a profound inquirer [Adam Smith] permit himself to abstain from an investigation at once so interesting and so fruitful in results? We can see no other reason than this – that it would have led to conclusions which would have tended but little to support his principle of absolute free trade. He would infallibly have been confronted with the fact that after free commercial intercourse with the Hansards had raised English agriculture from a state of barbarism, the protective commercial policy adopted by the English nation at the expense of the Hansards, the Belgians, and the Dutch helped England to attain to manufacturing supremacy, and that from the latter, aided by her Navigation Acts, arose her commercial supremacy.'[51]

List insisted: 'The source and origin of England's industrial and commercial greatness must be traced mainly to the breeding of sheep and to the woollen manufacture'.[52] This was brought about by England taking advantage of the knowledge and expertise of Hanseatic League imported into England coupled with a favourable environment created by the British government. It is estimated that during the reign of James I, the woollen manufactures exports amounted to 90% of all English exports.[53] The woollen industry and exports, coupled with the growth of coastal trade and fishing, supported by the Navigation Laws, which created England's maritime supremacy.[54] List wrote:

19

> 'The island kingdom borrowed from every country of the Continent its skill in special branches of industry, and planted them on English soil, under the protection of her customs system ... Once possessed of any one branch of industry, England bestowed upon it sedulous care and attention, for centuries treating it as a young tree which requires support and care.'[55]

In respect to those advocating free trade, List commented that:

> 'The theorists have since contended that England has attained to wealth and power not by means of, but in spite of, her commercial policy. As well might they argue that trees have grown to vigour and fruitfulness, not by means of, but *in spite of*, the props and fences with which they had been supported when they were first planted.'[56]

List highlighted the importance of the Navigation Acts:

> 'Both the fisheries and the coasting trade were previously in the hands of the Dutch. Stimulated by high customs duties and by bounties, the English now directed their own energies to the fishery trade, and by the Navigation Laws they secured chiefly to British sailors not only the transport of sea-borne coal, but the whole of the carrying trade by sea. The consequent increase in England's mercantile marine led to a proportionate augmentation of her naval power, which enabled the English to bid defiance to the Dutch fleet. Shortly after the passing of the Navigation Laws, a naval war broke out between England and Holland, whereby the trade of the Dutch with countries beyond the English Channel suffered almost total suspension, while their shipping in the North Sea and the Baltic was almost annihilated by English privateers. Hume estimates the number of Dutch vessels which thus fell into the hands of English cruisers at 1,600.'[57]

The British merchant fleet had benefited from a series of Navigation Acts initiated by Cromwell in 1651 when he reserved trade with the British colonies to British ships.[58] List fastened upon the completeness of England's protectionism:

> 'England prohibited the import of the goods dealt in by her own factories, the Indian cotton and silk fabrics. The prohibition was complete and peremptory. Not so much as a thread of them would England permit to be used.'[59]

This protection is contrary to the teachings of the free traders, such as Adam Smith and JB Say. Yet, 'English Ministers cared not for the acquisition of low-priced and perishable articles of manufacture, but for that of a more costly but enduring *manufacturing power'*.[60] List commented:

> 'We thus find that in all treaties of commerce concluded by the English, there is a tendency to extend the sale of their manufactures throughout all the countries with whom they negotiate, by offering them apparent advantages in respect of agricultural produce and raw materials. Everywhere their efforts are directed to ruining the native manufacturing power of those countries by means of cheaper goods and long credits. If they cannot obtain low tariffs, then they devote their exertions to defrauding the custom-houses and to organising a wholesale system of contraband trade. The former device, as we have seen, succeeded in Portugal, the latter in Spain. The collection of import dues upon the *ad valorem* principle has stood them in good stead in this matter, for which reason of late they have taken so much pains to represent the principle of paying duty by weight – as introduced by Prussia – as being injudicious.'[61]

Other countries' reliance on protectionist policies was not simply a matter of adopting a theory, but was born of experience as List himself eagerly highlighted:

> 'When, after a brief competition, the French manufacturers were brought to the brink of ruin, while French wine-growers had gained but little, then the French Government sought to arrest the progress of this ruin by terminating the treaty, but only acquired the conviction that it is much easier to ruin flourishing manufactories in a few years than to revive ruined manufactories in a whole generation. English competition had engendered a taste for English

goods in France, the consequence of which was an extensive and long-continued contraband trade which it was difficult to suppress. Meanwhile it was not so difficult for the English, after the termination of the treaty, to accustom their palates again to the wines of the Peninsula.'[62]

By contrast, during the Napoleonic wars, when English goods were barred from the French controlled countries, French manufacturing flourished.[63] List wrote:

'In France, although her ancient dynasty reascended the throne under the protection of the banner of England, or at any rate by the influence of English gold, the above arguments did not obtain currency for very long. England's free trade wrought such havoc amongst the manufacturing industries which had prospered and grown strong under the Continental blockade system, that a prohibitive *regime* was speedily resorted to, under the protecting aegis of which, according to Dupin's testimony, the producing power of French manufactories was doubled between the years 1815 and 1827.'[64]

The approach adopted by England was that national development required the import of raw materials and agricultural products and the export of manufactures. George I said: 'it is evident that nothing so much contributes to promote the public well-being as the exportation of manufactured goods and the importation of foreign raw material'.[65] However, having achieved complete dominance of manufacturing, it did not suit England's interests for others to develop their own manufacturing industry and so compete with England. William Pitt even exhorted the French to concentrate on wine growing and agriculture.[66] Henry Brougham MP said that, 'it was well worth while to incur a loss on the exportation of English manufactures in order to stifle in the cradle the foreign manufactures'. Another MP, Hume, hoped that, 'continental manufactures might be nipped in the bud'.[67] List wrote: 'The monopoly of all manufacturing industry by the mother country was one of the chief causes of the American Revolution; the tea duty merely afforded an opportunity for its outbreak'.[68]

After independence the USA embraced a policy of free trade. One speaker in Congress remarked:

> 'We did buy, according to the advice of modern theorists, where we could buy cheapest, and our markets were flooded with foreign goods; English goods sold cheaper in our seaport towns than in Liverpool or London. Our manufacturers were being ruined; our merchants, even those who thought to enrich themselves by importation, became bankrupt; and all these causes together were so detrimental to agriculture, that landed property became very generally worthless, and consequently bankruptcy became general even among our landowners.'[69]

Congress was inundated with demands for protection from all states. A small tariff was introduced with the result that manufacturing and the economy flourished. Even so, English manufacturing soon was able to reduce costs so as to regain the competitive advantage. Alexander Hamilton, in his *Report on the Manufacturers to the US Congress* in December 1791, as finance minister, argued that it was in the USA's best interests for certain industries to develop quickly and that US manufacturers needed to be protected, by tariffs on foreign goods, from the competition posed by European, especially British, industries.[70] This reasoning is often referred to as the 'infant industry' argument in that the tariffs are necessary to allow an industry to develop in its infancy before such tariffs are removed when the industry has developed sufficiently to compete with foreign firms. Hamilton's report was not fully adopted and encountered opposition from the southern states who wished to import manufactures cheaply, paid for by the export of agricultural products, including cotton.[71] Even so, the average tariff on imported manufactures was increased from around 5% to around 12.5%, which proved insufficient to achieve Hamilton's aims.[72] Congress increased the tariff to 15% in 1804 when it was also keen to raise more tax revenue. Even so, US manufacturing continued to struggle against the English competition.

Upon the outbreak of the Anglo-American war in 1812, the tariffs were immediately doubled to 25% and there was an embargo on British goods. This gave a boost to US manufacturing to such an extent that it was able to export. Increased prices led to increased prosperity. After the war, the American manufacturers wanted the tariffs to be not only continued but raised. Congress decided to double import duties for a period of one year. Under lobbying pressure these duties were reduced which in turn led to the return to the same pressures of foreign competition and falling prices as had followed the War of Independence.[73] In 1816, the tariffs were increased again to 35% and by 1820 the average tariff had been increased to 40%.[74] In 1824 the import tariffs were increased, not least due to the impact of the British Corn Laws on US agriculture, which made common cause with US manufacturers. This increased tariff was again increased in 1828.[75] List wrote:

> 'No nation has been so misconstrued and so misjudged as respects its future destiny and its national economy as the United States of North America, by theorists as well as by practical men. Adam Smith and JB Say had laid it down that the United States were, "like Poland", destined for agriculture. This comparison was not very flattering for the union of some dozen of new, aspiring, youthful republics, and the prospect thus held out to them for the future not very encouraging. The above-mentioned theorists had demonstrated that Nature herself had singled out the people of the United States exclusively for agriculture, so long as the richest arable land was to be had in their country for a mere trifle. Great was the commendation which had been bestowed upon them for so willingly acquiescing in Nature's ordinances, and thus supplying theorists with a beautiful example of the splendid working of the principle of free trade. The school (i.e. the free trade economists), however, soon had to experience the mortification of losing this cogent proof of the correctness and applicability of their theories in practice, and had to endure the spectacle of the United States seeking their nation's welfare in a direction exactly opposed to that of absolute freedom of trade.'[76]

Instead of concentrating on agricultural, be it by growing crops or herding cows, the US sought 'to promote their national prosperity by a return to that long-exploded mercantile system which had been clearly refuted by theory' much to the 'heaviest condemnation on the part of the theorists of every nation in Europe'.[77]

This is not to say that the USA did not appreciate the importance and potential of agriculture. During the American civil war, in 1862, the Republican Party passed the Homestead Act which granted 160 acres to any settler who would farm it for five years.[78]

Disagreement over the issue of trade policy was a major reason for the civil war. During the 1860 election campaign, Republicans in the more protectionist states demonized the Democrats as being the 'Southern-British-Antitariff-Disunion Party'.[79] President Lincoln increased tariffs on industrial goods and those tariffs remained in place after the civil war.

US vessels had a monopoly in coastal shipping from 1817 to WWI. Foreigners were not allowed to become directors of national banks and non-resident shareholders were barred from voting rights. Only US residents had logging rights (1878) and the 1887 Alien Property Act prohibited the ownership of land by aliens, or by companies more than 20% owned by aliens, in the territories (i.e. not fully fledged states). Even so, despite numerous restrictions, the USA was the world's largest importer of Foreign Direct Investment (FDI) up until WWI.[80]

US tariffs on manufactured imports were kept at between 40-50% until 1913, the highest in the world. In 1913, the newly elected Democrats introduced the Underwood Tariff bill which reduced tariffs on manufactured goods to 25%. Tariffs were raised again due to WWI and they were gradually raised to 37% by 1925. In 1930, the Smoot-Hawley tariff raised the tariffs to 48%, a move which has been blamed for initiating a tariff trade war.[81] The USA was the world's fastest growing economy up until the 1920s, and only adopted a free trade stance after WWII when it was the leading economic power and its competitors lay in financial ruin following the war.[82] Even then, the USA has been prepared to defend its interest by various methods of trade policy much more aggressively than Britain has ever done, such as anti-dumping legislation and 'voluntary' trade agreements with competitors, and has never had a zero tariffs. Up until the 1990s, between 50-70% of US Research & Development (R&D) was funded by the US federal government.[83] To this day, for example, The Jones Act requires that for goods shipped between US ports, then the ships must have been built in the USA, must be crewed largely by US citizens, must be owned by largely by Americans and registered as

US vessels. The Buy American Act requires a preference for American goods in direct government purchases, for manufactured goods then they must be produced containing more than 50% US components; and other acts including the Buy America Act and the Berry Amendment (for defence) which stipulate 100% US components.

A good example of the USA's determination to defend its economic interests is the Nixon Shock of 1971. On Sunday, 15th August 1971, President Richard Nixon made a live television announcement of his New Economic Policy, consisting of immediate wage and price controls, the suspension of convertibility of the US dollar into gold, and a 10% surtax on imports. The unilateral announcement became known as the Nixon Shock.[84] Nixon was aiming for a dollar devaluation against all the other major currencies and his 10% surtax was his method of achieving this as it was implemented immediately and would only be rescinded once Nixon had got the devaluation he sought. At the end of September, GATT met to decide whether or not the USA's import surtax was a contravention of its rules, which it clearly was. However, the other major trading nations were not minded to start a trade war with the USA and a G10 meeting was arranged in London, at which the USA demanded a $13billion swing in its trade balance in its favour and turning a $5billion deficit into an $8billion surplus. This demand was presented as non-negotiable and the other countries were told that it was up to them to decide how this was to be achieved. There was no early agreement on this but as the impact of the surtax took its toll the other countries gradually ceded ground. Eventually the dollar was devalued by 9% against gold and the other currencies were revalued upwards by between 3% and 8% against the dollar, giving a total adjustment of between 11% and 17%. In return, the USA agreed to remove the import surtax.

Nixon had acted in the US national interest, was prepared to ignore international treaties if necessary and was prepared to take on foreign governments too. He took a decision and implemented it. As List wrote:

> 'It is a fundamental error of the school when it represents the system of protection as a mere device of speculative politicians which is contrary to nature. History is there to prove that protective regulations originated either in the

natural efforts of nations to attain to prosperity, independence, and power, or in consequence of wars and of the hostile commercial legislation of predominating manufacturing nations.

The idea of independence and power originates in the very idea of "the nation". The school never takes this into consideration, because it does not make the economy of the separate nation, but the economy of society generally, i.e. of the whole human race, the object of its investigations.'[85]

The French economist François Quesnay (1694-1774) was the originator of the concept of universal free trade.[86] But he did not take account of the role of the nation. Adam Smith likewise downplayed the importance of the nation and his work is entitled *The Nature and Causes of the Wealth of Nations* – nations in the plural, i.e. the whole of humanity.[87] JB Say likewise takes a cosmopolitan view. List wrote: '*The popular school has assumed as being actually in existence a state of things which has yet to come into existence*. It assumes the existence of a universal union and a state of perpetual peace, and deduces therefrom the great benefits of free trade'.[88] A political alliance between nations precedes free trade and is not the result of it.[89] Adam Smith's real beliefs were not accurately set out by List as regards to a state of universal peace. Smith well recognised the need to defend the nation state and its possessions and of the necessity to be willing, if needs be, to wage war. The views of other free traders may be a different matter. List wrote:

> 'We ask, would not every sane person consider a government to be insane which, in consideration of the benefits and the reasonableness of a state of universal and perpetual peace, proposed to disband its armies, destroy its fleet, and demolish its fortresses? But such a government would be doing nothing different in principle from what the popular school requires from governments when, because of the advantages which would be derivable from general free trade, it urges that they should abandon the advantages derivable from protection.'[90]

List pointed out that, '*the power of producing wealth* is therefore infinitely more important than *wealth itself*'. By means of example,

List contrasted Germany, which had suffered major setbacks and wars, and yet had managed to bounce back to a state of prosperity due to its ability to create wealth; this is unlike 'rich and mighty but despot- and priest-ridden Spain, [which] notwithstanding her comparative enjoyment of internal peace, has sunk deeper into poverty and misery'.[91] List wrote:

> 'History teaches us how nations which have been endowed by Nature with all resources which are requisite for the attainment of the highest grade of wealth and power, may and must – without on that account forfeiting the end in view – modify their systems according to the measure of their own progress: in the first stage, adopting free trade with more advanced nations as a means of raising themselves from a state of barbarism, and of making advances in agriculture; in the second stage, promoting the growth of manufactures, fisheries, navigation, and foreign trade by means of commercial restrictions; and in the last stage, after reaching the highest degree of wealth and power, by gradually reverting to the principle of free trade and of unrestricted competition in the home as well as in foreign markets, that so their agriculturists, manufacturers, and merchants may be preserved from indolence, and stimulated to retain the supremacy which they have acquired. In the first stage, we see Spain, Portugal, and the Kingdom of Naples; in the second, Germany and the United States of North America; France apparently stands close upon the boundary line of the last stage; but Great Britain alone at the present time has actually reached it.'[92]

The point of this analysis is that it deals with the development of a national economy. (What we are now experiencing in Britain is the de-development of an economy. What is the trade policy response to that?) List emphasized the importance of manufacturing:

> 'With regard to the interchange of raw products, the school is perfectly correct in supposing that the most extensive liberty of commerce is, under all circumstances, most advantageous to the individual as well as to the entire State ... But the manufacturing productive power, on the

contrary, is governed by other laws, which have, unfortunately, entirely escaped the observation of the school.'[93]

List regarded the failure to develop manufacturing industry as a major reason for Poland's ruination.[94] List referred to Adam Smith's own admission that it is possible for a state to bring forward and speed up the development of manufacturing industry, and that, even so, Adam Smith rejected this as an option as such brought forward development could only be at the expense of other activities as the pool of savings out of which investment is made is fixed; therefore the development is a reallocation of resources away from other ventures and would be to support manufacturing development that would occur of its own accord anyway. List rejected this reasoning for a number of reasons, not only because Adam Smith's example of trying to develop vine growing in Scotland is not accurate for manufacturing, but also because the development of manufacturing also involves the development of the 'mental and bodily abilities of producers' which, as a form of capital, increases the capital available to the nation. Savings are not the only form of capital.[95] List argued:

> 'The building up of the material national capital takes place in quite another manner than by mere saving as in the case of the rentier, namely in the same manner as the building up of the productive powers, chiefly by means of the reciprocal action between the mental and material national capital, and between the agricultural, manufacturing and commercial capital.
> The augmentation of the national material capital is dependent on the augmentation of the national mental capital, and *vice versa*.
> The material commercial capital acts everywhere as an intermediary, helping and compensation between both.'[96]

Fundamental free traders have cited Adam Smith to justify themselves in the same way that Keynesians cite Keynes himself to justify their theories, even though Keynes may never have endorsed such theories. Likewise protectionism is condemned out of hand as being something positively damaging, immoral and backward, almost as if those advocating it were suggesting that we return to living in caves. List's arguments were well rounded and even Adam Smith was prepared to countenance protection in certain circumstances, as List criticized (List's argument is worth quoting in full):

> 'Moreover, the school itself does not condemn all protective duties. Adam Smith allows in three cases the special protection of internal industry: firstly as a measure of *retaliation* in case a foreign nation imposes restrictions on our imports, and there is hope of inducing it by means of reprisals to repeal those restrictions; secondly, for the *defence of the nation*, in case those manufacturing requirements which are necessary for defensive purposes could not under open competition be produced at home; thirdly, as a *means of equalisation* in case the products of foreigners are taxed lower than those of our home producers. J.B. Say objects to protection in all these cases, but admits it in a fourth case – namely, when some branch of industry is expected to become after the lapse of a few years so remunerative that it will then no longer need protection.
>
> Thus it is Adam Smith who wants to introduce the principle of retaliation into commercial policy – a principle which would lead to the most absurd and most ruinous measures, especially if the retaliatory duties, as Smith demands, are to be repealed as soon as the foreign nation agrees to abolish its restrictions. Supposing Germany made reprisals against England, because of the duties imposed by the latter on German corn and timber, by excluding from Germany English manufactured goods, and by this exclusion called artificially into existence a manufacturing power of her own; must Germany then allow this manufacturing industry, created at immense sacrifice, to come to grief in case England should be induced to reopen her ports to German corn and timber? What folly! It would have been ten times better than that if Germany had submitted quietly to all measures of restriction on the part of England, and had discouraged the growth of any manufacturing power of her own which might grow up notwithstanding the English import prohibitions, instead of stimulating its growth.

The principle of retaliation is reasonable and applicable only if it coincides with the principle of the *industrial development of the nation*, if it serves as it were as an assistance to this object.

Yes, it is reasonable and beneficial that other nations should retaliate against the English import restrictions on their agricultural products, by imposing restriction on the importation of manufactured goods, but only *when those nations are qualified to establish a manufacturing power of their own and to maintain it for all times*.

By the second exception, Adam Smith really justifies not merely the necessity of protecting such manufactures as supply the immediate requirements of war, such as, for instance, manufactories of arms and power, but the whole system of protection as we understand it; for by the establishment in the nation of a manufacturing power of its own, protection to native industry tends to the augmentation of the nation's population, of its material wealth, of its machine power, of its independence, and of all mental powers, and, therefore, of its means of national defence, in an infinitely higher degree than it could do by merely manufacturing arms and powder.

The same must be said of Adam Smith's third exception. If the burden of taxation to which our productions are subjected, affords a just ground for imposing protective duties on the less taxed products of foreign countries, why should not also the other disadvantages to which our manufacturing industry is subjected in comparison with that of the foreigner afford just grounds for protecting our native industry against the overwhelming competition of foreign industry?

J.B. Say has clearly perceived the contradictory character of this exception, but the exception substituted by him is no better; for in a nation qualified by nature and by its degree of culture to establish a manufacturing power of its own, almost every branch of industry must become remunerative under continued and powerful protection; and it is ridiculous to allow a nation merely a *few years* for the task of bringing to perfection one great branch of national industry or the whole industry of the nation.'[97]

SUMMARY

After Britain had alone experienced the industrial revolution and stood at its zenith, the most advanced and powerful country in the world, she needed to address and explain her hegemony. Ricardo's theory of comparative advantage offered a justification for other countries not to copy Britain's industrialization and instead import British manufactures while they concentrated on other economic output such as agricultural produce or tourism. The theory supported free trade and Britain duly adopted a policy of *unilateral* free trade.

List rejected free trade and the theory of comparative advantage. He advocated a national economic policy and urged countries, in particular his own country, Germany, to use tariffs and other protectionist methods to develop their own manufacturing industries just as Britain had done.

List went to great lengths to set out how other countries, highlighting both the USA and France, had been unable to compete with Britain and were reliant upon tariffs to give their own, infant, industries time to develop and prosper. List placed greater importance upon the ability to create wealth than upon an idealized efficient distribution of resources. He even went so far as to reject the use of tariffs as a bargaining weapon, as Adam Smith had contemplated, as once the effort had been put into developing a manufacturing industry then that investment should be followed through to realisation and not jettisoned.

List differed from both Keynes and Ricardo, who were theorists. List's rationale was drawn from history and he relied upon historical facts for his advocacy. He relied on facts to justify the need for tariffs.

While Ricardo's theory of comparative advantage and the benefits of free trade dominated economic policy in Britain, List's historical analysis of the benefits of tariffs for the development of manufacturing industry proved persuasive everywhere else. List cited a failure to develop manufacturing industry as a reason for countries failing to reach their potential. For List, manufacturing was key; and a protectionist policy was the key to the development of manufacturing.

4 JOSEPH CHAMBERLAIN AND THE TARIFF REFORM CAMPAIGN

'Russia and the United States will surpass in power the states now called great as much as the great country-states of the sixteenth century surpassed Florence. Is not this a serious consideration, and is it not especially so for a state like England, which has at the present time the choice in its hands between two courses of action, the one of which may set it in that future age on a level with the greatest of these great states of the future, while the other will reduce it to the level of a purely European Power, looking back, as Spain does now, to the great days when she pretended to be a world-state.' – The English historian, J.R. Seeley (1834-1895), writing in 1884

'Now, today in England, we are fighting to a finish – "damned badly", I admit ... Two ideals, and only two, emerge from the vortex:-
1. Imperialism which demands Unity at Home between classes, and Unity throughout the Empire; and which *prescribes* Fiscal reform to secure both.
2. Insular Socialism, and Class Antagonism ...

Between these two ideals a great battle will be fought. I do not know which will win. If Imperialism wins, we shall go on and be a great Empire. If Socialism wins we shall cease to be. The rich will be plundered. The poor will suffer. We shall perish with Babylon, Rome and Constantinople.'[98] – The Conservative George Wyndham MP (1863-1913)

In the closing decades of the 19th century there was an increasing sense of foreboding in Britain. Britain had been the world's dominant economic power with the world's greatest empire, and the first industrial nation. However, a depression which started in 1873 was a setback that heralded the end of British supremacy. By the late 19th century the threat posed by the newly industrialised competitors, in particular Germany and the

USA, meant that Britain no longer had a monopoly on advanced industrial and manufacturing production. Britain's long-term economic decline had begun. Some realised it at the time and sought to rally the nation to take steps to reverse that decline. Others believed that Britain's existing economic structure and national culture was sound and that no dramatic changes were needed.

In the years 1882 to 1899 Britain's growth rate was 2.5% and this fell to only 1.1% per annum from 1899 to 1913. Productivity growth rate declined from 1.4% per annum in the mid-Victorian era to an average of 0.5% in the 40 years to 1913.[99]

The volume of Britain's production of steel was surpassed by the USA in 1890 and by Germany in 1893. In 1896 US steel production, at just over 5million tonnes, was slightly higher than that of Britain. By 1913 US steel production had increased sixfold to 32million tonnes whereas the British output had less than doubled to eight million tonnes.[100] Taking the steel industry as an example, to cite Correlli Barnett:

> 'One successful Scottish emigrant to the US who returned to give a paper to the British Iron and Steel Trades Federation in 1902 on the superiority of US rolling mills informed his audience that the entire British steel industry had spent less in a decade than the Carnegie Company in two years. He recounted how when he suggested to a British steel maker that the adoption of American methods could help the British industry, the Englishman replied: "Why should I? I made over 30 per cent on my capital last year, and I am satisfied with that". This stalwart was producing some 10 tons per shift of hand-rolled ¾-inch bars, the operation being powered by a single engine which "appeared to have been designed by Watt himself". Also in 1902 a British exponent of electric power in steel-making operations vainly asked why British works were content to jog on with low-pressure steam boilers 30 years old and "the same old beam engine constructed in the days of Watt and Stephenson". A similar inertness prevailed in pig-iron production, as an Iron and Steel Institute meeting was told by a manager from Palmer's Jarrow works in 1901: "The blast furnace owners in this country were very conservative,

and had a very great objection to spending money unless they saw someone else had done so".[101]

This poor performance was typical across a range of industries where both the USA and Germany overtook Britain and forged ahead. Even so, Britain still dominated shipbuilding, accounting for 60% of the world's tonnage in the decades before 1914, as well as showing potential for dominating car building and the establishment of retail chains. In 1914, Britain had 9,000 full-time scientists. Germany had 58,000. Britain's share of world trade in manufactures had fallen from 31% in 1870 to 14% in 1914, and it was only large imports of US steel that prevented Germany, which was producing twice as much steel as Britain, from winning the war in 1916. Britain's investment rate was 9% of GDP, which was half that of the USA, Germany and France. Britain invested heavily overseas. Overseas investments increased from £1.2billion in 1870 to £4billion in 1914, with an increase in income stream from £44million to £200million that helped mask Britain's declining economic position.[102]

There was concern that Britain was falling behind technologically. That the size of firms and of plant was too small to compete effectively against the much larger US and German cartels; that the production processes were out of date and that new methods of production were not being adopted as they should have been. There was a reluctance to change. In some ways there was an inevitable obsolescence as Britain's industrial infrastructure had aged in the earlier years of the industrial revolution. Coal fields had been exhausted and steel plant had been sited in locations not suited to new production techniques. This was not helped by British institutions channelling finance overseas to take advantage of opportunities in other countries and the Empire instead of targeting that funding on British industry.

A long-standing criticism is that because of the manner of the industrialisation in Britain, relying on individual entrepreneurship, that Britain relied upon the cult of the practical man rather than professionalism and training – unlike competitors who had industrialised with the active support of government and had to adapt to new technology and production techniques that had already been invented; that required expertise and training. Practical men were less suited to the newer more scientific industries and products. Furthermore, the class structure in Britain was more suited to the running of the Empire than with the nurturing and implementation of industrial economics. Those businessmen who had succeeded in industry aspired to join the gentry rather than to further their industrial successes. The Empire, and the military, took the best of British youth leaving industry starved of the best brains available.

It has been said that the Empire, far from being a source of British power was a weakness. It was expensive and lured Britain into otherwise needless military commitments and wars. As a market, it was an easy escape from the more cutting competition of the home markets of Britain's competitors. British business could escape the competition in Europe and America by retreating into the safe haven of the slow-growing and backward Empire. Although Britain did export more manufactures than other industrialised countries to the Third World, it did represent a growing market for all industrial nations.[103]

The Empire was bound to account for an increasing share of British trade and bound to be of increasing importance. Between 1870 and 1914 the British Empire more than doubled in size, from 4,485million to 11.1million square miles, and from a population of 202.3million to 372.1million. This growth affected the pattern of trade and it is not surprising that there was a growth of trade with the Empire. Imports from the Empire grew from £64.4million, 21.4% of the total, in 1870 to £187.8million, 27% of the total, in 1914; exports to the Empire grew from £55.4million, 22.7% of the total, in 1870 to £183.9million, 34.9% of the total, in 1914. Imports from the Empire almost trebled while exports to the Empire more than trebled. By comparison, imports from foreign countries a little more than doubled, from £238.4million to £508.8million (78.6% to 73% of the total), and exports to foreign countries did not even double, from £188.7million to £342.3million (77.3% to 65.1% of the total). In 1914, India, Australia, North American colonies, South Africa and New Zealand were the five main destinations for British exports accounting for 80-85% of all exports to and imports from the Empire.[104]

The increase in trade with the Empire was in part due to the protectionist policies adopted by Britain's industrial competitors. Germany returned to a protectionist stance in 1878 and increased its tariffs again in 1903. The USA introduced the McKinley tariff in 1890 and the Dingley tariff in 1897. France introduced tariffs in

1892. By 1910, the average *ad valorem* tariffs on *all* imports were 8.4% in Germany, 8% in France, 9.6% in Italy, 13.4% in Spain and 38.9% in Russia. By the mid-1920s, the tariffs had been increased to 15% in Germany, 16% in France, 16% in Italy and 30% in Spain. Japan in 1914 was imposing tariffs as high as 40-50% on some imports.[105]

While British economic policy in the 19th century can be summarised as laissez-faire and free trade, this could not be said of the other industrialised nations where the state played a significant part in their industrialisation and where protectionism was the norm. British economic and trade policy had not always been laissez-faire and free trade. The 'glorious revolution' of 1688 had heralded a Mercantalist policy for the advantage of the landed aristocracy and the City, dominated by merchants and financiers. The Corn Laws of 1815 were the embodiment of this Mercantalist sentiment and their bitter fought repeal in 1846, in a campaign led by Richard Cobden, heralded the era of unilateral free trade, not merely as a policy, but as a national ideology that drew active support from across the nation and was extolled as a civilizing and *moral* crusade.[106] Europe came close to full free trade in the 1860s and 1870s, but the continental countries reverted to their protectionist stance leaving Britain alone with zero tariffs.[107]

At the time, the repeal of the Corn Laws and the policy of free trade was for rational and patriotic reasons, and was combined with a determined effort to open up foreign markets. There was a desire to increase exports in order to boost business and to reduce unemployment. Britain was more competitive than her rivals and so free trade would lead to more British goods being sold. Also, the growth of the British population had exceeded the capacity of British agriculture to feed that population. The Irish famine demonstrated this.[108] It suited Britain to import cheap food to feed its expanding population while selling manufactures as exports.

Another factor in the move towards free trade is that the British Empire at that time was far smaller than it was fifty years later, especially after the Scramble for Africa, with comparatively fledgling colonies in Australia and Canada, and only a foothold in Africa (the main presence being in South Africa). In addition to which there was the informal influence of Britain where countries may not have been incorporated into the Empire but which were nevertheless subject to significant British influence, South America being a principal example and where Britain was keen to develop her commercial interests.

Another key factor was that practical adoption of the free trade policy was accompanied with a robust defence of British interests. The 19th century was the era of British gunboat diplomacy. Free trade was pointless if members of certain countries were disinclined to pay for that which they had bought, or if the seas were not safe for the passage of goods. Lord Palmerston (1784-1865), the Foreign Secretary, explained to parliament in September 1850:

> 'These half-civilized governments such as those of China, Portugal, Spanish America, all require a dressing down every eight or ten years to keep them in order. Their minds are too shallow to receive an impression that will last longer than some such period and warning is of little use. They care little for words and they must not only see the stick but actually feel it on their shoulders before they yield to that argument which brings conviction.'[109]

In January 1850 Palmerston had sent seven battleships and five steamers to Salamis Bay after the Greek government had refused to pay compensation for losses suffered by a number of British subjects. The local admiral had been ordered to take 'measures' to ensure the Greek government understood that Britain meant to defend its subjects' interests. The Greek navy was seized, Greek merchantmen were arrested, and an embargo was imposed on Greek shipping.[110]

The Royal Navy was heavily engaged in the war against piracy. When pirates seized two dhows in the Persian Gulf in 1855, the local sheik was ordered to find the culprits or else he would have to pay blood money and compensation if he wanted to avoid having the Royal Navy bombard his village. The war could turn brutal. Cobden protested at the reward of £20 to sailors for each dead or captured pirate. Colonel Charles Sibthorp, a Tory, enquired whether Cobden's humanitarian concerns for Borneo pirates would likewise extend to his own factory workers.[111]

In the same way that Palmerston would back the local men in difficulties, so too did the electorate back Palmerston. In a debate about aggressive measures taken against China by Hong Kong authorities in 1856, Palmerston, now Prime Minister, asked MPs whether they were prepared to 'abandon a large community of British subjects at the extreme end of the globe to a set of barbarians – a set of kidnapping, murdering, poisoning barbarians'. Palmerston lost the vote in the House of Commons. He called a general election. The British voters re-elected Palmerston's government, with his principal opponents, Cobden and John Bright (a pacifist), both losing their seats.[112] The high-minded moralizing about free trade being the route to universal peace cut no ice with Palmerston nor the electorate, who embraced free trade so long as it was in British interests and who expected those interests to be defended.

By 1870, Britain's position as the centre of the world economy had reached its zenith, with Britain exporting both manufactured goods and substantial long-term capital investment, this investment overseas being one factor in the development of Britain's competitors and the demise of British supremacy. Britain's share of world exports of manufactures fell from 40.7% in 1890 to 29.9% in 1913. In the half century to 1914, imports were growing faster than exports both in value and volume. This trend of British decline was against the background of increasing protectionism in Europe after 1878, following the Great Depression, and increased US tariffs from 1890.[113] This protection was high and directed at British exports. In 1902, nominal tariffs on manufactures were 131% in Russia, 73% in the USA, 34% in France and 25% in Germany.[114] However, for Britain the evangelical cause of free trade remained absolute and unilateral free trade remained the policy.[115] In 1904 the great and the good gathered at Alexandra Palace to commemorate Cobden's centenary; after a rousing speech extolling the virtues of free trade, Sir Henry Campbell-Bannerman, the Liberal leader and future prime minister, left the gathering flanked by a guard of honour including 300 torchbearers.[116]

By the end of the 19th century most of the industrialised countries experienced rapid economic growth. Britain did not. Industrial growth in Britain was very low and for a time was almost nil. More industries blamed this on foreign competition and there was a growing demand for the abandonment of free trade and the adoption of a more protectionist policy. In 1881, the National Fair Trade League was formed. There were demands for protection from foreign competition and also for imperial preference, including from the white Dominions which wanted something in return for the preference they had given to British goods. At its inaugural meeting in July 1903, the Tariff Reform League declared that it stood for 'the defence and development of the industrial interests of the British Empire'.[117] Protectionism and free trade had been a highly contentious issue in Britain. Free trade and Empire were seen as synonymous.

Protectionism was portrayed as backward even if it was a resort often used in difficult economic times. It was something that foreigners did. The Conservatives were more sympathetic to tariff reform, although the issue had the potential to divide the party (as membership of the EU can divide it today). Labour and the Liberals were more internationalist in outlook and favoured free trade strongly. Keynes also opposed protectionism and wrote (italics Keynes' own):

> 'If there is one thing Protection can *not* do, it is to cure Unemployment. There are some arguments for Protection, based upon its securing possible but improbable advantages to which there is no simple answer. But the claim to cure Unemployment involves the Protectionist fallacy in its grossest and crudest form.'[118]

The demands for reform went beyond pure tariff reform and those campaigning for change became known as social imperialists and the unification of the British Empire was one of their major goals. This was against a backdrop of the increasing naval threat from Germany, which had undertaken a battleship building programme with the clear intention of challenging British naval supremacy. Germany's Second Navy Law of 1900 increased the planned German fleet to four battle squadrons and a total of 38 battleships, stated:

> 'It is not absolutely necessary that the German battle fleet should be as strong as that of the greatest naval Power because a great naval Power will not, as a rule, be in a position to concentrate all its striking forces against us. But even if it should succeed in meeting us with considerable superiority of strength the defeat of a strong German fleet would so substantially weaken the enemy that, in spite of a victory he might have obtained, his own position in the world would no longer be secured by an adequate fleet.'[119]

Germany, unlike Britain, was a land power and did not need a formidable navy. The German battleships were purely an aggressive weapon aimed against Britain. The British Admiralty was slow to see the German threat, but once bestirred reacted by withdrawing warships from other parts of the world to concentrate them in the home waters to defend Britain, and successfully demanded that Britain undertake its own battleship building programme with the construction and launching of the revolutionary, powerful dreadnought battleships.

However, military power ultimately stems from economic power and it was the issue of tariff reform that was the central plank of the social imperialist campaign. The issue split the Unionist Party (an alliance comprised of the Conservative Party and the Liberal Unionists who had split from the Liberal Party over the issue of home rule for Ireland) and was a major issue in the general election of 1906. The leader of the tariff reform campaign at the time was the mighty figure of Joseph Chamberlain (1836-1914), who was not only a man of strong principles and a great orator, but also a highly effective organiser. He had had a very successful business career, a distinguished period as mayor of Birmingham prior to entering parliament and, despite the pressure of being Colonial Secretary at the time, was also instrumental in the setting up of a university in Birmingham that would engage in applied science, original research and train the captains of industry as well as its other activities. Chamberlain secured the University's charter, set the curriculum, hired its principle officers and management, as well as securing its funding from a number of friends, relations, businesses and philanthropists and even persuaded Lord Calthorpe to donate 25 acres of land in Edgbaston to site the campus.[120] When Lord Rosebey's Liberal government fell in June 1895, Lord Salisbury joined together a coalition of the Conservatives with the Liberal Unionists to form a minority government. Chamberlain was the leader of the Liberal Unionists in the House of Commons with the Duke of Devonshire being the Liberal Unionist leader in the House of Lords. Chamberlain had the choice of any post he wanted, including Chancellor of the Exchequer, Foreign Secretary and Home Secretary, and yet chose the Colonial Secretary, a decision which puzzled many as the Colonial Office was seen as a backwater notorious for bungling and caught between the powerful Foreign Office and the tight-fisted Treasury.[121] However, it was a post that he wanted and he saw it as his role to develop the Empire:

'It is not enough to occupy great spaces of the world's surface unless you can make the best of them. It is the duty of a landlord to develop his estate'.[122] This choice and attitude is to his credit as his ambition was to govern well and develop the Empire rather than to make a smart career move. Chamberlain was Colonial Secretary during the Boer War, often referred to as 'Joe's War', which had shaken the Empire and many in Britain were concerned at Britain's isolation and the threat posed by Germany, which had been supportive of the Boers. As Colonial Secretary, Chamberlain had been consistently in receipt of calls from the White Dominions for preferential treatment from the Mother Country in trade, which had been denied them. Chamberlain was sympathetic to their plight.

Chamberlain attracted both strong support and equally strong hatred. His distinctive image – with a monocle and button-hole orchid – made him a media celebrity. In politics he held passionate beliefs and had a combative style, believing that there should be 'no fraternizing in the trenches and no wandering about in no-man's land'.[123] To his supporters 'good ol' Joe' was the greatest prime minister Britain never had.[124] Keynes dismissed him as a 'fanatical charlatan'. Others resented 'Pushful Joe'.[125] Shaw Lefevre, who had held several ministerial positions in Liberal governments since the 1860s, thought that Chamberlain 'has shown himself totally unfit for the higher spheres of politics. He thought he could carry on the game in the same manner as that by which he succeeded in his screw business by bluffing his competitors in trade and establishing a monopoly. There ought to be no mincing of words with regard to him'.[126] Lord Robert Cecil (1864-1958), a committed free trader, was contemptuous of the Chamberlainites: 'Their whole way of looking at politics ... appears to me entirely sordid and materialistic, not yet corrupt, but on the high-road to corruption'.[127]

Chamberlain's campaign of 1903 could trace its origins back to the 1880s with the Imperial Federation League and the Fair Trade League, the concept of 'fair' trade gaining considerable support from certain sections of the Conservative Party, including Lord Randolph Churchill who campaigned for Fair Trade in 1885.[128]

Chamberlain argued that 'the presence of hostile tariffs, the presence of bounties, the presence of subsidies' made the costs of production largely irrelevant to the final selling price of goods in foreign markets; in consequence, he believed that a stable home and imperial market was more important and should be protected against subsidized foreign competition. He believed that the government should promote trade with the colonies rather than with foreign countries and that the Empire should be a self-sustaining single unit. Chamberlain also advocated tariff reform as a means of raising tax revenues to pay for social expenditure such as pensions.[129]

The ideological commitment to free trade verged on the religious and was bound up with the existence of the British Empire, which was deemed a product of the free trade ethos. Liberals declared that tariff reform would be 'turning back the hand on the dial of civilization'.[130] The reaction of the free traders was therefore aggressive and they fought a very determined and well-funded campaign to oppose the tariff reform cause. By comparison the tariff reform position was a fudge between the demands for tariff reform as a means of unifying the Empire on the one hand, and those who saw it merely as a bargaining or retaliatory weapon to react against those other industrialised countries who had taken protectionist measures against Britain on the other.

Free traders managed to occupy the moral high ground. Lloyd George condemned the 'wholesale ... and insidious appeal to human selfishness' of Chamberlain's tariff reform proposals, which were an attempt to 'reorganize society on a principle of universal loot' and that Chamberlain's rallying cry was '"Down with freedom! Long live King Greed!"'.[131] Lloyd George told audiences that Chamberlain was a 'new Joshua' leading people to 'a land, not flowing with milk and honey, but rolling with black bread and German sausages'.[132] Tariffs allegedly forced the Germans to eat horses and dogs, which they also put in their sausages. Lloyd George said: 'Three months of black-bread diet and the most juicy horseflesh rump steaks' would make the peers pass the Liberal budget within three days during the 1910 election campaign. He further announced that he 'was not afraid of the German navy; he was not afraid of German trade competition; but he had a real dread of the German sausage' and he told a meeting in York that 'if this country wanted German tariffs, it must have German wages ... German militarism and German sausages'.[133] One poster showed the Tariff Reformers waiting to ambush Little Red Riding Hood and tax her shoes, clothes, and bread. It was even alleged that 'the slum child is to have the treacle upon his bread taxed'.[134] A Liberal postcard declared 'Stop Thief!' as the hand of tariff reform reached through the window to rob the family cupboard.[135]

Britain was seriously divided over the tariff reform issue and, contrary to present day myths, the outcome owed more to political and personality factors than to any intellectual economic analysis, and therefore needs to be examined in detail. The split began quietly over the issue of preference for the Empire relating to a duty on corn. The duty had been reintroduced as a means of raising revenues to help pay for the Boer War (1899-1902), in which Britain had put nearly 450,000 troops into the field,[136] in the Budget of April 1902 by the then Unionist Chancellor, Hicks Beach. When announced in the House of Commons the immediate response by the Liberal opposition was to denounce the move as an attack on free trade. When it came to the vote, only two Unionist MPs voted against with the others accepting Hicks Beach's assertion that: 'a duty which, when it existed, nobody felt, for the removal of which nobody was grateful because nobody desired it, will no more in the future than in the past have ... any practical effect on the cost of food'.[137] Public opinion was disinterested and food prices were not affected by the measure. Press comment was restrained although the *National Review* observed: 'Though there is no rebate on Colonial corn, such as there ought to be, the slow-moving mother-country is gradually working towards the position in which she will be able to enter into preferential trade relations with the daughter nations'.[138]

The *National Review* was not alone in seeing the opportunity for preferential trade between Britain and the daughter nations; the daughter nations themselves were quick to spot the opportunity and had already been lobbying Chamberlain, as Colonial Secretary, before the duty was introduced. In particular, Sir Wilfrid Laurier, the Canadian prime minister, publicly expressed a hope that a preferential trade agreement could be arranged; this hope was rejected at once by Balfour, but Chamberlain, in a speech in Birmingham on the 16th May, after lampooning the Liberal leader Sir Henry Campbell-Bannerman for attacking the corn duty 'with bated breath and in tones of horror' (to much laughter), continued:

> 'At the present moment, the Empire is being attacked on all sides and, in our isolation, we must look to ourselves. We must draw closer our internal relations, the ties of sentiment, the ties of sympathy, yes, and the ties of interest. If by adherence to economic pedantry, to old shibboleths, we are to lose opportunities of closer union which are

> offered us by our colonies, if we are to put aside occasions now within our grasp, if we do not take every chance in our power to keep British trade in British hands, I am certain that we shall deserve the disasters which will infallibly come upon us (cheers).'[139]

This speech attracted minor attention, but the move towards Preference was noticed. At an Imperial Conference shortly thereafter, the Dominions, which were self-governing and protectionist, once again called for reciprocal preference with Britain, with Canada leading clamour not least because in 1900 she had unilaterally given Britain a 33⅓% preference on British goods. Laurier pointed out that:

> 'Foreign nations ... are practically engaged in developing a commercial war ... I speak of our neighbour, the United States, whose tariff is absolutely prohibitory. Their policy is to sell to the foreign nations as much as they can and not to buy.'[140]

The conference passed a resolution urging preferential trade between the colonies and Britain and urged that Britain to grant 'preferential treatment to the products and manufactures of the Colonies either by exemption from or reduction of duties now or hereafter imposed'.[141] Chamberlain was impressed upon by the Canadians that they were expecting something to be done before they flew off to Paris to discuss trade relations with France (this was seen, and was intended to be seen, as an implied threat).

Chamberlain raised the issue of granting Canada a preference at the Cabinet meeting of October 1902 although the matter was deferred to the November meeting, before which Richie, the new Chancellor, circulated a memo setting out his opposition. Even so, the Cabinet decided after a 'long and elaborate' discussion to maintain to duty on foreign corn only, with Empire corn thus gaining a preference that was of particular importance to Canada as a major corn producing country. Ritchie, had been in a minority of two in the Cabinet vote but was expected to introduce the measure in the next budget in May 1903. Days later, Chamberlain embarked on an African tour to include South Africa.

The African tour was a major event. It was not usual for minsters to embark on such an exercise, it captivated public interest, and other colonies invited Chamberlain to visit them in the near future. Chamberlain was minded to do so, especially now that he had Imperial Preference to offer them. He departed on his African tour with a grand banquet at Birmingham Town Hall, followed by a parade escorted by the Warwickshire Imperial Yeomanry and 4,000 torch bearers to cheering crowds. He departed for Portsmouth from Victoria Station in London where he had been greeted by Balfour, Field Marshal Roberts, half the Cabinet and a number of other dignitaries. He set sail on *HMS Good Hope* on her maiden voyage.[142] The tour lasted three months.

While Chamberlain was away, the Unionist government's fortunes worsened. A contentious Education Bill continued its bloody progress through parliament, with controversy and revolts along its way. One particular group of Unionists, known as the Hughligans after one of its members (Lord Hugh Cecil), which included Winston Churchill, had formed a rebel 'Cave' with encouragement from former Liberal leader the Earl of Rosebery (1847-1929) and were having some sport attacking a proposed reform of the Army. At one Hughligan dinner threats were made about Chamberlain ('Just you wait till Joe comes back from South Africa' and 'We must pull Joe down a peg or two'). The Liberal opposition awaited Chamberlain's return with trepidation and Campbell-Bannerman suspected 'on the way home, if not actually on the illimitable veld, his busy brain would be spinning new schemes to revive the fortunes of his party'.[143]

More importantly, Ritchie, after quietly lobbying members of the Cabinet concerning his hostility towards the November decision about giving preference on corn, threatened to resign two weeks before Chamberlain was due back. It was recognised that Ritchie, who had once been a Fair Trader (and therefore leaning towards protection) as opposed to a Free Trader, had gone native at the Treasury with its 'Gladstonian garrison'. Balfour commented that Ritchie as being 'completely under the control of Mowatt and E. Hamilton' (2 of the senior Treasury mandarins).[144] Although Ritchie said that he was concerned about the corn duty's unpopularity in the constituencies as well as its potential for use for Imperial preference, there were darker motives. JS Sanders, Balfour's Private Secretary and who likewise recognised that Ritchie had gone native at the Treasury ('Ritchie became a mere puppet in their hands'), wrote:

'Ritchie made no pretence to conceal his dislike of Chamberlain. He saw in him a man, who, though he only became a member of a Unionist Administration in 1895, had passed him in a stride; and it was evident that from the moment that the fiscal issue arose he was determined to thwart the famous member for Birmingham. Ritchie bitterly resented Balfour's appreciation of Chamberlain's character and abilities as well as the popularity which the latter had won among representatives of Conservative opinion – especially in the House of Commons. Hence it is impossible to doubt that in seeking a counterpoise to the large reduction of income tax in the Budget of 1903 – at the close of the South African War – he deliberately selected the repeal of the small Registration Duty on Corn with a view to defeating Chamberlain's project of fiscal reform in its Imperial connection. In this way he hoped to dethrone the Colonial Secretary from his commanding position in Parliament and in the country.'[145]

Balfour's response to Ritchie's threatened resignation was to defer a decision until Chamberlain returned.

Meanwhile, Chamberlain on his way back on a Union-Castle liner had had a bad attack of gout as he neared Madeira which had prepared a banquet in his honour. The King of Portugal sent a cruiser to greet him at the island. On arrival he felt a little better and so forced his affected foot into a shoe and went ashore to be met by the Civil Governor, the Military Governor and the Admiral and their wives at the pier. Chamberlain walked without a limp despite the pain and ate and drank heartily at lunch, ending the meal with an old brandy which he claimed was the best he had ever had. The gout was gone and the Chamberlains enjoyed sightseeing the island.

Early on the 14th March, Chamberlain arrived back at Southampton. Mrs Chamberlain (this was Chamberlain's third wife, an American who he had married when she was 23 and he was 51, his first two wives having died after giving birth to sons: Austen and Neville) wrote to her mother:

'It was a misty grey morning as we steamed up Southampton Water and when the first communication came with land – the Medical Officer's tug – what was my surprise to find myself in the midst of a deputation of Joe's constituents – headed by Mr Harry Peyton, his Chairman. They were all beaming, and when I expressed my surprise at seeing them there, they exclaimed: "*Didn't* you know we were coming? *Doesn't* Mr Chamberlain know?" I cautiously said that I did not think he did, but perhaps I was mistaken – though how we should divine it at sea with no telegram to Madeira to tell us I could not quite imagine to myself. Then I had to break it to them that Joe was still in his room (time 8 a.m.) – as a matter of fact he was in his bath – but that I would go and tell him. "Oh, *please* don't do that," exclaimed Mr Titterton, "it won't be any surprise if you do." So I refrained at the moment, but later gave him a surreptitious hint. They were enchanted with the success of their coming and a little ceremony of presenting an Address took place in the library. Their great delight was in having been the first to greet him, even before the family, and Southampton. All parties were represented in the group and they were, as ever, full of loyalty and admiration for their Member. Then as we slowly steamed up to the pier our eyes were delighted by the three girls and Austen and Neville, and while the Civic Dignitaries – all arrayed in their robes of office and bearing their ancient maces of Southampton – waited, they all came on board to welcome us. As soon as the family re-union was accomplished, the Mayor and Mayoress followed, and we received them in the library. A bouquet was presented to me and a boutonniére to Joe, and after taking leave of the Captain we departed in procession, to the interest and amusement of our fellow passengers, who lined the decks and who, together with the crew, sent up resounding cheers as we stepped ashore.'[146]

The press had highlighted the times when Chamberlain's train would progress through the different stations, and despite the cold weather people had gathered to witness the train's journey, Mrs Chamberlain wrote: 'little crowds were gathered to see the train go by, and that in the fields groups were assembled, and from back gardens and windows flags and handkerchiefs and hats were waving to us as the train flew by'. They arrived at Waterloo early to be greeted by 'much the same group which waved us "Godspeed" in November', including Balfour, 'Joe's quaint little cousins' Miss Chamberlain and Miss Preston, most of the Cabinet, Colonial Office staff, friends and MPs, many with their wives. Mrs Chamberlain wrote: 'Just as we were moving down the platform … a large figure loomed in front of me and there was the Duke of Devonshire, smiling and breathless. "I am afraid I am rather late. I went to the wrong platform", – at which he haw-hawed at his own expense, and then said how glad he was to see us back'.[147] As Chamberlain emerged from the station a crowd outside let out a great cheer. 'From Waterloo Station, over Westminster Bridge, past the Houses of Parliament, nearly to Birdcage Walk, there was a crowd several people deep, who waved and cheered and shouted: "Glad to see you back" – "Well done, Joey!" – "Welcome home, Sir!" etc., etc.'.[148] More crowds awaited at their destination and there was a three-deep crowd in St James's Street and the windows in Pall Mall and Piccadilly were full (wrongly believing that Chamberlain would be passing by due to 'an invention of an enterprising reporter'). Mrs Chamberlain continued that they spent a quiet afternoon on Saturday with the family, then:

> 'On Sunday afternoon I had a stream of visitors, all very cordial and nice, while Joe went to see His Majesty. He had a most gracious reception and afterwards the Queen sent for him and was also full of interest in his journey. They both sent messages to me and the Queen sent word that she wanted me to come and see her and would write me – and so I am wondering whether and when I shall receive a summons. I hope it will not come as Joe's has! The King has commanded him to dinner on Saturday, which cuts into the visit we mean to make to Ethel at Eastbourne. I shall, however, go down on Saturday and he will follow.'[149]

What Chamberlain's enemies, rivals and the Liberal opposition made of all this does not require too much imagination.

At the next Cabinet meeting after Chamberlain returned after Ritchie insisted on sticking to his determination to resign unless he got his own way regarding preference on the Corn Duty, Chamberlain backed down. He did however successfully argue that the Corn Duty should be abolished altogether, and not the Tea Duty, as this would be less offensive to Canada. Chamberlain subsequently explained that his own failure to press the point and if necessary resign himself, given that the majority of the Cabinet was still in his favour, was that there was insufficient time to properly deal with the issue before the Budget, for which Ritchie was responsible, and that he expected the matter to be investigated over the summer.[150] Even so, with the benefit of hindsight, although it is understandable that he had yet to fully get a grip on matters since he had returned (the resignation threat had been a shock and that there would be a natural inclination not to cause a major ruction), Chamberlain would have been better to have fought to the finish then and there. Another factor is that Balfour noted that Chamberlain had returned from South Africa 'rather ill, rather irritable, and very tired'.[151] Tactically, it would have been far easier to sell the issue of preference on an existing duty, than to have to introduce a duty in order to give a preference on it. As it was, Chamberlain had the majority of the Cabinet on his side and also had the support of the Prime Minister, so his nonchalance is understandable. Chamberlain abandoned any intention of touring other colonies given that he now had nothing to offer them.

The Corn Duty was abolished in the Budget to a puzzled response as it was difficult to understand why the government had taken the trouble to introduce the contentious tax only to abolish it twelve months later even though it had been readily accepted. However, the reaction from the colonies was one of disappointment. In Canada there were even moves to end the preferences given to Britain. On the Unionist backbenches a revolt started to form as those who supported Chamberlain made their views known and a deputation led by the Conservative MP Chaplin (1840-1923) even met with Balfour to express those views. At a Cabinet meeting the day after the deputation's meeting with Balfour, 12th May 1903, at which the matter was discussed and how Balfour should deal with it, Chamberlain mentioned that he would be making a speech in Birmingham, which he did on 15th May 1903, at which before getting up to speak he told the event organizer: 'You can burn your leaflets. We are going to talk about something else'.[152]

'You will excuse me if I am a little out of practice (laughter)', Chamberlain began his speech, before proceeding to set out the development, the importance of the Empire and 'Imperial patriotism'. He believed that Britain should appreciate and reciprocate steps taken by the colonies to show Imperial solidarity – as had been shown in the Boer War and in other ways too including preferential tariffs, which Canada in particular granted in favour of Britain. Yet they had had nothing in return. Chamberlain told the audience that Canada had offered more preferences to Britain provided that Britain reciprocated and that they wanted a preference on the Corn Duty. Chamberlain continued:

> 'That was a definite offer, which we had to refuse. I need not say that, if I could treat matters of this kind solely in regard to my position as Secretary of State for the Colonies, I should have said, "That is a fair offer, that is a generous offer, from your point of view, and it is an offer which we might ask our people to accept". But, speaking for the Government as a whole, and not solely in the interests of the Colonies, I am obliged to say that it is contrary to the established fiscal policy of this country; that we hold ourselves bound to keep open market for all the world, even if they close their markets to us (laughter); and that, therefore, so long as that is the mandate of the British public, we are not in a position to offer any preference or favour whatever, even to our own children. We cannot make any difference between those who treat us well and those who treat us badly (shame). Yes, but that is the doctrine which, I am told, is the accepted doctrine of Free Traders, and we are all Free Traders (cries of "No, no", and laughter). Well I am (loud laughter). I have considerable doubt whether the interpretation of Free Trade which is current among a certain limited section is the true interpretation (applause). I am perfectly certain that I am not a Protectionist; but I want to point out that, if the interpretation is that our only duty is to buy in the cheapest market without regard to where we can sell, – if that is the theory of Free Trade that finds acceptance, then, in pursuance of that policy, you will lose the advantage of the further reduction in duty which your great Colony of Canada offers to you, the manufacturers of this country. And you may lose a great deal more; because in the speech which the Minister of Finance made to the Canadian Parliament the other day he says that if they are told definitely that Great Britain, the Mother Country, can do nothing for them in the way of reciprocity, they must

reconsider their position and reconsider the preference that they have already given us.'[153]

Chamberlain then pointed out that Germany was targeting and penalising Canada by imposing an additional tariff on Canadian goods in response to its preference to Britain, and that the German press was being quite open that the policy or reprisal was not only to bully Canada but also to deter other Colonies from giving Britain preference in trade. Germany was treating Canada as a separate country despite the fact that it was a part of the British Empire. For Chamberlain, this was a new situation unforeseen by the original authors of Free Trade and that a new policy was called for.

Chamberlain saw two alternatives. Either Britain could continue with its current interpretation of Free Trade as dictated by 'a small remnant of Little Englanders of the Manchester School, who now profess to be the sole repositories of the doctrines of [Free Trade]'. In that case Britain will be precluded from giving preference to Colonies or even protecting those Colonies from foreign threat. Or, Britain should no longer 'be bound by any purely technical definition of Free Trade', and that while seeking 'free interchange of trade and commerce between ourselves and all the nations of the world', nevertheless Britain should recover its 'freedom, resume the power of negotiation, and, if necessary, retaliation (loud cheers), whenever our own interests or our relations between our Colonies and ourselves are threatened by other people (renewed cheers)'.[154] Chamberlain concluded by saying that he wanted to open discussion on these matters and that:

> 'For my own part, I believe in a British Empire, in an Empire which, although it should be one of its first duties to cultivate friendship with all the nations of the world, should yet, even if alone, be self-sustaining and self-sufficient, able to maintain itself against the competition of all its rivals. And I do not believe in a Little England which shall be separated from all those to whom it should in the natural course look for support and affection – a Little England which shall thus be dependent absolutely on the mercy of those who envy its present prosperity, and who have shown they are ready to do all in their power to

prevent its future union with the British race throughout the world (loud and continuous cheers).'[155]

The reaction to the speech and the consequences of it were momentous. Chamberlain did not expect speed or the scale of the reaction and was unprepared to cope with the volume of letters which poured in. *The Times* described the speech as 'great and stirring' and was sympathetic to Chamberlain's argument. *The Telegraph* was pro-Chamberlain as was *The Express* and the *Daily Mail*, after opposing the 'stomach tax' swapped sides and joined the Chamberlain camp. The response in the colonies was favourable. Borden, the leader of the Opposition in Canada remarked: 'It seems to us that the hour has come and with it the man'.[156] Chamberlain was inundated with letters of support and the bulk of the Unionist Party were excited by the issues raised and the vision offered. However, senior Unionist figures committed to free trade were hostile as was the Liberal Party Opposition. Campbell-Bannerman wrote:

> 'This reckless criminal escapade of Joe's is the great event of our time. It is playing old Harry with all party relations. Hicks Beach will take the lead in denouncing it; he is violently (not to say viciously and even vindictively) opposed to anything in the way of protection, especially from that quarter. Young Churchill too and that lot are furious. All the old war-horses about me – Ripon, Harcourt, for instance, are snorting with excitement. We are in for a great time.'[157]

Soon after the speech, the Mayor of Liverpool had been invited to a Hughligans dinner at parliament by Winston Churchill at which Hicks Beach was in attendance. After dinner, discussion turned to how to scupper Chamberlain. The Mayor told the diners that: 'With all respect ... I have come here under some misapprehension as to the nature of the gathering. I look upon it as ... a plot against one of the leaders of our party – a leader who means more to the masses of the Industrial Midlands and North than all of us put together. I am sorry to make such a poor return for hospitality, but I think it would facilitate the business in hand if I now withdrew from the table'.[158] At which point the Mayor sought out Chamberlain and told him of what had happened before inviting him to a meeting of the Liverpool Working Men's Conservative Association. Chamberlain accepted.

The Cabinet Free Traders were angry, with Ritchie describing Chamberlain's speech as 'scandalous'. Balfour managed to get the Cabinet to agree that 'the question of the preferential treatment of the Colonies should be discussed and inquired into'.[159] Cabinet members were required to refrain from making controversial statements – although leaflets were exempted at Chamberlain's request (a decision the Free Traders acquiesced to, overlooking Chamberlain's organizational and campaigning track record, and which they quickly regretted). This Cabinet truce may well have been the official policy, but behind the scenes a battle raged. The Chamberlainites had the upper hand in the constituencies. Donations came in and on the 25th June there was a meeting of the leaders of the iron, steel and electrical manufacturing industries in the House of Commons to discuss the creation of 'a war chest ... in order that there may be a vigorous crusade in favour of the Colonial Secretary's scheme'.[160] Chamberlain created a Tariff Committee of the Birmingham Liberal Unionist Association with Chamberlain's allies in charge (the inaugural meeting of the Tariff Reform League was held on the 21st July); by July the committee claimed to have already distributed nine leaflets and another six were on the way – including a 'short handbook for speakers and students of the policy of Preferential Tariffs'. Churchill complained that Chamberlain had 'captured the party machine' and that there had been attempts to get his own agent to circulate protectionist propaganda.[161]

The Unionist Free Traders were strong in parliament and were aided by the Liberal Opposition, who were contemptuous of Balfour's fudging. Of Balfour, the Liberal MP Sir Wilfred Lawson penned a verse:

> *I'm all for Free Trade, and I'm not for Protection*
> *I approve of them both, and to both have objection*
> *In going through life I continually find*
> *It's a terrible business to make up one's mind*
> *So in spite of all comments, reproach and predictions*
> *I firmly adhere to unsettled convictions*[162]

In a debate about a Bill prohibiting 'bounty-fed' sugar, which was a minor deviation from free trade, the Free Traders launched an attack on the Government. On the second day of the debate, Churchill, the MP for Oldham, made what was lauded as a brilliant speech attacking both the Sugar Convention and Chamberlain personally. Chamberlain, as Colonial Secretary, replied for the Government and chided his critics for their use of 'extravagant language' of which he cited some examples before advising that his adversaries 'not to exhaust their vocabulary of violent adjectives, and not to turn an economic fight into a personal fight (cheers). I am told have all the logic is on their side; let them be content, and do not let them add to it abuse (cheers)'. Chamberlain then turned to Churchill's speech:

> 'We had an interesting speech today, which has earned an unusual compliment as being paid by the leader of the Opposition to the member for Oldham (cheers). I really do not know whether to congratulate my honourable friend on the ability of his speech or to condole with him in the painful position in which he finds himself. I remember my honourable friend at the time he came into Parliament, and I did the best I could then. I remember how, in the heyday of his enthusiasm, he was going to give his ready and cordial support to his own party (laughter and cheers) – and to his own Government … but it is clear that all those expectations of my honourable friend have been disappointed. One by one his fond delusions have vanished. First he discovered that the Prime Minister was unworthy of his confidence. Then came the Secretary for War, who was also found unworthy. Next it was the Foreign Secretary; then it was the President of the Board of Trade; and after all that – it is with deep regret I have to say it (loud laughter) – he came to the Colonial Secretary. But my honourable friend has still one hope – he clings to the Chancellor of the Exchequer (prolonged laughter and Opposition cheers). Well, I hope that the confidence of my honourable friend will not be again misplaced; but I warn my right honourable friend not to place too much faith in the valued and continued confidence of my honourable friend (laughter).'[163]

The issue of Tariff Reform (aka Fiscal Reform) united the Liberal Party in their opposition to it, and divided the Unionists into three camps: There were the Free Traders; there were the

Chamberlainites who supported Preference; and there were those who supported Balfour's line that there needed to be flexibility to allow retaliation against those countries which had tariff barriers against British goods. Chamberlain had made headway in the country but, not in parliament or Whitehall, and he realised that Preference was still not as popular as retaliation. His response was to plan a series of meetings as part of an educational campaign in the autumn of 1903 with a view of the Government calling a general election in 1904 with a commitment to its new policy. The Government was undergoing a bad period on fronts other than the issue of tariffs, with its Education Act remaining contentious, a reorganization of the army which was attracting much criticism, and the publication of a report into the Boer War in which several ministers and military commanders were strongly criticised, leading to adverse reports in the press and even calls for the Secretary of State for War, Lansdowne, to be impeached. (Chamberlain emerged well in the report as he had warned the War Office of the Boer build up of arms at a time of rising tensions).

A key figure in the power struggle in the Cabinet was the Duke of Devonshire (the Duke). The Duke was the Liberal Unionist leader in the House of Lords and a Free Trader, although, so both Balfour and Chamberlain believed, someone who might be persuaded to their point of view. In this they were seriously wrong. The Duke was more committed to Free Trade than they realised, was in closer contact with the hard line Free Traders than they realised, and was prone to saying that 'You can't stop halfway down Niagara' during the summer of 1903, in reference to the attempt to find a middle way rather than full Preference as advocated by Chamberlain, the Duke being convinced that Chamberlain would take the whole Unionist Party down the Preference route if any quarter was given.[164] Although the Duke readily admitted that he did not understand the tariff issue or even the economic arguments for free trade, he was nevertheless sufficiently wily not to reject Balfour and Chamberlain outright which led them on into thinking that he was open to persuasion. Basically, the Duke was a man of influence who was more interested in the races and playing cards than the details of Fiscal Reform, was forgetful, and prone to falling asleep during Cabinet meetings.[165] Yet he was to play a pivotal role in an impending bust up that became a political farce of historical proportions.

Balfour's top priority was to keep the Unionist Party together and believed that a compromise was necessary, as he wrote to the Duke, because a failure to so compromise 'will not merely break up the Unionist Party; it will shatter each separate wing ... dividing Tory from Tory, and Liberal from Liberal. This is dynamite with a vengeance! I still hope for better things'.[166] The Free Traders were not happy with Balfour's willingness to compromise with Chamberlain and were worried that without Balfour taking a firmer stand then they would 'have to face Joe at his best in the country with all his immense skill & ability, his unequalled prestige & his electioneering dexterity and unscrupulousness' and that by comparison they were not 'within a mile of him'.[167]

Chamberlain was prepared to compromise in order to help Balfour keep the Unionist Party together and to keep the Duke in the Cabinet. However, he also offered to resign from the Government in order to defuse the crisis and free himself to speak out for Preference in a personal capacity to educate public opinion. At this time the Duke hardened his stance, as he set out to Balfour in a letter:

> 'I am more and more convinced that this is and must be a fight between Free Trade and Protection, and that no real compromise is possible between them. I do not know whether you have seen the article in the *National Review* which Chamberlain told me expresses his views. I have now read it, and although there is a good deal in it which I cannot follow, it seems to me that it is an argument for pure, unmitigated Protection.'[168]

On the same day that Balfour received this letter, he also received a memorandum from Ritchie, the Chancellor of the Exchequer, in which he made it clear that he would rather resign than accept any introduction of tariffs. This stance was the same as that adopted by another Cabinet Free Trader, Balfour of Burleigh, in his own memorandum.[169] Balfour then received a letter from Chamberlain in which he reiterated what he had already said to Balfour in that he recommended that 'if you cut out the preference part of our scheme you might keep the Duke and possibly the other recalcitrants in the Cabinet for a moderate policy of Retaliation against dumping or unfair competition of any kind'. Chamberlain continued to say that he believed Preference would become inevitable with such a policy anyhow. He further wrote that: 'Of course if this were done I must leave the Cabinet, but I should do so gladly and without the slightest trace of bitterness'. He believed this as to do otherwise would be a betrayal of the Colonies and he also wanted to be able to speak and campaign freely.[170]

The Cabinet was due to meet on the 14th September 1903 and on the 13th September the Duke conferred with other Free Trade ministers from late morning to late afternoon. Before the Cabinet meeting Balfour met with Chamberlain again and they agreed that Chamberlain would be prepared to resign with a view to launching a campaign to win public opinion and in the expectation that Balfour would then swing full Government support behind Chamberlain's campaign once that had been done. Chamberlain would also seek to persuade his son and Cabinet member, Austen, to remain in the Government. The Cabinet Free Traders knew nothing of Balfour's dealings with Chamberlain. At the Cabinet meeting Balfour described Preference as not being practical politics at the present time but wanted the Government to adopt a policy of Fiscal flexibility to allow retaliation. Although Chamberlain told the Cabinet that he would go if Preference were dropped, they did not fully grasp that Chamberlain meant it and that, since Balfour was not pursuing Preference, then Chamberlain would in fact resign. Balfour told both Ritchie and Balfour of Burleigh that he expected them to resign due to their memorandums and their unwillingness to support Fiscal flexibility.

The Duke, Ritchie, Balfour of Burleigh and Lord George Hamilton all met immediately following the Cabinet. They resolved to all resign, but would await the outcome of another Cabinet meeting the next day. However, the Duke said that he wanted to see Balfour that evening and he duly visited Downing Street where, according to the Duke, Balfour hinted that Chamberlain might resign. Balfour claimed to have told the Duke that since Preference was impractical then Chamberlain would resign as he had told the Cabinet. The Duke wrote to Balfour that evening in which he stated that it would take a rejection of Preference by Balfour to alter the Duke's views.

The Cabinet meeting the following day was concerned with foreign affairs. The Free Traders met again afterwards and, allegedly, they all agreed to send in their resignations that afternoon. However, the Duke said that his resignation, which he had already written and shown to the others, was dependent upon the outcome of another meeting with Balfour. At this meeting, Balfour told the Duke that Chamberlain would probably resign and asked the Duke to keep this secret.[171] Ritchie insisted that he resigned in the belief that his resignation would be accompanied by those of Lord Balfour of Burleigh, Lord George Hamilton *and the Duke*. All the letters were sent. However, the Duke sent in a covering letter in which he invited Balfour to correct any 'misapprehension'. Balfour accepted the resignations apart from that from the Duke, to whom he urgently sent a Cabinet dispatch box saying that Chamberlain had definitely offered to resign. The Duke, who was dining at the house of Lord Edward Stanley did not have his key to the dispatch box with him when the box arrived halfway through dinner, and so he took it back home with him unopened. Feeling sleepy, he left the box downstairs and retired to bed. Next morning the Duke had forgotten all about the dispatch box, and was still hoping that Balfour would 'still find him a loophole' allowing him to withdraw his resignation.[172] While Balfour awaited the Duke's reply, Edward Stanley visited the Duke, then called in at 12 Downing Street, spoke to Sanders, was told of the dispatch box and so dashed back to the Duke to get the dispatch box urgently opened. The Duke sent word that he wanted to meet with Balfour and Balfour immediately attended the Duke, and read him Chamberlain's resignation letter and confirmed that he would speak out against Preference at a Party conference in Sheffield. The Duke agreed to withdraw his resignation, and so Balfour wrote to Chamberlain, who in contemporaneous correspondence to his supporters did not know for sure whether or not he would be required to leave office, to accept his resignation.

The fallout was scathing of particularly Balfour and the Duke. Balfour had been less than open and honest with his colleagues and the Duke was criticised for not resigning with the others – as they alleged they understood he would. Chamberlain was angry that the Duke had stated that he had been willing to stay only when Chamberlain was gone. The Duke was under substantial pressure from the Unionist Free Traders, who felt betrayed (especially Ritchie), and was feeling very sorry for himself, telling Sanders that: 'he ought never to have had anything to do with them, that he ought to have left them to take their own course, but by degrees he had been led into the position of giving them advice, and it was a position he frankly owned he ought never to have taken up'.[173] The

Duke was made to feel that he had acted dishonourably and complained to Edward Stanley: 'To think I have gone through all my life and now at the end of it to have these sort of accusations levelled against me'.[174] The Duke was at the races when he heard that Ritchie was about to publish his own version of events; he dashed off the racecourse and back to London to try and persuade him not to.

At the Sheffield conference the Free Traders were mostly shouted down during the relevant debate. Balfour's speech was an anticlimax and was spoiled when several members shouted 'What about Joe?', and ended in chaos. However, of the Duke, Winston Churchill wrote:

> 'Never did a grand inquisitor scrutinize more searchingly the utterance of a suspected heretic than did this able yet simple old man his leader's speech; and to his immense relief he found a phrase which went beyond, at least in some of its implications, the formula to which he had bound himself. He literally hurled in his resignation.'[175]

Now it was Balfour and his supporters who were critical of the Duke. Balfour even fired off an angry letter before he had had his bath in which he challenged:

> 'You were intimately acquainted during the whole fortnight in which you lent your countenance to the Government after the recent resignations. I must suppose, therefore, that it is some unintentional discrepancy between the written and the spoken word that now drives you to desert the Administration you have so long adorned. Such unintentional discrepancies are no doubt hard to avoid. Not every one, certainly not I, can always be sure of finding on the spur of the moment, before an eager audience of 5,000 people, the precise phrase which shall so dexterously express the exact opinion of the speaker on a difficult and abstract subject, as to foil the opponents who would wrest it either to the right hand or the left. But till one o'clock this afternoon I had, I confess, counted on you not as an opponent, but as a colleague – a colleague in spirit as well as name. To such a one it would have seemed natural (so at least I should have thought) to take, in cases of apparent

discrepancy, the written rather than the spoken word as expressing the true meaning of the author, or (if this be asking too much) at least to make enquiries before arriving at a final and hostile conclusion.'[176]

The Duke explained himself in a letter to a colleague, saying:

'The strain of the continuous discussions and interviews ... completely tired and wore me out ... on the Wednesday afternoon my mind was more occupied [with the various resignations] ... When therefore Balfour read me his correspondence with Chamberlain, or part of it, I altogether failed to grasp its full effect.

When I had read and considered it more carefully I became extremely uneasy. But I had made up my mind to stick to the ship and should have done so, but for the, to me, quite unexpected declarations in the Sheffield speech. It is, however, a great relief to me that the final declarations in the speech were so clear and decided (in my opinion) on the side of Protection that I had no alternative.

I suppose that now I shall be re-admitted into the fold of Free-Traders.'[177]

In the space of weeks, Balfour had managed to lose his Chancellor, Ritchie; two other Cabinet members; the Duke with all his influence; and the Government's big hitter and Colonial Secretary – Joseph Chamberlain. The Government was split and the Unionist Party in a state of civil war. It should be recalled, that this all started with Ritchie's threatened resignation in response to a Cabinet decision that there be preference shown to Canada on an existing duty on corn. This had been granted in response to Canada's request and in return to a preference given by Canada to British goods.

While Balfour and his supporters and the Free Traders argued among themselves as to who had agreed what with whom and when and who was to blame, all in full public view, Chamberlain prepared for his nationwide campaign meetings. Although Chamberlain had been caught by surprise by the speed and strength of the response to his May speech, he quickly set about the task before him. He pulled together a group of economists and journalists for advice and he had personally undertaken substantial research in addition. In the autumn of 1903 the economy was preforming poorly with shipping, railways, cotton and coal mining all struggling (coal miners wages had been cut). Unemployment was rising and *The Times* had begun an enquiry into 'pauperism'.[178]

Chamberlain's first meeting was in Glasgow on the 6th October. Chamberlain and his wife were honoured with a banquet arranged by local dignitaries before setting off for the meeting at St Andrews Hall at 8 pm. *The Times* described that Chamberlain was welcomed by a crowd of 5,000 with waving hats and handkerchiefs and loud cheers, followed by rounds of 'For he's a jolly good fellow', followed by an organ playing the national anthem. This continued for 15 minutes.[179]

Chamberlain spoke for just under two hours and began by acknowledging that Glasgow was the City in which 'Free Trade took its birth' and cited Adam Smith:

> 'When I read his books I see how even then he was aware of the importance of home markets as compared with foreign; how he supported the Navigation Laws; how he was the author of the sentence which we ought never to forget, that "Defence is greater than opulence' ... he had a broader mind ... than some ... who claim to be his successors'.[180]

Chamberlain continued his speech and turned to trade:

> 'The year 1900 was the record year of British trade. The exports were the largest we had ever known. The year 1902 – the last year – was nearly as good, and yet, if you will compare your trade in 1872, thirty years ago, with the trade of 1902 – the export trade – you will find that there has been a moderate increase of £22,000,000. That, I think, is something like 7½ per cent. Meanwhile, the population has increased 30 per cent ... In the same time the increase in the United States of America was £110,000,000, and the increase in Germany was £56,000,000 ... Meanwhile the protected countries which you have been told, and which I myself at one time believed, were going rapidly to wreck and ruin, have progressed in a much greater proportion than ours. That is not all ... When Mr Cobden preached his doctrine, he believed ... that while foreign countries would supply us with our food-stuffs and raw materials, we should

> ... send them in exchange our manufactures. But that is exactly what we have not done. On the contrary, in the period to which I have referred, we are sending less and less of our manufactures to them, and they are sending more and more of their manufactures to us.'[181]

Chamberlain then referred to a table he had compiled for British manufactures exports from 1872 to 1902, which showed exports to the USA, Germany and protected European countries fell by £42,500,000; exports to low tariff countries such as Egypt, China and those in South America increased by £35,000,000; and that exports to British Colonies increased by £40,000,000. From these figures Chamberlain concluded that:

> 'Our Imperial trade is absolutely essential to our prosperity at the present time. If that trade declines, or if it does not increase in proportion to our population and to the loss of trade with foreign countries, then we sink at once into a fifth-rate nation. Our fate will be the fate of the empires and kingdoms of the past. We shall have reached our highest point, and indeed I am not certain that there are not some of my opponents who regard that with absolute complacency. I do not. As I have said, I have the misfortune to be an optimist. I do not believe in the setting of the British star, but then, I do not believe in the folly of the British people. I trust them. I trust the working classes of this country, and I have confidence that they who are our masters, electorally speaking, will have the intelligence to see that they must wake up. They must modify their policy to suit new conditions. They must meet those conditions with altogether a new policy.'[182]

Chamberlain said that he believed that we had lost export trade with the USA and Europe because they had become protectionist, and thus had been able to industrialise. Now, the Colonies were also protectionist and were also industrialising and unless we offered them reciprocity and preference they too would steadily close their markets to us: 'I predict with certainty, that Canada will fall to the level of the United States ... The Colonies are prepared to meet us. In return for a very moderate preference they will give us substantial advantage'. Chamberlain had calculated that

£26,000,000 worth of foreign goods imported by the Colonies would be imported from Britain with a preferential system:[183]

> 'What does this mean? The Board of Trade assumes that of manufactured goods one-half the value is expended in labour – I think it is a great deal more, but take the Board of Trade figures – £13,000,000 a year of new employment. What does that mean to the United Kingdom? It means the employment of 166,000 men at 30s a week. It means the subsistence, if you include their families, of 830,000 persons; and now, if you will only add to that our present export to the British possessions of £96,000,000, you will find that that gives, on the same calculation, £48,000,000 for wages, or employment at 30s a week to 615,000 work people, and it funds subsistence for 3,075,000 persons. In other words, your Colonial trade as it stands at present with the prospective advantage of a preference against the foreigner means employment and fair wages for three-quarters of a million workmen, and subsistence for nearly four millions of our population.'[184]

Chamberlain then made an appeal to Imperial patriotism and warned that 'we must either draw closer together or we shall drift apart'.[185] He reminded the audience that the Colonies were either already giving Britain a preference and others were promising to give a preference – but that they expected something in return.

The following night, Chamberlain spoke at Greenock. This time he concentrated on the case for retaliation. He argued that he had himself been a committed believer in free trade 30 years ago, but since then the world had changed and that a new policy was needed. He said:

> 'We are a great people, but, after all, I have never been able to believe that all the wisdom in the world was absolutely domiciled in this country. I have a great opinion of our American cousins ... I have some considerable respect for the German people ... I have a great regard for our neighbours the French ... I do not believe that all these people are fools ... What is the policy of these ... nations? It has been, not a haphazard policy, but a policy deliberately adopted and deliberately pursued. It is a policy

to use tariffs to increase home trade, and, if you like, to exclude foreign trade. All these nations to which I have referred, and every other civilised nation on the face of the earth, have adopted a tariff with the object of keeping the home market to the home population and not from any want of friendship to us. I do not believe they have been in the slightest degree actuated by ill-feeling to Great Britain; but because they thought it was necessary for their own security and prosperity, they have done everything in their power to shut out British goods ... That was a deliberate policy; there is no doubt about that. Has it succeeded? It has, whether it was right or wrong. What these people intended to do they have done; and if you look back for any term of years you will find that the exports of British manufactures have fallen off to these countries, while their exports to us have risen ... I am a Free Trader. I want to have exchange with all the nations of the world, but if they will not exchange with me, then I am nor a Free Trader at any price.'[186]

Chamberlain proceeded to argue that it was illogical to introduce workplace legislation to promote welfare and higher standards of living if foreign imports were still allowed when they were not burdened with such legislation: 'If these foreign goods come in cheaper, one of two things will follow: either you will have to give up the conditions you have gained ... either you will have to take lower wages, or you will lose your work. You cannot keep your work at this higher standard of living and wages if at the same time you allow foreigners at a lower standard and lower rate of pay to send their goods freely in competition with yours'.[187] Chamberlain turned his attention to the sugar industry of which Greenock had been 'a great centre'. Despite a large increase in the demand for sugar, the number of refineries had fallen and jobs had been lost, including in the subsidiary industries. Foreign competition, aided by bounties, had damaged Greenock's sugar industry:

'Free imports have destroyed this industry, at all events for the time and it is not easy to recover an industry when it has once been lost. They have destroyed sugar-refining for a time as one of the great staple industries of the country, which it always to have remained. They have destroyed agriculture ... Agriculture, as the greatest of all trades and industries of this country, has been practically destroyed. Sugar has gone; silk has gone; iron is threatened; wool is threatened; cotton will go! How long are you going to stand it? At the present moment these industries, and the working men who depend upon them, are like sheep in a field. One by one they allow themselves to be led to the slaughter, and there is no combination, no apparent prevision of what is in store for the rest of them. Do you think, if you belong at present to a prosperous industry, that your industry will be allowed to continue? Do you think that the same causes which have destroyed some of our industries, and which are in the course of destroying others, will not be equally applicable to you when your turn comes? ...

What is the remedy? What is it that the Prime Minister proposed at Sheffield? He said – I am not quoting his exact words – Let us get rid of the chains which we ourselves have forged, and which have fettered our action. Let us claim some protection like every other civilised nation.

Then we are told that if we do this the foreigners will be angry with us! Has it come to that with Great Britain? It is a craven argument; it is worthy of the Little Englander; it is not possible for any man who believes in his own country. The argument is absurd. Who is to suffer? Are we so poor that we are at the mercy of every foreign State – that we cannot hold our own – that we are to fear their resentment if we imitate their own policy? Are we to receive their orders "with bated breath and whispering humbleness"? No, if that were true, I should say that the star of England has already set; it would not be worth anyone's while to care to speculate on her possible future. But it is not true. There is not a word of truth in it. We have nothing to fear from the foreigners. I do not believe in a war of tariffs, but if there were to be a war of tariffs, I know we should not come out second best. Why, at the present time ours is the greatest market in the whole world. We are the best customers of all those countries. There are many suitors for our markets. We may reject the addresses of some, but there is no fear that we shall not have other offers. It is absolutely absurd to suppose that all these countries, keenly competitive among themselves, would agree among themselves to fight with us when they might benefit at the expense of their neighbours. Why, at the present time, we take from Germany about twice as much as she takes from us. We take from France about three times as much, and from the United States of America we take about six times as much as they take from us. After all that, do we stand to lose if there is to be a war of tariffs?'[188]

One lesson of the Greenock meeting was that the arguments against the threat of foreign competition had had a greater impact than those advocating Preference. Chamberlain was content with the start of his campaign and left Scotland feeling optimistic. His speeches provoked seven speeches from Liberal leaders within a week. Asquith was the first to speak the day after Chamberlain's Greenock speech and he proceeded to pursue Chamberlain across the country, which established his own reputation. His first speech at Cinderford began by mocking Balfour's stance:

> 'He is asked to give a lead, and what is the lead he gives? In effect what he says to his followers is this: For the moment we will all combine to talk generalities about retaliation or freedom of negotiation, which may mean anything or which may mean nothing, so that the unity of our party will be secured; but none the less our lamented colleague, Mr Chamberlain ... will continue to conduct ostensibly from outside, his propaganda for the taxation of bread and meat. In the meantime, I, the Prime Minister, having shed my Free Trade colleagues, will contemplate his operations from afar with undisguised, though for the moment inactive, sympathy.'[189]

Asquith regarded free imports as necessary to the export trade and said that Britain's export trade to the Protectionist countries was greater than they were exporting to each other. According to him, the overwhelming bulk of the imports from Russia and the USA were food and raw materials and that there was therefore no need for tariffs on imports. Asquith shared Chamberlain's desire for Imperial unity and British prosperity but did not share Chamberlain's methods of trying to achieve them, and further rejected Chamberlain's gloomy analysis:

'Let me ask my fellow countrymen to see what has been our condition during this era of stagnant trade. During that period the amount assessed to the income tax has doubled; the interest upon our foreign investments has more than doubled; the deposits in our savings banks have multiplied two and three fold ... and last, but not least, the wages of the working classes have risen, measured not merely in terms of money, though there has been a considerable rise in our money wages, but much more measured in their real terms, in the terms of that which the money can buy. As the Board of Trade has told us, 100s buys as much as 140s twenty years ago. Talk about Germany and the wages of a protectionist country! I hope you will compare, from the material the Blue-books place at your disposal, the wages, the standard of living, and the hours of labour of the German workman and your own.'[190]

Asquith emphasized the importance of the home market as the export trade did 'not employ more than one-fifth or one-sixth of the whole labour of the country'. Asquith further condemned the statistics Chamberlain had used by leaving out earnings from shipping, investment and services and also the choice of the year 1872, which was the year after the Franco-Prussian war and was therefore not typical and Chamberlain's choice was therefore 'an absolutely unpardonable error'.[191] Asquith did not regard the small preferences suggested as being likely to make much difference were the Empire to be breaking up, and he regarded Canada's tariffs to be too high for a small preference in our favour to make much difference.

Other Free Traders made speeches in quick succession. Elsewhere the temperature was raised. Ritchie, when trying to explain matters to his constituents, was drowned out by the singing of *Rule Britannia*. Lord Spencer, the Liberal Party leader in the House of Lords, called Chamberlain 'one of the most ruthless and unscrupulous of statesmen who never hesitated to use any weapon that could advance his cause'. Austen described this as 'vulgar abuse'.[192] The Duke was elected as President of the Free Food League with Hicks Beach and Ritchie elected as Vice-Presidents.

Meanwhile, Chamberlain, during the Birmingham music festival, had a bad attack of gout and spent two days in bed. On the third day a visitor arrived to find him sitting with a tankard of champagne. The visitor enquired whether his doctor approved of his diet and Chamberlain replied that 'He wouldn't be my doctor for long if he didn't'.[193] The day before Chamberlain was due to speak in Newcastle, the gout returned, although Chamberlain managed to limp there and with a worsening headache. He made a speech that night and another in Tynemouth the next day. The following week he spoke at the invitation of the Mayor of Liverpool at the Hippodrome, as arranged following the Hughligans diner. During the speech he highlighted that France had reserved the trade to Madagascar and the USA the Cuban trade as coastal trade for their own ships only, which were heavily subsidized. He asked whether Britain should not likewise reserve trade with the Colonies as coastal trade. He believed that we should prioritise trade with 'our own kith and kin across the seas'.[194] He told the audience that by comparison with the struggles of previous generations they had 'a mere trifle ... only ... to keep the fruits of the victory that they have won' and that 'if indeed we are called upon to give up some antiquated and nevertheless dearly beloved prejudice or superstition, if indeed we are called upon for more than that, let us show that prosperity has not corrupted our blood – that it has not weakened our nerve or destroyed our fibre'.[195] *The Liverpool Courier* published a full text of the speech in a special edition that evening. Chamberlain made another two speeches the following day, in the second of which he referred to the impact of foreign competition on trades including the local watch trade:

> 'What does it matter? You have lost all these trades. You are losing others, but there is something that remains. The men who made watches are doing something else. Yes and what do they do? Here is a man who makes a watch. For that he required a fineness of touch that often is hereditary, which can only be obtained after years of work, obtained only in youth and never obtained in after-life; and the moment the watch trade ceases, or does not continue to employ the same number of workpeople, this man, who has acquired the special gift that is worth much to himself and his family, has to throw it away, to destroy it. He has to go and act as a porter or a dock labourer, or to sweep the streets, and if afterwards we restore him to his trade he would no longer be able to take advantage of it. He is

dropped into the ranks of casual employment, dropped down into the 13,000,000, be they more be they less, who are always on the verge of hunger.'[196]

A week late Chamberlain spoke in Birmingham. On this occasion he compared two loaves of bread. One was baked with 'a few ounces less flour' as would allegedly be the case with a corn duty. The two loaves were indistinguishable despite Free Trader allegations that the corn duty would produce a small loaf.

The Unionist Free Traders were very active with their own speeches and Churchill even went to Birmingham himself. Hicks Beach came out in favour or Balfour's compromise. The Duke attributed Hicks Beach's conversion to pressure from constituents.

At a meeting in Cardiff, in a scarcely prepared speech Chamberlain picked up on the issue of dumping, which the Free Traders were claiming was a good thing:

> 'We are the only free country that admits ... dumped goods, and we become in consequence the dumping-ground and the dust-heap of all Europe and America (shame) ... Mr Asquith has devoted himself to this subject of dumping, and still has a good deal to learn. He has made some astounding discoveries, which I am sure will surprise you very much. He is satisfied, and I think that others who follow the same line – Sir William Harcourt and other members of the Opposition – they have come to the conclusion that dumping is a positive benefit, that it is really a good thing that you should have sent over to this country goods below any fair price ... These gentlemen believe that foreign countries are making us a present when they dump their goods below our cost. Now, is not that rather silly? Here are these people, the Americans and the Germans, the keenest men of business in the world, the most intelligent, as intelligent as any – do you really think that they are spending millions of money in order to promote our interests (laughter)? Do you think they are ruining themselves in order to make us a present? No, they are doing nothing of the kind. The whole defence of this system is based on an utter misapprehension of what this is. They can afford to dump because it does not cost them anything; but we, who have to take the dumped goods – it costs us our

employment, our profit, our trade (cheers and a voice: "Let us alter it; it's time"). Now, Mr Asquith said the other day: "Suppose there is some dumping done by the foreign country. It is at a loss, and can't go on for ever". But that is pretty poor comfort (hear, hear). I don't suppose I can hold Mr Asquith's head under water for ever (laughter) – but I can hold it there long enough to drown him (loud cheers and laughter).

Now let us come home to Newport (hear, hear). Let us ask is this matter affecting you in this present year, 1903. it is estimated that 250,000 tons of steel bars, billets and blooms will have been imported into Newport alone; at all events into South Wales ... What is going to be saved to anybody by that 250,000 tons of steel? ... Suppose that the whole is put down at 10s below the lowest English price. They say the manufacturers that use the bars and the blooms and the billets will profit to the extent of £125,000 a year and that is what Messrs Harcourt and Asquith are always dwelling upon. They dwell upon the profit. Somebody or another gains the £125,000 a year by buying billets so much cheaper. Yes; but how much is lost (hear, hear)? Do you know how much wages there are in 250,000 tons of this stuff, if you take the cost of what has to be done to make the bars? If you supposed that they were made in this country from the ore we should get from abroad ... that 250,000 tons would involve £500,000 worth of wages – wages alone paid to the workmen ... Every man employed on each stage – the miner, the overground workman, the furnace men, the roller – every man employed in every branch of this industry from beginning to end would have a share in the advantage, and the total sum in wages gained by the country would have been £500,000 a year, which you are throwing away for the sake of a profit of £125,000 to a particular trade ...

I ask on all these occasions where does the individual come in (hear, hear)? What becomes of the men who lose their employment? They are always supposed, on the happy-go-lucky theory of Mr Asquith, to find other employment. Well, they do not (hear, hear). In many cases the only employment they find is at the workhouse (hear, hear). In other cases they emigrate. In others they go into inferior employments. The other day I had a story told me by a railway servant, and it seemed to me rather pathetic. He was at a station near Birmingham, and he saw three men unloading trucks, and the trucks contained German wire. As he passed, one of the men said, "This is rather hard; we used to make these". These were men who had been in Birmingham or elsewhere as wire makers. They formerly got good wages, and had acquired a special aptitude, but they lost their employment, and then, according to Mr Asquith's beneficent theory, they have been transferred to other employments, being now engaged like common labourers – all their skill thrown away and no longer the slightest advantage to them, as they worked at unloading German wire. Who profits from this?'[197]

The following day *The Times* commented: 'Nothing bears more eloquent witness, not merely to his physical energy, but to the mastery of the subject and the abundance of the resources on which he draws, than the way in which he is thus able, time after time, to follow up one remarkable utterance with another, perfectly new in character, and not less impressive'.[198]

There was a stark contrast between Chamberlain's campaign and that of those favouring Free Trade. The Free Traders were active, including the Unionist Free Traders, whereas Chamberlain was alone. The Free Traders themselves claimed to be getting support, although other reports were less favourable. At the end of November, the National Union of Conservative Associations elected a substantial majority of Chamberlainites to their executive; and *The Sun* newspaper came out in favour of Chamberlain. In the first week of December the Council of the Chamber of Agriculture passed a resolution in favour of a full Tariff Reform policy and Field Marshal Wolseley declared for Chamberlain.

There were five by-elections due, and the first two in Dulwich and Lewisham, both marginal seats, were held on the 15th December. Despite being requested by Central Office to stick to the Balfour line, both candidates declared for a full Chamberlain policy. The Duke published a letter, supported by Ritchie, Balfour of Burleigh and George Hamilton which stated: 'The Duke of Devonshire, as President of the Unionist Free Food League, is of opinion that an elector who sympathises with the objects of that

League would be well advised to decline to give his support, at any election, to a Unionist candidate who expresses his sympathy with the policy of Mr Chamberlain and the Tariff Reform League'.[199] The Unionist by-election candidates thus had to fight off opposition from a section of their own party, which was in an open state of civil war. The results were good victories for both Chamberlainite Unionist candidates and exceeded Chamberlain's own expectations. The next day Chamberlain had a meeting in Leeds when they were mobbed by a crowd as Mrs Chamberlain wrote to her mother: 'On arriving at Leeds to our surprise nobody was on the platform to receive us, though an enthusiastic crowd quickly sprang out of the ground, and then as we walked along the platform to the hotel at the end it gathered in such numbers that the two stalwart policemen in front were quite unable to stem the tide – and we were so closely pressed by friendly admirers that I began to wonder whether we should be carried off our feet ...'[200] Chamberlain began his speech by acknowledging his opponents:

> 'I am not so much impressed as I ought to be with the authority which they carry. It is true that Mr Ritchie has called my attention to the fact that there are four Chancellors of the Exchequer among them, and that one of them is himself (laughter). I have a doubt whether the magnificent robes which the Chancellor of the Exchequer wears upon occasion carry with them all the virtues and all the wisdom of all his predecessors (laughter) – and I am quite unable – with no disrespect to him – to accept Mr Ritchie as a great financial authority, because he happened to be under the tuition of the permanent officials of the Treasury for the space of a few months.'[201]

On the 23rd December the Chamberlainite Unionist candidate won the next by-election in Ludlow despite Churchill supporting the opponent. A few days later both George Hamilton and Churchill were repudiated by their constituency associations.

At this point the fatal flaw in Chamberlain's strategy became increasingly obvious. The Unionists were winning by-elections and Chamberlain was receiving rapturous support with his speaking campaign. A large section of the press was backing him and he had the overwhelming support of the ordinary Unionist members. Unionism had been reinvigorated and had regained the political initiative. Yet as he looked for Balfour to weigh in and support him, as they had agreed, Balfour sat tight. Chamberlain was left to fight on with his campaign without Government support and not as part of an electoral strategy.

Balfour was more fixated on trying to maintain a compromise between the Chamberlainites and the Free Traders and keep the Unionist Party together. The consequence of this strategy was that the Unionist Party continued to rip itself apart. Balfour failed to see that it was more important to keep the Unionist voters than it was to keep some Free Trade party grandees. The Unionists lost the next two by-elections where the candidates stuck to Balfour's line.

Chamberlain was suffering from ill health, both from gout and a strained heart. In early 1904 he took two months holiday (his doctors had recommended four months). In May 1904, Chamberlain made a speech in Birmingham to the Grand Committee of the Birmingham Liberal Unionist Association, where he dealt with the by-election losses (There were 37 parliamentary by-elections in 1904 and 1905. The Unionists lost 28 and won only 9.)[202]:

> 'Where we have had our won our greatest successes has been in London, in Rochester, in Shropshire, and, above all, in South Birmingham; where we have had candidates who have had a little courage, and who have dared to call their souls their own (laughter) – who have supported with all their might whole-heartedly the policy in which they believe, and who have earned and deserved to earn, the result of their courage. Victories in politics are like victories in war: they are won by enthusiasm; they are lost by timidity. It is not, after all, good policy – to say nothing at all about morality – it is not good policy to sit on a fence (hear, hear). Now, I say, at the next election, whatever its result is to be, let us hold our banner high (cheers) – and we shall have plenty who will come to the standard. Let us fight, if we must fight, for something worth fighting for. I do not much like the modern political nomenclature, and I will not use it; but I will say that on the whole I believe that those who take "Thorough" as their guiding motto will be much more likely to be successful than those who are half-hearted and weak-kneed and trying to catch a breeze that will never come.'[203]

By May 1904 the Unionists were openly split and the venom was scarcely contained. Hugh Cecil accused Chamberlain of physical cowardice in the House of Commons.[204] Other Free Traders defected. Churchill who had been in the habit of saying: 'Thank God we have a Liberal Party' and who had been intriguing to form a coalition government with the Duke as Prime Minister also defected shortly after being snubbed by Balfour, who left the House of Commons as Churchill started to speak and was closely and noisily followed by others when Churchill objected (some even stopped to jeer at Churchill as they left).[205] When Churchill crossed the House of Commons to sit with the Liberals, he did so to Unionist cries of 'Blenheim Rat' and 'Blackleg Blueblood'.[206] Churchill was scathing of the Government: 'To keep in office for a few weeks and months there is no principle which the Government is not prepared to abandon, and no quantity of dust and filth they are not prepared to eat', and of Balfour: 'The dignity of a Prime Minister, like a lady's virtue, is not susceptible to partial diminution'.[207]

Chamberlain continued his campaign from outside the Government while Balfour concentrated on clinging on to office and surviving various motions on the Fiscal issue in the House of Commons. There was a suggestion that there be a Colonial Conference to take the matter of tariff reform further; Balfour was not inclined to agree to this 'at present' (August 1904).[208] Eventually Balfour came up with a counter proposal that there could be a Colonial Conference to discuss the issue, but that it would require a mandate at a general election at first and then any decisions made at the conference would have to be put to the electorate in another election afterwards.[209] Thus was born Balfour's twin election strategy which he put forward in private correspondence and averred to in a speech in October 1904: 'Any large plan for Imperial union on fiscal or other lines, ought not to be regarded as accepted by any of the parties ... unless their various electorates have given their adhesion to the scheme'. Balfour stated that this 'may take, and indeed must take, some time to carry out'.[210] Hicks Beach commented that: 'both he and Joe would be under ground before anything could be done'.[211] Balfour was simply kicking the matter into the long grass. Meanwhile Chamberlain continued to campaign.

As the failure to move towards *any* kind of tariff reform continued, Balfour not even trying to implement his own version of it, Chamberlain suggested a private meeting and this occurred in February 1905. The meeting, over dinner, did not go well and Balfour was obstinate. They even disagreed about the effect of and the reason for candidates going down to defeat in by-elections. Chamberlain believed that his stance aroused enthusiasm and yet the candidates were being forced by Central Office to adopt the Balfour line. Balfour insisted that the candidates 'in every case' had adopted the retaliation stance due to 'local not central influence'.[212] In March there were two more by-elections. One candidate adopted Balfour's retaliation line and lost not least, according to the election agent, due to the intervention of the Free Food League and there being 'no corresponding reply from our side' and that 'it was the lies of the Free Food League that frightened' the voters (The Tariff Reform League advocated a Chamberlainite policy and was therefore excluded); in the other by-election, in Liverpool, the candidate was a Chamberlainite and won.[213]

In parliament the Government spent much time trying to avoid defeat in debates related to Fiscal reform with either the Free Trade Unionists or the Liberal Party Opposition initiated. At one point, in the face of four resolutions of which half were attacking Chamberlain's position alone, one attacking Balfour's position and one attacked both, Balfour instructed the Unionist Party to abstain in a compromise to avoid a Unionist split and a defeat, after originally being prepared to go back on a deal reached with Chamberlain as to how to handle this scenario. Balfour announced his intention to abstain and got up and left the House of Commons with his supporters following him. This farce led to very adverse comment in the press, seeing the manner in which Balfour had been prepared to disown Chamberlain and which realised, if Balfour and his supporters did not, that the Unionist Party was headed for crushing electoral defeat at the next election. Tariff Reformers were also becoming increasingly angry and believed that the longer the present Government stayed in office the worse would be its ultimate defeat. In the constituencies matters were unsettled, not least because the Free Traders risked being deselected, as had happened to Hugh Cecil when a Chamberlainite candidate was chosen to replace him. Hugh Cecil was a particular target due to his accusation of cowardice against Chamberlain.[214] Balfour instructed the Government Chief Whip to lobby on behalf of Cecil to the local association, and Chamberlain offered the full resources of the Tariff Reform League, which had branches in the constituencies,[215] for the new candidate.[216] In reply to a plea for help from Hugh Cecil, in an exercise of fence-sitting, Balfour wrote:

> 'Just as I think Chamberlain has done much injury to what I believe to be his fundamental object – Imperial Unity – by his attempts to harness all sorts of particular and selfish interests to his Imperial car; so I think the free fooders have also done great injury to free trade by their appeals to ignorance and prejudice and by the exaggerated importance they have given to any objections that may be made to a re-arrangement of our duties on food.'[217]

In May 1905 at a meeting with some of the Tariff Reformers and Balfour's supporters at the House of Commons, Chamberlain offered to rejoin the Cabinet, without portfolio, provided the Cabinet would adopt a policy of Colonial Preference. Balfour declined the offer, although in the discussion afterwards he agreed that: tariff reform would be the leading policy in the Unionist programme at the next general election; that there should be an 'all-round' tariff; and that the outcome of a Colonial Conference should be acted upon (i.e. there would be no delay until another general election). Chamberlain warned his jubilant supporters, who thought that they had got all they wanted, that they needed to be cautious. Chamberlain was correct, as they discovered that Balfour had told the Free Fooders that he had agreed nothing with Chamberlain.[218] Eventually Balfour did make a speech in which he committed broadly to that which he had agreed. Chamberlain subsequently interpreted the speech in terms which left the Free Traders aghast. Balfour insisted that: 'Those who wish to know the views I hold had better get them from my own speeches not from those of the Right Honourable member for West Birmingham'.[219]

By the middle of 1905, Chamberlain's health had deteriorated; he had had repeated headaches, gout and memory lapses. His recovery from his illnesses was slow. On one occasion he had found himself unable to speak or even write for a few minutes before recovering. Even so, he insisted, against doctor's orders, in making a speech two days later.[220]

At a mass meeting of the Tariff Reform League at the Albert Hall, Chamberlain made a speech in which he contrasted the League's position to that of the Balfour supporters:

> 'We do not only exist for inquiry (cheers). We are not where we are merely to ask questions – we are determined to carry inquiry into action (loud and prolonged cheers).
>
> Let no man join us under any mistake. We are a fighting force (renewed cheers). We have a definite and a constructive policy. Let no man join us who does not agree with the whole of it (prolonged cheering) ... There is no object in concealing anything. We do not shrink from the logical consequences of the action we have undertaken (cheers). Why are we an independent association? In order that we may be independent, that we may speak our minds ...
>
> I am a politician – with all the faults of a politician, and I know if I was speaking and acting as a politician alone I should recognise the value in politics of a discreet obscurity (laughter). I am not speaking to you tonight in that capacity, and while what I say may not be universally popular, I cannot help believing that in the long run it will be the wisest course to take even for a hardened politician (laughter). I know very well that there are men on both sides of politics who, when some forward movement is in progress, are led by their excessive modesty to creep to the rear (laughter). They are the men who tell you that rapid advance – too rapid advance – should be avoided. They are the men who are afraid to commit themselves prematurely (laughter), and it is only when the battle has been fought and won (cheers), that they emerge to congratulate the victors (laughter).'[221]

By August when the House of Commons rose for its summer break, Chamberlain was exhausted. He left for Aix-les-Bains to take a cure and then spent several weeks on holiday. He returned to Britain refreshed and reinvigorated. By October he was openly speaking of the desirability of calling an election – which he fully expected to lose given the state of the Unionist Party. Fresh attempts to find a compromise between Chamberlain and the Free Traders came to nothing. On a train journey to Windsor to meet the

King of Greece, who was on a state visit, Balfour and Chamberlain (and Mrs Chamberlain) shared a carriage and had a frank discussion. Chamberlain told Balfour: 'I tell you Arthur, you will wreck the Party if you go on. You should have dissolved two years ago'. Balfour eventually acknowledged that Chamberlain might be right after initial reluctance. In a speech soon later in Bristol, Chamberlain referred to the prospect of an impending election and said:

> 'If you want to win now or later – if your policy is to bring with it the full application of the principles which you have desired to establish, believe me you must have a forward policy (cheers) – you must not suffer it to be whittled down by the timid or the half-hearted minority of your party (cheers) – you must not ask the majority, be it nine-tenths, or, as I think, ninety-nine-hundredths (hear, hear) – you must not ask them to sacrifice their convictions to the prejudices of the minority (cheers). No army was ever led successfully to battle on the principle that the lamest man should govern the march of the army (hear, hear).'[222]

After saying that 'We lost some of the friends whom we would very gladly have kept if they had agreed with us (laughter)' and that those losses were minute compared to the new supporters his campaign had attracted, Chamberlain continued and set out his own stance:

> 'I see in papers, I hear in speeches, talk about the divisions in the Unionist party. Where are they (hear, hear)? There is a most grotesque exaggeration on the part of the people who make the divisions (hear, hear). Of course, if there are a thousand people on one side and one on the other it is a division (laughter and cheers) ... No honest man will doubt for a moment that the Unionist party is substantially agreed (hear, hear) upon the two main objects of the future constructive policy. We are agreed upon Retaliation (loud cheers) – we are agreed upon Preference (renewed cheers). I will add to that, because I am determined to withhold nothing in my appeal to the country (cheers) – you can't have Retaliation, and the more you look at it the more it will be clear to you, without a general tariff; you can't have

> Preference – that is to say, you can't secure from your kinsmen abroad the advantages which will secure to you their trade, their ever-increasing trade, unless you think in the same spirit (cheers) – unless you will treat with them a little better than our rivals and competitors, unless you will give to them, in return for a Preference on you manufactures, a Preference on their chief product, even although that product may be described as a principal part of the food of this country (hear, hear). It is useless to hide yourselves in the sand, and because our opponents indulge in the grossest misrepresentations and the most colossal lies (cheers) – I say it is perfectly absurd for us to think that we can meet these misrepresentations by trying to hide what our policy is. Let us defend our policy (hear, hear). My object is to make clear what it is ... [It is] more work for the people of this country (cheers) and a closer union between the different parts of the Empire (renewed cheers).[223]

The Times and *The Telegraph* both ran leading articles to the effect that Chamberlain's Bristol speech had left the Government little option but to resign. *The Times* said that what Chamberlain had called for was that the Unionist Party should unite behind *his* policy. Balfour announced his resignation to the King on the 4th December 1905.

Ritchie attended Downing Street soon after the Government's fall to inquire after a Viscounty and ran into Sanders, who held Ritchie responsible for the Government's troubles. Sanders rudely told Ritchie that he deserved nothing. In the event, Balfour awarded him a barony. It should not be forgotten that Ritchie was responsible, in his threat to resign in response to a Cabinet decision to give preference on an existing duty on corn, for precipitating a prolonged division and power struggle that ended the Unionist administration.

The Liberal Party leader, Campbell-Bannerman, put together a new government within days. On the 23rd December 1905 he told a meeting at the Albert Hall:

> 'We were told – told emphatically and abundantly – that the method of their (the Government's) going would be a masterpiece of tactical skill. Tactics! Tactics! Ladies and

gentlemen, the country is tired of their tactics. It would have been better for them if they had had less of tactics and more of reality. But they have lived for some years on nothing but tactics and now they have died of tactics.'[224]

The various factions of the Unionist Party went their own way. Balfour was no longer able to control them or demand their allegiance. Chamberlain had won control of the Unionist local committees, both the Liberal Unionist and Conservative national organizations, and the Unionist press; only Central Office remained beyond his influence.[225] Chamberlain was 'tired of this word splitting' and resolved to fight his own campaign without referring to Balfour.[226] The Liberal Party secured a victory in the following general election of January 1906, with even Balfour losing his seat, when they won 377 out of 670 seats; Labour won 53; the Irish nationalists 83; and the Unionists 157, of whom an estimated 11 were Free Fooders, 32 were Balfourites and 109 Chamberlainites (5 were deemed uncertain).[227] Thus although the Unionist Party was comprehensively defeated, for a variety of reasons including a booming economy between 1905 and 1907 (which undermined the argument that the economy was suffering due to free trade),[228] and a public hostility to the importation of Chinese labour into South Africa that was described as having 'enormous influence',[229] the Chamberlain supporters were by far the majority of the Unionists and the Birmingham seats were all held by hugely *increased* majorities (Chamberlain himself had a majority of 5,079 – an increase of 801).[230] The Unionists did not lose because of tariff reform and some even went so far as to attribute fighting robustly advocating that cause as the main reason for their success; Wyndham wrote [italics his own]: 'I won *solely* on Fiscal Reform ... The working-men poled right out for Fiscal Reform & the Empire. I won on that, & nothing else'.[231] Britain did not vote against tariff reform, they voted the fragmented Unionist government out. They voted against the importation of cheap Chinese labour into South Africa. They voted for change.

Chamberlain led the Unionists in the House of Commons until Balfour was able to return and remained loyal to Balfour. He did not entertain leadership ambitions himself. The 8th July was his seventieth birthday and he had also now reached 30 years as a Birmingham MP. The Birmingham civic leaders and dignitaries agreed to celebrate this, irrespective of party. His birthday fell on the Sunday and Friday was spent quietly with his family. Flags were flown from public buildings and as well as private properties. Commemorative medals were given to elementary school children and the Faculty and students of the University of Birmingham sent Chamberlain their congratulations. On the Friday evening bunting was spontaneously put up in several streets. On Saturday the celebrations started in earnest with a lunch given by the Lord Mayor and attended by 200 dignitaries, after which Chamberlain gave a speech and expressed his gratitude. Chamberlain emerged at 3.30pm to cheering crowds and commenced a 17-mile tour of the city in a cavalcade of 80 cars. There was an estimated 50,000 crowd along the route. In the evening there was a fireworks display. Chamberlain said that he felt very tired and was still feeling so the following day – his birthday. He spent the day with his family, going through the large volume of telegrams from across the globe. On Monday, there was a meeting at which 10,000 people attended. After some pomp, Chamberlain made a speech in which he reflected upon his career and thanked the people of Birmingham for their support. The next day he returned to London for a dinner at which he was host. The day after Chamberlain, despite complaining of tiredness, attended a meeting of the Tariff Commission and made a speech before returning home. He was due to go out to dinner that evening, but was in his library and was late. Mrs Chamberlain went to investigate and found the library door locked and Chamberlain faintly spoke that he could not get out. While a footman went to fetch a crowbar Chamberlain managed to open the door. Mrs Chamberlain found him on the floor and paralysed down the right side. He had suffered a stroke.

Chamberlain made some initial recovery but had difficulty speaking and writing properly. While his mental faculties remained sharp, physically he became increasingly frail. His days in the front line of politics were over, although he retained his seat and was re-elected uncontested by the Liberal Party. He maintained some considerable influence behind the scenes and was very active in the run up to the two general elections of 1910.

The battle for Tariff Reform continued. Between January 1909 and the January 1910 election, the Tariff Reform League held 7,763 meetings, circulated 53million leaflets and pamphlets and organized 161 Dump Shops, motor omnibuses, and caravans; 900,000 copies of a cartoon *Fiscal Facts* were distributed and during the election no less than 166,000 posters were dispatched.

Meanwhile the Free Trade Union had sponsored more than 5,000 meetings between 1903 and 1909, and in 1910, when there were two general elections, it held 12,471 meetings.[232]

The outcome of the election of January 1910 was: Liberals 275; Labour 40; Irish Nationalists 82; Unionists 273. the result meant that the Liberals held on to office. The Unionists had fought on a tariff reform policy. In the second general election of that year it was expected that that policy would be adhered to. However, after pressure from Lancashire free traders, Balfour announced in a speech at a public meeting that any tariff on food items would be subject to a referendum approval first. Mrs Chamberlain wrote: 'A bolt from the blue fell upon us on Tuesday night and I could not believe my eyes when I saw what Mr Balfour had committed himself to at the Albert Hall ... and agreed to submit Tariff Reform to a referendum!!! I could have cried. Poor Joe! Poor Austen! Just when their efforts seemed ready to be crowned with success and the whole Party brought into line, Mr Balfour strong for the policy and all going well ... Joe is his usual controlled self over it'.[233] Balfour's referendum commitment meant not only that there would not necessarily be full tariff reform, but also gave a minority of free traders in the Unionist Party the ability to vote against the referendum and so scupper the whole project; from their track record, this was a very real danger. Austen held that the referendum commitment cost the Unionists more votes than they might possibly have gained. The general election result was: Liberals 272; Labour 42; Irish Nationalists 84; and Unionists 272. Hugh Cecil, representing a university constituency, was the sole remaining Unionist Free Trader.[234]

Chamberlain died peacefully following a heart attack in July 1914. The Dean of Westminster offered that he be buried at Westminster Abbey; this was declined as it had been Chamberlain's desire to be buried, as had other members of his family, in Key Hill Cemetery, in Birmingham.

SUMMARY

Britain may well have been the first industrial nation, but by the end of the 19th century she was already in long term economic decline. The USA and Germany, in particular, were overtaking Britain economically (and hence inevitably would do so militarily in due course). Britain's decline was not inevitable and there were those who believed that they knew the causes and sought to rectify them. Tariff Reform was the major issue and Britain's policy of unilateral free trade – adhered to with religious fervour – was held to be the major obstacle to arresting the decline of British industry and the unification of the British Empire. Tariff Reform was therefore advocated for two reasons: to retaliate against protectionist foreign countries; and to enhance the Empire's economic development and further its unification.

Joseph Chamberlain led a determined campaign to overturn an interpretation of free trade that was destructive to Britain's continuance, as he and his supporters saw it, as the world's leading power and economic prosperity. Chamberlain galvanised support from ordinary party activists, the press and the wider public and by-elections were being won. The establishment opposed him with all its might. A handful of Unionist Party grandees held their party to ransom and ultimately split it apart, sending it into electoral oblivion. Balfour was as inept as he was treacherous and unprincipled, not seeing that it was more important to present an appealing programme to the voters and wider party. Instead, Balfour tried to trick his way through a series of Cabinet and parliamentary crises and resignations. The Unionist Party ceased to be a cohesive organization and split into warring factions.

The trigger for the animosity was a decision to give preference to Canada on a piddling corn duty. Yet the purity of free trade theories, and the degree of intolerance of any deviation from a particular interpretation of free trade, was such that the Free Traders were happy to destroy any proposals to address the protectionist trading practices of Britain's rivals and competitors – no matter the consequences. This puritanical allegiance to free trade was in contrast to the hard-headed approach adopted by Lord Palmerston who vigorously defended the national interest.

There are those who say that free trade won and that protectionism lost in the fight for Tariff Reform before WWI. That is a gross distortion. Any victory for free trade was confined to Britain only. In fact the defeat of the social imperialists and the Tariff Reform campaign was more about the defeat of the Unionist Party in the 1906 election and its failure to recover afterwards. That electoral defeat was for a multitude of reasons including its general unpopularity, the mood for change given the length of time that the Unionist Party had been in office and the general incompetence of Balfour leading to the resignations, defections and divisions. The Unionist Party in 1906 was no longer a credible party of office. The opposition to and defeat of Tariff Reform owed as much to personal animosity and political opportunism as to the free trade religion. Chamberlain had very successfully pulled together a formidable campaign across the country and had won support from a variety of leading newspapers. He had a strong following among ordinary people and had Balfour honoured his deal with Chamberlain to swing the government behind Chamberlain's campaign in 1904 then history may well have been very different.

Before continuing the historical narrative into the inter-war years, which were a turning point for Britain, first there will be an examination of Keynes' thinking and his *General Theory*. It is vital to recognise that the *General Theory* is just that – a theory. It is not an analysis born of historical fact. It is an abstract theory. Keynes may well have had strong views on what was wrong in the inter-war years, but, as will be seen, the facts of the extent of Keynes' influence do not match the myth. It is therefore beneficial to examine the theory before examining the historical facts in order to appreciate its irrelevance and the importance of what actually did happen and the lessons to be learnt.

5 THE GENERAL THEORY

Keynes had been advocating higher government spending as a solution to unemployment for some time before he wrote the *General Theory*. His rationale changed as he grappled the justification for his preferred policy, in particular how to pay for it. His thinking was further a reaction against the various policies pursued by governments of the inter-war period, as well as a reaction against the prevailing classical economic theory. Keynes' efforts were therefore directed at debunking classical economic theory, criticizing government policy, and developing a theory to justify his demands for more government intervention and more government spending.

Keynes' voluminous writing for newspapers, on both sides of the Atlantic, essays, pamphlets for elections (he supported the Liberal Party) and books culminated in *Treatise* and, in particular, the *General Theory*. Keynes' thinking continually changed as he tried to grapple with the task he had set himself and under the influence of The Circus – a group of economist colleagues with whom he discussed his work (The Circus was disbanded in 1931).[235] After seven years writing the *Treatise*, he told his wife that 'artistically it is a failure – I have changed my mind too much during the course of it for it to be a proper unity'.[236] Friedrich Hayek (1899-1992) wrote a long critique to the *Treatise* in the London School of Economics (LSE) house journal in a two part article. After the second instalment had been published in February 1932, in reference to Keynes, Hayek claimed: 'Great was my disappointment when all this effort seemed wasted because after the appearance of the second part of my article he told me that he had in the meantime changed his mind and no longer believed what he had said in that work'.[237] Indeed by May Keynes was speaking of 'working it out all over again'.[238]

Keynes' *General Theory*, the basis of what was subsequently defined as Keynesianism, dealt with how to reduce unemployment. A major attention has been focused on the *General Theory's* rejection of Say's Law. Keynes interpreted Say's Law as to mean that there could be 'no such thing as involuntary unemployment in the strict sense'. Obviously, were supply to create its own demand then a supply of workers will create a demand for workers and hence Keynes' interpretation is valid.[239] Keynes defined involuntary unemployment thus:

> 'Men are involuntarily unemployed if, in the event of a small rise in the price of wage-goods relatively to the money-wage, both the aggregate supply of labour willing to work for the current money-wage and the aggregate demand for it at that wage would be greater than the existing volume of employment.'[240]

It should be noted that this definition is not one relying upon money wages, but implicitly on real wages. Keynes took the view that a cut in real wages might be necessary to increase employment but that to achieve this by cutting money wages was difficult. He believed that to reduce the value of money, which the employed would either not realise or not care about too much, was a better way to achieve a desired cut in real wages. The definition he therefore gives is one which facilitates his preferred policy option, which he had been advocating for a long period before he actually wrote the *General Theory*. Keynes relied upon *Treatise*, despite changing his opinions, when writing the *General Theory* and the *General Theory's* reading at the time was expected to be by those who had already read *Treatise*.[241]

Keynes persistently argued that there should be an increase in government spending to create extra demand and jobs. As to where the money was to come from to pay for his much vaunted public works, Keynes had, in October 1928, three sources to hand. Firstly, by increasing the bank rate to attract home savings; secondly, to attract foreign savings (this could not be done on an international scale as each country could not attract foreign savings); and finally by credit inflation to transfer income into the pockets of businessmen. It was not until February 1929 that he hit on another scheme, in which he argued that more resources would become available 'by restoring the equilibrium between savings and investment'.[242] Keynes argued that: 'The volume of real investment is falling short of the volume of money savings. Industry is too depressed to absorb all the savings which the public is ready to place at its disposal'.[243]

Keynes went to great lengths to advance a theory that savings could exceed investment and that such would cause unemployment, to some success with his followers, and with considerable lack of success for the classical economists who remained unconvinced at Keynesian theorising; for classical economists interest rates ensured that savings matched investment. There was no meeting ground on this point and no empirical evidence is available to prove the issue and it remains unproven.[244]

The *Treatise* made its sums add up by defining income as expected income, including expected profit, excluding windfall gains or losses. If expected income is realised then savings are equal to investment. But even if the expected profit is not realised then it is still counted as being a part of income. Since savings are this theoretical income less actual consumption, then the savings figure is also an artificial one. In a recession with falling profits, then the expected profit figure is not realised and the difference between the outcome profit figure and the expected profit figure is a loss equal, in theory, to an excess of savings. The flaw in this theory is that none of the figures being used to establish that savings exceed investment exist in reality. It is an abstract theory based on expectations and not reality.[245] Mathematical equations can only be as good as the assumptions on which they were based and Keynes subsequently backtracked from the assumptions he had made.

Keynes developed this thinking further in a modification of his reasoning. He came to believe that savings were passive and a product of the demand for investment. The level of savings were determined by the demand for investment. Therefore the amount of investment, and therefore the level of output, was not determined by the available savings, but determined the level of savings.[246]

A key aspect of Keynes' logic was the multiplier. Richard Ferdinand Kahn (1905-1989), an economist who was a member of The Circus, first voiced the concept of the multiplier in *Can Lloyd George Do It?* (1929) when he wrote: 'The fact that many workpeople who are now unemployed would be receiving wages instead of unemployment pay would mean an increase in effective purchasing power which would give a general stimulus to trade'.[247] Keynes did not immediately embrace the views of his Circus colleagues and Joan Robinson (1903-1983), an economist and another member of the Circus, commented that 'there were moments when we had some trouble in getting Maynard to see what the point of his revolution really was'.[248] Kahn went on to quantify the multiplier effect by calculating that if half of all the extra income was spent and those in receipt of this extra expenditure would likewise spend half of their new income, then the original expenditure will be multiplied by two once the subsequent expenditure is taken into account (hence the multiplier is two). This meant that the impact of extra expenditure on the economy could be calculated with some precision if the amount of the extra income that would be spent were known accurately (thus allowing the multiplier figure to be known accurately). To Keynes the propensity to consume determined the extent of the multiplier. At the time of writing *General Theory*, Keynes assumed that the multiplier would be slightly higher than 2.[249]

Versions of the multiplier theory were developed at this time by four economists: LF Giblin in Australia, Ralph Hawtrey at the Treasury, Richard Kahn at Cambridge University and by Jens Warming in Denmark.[250] Hawtrey refined his own thinking and focused on what he described as secondary consumption, in the same way in which Kahn had focused on secondary employment. It was another way of presenting the multiplier.[251] Kahn, assuming that supply was elastic and that prices would not rise, calculated that the secondary employment generated would be determined by the proportion of extra expenditure created by the new investment.[252]

Keynes wrote: 'Mr Kahn has produced an argument, which seems to me convincing, for supposing that in present conditions in Great Britain a given amount of primary employment gives rise to an approximately equal amount of secondary employment'.[253] Keynes recognised that it was necessary for there to be unused resources for the multiplier to work as expected and that the impact of the multiplier was limited by leakages such as imports.[254] This gave rise to a questioning of free trade.

Having developed this concept, attention was then turned to perfecting the theory. 'Leakages', as Keynes subsequently called them, were a source of difficulty in determining the extra output that would arise from extra spending. These leakages included personal savings, reduced unemployment benefit payments as people become employed, increases in unspent profits *and imports*, which amount to spending being transferred abroad rather than being spent in the home economy. Unspent profits would amount to an increase in savings.

The conclusion reached was that the initial borrowing incurred would pay for itself through higher economic activity as a result of the increased public investment and the multiplier effect flowing from that increased public investment. There would not therefore be an increased burden of debt to be funded from future tax receipts, as those tax receipts will have been increased by the public investment. Key to this theory is the belief that savings would increase to fund the investment. One of those at the centre of the Circus, James Meade, subsequently wrote:

> 'Keynes's intellectual revolution was to shift economists from thinking normally in terms of a model of reality in which a dog called *savings* wagged his tail labelled *investment* to thinking in term of a model in which a dog called *investment* wagged his tail labelled *savings*.'[255]

Keynes was still attached to his earlier position regarding the mismatch between savings and investment as set out in *Treatise* as the Circus was developing this new view of savings. In the summer of 1931, Keynes was still denying that savings and investment were necessarily equal in public lectures in Chicago. One of the better known of Keynes parables was the banana parable, which he first explained before the Macmillan Committee (which had been formed after the 1929 Wall Street Crash to investigate the perilous state of the British economy). In this parable, a community owns only banana plantations and they only produce and consume bananas. What is not spent on bananas is saved. The investment in the banana plantations equals exactly the amount saved. However, Keynes said, 'into this Eden there enters a thrift campaign urging the members of the public to abate their improvident practice of spending nearly all their current incomes on buying bananas for food'. This leads to an increase in savings which is not matched by an increase in investment. There is no reason for an increase in investment as the bananas are still being produced in the same quantity but, as they will not keep, they have to be sold. As the public is now spending less on bananas the same quantity of bananas are therefore sold for lower prices. Keynes claimed that: 'the only effect has been to transfer the wealth of the entrepreneurs out of their pockets into the pockets of the public'. Keynes then pointed out that: 'The only thing that increases the actual wealth of the world is actual investment'.[256] Investment might be the only way to increase wealth in the long run as it increases the productive capacity. The parable does not take account of a fall in the incomes of those employed on the banana plantations that would occur if the bananas are selling for less, or of a reduction of banana production if it becomes unprofitable, or of the fall in savings that would occur if people were being paid less as they would have less income out of which savings are to be made. However, Keynes was setting out a danger that might befall a country in a recession where the multiplier effect would worsen the fall in output in a downwards direction.

When interest rates had been cut to 2% and the interest rates on savings were down to 0.5%, Keynes believed that Britain had reached what he described as a liquidity trap, especially at a time of high deflation: 'When prices are falling 30 to 40 per cent between the average of one year and that of the next, as they were in Great Britain and in the United States during 1921, even a bank rate of 1 per cent would have been oppressive to business since it would have corresponded to a very high rate of real interest'.[257] Keynes was now advocating the same policies of public spending etc. albeit for entirely different reasons.[258] He no longer argued that there were rigidities which allowed a state of disequilibrium to persist, and hence there was a need to artificially cut real wages in order to price people back into work, for example, but that the equilibrium level of output might not necessarily involve full employment anyway and that an increase in effective demand was necessary to create a new equilibrium at which full employment could be achieved.[259] Thus Keynes' thinking changed and continued to change.

The belief that the failure of the cut in interest rates to achieve full employment was because of a lack of competitiveness, and that a cut in wages was therefore needed, was undermined by the high levels of unemployment worldwide as the leading economies plunged into the Slump. They could not all be uncompetitive with each other, and so wage cuts in each country were not seen by Keynes to be a solution. Interest rates cuts had failed to revive economic fortunes. To Keynes a new equilibrium had brought investment and savings into balance, but at a level of output that meant many people remained unemployed. To Keynes the economy was not self-correcting, as the classical economists believed it would be, and the mass unemployment was liable to continue.

Even before Keynes set out his new thinking in the *General Theory*, he had begun to articulate the vision he now held. He was especially critical of the British government's attempts to balance the budget in the midst of the Slump: 'you will never balance the Budget through measures which reduce national income'.[260] He believed that cuts in government spending were counterproductive. He advised: 'Look after the unemployment, and the Budget will look after itself'.[261] A point that Keynes latched onto and made much of was that the continuing high rate of unemployment was, according to prevailing economic theory, impossible. According to the classical theory markets regulated supply and demand. Supply would always equal demand and the price mechanism would ensure this. A surplus of a commodity would result in a fall in price for that commodity and hence a greater demand as many could now afford to buy more of the cheaper good on offer. Conversely, a shortage of a particular commodity would push up its price; this increased price would prove too much for some to afford, or would wish to pay, and so decrease demand, whereas more would wish to supply the commodity as they could now make a greater profit. The change in the price mechanism therefore ensured that demand would always equal supply. However, there was a surplus of the supply of labour over the demand for labour – i.e. unemployment. The *General Theory* was primarily concerned with how to solve this unemployment problem and ensure full employment, as Keynes himself stated: 'The ultimate object of our analysis is to discover what determines the volume of employment'.[262]

Keynes was concerned with involuntary unemployment that occurred across the whole economy and was the result of the trade cycle. The *General Theory* did address the trade cycle and the reasons for it, but this was not the main thrust of the book. Keynes was also concerned with only the short term and did not intend to deal with the long term. His solutions were short-term solutions to what he saw as a short-term problem of mass unemployment caused by the trade cycle. His analysis did have a long-term dimension in that he did not believe that the market would necessarily self-correct. Keynes did not therefore assume full employment as a normal state of affairs. The level of employment was determined by the level of output, which was in turn determined by the level of effective demand. Demand equalled output. Demand itself, argued Keynes, consisted of consumption and investment (e.g. a firm invests in the purchase of new plant and machinery; housing is also classed as investment). For Britain, approximately one fifth of economic output will consist of investment and the remainder is consumption.

Consumption is determined mainly by income. Most individuals may save some of their income and so, in the long term, their consumption will be less than their income. In a recession, when income might fall, then individuals may save less or draw upon some of their savings to maintain their living standards in the short term. Broadly speaking, however, consumption is dependent upon income and is less than income. Wealthier people tend to save more than the poor who have less money to save as they need their income to live on. Emerging from a recession, people tend to save more even when their incomes might be increasing as it tends to take a while for them to adjust their consumption expenditure to take account of their increased earnings. Keynes focused on what he described as the *marginal propensity to consume*. This is the proportion of any *increase* in income that is spent on consumption. The marginal propensity to consume may be lower then normal when an economy is emerging from recession due to the lag before individuals take account of their increased earnings.

Keynes summarised the level of output with an equation: $C + I = Y$, in which C is consumption, I is investment and Y is the National Income or output. Since output determined employment, then consumption and investment determined employment. Keynes then questioned why the level of employment, that is the level of consumption and investment, be at such a level as to produce full employment. He did not believe that the investment decisions taken by businessmen or the consumption expenditure of households would necessarily produce a level of output which just happened to be that level of output that might employ everyone who is looking for work. Keynes, rejecting the classical view that unemployment was a temporary deviation from normality and that the market was self-correcting, argued that what was needed was for government intervention to ensure full employment: 'The central controls necessary to ensure full employment would, of course, involve a large extension of the traditional functions of government'.[263]

This new role for government, the responsibility for ensuring full employment, would require, Keynes argued, that government needed to intervene to boost consumption and investment. This would mean that the government should be prepared to run a budget deficit and should prioritise the goal of full employment rather than eliminating a budget deficit. This requirement was made all the more necessary by the relationship between savings and investment, which might always be equal, but not necessarily in equilibrium. However, disequilibrium cannot continue for long and so savings and investment will reach an equilibrium and produce an equilibrium level of output, or National Income. That level of output might be at a level involving significant unemployment. For Keynes, an equilibrium would only be achieved if the amount that businessmen *wanted* to invest was equal to the amount people *wanted* to save. In practice it is the level of investment which is most variable, as firms become or lose confidence in the health of the economy and so adjust their investment accordingly. The impact of these changes is compounded by the multiplier effect. Of any increase in income the greater portion, say 80%, is spent and 20% is thus saved. This extra expenditure likewise increases the income of others who in turn spend 80% on consumption and save 20%. This multiplier effect is dependent upon the marginal propensity to consume or save and can also work in reverse, with a decrease in investment having a ripple effect as the multiplier reduces incomes accordingly. These changes will temporarily put the economy into disequilibrium until a new equilibrium is established. This new equilibrium is determined by the changes in investment, the marginal propensity to consume or save, and the size of the multiplier. According to Keynes, they were not brought about by the need to establish full employment and there is no reason why the new equilibrium should be at a level of output involving full employment. Relatively small changes in investment, due to the multiplier effect, could produce fairly significant changes in the level of output, which may result in substantial unemployment. This new equilibrium may continue for some time with the resultant continuation of high unemployment. Therefore, there was a need for the government to encourage business investment, or encourage consumption – alternatively, especially if the measures to boost investment or consumption in the private sector failed, the government should itself undertake large scale public expenditure and investment, which due to the multiplier would have a ripple effect in the wider economy. The government should be prepared to run budget deficits to boost consumption and investment to ensure full employment. Keynes did not see budget deficits as a problem and gave priority to full employment.

Keynes' theory would entail a major change in government policy, although it might be said that governments were already struggling to eliminate their budget deficits and so it might be said that Keynes was merely justifying policies that were already being carried out. Even so, Keynes had given a new theory which, if accepted, required a re-prioritisation away from trying to reduce the budget deficit towards being prepared to increase it in order to create demand and jobs.

Classical economists were confident that all savings were invested and that there would be full employment. This was the experience of the 19th century when there was full employment as the industrial revolution surged ahead. With a small business, owned by its managers, the profits of the business would be reinvested. Those taking the decisions to save were the same as those who did the investing. However, as the 19th century progressed, it became more common for firms to have shareholders and to borrow money from the bank to aid the investment. Those who saved were increasingly different people from those who did the investing. Nevertheless, classical economists remained confident that savings would fuel investment and that savings would equal investment. This would occur due to free market principles and the price mechanism in the form in interest rates. Interest rates would fall if savings were increasing ahead of investment, and would rise if investment, the demand for savings, was increasing faster than savings; such changes in interest rates would ensure that savings and investment would always be in balance. A fall in interest rates will discourage saving while at the same time make profitable projects which would be otherwise unprofitable or of low profitability. Conversely, an increase in interest rates will encourage savings and reduce or eliminate the profitability of those investment projects dependent on borrowed funds. If individuals decide to reduce consumption and save more, then the sales of consumer goods might fall but the demand for investment goods, such as plant and machinery, will increase as businesses increase their investment. The overall output of the economy will be unaffected.

Keynes argued that a fall in consumption, even if it was matched by an increase in savings, would push the economy into recession as the fall in the demand in consumer goods would lead to a fall in incomes of those producing such goods. Due to the multiplier effect, such a fall in incomes would have a knock-on effect as those with less income would in turn spend less and so others would find that their incomes would also fall. Unemployment would result, despite the increased spending on investment goods that might occur elsewhere in the economy, especially if this was compounded by a fall in investment as businesses became less confident of the profitability of investment projects due to the falling consumer demand. Keynes rejected the notion that interest rates could be relied upon to distribute savings towards investment smoothly and regulate the amount saved and invested. Nor did the operation of interest rates guarantee full employment.

Classical economists believed that unemployment would be solved by the market mechanism of an adjustment of wages. If there was unemployment, a surplus of labour, then wage rates would fall, thus making it more attractive for firms to employ more workers. Conversely, if there were a shortage of labour then firms would increase wages, and workers would demand higher wages, thus making it more attractive for people to work and less attractive to employ people. Unemployment would therefore be solved by a fall in wage rates. The solution to unemployment then was not only the movement in interest rates, which would make investment more attractive, but also the fall in wages, which would make the employment of more workers more attractive.

Although Keynes accepted the classical theory regarding the wages and employment, he disputed the reality of the theory in practice. Keynes focused on real wages as opposed to money wages. He argued that a money wage increase of 5% is only a real wage increase of 5% if prices do not change. If prices also increase by 5% then, he argued, the real wage is unchanged. Conversely, if the money wage is cut by 5% and prices also fall by 5%, then the real wage is unchanged. Keynes believed that the classical theory was deficient as it did not take account of the difference between real and money wages.[264] Keynes reasoned that although individual firms and industries might be able to increase employment and sales by cutting wages and prices for their goods, if the entire economy acted in such a way, with wages and prices for goods falling by 5%, say, then the real wage rate would have remained unchanged across the board. Consequently, Keynes argued, according to classical theory, there was would be no reduction in unemployment as there had been no cut in wages (this argument was particularly relevant to the problems in Britain in the 1920s/30s when the government had rejoined the Gold Standard at pre-war parity and had hence rendered export industries uncompetitive at a stroke; they expected to solve this uncompetitiveness by cutting wages). A general reduction in money wages would, as people had less to spend on consumption, be bound to exert a downward pressure on the prices of consumer goods. In practice, a general fall in money wages would lead to a smaller reduction in real wages. Therefore a general fall in wages would not necessarily lead to a general fall in real wages and so would not necessarily lead to greater employment. Keynes believed that it would be preferable to increase the money supply and not cut money wages, rather than to leave the money supply unchanged and cut money wages:

> 'Having regard to human nature and our institutions, it can only be a foolish person who would prefer a flexible wage policy to a flexible money policy, unless he can point to advantages from the former which are not obtainable from the latter. Moreover, other things being equal, a method which it is comparatively easy to apply should be deemed preferable to a method which is probably so difficult is to be impracticable.'[265]

Keynes was opposed to flexible wages, not only for reasons of convenience, or efficacy, but also for economic reasons as he saw flexible wages to be damaging:

> 'If labour were to respond to conditions of gradually diminishing employment by offering its services at a gradually diminishing money-wage, this would not, as a rule, have the effect of reducing real wages and might even have the effect of increasing them, through its adverse influence on the volume of output. The chief result of this policy would be to cause a great instability of prices, so violent perhaps as to make business calculations futile in an economic society functioning after the manner of that in which we live. To suppose that a flexible wage policy is a right and proper adjunct of a system which on the whole is one of laissez-faire, is the opposite of the truth. It is only in a highly authoritarian society, where sudden, substantial, all-round changes could be decreed that a flexible wage policy could function with success.'[266]

Not only did Keynes believe that it was preferable to avoid cutting wages, he also believed, stating the seemingly obvious, that wages were downwards inflexible as workers would be reluctant to see a fall in their living standards:

> 'No section of labour will readily accept lower wages merely in response to sentimental speeches, however genuine ... We are depending for the reduction of wages on the pressure of unemployment and of strikes and lockouts; and in order to make sure of this result we are deliberately intensifying the unemployment'.[267]

Keynes further said: 'I do not think it is any more economic law that wages should go down easily than that they should not. It is a question of facts. Economic law does not lay down the facts, it tells you what the consequences are'.[268] Keynes believed that a cut in money wages would lead to a fall in effective demand and hence employment. He believed that it would be preferable to increase the money supply and increase effective demand by government intervention. This intervention should consist of the central bank trying to reduce interest rates in order to encourage investment; tax cuts to increase the amount of money people have to spend and so stimulate demand; and the government should increase public expenditure. The increased economic activity would lead to increased prices, especially with an increased money supply, which would therefore reduce the real wages of workers even if their money wages remained unchanged. Keynes 'enunciated' the quantity theory of money thus:

> 'So long as there is unemployment, employment will change in the same proportion as the quantity of money; and when there is full employment, prices will change in the same proportion as the quantity of money.'[269]

In setting this out, Keynes made two simplifying assumptions: firstly that all unemployed resources are homogeneous and interchangeable in their efficiency; secondly, that so long as there is a surplus unemployed, the factors of production entering into marginal cost will do so at the same money-wage. Having made these assumptions, Keynes then set out some possible complications:

1. Effective demand would not change in exact proportion to the quantity of money.
2. There will be diminishing, not constant, returns as employment increases as resources are not homogeneous.
3. Resources are not interchangeable and so some commodities will experience inelastic supply even though there will still be unemployed resources available for the production of other commodities. This will be a particular problem once bottlenecks are reached.
4. Wages will increase before a state of full employment is achieved.
5. The cost factors will not all change in the same proportion.

The classical response to Keynes's *General Theory* was centred mainly on what was described as the 'Pigou effect'.[270] This was the case put against the *General Theory* by the economist the Cambridge economist, Arthur Pigou, that the economy was more self-stabilizing than Keynes asserted and that the classical theory was correct and that Keynes was wrong. When the economy entered a recession, then both prices and wages would fall and so the purchasing power of a sum of money would increase. As money would now buy more then more would in fact be bought. Output would increase and so would employment, eventually bringing the economy back to a state of full employment. Keynes was aware of the merits of the argument of the classical theory, but believed that wages were not as flexible downwards as the classical economists assumed and that consequently their understanding that the economy would self-correct was wrong. Keynes went further by asserting that interest rates would not necessarily fall far enough and fast enough, along with wages and prices, and that the multiplier effect would exacerbate the downturn leading to the establishment of a lower level of output equilibrium which would involve continuing high levels of unemployment. Keynes dismissed the classical economic theory as being a solution to the problem in his well-known statement that:

'Many people are trying to solve the problem of unemployment with a theory which is based on the assumption that there is no unemployment'.[271] Keynes was heavily critical of Pigou. Regarding unemployment Pigou wrote:

> 'Our conclusion, that the long-run effect of expansionist State policies – and under this head must be included not only the undertakings of large-scale public works, but bounties, guarantees of interest, and, if successful in the purpose, protective duties – does not touch employment, affords, of course, no argument against the State's adopting these devices as "remedies" for unemployment in times of exceptional depression. For here it is not their long-run, but their short-run, consequences that are significant. Nor need we mean here by "exceptional depression" merely the lower extremity of a normal trade cycle. Thus, though the heavy unemployment that prevailed in this country for the decade following the post-Armistice boom – the intractable million – was not associated with a cyclical depression in the narrow sense, there was, nevertheless, some reason to believe that it was a short-period malady, needing treatment for only a few difficult years. The situation was such that improvements in industrial technique and capital equipment might well have made the normal real demand for British labour expand at more than the usual rate, while, at the same time, owing to the low birth-rate of the pre-war, and, still more, of the war years, the number of the wage-earning population of working age was expanding at much less than the usual rate. This double change must clearly in the near future have made the absorption of the whole body of potential workers at a given wage-rate – real rate and money rate alike – much easier than it would otherwise have been. Thus a temporary campaign maintained for a few years – apart from the great slump that began in 1930 – might have proved successful.
>
> Moreover, a lasting favourable effect on employment might be produced if the State undertook – and succeeded in its undertaking – not merely to make the real demand for labour higher than it would otherwise have been, but to make it progressively higher.'[272]

Keynes's attacks on Pigou and the caricature he painted of Pigou's beliefs were inaccurate and unfair. Pigou said: 'with perfectly free competition among workpeople and labour perfectly mobile ... there will always be at work a strong tendency for wage rates to be so related to demand that everybody is employed ... The implication is that such unemployment as exists at any time is due wholly to the fact that changes in demand conditions are continually taking place and that frictional resistances prevent the appropriate wage adjustments from being made instantaneously'.[273] Pigou agreed with Keynes on the need for a public works programme, lower interest rates and, due to problems posed by the Gold Standard, on the need for tariffs.[274]

The classical position did concede that in the short term, an increase in the money-supply would boost economic output. But the classical economists believed that the oncoming inflation caused by the surge in the money-supply coupled with the mal-investment it would also cause (as organizations would be investing based on a surge in the money-supply and not the genuine demands of the real economy), would wipe out the temporary boost in the medium to long term or else there would be an adverse outcome overall. The real economy could not be influenced by the money-supply in a positive way. Of the likelihood of the assertion that to increase the quantity of money would have no impact on consumption as money prices would simply change, Keynes, like Malthus, focusing on the short term, said:

> 'Now, "in the long run" this is probably true. But this long run is a misleading guide to current affairs. *In the long run we are all dead.* Economists set themselves too easy, too useless a task if in tempestuous seasons they can only tell us that when the storm is long past the ocean is flat again.'[275]

Hayek and many other economists rejected Keynes' arguments. Some professed not to understand what he was talking about and concluded that he did not either. This book will focus upon the arguments put by Hayek and the Austrian economist Ludwig von Mises (1881-1973) to give a flavour of the counterattack against Keynes.

Hayek believed that it was untrue that all unemployment was down to an insufficiency of demand or could be cured by an increase in such demand in the long term. With certain industries producing goods for which demand is limited due to customers choosing other products, low wages will be the consequence of unemployment and not a cause of it. In this situation only a redistribution of labour to those industries producing goods which the customer wants will be a solution to the problem, and an increase in the amount of money may well lead to an increase in the output of the unwanted products, but the underlying problem will remain and will reassert itself once the monetary pressure fades.[276]

(Thus Keynesian monetary expansion merely hides the underlying problem and does not resolve it. It masks the misdistribution of labour and prevents the labour market, by means of wage differentials from correcting that misdistribution. The same applies when an economy has become reliant upon immigration to fill jobs which are supposedly experiencing a shortage of workers. The labour market will be distorted and the corrective mechanism of a change in the wage rates will not correct that problem. Immigration will merely hide the problem and not allow workers from declining sectors to move to expanding sectors.)

If the government pursues a policy of monetary expansion in order to maintain full employment which would otherwise not be achieved, due to decline of certain sectors or industries, then the effect will be to sustain people in those industries when they should be relocating to other jobs. This means that what might have been a gradual process achieved over time, due to the delayed effect as a result of the monetary expansion, may become a sudden event requiring mass relocation which makes the taking up of new jobs much more difficult. The attempt to sustain full employment when certain sectors are declining with the blunderbuss approach of monetary expansion, affecting all sectors, means that those sectors not in decline and where demand is already employing resources at maximum capacity, may tend to experience inflation well before the declining sectors achieve their own full utilisation of resources. The economy may therefore experience overall inflation before full employment is achieved and a government may be forced to counter its own policies by then pursuing a deflationary policy to counter the inflation its previous policy had caused; this will increase the unemployment in the declining sector which is contrary to the intention of the government's interference.

Creating full employment, or even increasing it, when it may simply be preventing the reallocation of labour merely postpones the problem rather than solving it – and may even make this worse by so doing. Once the inflation reaches such a level that it must be tackled by deflationary policies, then the sudden denial of monetary expansion will cause the loss of jobs in declining sectors to be sudden and dramatic as the true level of demand is thrust on those sectors in one blow and will be made worse still be the impact of the deflationary measures. Hayek wrote:

> 'The conclusion which Lord Keynes drew from this, and which the whole of his theoretical system was intended to justify, was that since money wages can in practice not be lowered, the adjustment necessary, whenever wages have become too high to allow "full employment", must be effected by the devious process of reducing the value of money. A society which accepts this is bound for a continuous process of inflation.'[277]

Hayek argued that inflation can only produce prosperity when it is larger than expected – that is a progressively increasing rate of inflation. This is because a with a constant rate of inflation the people take account of the expected inflation rate and so factor in such a rate into their price and wage expectations. It is only if inflation turns out higher that bigger profits are made. The problem with a progressively increasing rate of inflation is that it is unsustainable in the long run. Eventually it must reach such a rate that the currency becomes worthless.

The trick of reducing wages by a dose of inflation can only work so long as the workers, and the trades unions, are oblivious to the trick. The government, by taking responsibility for securing full employment, is making the mistake of letting the unions, the wage demands and the willingness of employers to grant wage increases, off the hook as it is these factors which are the real causes of unemployment. It allows unions to demand whatever wage increases they wish, to take whatever industrial action they wish, regardless of the disruption to the employers and the economy as a whole, and then simply assume that it is up to the government to increase the money in circulation, if necessary by printing it, in order to boost demand to ensure full employment. This is a recipe for continuous inflation and is not feasible as a means of securing full employment, as the consequences of the wage increases and industrial unrest damage both the rate of growth of the economy and the competitiveness of industry – especially against foreign competition in the home market and in export markets, as the foreign producers will not all have been affected by the same problems. It will produce in the long term a battle between the government's ability to boost effective demand and the loss of competitiveness due to the activities of the unions, compounded by an ever-increasing inflation rate.

The government's response to the inflationary pressures is to resort to more interference with the introduction of controls to try and prevent the symptoms of inflation. Wages and price controls are an obvious example. Ultimately measures such as rationing and criminal sanctions may be applied. The aim of the monetary expansion is to create demand and hence create jobs. The government must therefore try to direct that extra money at those industries and sectors where it believes the extra jobs will be created and prevent expenditure on undesirable or unplanned goods, services or expenditure. Hayek said:

> 'It is easy to see how such belief, according to which the creation of additional money will lead to the creation of a corresponding amount of goods, was bound to lead to a revival of the more naïve inflationist fallacies which we thought economics had once and for all exterminated. And I have little doubt that we owe much of the post-war inflation to the great influence of such over-simplified Keynesianism. Not that Keynes himself would have approved of this. Indeed, I am fairly certain that if he had lived he would in that period have been one of the most determined fighters against inflation. About the last time I saw him, a few weeks before his death, he more or less plainly told me so. As his remark on that occasion is illuminating in other respects, it is worth reporting. I had asked him whether he was not getting alarmed about the use to which some of his disciples were putting his theories. His reply was that these theories had been greatly needed in the 1930s, but if these theories should ever become harmful, I could be assured that he would quickly bring about a change in public opinion. What I blame him

for is that he had called such a tract for the times the *General Theory*'.[278]

Hayek revealed that Keynes had actually believed that 'England had reached practically full employment though the unemployment figure was still well over one million'. This was not what many other Keynesians understood full employment to be. This meant that there would be 'intense pressure for more of the same medicine' so long as there remained a substantial unemployment number, despite the fact that according the Keynes himself, according to Hayek, 'it can do only harm and no good in such a situation'.[279] Despite his interventionist beliefs, Keynes still claimed that he agreed 'morally and philosophically' with 'virtually the whole' of Hayek's *The Road to Serfdom*.

A period of high growth leads to conditions for a recession as the economy needs to readjust to bring itself back into equilibrium. An expansive boom or bubble will inevitably lead to a bust or recession. Over-expanded industries are made to contract and overpriced commodities and goods lose their inflated values as prices fall. The danger of a Keynesian approach is that once the readjustment starts and a recession begins then an increased flow of money is used to try and sustain the boom and prevent the readjustment. Of course one would wish to avoid a recession, but the concept of demand management, where demand is boosted continuously to keep the unemployment figure at a certain level, irrespective of the health of the economy or the cause of the unemployment (e.g. by the scale of mass immigration or the lack of competitiveness), can only lead to a misdistribution of resources, where goods are produced to satisfy the artificial demand created by government and not by the genuine demand of consumers. If the economy is sustained in what would otherwise be an unsustainable boom, then for how long can that artificial condition be maintained and at what cost?

In an article written in 1950, Ludwig von Mises, professor of economics at New York University, pointed out:

> 'The policies which the *General Theory* recommended were precisely those which the "monetary cranks" had advanced long before and which most governments espoused in the depression of 1929 and the following years. Some people believe that Keynes' earlier writings played an important

part in the process which converted the world's most powerful governments to the doctrines of reckless spending, credit expansion and inflation ... At any rate it cannot be denied that the governments and peoples did not wait for the General Theory to embark upon these "Keynesian" – or more correctly, Gesellian, policies.'[280]

Gesell (1862-1930) who has been described as a 'vagrant thinker', served for a period of days as a Minister of Finance in the Soviet cabinet of Bavaria in 1919 (it was quickly overthrown and Gesell was detained for several months before being acquitted of treason). He was of the opinion that interest charges were an obstacle to capital growth. He believed that if this obstacle was removed then real capital would grow so quickly that 'a zero money-rate of interest would probably be justified ... within a comparatively short period of time'.[281] Ludwig von Mises was scathing towards those who opposed Say:

> 'Say emerged victoriously from his polemics with Malthus and Sismondi. He proved his case, while his adversaries could not prove theirs. Henceforth, during the whole rest of the nineteenth century, the acknowledgement of the truth contained in Say's Law was the distinctive mark of an economist. Those authors and politicians who made the alleged scarcity of money responsible for all ills and advocated inflation as the panacea were no longer considered economists but "monetary cranks."
>
> The struggle between the champions of sound money and the inflationists went on for many decades. But it was no longer considered a controversy between various schools of economists. It was viewed as a conflict between economists and anti-economists, between reasonable men and ignorant zealots.'[282]

Ludwig von Mises continued:

> 'The economists did not contest the fact that a credit expansion in its initial stages makes business boom. But they pointed out how such a contrived boom must inevitably collapse after a while and produce a general depression. This demonstration could appeal to statesmen

intent on promoting the enduring well-being of their nation. It could not influence demagogues who care for nothing but success in the impending election campaign and are not in the least troubled about what will happen the day after tomorrow. But it is precisely such people who have become supreme in the political life of this age of wars and revolutions. In defiance of all the teachings of the economists, inflation and credit expansion have been elevated to the dignity of the first principle of economic policy. Nearly all governments are now committed to reckless spending, and finance their deficits by issuing additional quantities of irredeemable paper money and by boundless credit expansion.'[283]

Governments were at a loss to explain the continuation of the high levels of unemployment and people were desperate to return to a more prosperous society. Socialism was gaining ground; in Britain this was reflected by the electoral rise of the Labour Party (and the accompanying demise of the Liberal Party), and the establishment parties were keen to head off this drift to a revolutionary creed, many of whose adherents looked enviously towards the communist regime in Russia. Keynes also offered a way out from the economic slump and made justification for deficit spending, which he actually encouraged. This was something that politicians then and now love to hear. They are being told that their financial largesse with taxpayers' monies is desirable and for the taxpayers' own benefit. Taxpayers should be grateful for the sheer scale of the public spending programmes. The mathematical formula added a specious credence to the discredited inflationist dogma. This allowed the political elites to adopt his recommendations without the obvious ridicule that otherwise might be the reaction.

In the eyes of the politician, Keynes takes away the need for personal incentive and business success. The economy succeeds if politicians direct and control savings and investment; they have a duty to take responsibility for the economic output which, according to the mathematical formulae developed by Keynes, they can manipulate to achieve full employment; they need no longer bother to balance the government budget, instead they have a duty to increase it for the public good.

SUMMARY

Despite its all encompassing title, Keynes was writing *General Theory* in the 1930s to deal with a specific problem of unemployment at that time and was doing so when the size of government was far smaller than it is today. Excluding defence expenditure and interest on the national debt, government spending had been less than 6% of GNP before WWI and was approximately 14% in the 1960s. It rose even higher in the 1970s. Keynes' call for more government spending was therefore made to governments who had some flexibility to expand the size of government activity. Today, with governments across the EU teetering on the brink of insolvency, with the Greece debt problem and the economic collapse Greece with falling GDP, and with other Mediterranean countries in serious difficulties of their own, and with even the USA witnessing its own ballooning budget deficit, the room for manoeuvre is greatly reduced. Governments do not have the borrowing capacity to carry out Keynesian expansionism even if they wanted to, without running the risk of being forced into default in the same way that the banks collapsed when they could no longer borrow more money.

Keynes rejected the classical school's insistence that markets would always ensure that supply would equal demand and rejected Say's Law. He could rightly point to the large numbers of unemployment in the inter-war years as evidence of his belief. He therefore reopened the debate that the classical school believed had been settled in the previous century. Keynes believed that the government should intervene to reduce unemployment by encouraging private consumption and investment, by increasing its own expenditure and by reducing the value of money to reduce real wage rates. He wanted the government to actively intervene in the functioning of the market.

Keynes had a journey of convoluted rationale as he tried to justify his preferred policy recommendations and changed his mind often, and at times advocated the same policy for completely different reasons. He failed to convince his classical school opponents.

The development of the understanding of the multiplier, a concept that he pushed once he had embraced it, was an important advancement in economics. He used the multiplier to argue that the extra expenditure he advocated could be self-financing. His assertion that savings did not match investment was convoluted, unconvincing, unproven and failed to impress the classical school of economists.

Keynes' method of defining real wages fitted with the theory he wanted to pursue and was nonsense. If wages rates fell then this was a matter of fact unaffected by any corresponding fall in prices. If both wages and prices fall, as is often the case in a recession, then they have both fallen. It is untrue that real wages are unchanged any more than real prices are unchanged. A given quantity of money would be able to buy more of each. What may be the true is that living standards are better preserved if prices fall in line with wages. But as a point of fact they have both fallen.

The classical economists did concede that, *in the short term*, then it might be possible to cut unemployment by an increase in government spending. But they believed that this would be counterproductive in the long term as the effect of the increased spending would be to prevent the needed market correction and that goods would be produced to meet the increased expenditure rather than the true consumer desires. They believed that in the long run an increase in the quantity of money would not change consumption but would merely change prices. Keynes did not necessarily disagree with this, but believed that the short term mattered as 'in the long run we are all dead'.

In the eighteenth chapter of the *General Theory* Keynes announces that in deriving his theory, and the mathematical equations contained within it, that 'in this place and context, we are not considering or taking into account' the effects and consequence of changes in: technical changes or invention; changes in taste; changes in population or resources; changes in the preferences between work or goods and leisure.[284] In other words he excludes a large part of the factors which affect the working of the economy and causes of unemployment. He restricts himself to a scenario which is unreal and does so in order to validate his own theory and his own mathematical equations.

A problem with focusing on full employment as the criteria by which the economy is operating at its full capacity is that it ignores other constraints posed by other factors of production. Machines, other equipment, factory space for example might also be underutilised. Yet Keynes does not advocate an increase in demand or that such an increase would not cause inflation if those other factors of production are underutilised. Nor does he see that reaching the full capacity of these other factors might lead to a limit on the ability to increase output rather than prices. Although Keynes does acknowledge the potential for reaching bottlenecks and the constraints that they pose. Full employment is desirable for social reasons. It is the social hardship caused by unemployment that makes it important. Yet focusing on solving the social problem by manipulating the market forces which control the economic output is not necessarily a way to deal with a social problem. Unemployment may have many causes, such as mass immigration or inefficient working practices, and may therefore be solvable by dealing with those other causes.

From a strictly economic point of view, it may be possible to temporarily solve unemployment if one creates jobs irrespective of the productivity involved and irrespective of the cost entailed. But the long-term consequences flowing from the extra public debt and maldistribution of resources make this problematic. One therefore has to set the short-term advantages against the long-term costs.

6 THE INTER-WAR YEARS

At the outbreak of WWI, Britain found itself in difficulty as it was dependent upon supplies from Germany for many key products, such as tungsten, dyes, scientific instruments and magnetos. Up until June 1915, Britain remained faithful to laissez-faire liberalism and free market principles were adhered to with even munitions production being put out to tender. When British troops had to be rationed to four rounds each per day due to supply shortages, then something had to be done. Lloyd George told an audience in Manchester:

> 'We are fighting against the best organized community in the world, the best organized either for peace or war, and we have been employing too much the haphazared, leisurely, go-as-you-please methods, which, believe me, would not have enabled us to maintain our place as a nation even in peace very much longer.'[285]

To remedy its industrial deficiency, Britain even went so far as to adopt the classic infant industry measure of the government creating new companies to manufacture certain products. Extensions to private factories were built using government monies and 218 national factories were established to make a variety of products including ball-bearings, aircraft, explosives, gauges, tools, chemicals, and even reinforced concrete slabs, with modern machine tools being imported from the USA, Switzerland and Sweden.[286] *The Times* commented in November 1915:

> 'One of the new factories has grown up on a spot which last November was green fields. Now there are 25 acres covered with buildings packed full of machinery. Most of the machines are of American make, and some are marvels of ingenuity. Herein the war will prove a permanent benefactor to Birmingham. For it would be flattery to pretend that the prevailing Birmingham type of workshop is anything to boast about. It is on the whole conspicuously antiquated.'[287]

An important element was that government support, including cheap finance, was not short term for the duration of the war, but would continue after the war.[288] The new magnetos manufacturers were especially concerned about potential post-war US and German dumping on the British market. Before the war German dumping had prevented British producers of tungsten from entering the market. Dumping could take three forms: strategic dumping, as with tungsten, to prevent competition from developing; systematic dumping where unfair advantages such as cheap, unregulated labour, low taxes or a depreciated currency led to a flood of cheap goods; and also dual pricing where foreign firms used a higher price in a, usually protected, home market to subsidize a lower price for exports.

Britain had to resort to protectionism and introduced the McKenna Duties in 1915, which were presented as an emergency wartime measure, and were renewable annually during the war. However they were retained after the war (Labour repealed the duties in 1924 but they were restored by the Conserrvative government in 1925). They were levied at a rate of 33⅓% *ad valorem* on certain luxury items: motor cars, clocks, watches, musical instruments and a specific duty on cinematograph film.[289]

The Safeguarding Act of 1921 introduced duties of 33⅓% on 6,500 items of goods considered to be of strategic importance (e.g. scientific instruments, some chemicals, glassware, wireless valves, ignition magnetos, hosiery latch needles); the duty was 50% on optical glass. Commonwealth products were exempt.[290] The Act was limited to five years, which was considered to be enough time to allow domestic industries to become competitive. Even so, the Act was renewed for a further five years in 1926 and the range of goods extended. Part II of the Act was concerned with anti-dumping (including that arising out of countries depreciating their currencies), but of the 24 applications for protection citing this in the first five months none were granted. In 1929, the Labour government allowed some of the safeguarding duties to lapse and repealed the anti-dumping provisions in the Finance Act of 1930.[291]

Although the items covered by these protectionist measures were insignificant in terms of the volume of imports, the actions did represent an erosion of free trade hegemony. In 1930, almost 85% of Britain's imports were free of any tariff.[292] After WWI, the desire to return to the perceived normality of free trade was reinforced by the perceived extent of the German collapse in 1918 and the assessment that Germany would no longer be an economic competitor in the same way it had been before the war.[293]

There was a boom as the wartime repressed demand for consumer goods was unleashed. There was further large investment in new plant, machinery and buildings.[294] Between spring 1919 and summer 1920, the money supply soared, as did consumer spending, and prices rose by 25%. The Bank of England brought the boom to an end by pushing up interest rates to 7%.[295] By the end of 1920 the boom had exhausted itself and a recession was under way with output, employment, wages and prices all beginning to fall. After a couple of years the down-swing bottomed out but there was no signs of the usual economic recovery. Unemployment remained very high with more than one million people unemployed and at times up to two million. Unemployment in Britain was around 10% through the 1920s, was an average of 16% in 1930 and reached more than 21% in 1931.[296]

The traditional export industries were the worst affected. Partly this was due to the loss of overseas markets during WWI, and partly due to the lack of competitiveness of British industry. Export prices were too high. During WWI and the boom afterwards, wages, prices (including those of the export industries such as coal, cotton and shipbuilding) and profits had almost trebled. This increase was greater than experienced by other countries and had significantly reduced British export competitiveness. By the early 1920s, British exports were only two thirds of the volume they had been in 1913, resulting in lower output and less employment.

The response to this export uncompetitiveness was to urge wage and price reductions of export goods. Driving down the costs of producing export goods would allow for those goods to sell for less and so they would regain their lost competitiveness. Cuts in wages and prices were the normal response to a recession and were seen to be a necessary pre-requisite for economic recovery. The alternative to cutting wages and prices would have been to have devalued sterling and so cutting the price of British exports in the overseas markets. However, the government was strongly opposed to this devaluation option, not least because of the commitment to the Gold Standard.

Gold is a premium form of money as it is so rare. Its supply from mining expands at only about 1.5% each year and therefore cannot facilitate any serious inflation and its shortage is more likely to create a steady deflation.[297] As Keynes wrote:

> 'Approximately the *same* level of price ruled in or about the years 1826, 1841, 1855, 1862, 1867, 1871, and 1915. Prices were also level in the years 1844, 1881, and 1914. if we call the index number of these latter years 100, we find that, for the period of close on a century from 1826 to the outbreak of war, the maximum fluctuation in either direction was 30 points, the index number never rising above 130 and never falling below 70. No wonder that we came to believe in the stability of money contracts over a long period. The metal *gold* might not possess all the theoretical advantages of an artificially regulated standard, but it could not be tampered with and had proved reliable in practice.'[298]

The period 1870 to 1914, when the gold standard operated, was a golden age of benign deflation in the more industrialized economies, as a result of increases in productivity and technical innovation. It was also a period of rising living standards.[299] A national currency was backed by gold and a unit of the paper currency could be exchanged for gold. This required that exchange rates between countries on the Gold Standard were fixed. International payments were made in gold. A country which ran a trade deficit would witness an outflow of gold. In theory, this reduction in gold at the central bank would, in order to maintain the relationship between the value of the currency on the value of gold, lead to a fall in the money supply, which in turn would decrease demand and economic activity and so reduce imports and hence bring the trade back into balance. Prices and wages would also be reduced due to the economic down-turn and this in turn would help reduce the cost of exports. On the other hand, a country running a trade surplus would have an expanded money supply and so would suck in more imports while, due to increasing prices and wages, its own exports would tend to increase in price and so its trade balance would be restored to balance again – in theory.[300] The Gold Standard was a self-correcting mechanism and it was regarded as a good system for the conduct of international trade; in the 19th century international trade had grown without major difficulties in dealing with trade imbalances.

Britain had been at the centre of the Gold Standard. The Bank of England had been able to ensure the smooth running of the system and Britain's status as the world's greatest economic power increased its influence. WWI led to a suspension of the Gold Standard. One day after Britain declared war on Germany, the government passed the *Currency and Bank Notes Act, 1914*: 'A Bill, To authorise the issue of Currency Notes, and to make provision with respect to the Note Issue of Banks', which allowed the government to print notes as legal tender in place of gold sovereigns and half-sovereigns. By withdrawing gold from internal circulation, the Gold Standard had been effectively suspended and the government was able to expand the money supply to fund the war effort. Although the Royal Mint continued to produce gold sovereigns until 1917, gold coins were soon withdrawn from circulation.

But this war measure was regarded as only temporary and that Britain would rejoin the Gold Standard as soon as possible. This was seen as necessary to ensure sterling remained the world's primary currency and to ensure the position of the City of London as the centre of the world's financial system. The City demanded that Britain re-joined the Gold Standard at pre-war parity, despite the lower level that in reality the currency was worth. The City was keen to protect the interests of foreigners who held sterling or had invested in Britain, who would find that they had lost money compared to what they would have had if Britain retained pre-war parity. To re-join at a lower level was regarded by most politicians and economists, as well as the City, as being a default to foreigners on their investments and would make it more difficult to re-establish sterling's and the City's former status. In reference to joining at pre-war parity, the governor of the Bank of England, Montagu Norman, said: 'I think that the disadvantages to the internal position are relatively small compared with the advantage to the external position'.[301]

The new gold exchange standard that was created post-WWI effectively ended the circulation of gold as a currency and was less stable that the classical gold standard that had prevailed in the 19th century. The movements in interest rates and contractions or expansions of national economies that were supposed to happen automatically did not as national governments were struggling to remedy their domestic economic problems and so were not prepared to play by the rules of the game.[302] Not only was

Germany faced with the financial strain of paying reparations, but the allies themselves were in serious financial difficulties. Both Britain and France had loaned large sums to Russia, which defaulted on its debts following the Bolshevik revolution. Both Britain and France owed large sums to the USA that they could not afford to repay and France also owed a large sum to Britain.[303]

Britain had managed to run the gold standard up until the outbreak of WWI as it consistently ran a small surplus. Post WWI, the fall in British exports reduced the surplus and the increase in interest rates which had a remedial effect of correcting the trade balance, by also driving down prices, due to the fall in economic activity, put pressure on the need to cut costs – in particular wages.[304] Keynes took the view that it was better to allow in imports rather than to run an export surplus and so export capital.[305] This idea that Britain could easily generate an export surplus was increasingly questionable as the 1920s progressed.

There was considerable economic and political turmoil after WWI. Britain was undergoing a period of political change that made managing the economy more difficult. Tariff reform remained a live issue. In the general election of the autumn of 1918 the National Government, consisting of the Tories with some Liberals loyal to Lloyd George, was returned to office with Lloyd George as Prime Minister. Lloyd George was removed as prime minister in October 1922 following a Tory revolt due to the Chanak Crisis when Lloyd George nearly embroiled Britain in a war with Turkey. The Tory Bonar Law took office as prime minister but, fatally ill, handed over to Baldwin early in 1923. At the October 1923 Imperial Conference, once again there were calls for Preference, especially from New Zealand, Australia and South Africa, because of the difficult economic circumstances. Some preferences were introduced. Baldwin told his Cabinet that he wanted an early election with a programme of Tariff Reform and Imperial Preference.[306] Most of the Cabinet urged a delay before calling an election. Lloyd George, who was on a tour of the USA and Canada, heard of Baldwin's plans and, being urged by allies to adopt a policy of Imperial Preference himself, decided to do just that. Baldwin learnt of Lloyd George's plans and declared publicly that he intended to adopt Imperial Preference and called a general election. Hearing this Lloyd George resolved to fight on a platform of Free Trade: 'Baldwin knifed me and I shall knife him'.[307] The election result was a disaster for the Tories, who lost 88 seats and a minority *Labour* government took office with Ramsey MacDonald as prime minister in January 1924. For MacDonald, free trade was a 'preliminary stage in the progress of socialism'.[308]

The incoming Chancellor, Philip Snowden (1864-1937), abolished the McKenna Duties and also other preferences granted to the Dominions. The minority Labour government did not last long and in the general election of October 1924, Baldwin pledged that he would not introduce a general tariff and that only particular industries would be safeguarded. The Tories won the election 412 seats; Labour won 151; and the Liberals won 40.

Baldwin's appointment of Winston Churchill as Chancellor of the Exchequer in 1924 thwarted protectionist sentiments of many of his colleagues. Leopold Amery MP (1873-1955) succeeded in persuading Baldwin and the Cabinet to reintroduce the McKenna Duties and some other preferences from 1919, but Churchill argued that the election pledges made by Baldwin prevented a reintroduction of those Preferences given in 1923; a compromise was reached with the creation of the Empire Marketing Board the budget of which approximated to the cash value of the Preferences and which successfully marketed Empire goods in Britain.[309] But Churchill's major impact as Chancellor was the decision to re-join the Gold Standard. The City and its interests – banking, bankers, international finance and capital flows – has a special appeal to free traders who focus on picking winners rather than making winners.

Since the value of sterling had in fact fallen considerably against the US dollar (the USA had remained on the Gold Standard), then to rejoin at pre-war parity, which was the decision, entailed the need for significant cuts in wages and prices as British exports were not only uncompetitive due to the raised prices that had occurred during WWI and the short boom afterwards, but also because of the deliberately overvalued sterling due to joining the Gold Standard at pre-war parity in 1925.[310] Although he had his doubts; Churchill had confessed that: 'I would rather see Finance less proud and Industry more content'.[311] However, he presented the move to the House of Commons as being inevitable:

> 'A return to an effective gold standard has long been the settled and declared policy of this country. Every Expert Conference since the War — Brussels, Genoa — every expert Committee in this country, airs urged the principle of

a return to the gold standard. No responsible authority has advocated any other policy. No British Government — and every party has held office — no political party, no previous holder of the Office of Chancellor of the Exchequer has challenged, or so far as I am aware is now challenging, the principle of a reversion to the gold standard in international affairs at the earliest possible moment. It has always been taken as a matter of course that we should return to it, and the only questions open have been the difficult and the very delicate questions of how and when.'[312]

What this meant was that far from using tariffs and protection to help industry compete with foreigners, the government was now deliberately rendering industry even more uncompetitive. To join at an overvalued exchange rate is the exact opposite of the aims of protection, and openly subordinated the interests of British industry to the interests of the City and foreign investors. The American economist, JK Galbraith wrote:

'In 1925, under the aegis of the then Chancellor of the Exchequer, Mr Winston Churchill, Britain returned to the gold standard at the old or pre-World War I relationship between gold, dollars, and the pound. There is no doubt that Churchill was more impressed by the grandeur of the traditional, or $4.86, pound than by the more subtle consequences of overvaluation, which he is widely assumed not to have understood. The consequences, nonetheless, were real and severe. Customers of Britain had now to use these costly pounds to buy goods at prices that still reflected wartime inflation.'[313]

Deflation is benevolent when it is the result of increased productivity and product innovation, but is malign when it is sudden, the result of monetary contraction and a general economic downturn with mass unemployment. Deflation, resulting from the attempt to get sterling back onto the gold standard at pre-war parity, led to a dramatic fall in prices in Britain with accompanying business failures and unemployment.[314] Unlike Britain, both France and Germany devalued their currencies to take account of the war inflation. Churchill later admitted that the return to the Gold

Standard had been 'the biggest blunder' of his political life. Keynes had the foresight (that it was foresight gave his opinion all the more credibility) to predict the outcome in his book *The Economic Consequences of Mr Churchill,* in which he argued that he was 'against having restored gold in conditions which required a substantial readjustment of all our money values', and accused Churchill of 'committing himself to force down money wages and all money values, without any idea how it was to be done. Why did he do such a silly thing?'[315] Keynes believed that the only way that the government could bring down real wages was '*in no other way than by the deliberate intensification of unemployment*'.[316] To return to the Gold Standard at a dollar value of $4.86, the value sterling had been in 1914, meant that wages needed to be forced down by at least 10%.

Winston Churchill, rejected Keynes' arguments and in a speech on Budget Day extolled 'the orthodox Treasury dogma, which is steadfastly held, that whatever might be the political or social advantages, very little additional employment and no permanent additional employment can in fact, and as a general rule, be created by State borrowing and State expenditure'. Keynes was quick to pick up on the notion of the 'Treasury view' which he described as 'a pure logical delusion, without any foundation at all in sound thinking'. Keynes believed that the Treasury had failed to distinguish between savings and investment: 'the Treasury view only demonstrates that home investment is not a cure for unemployment, by first of all assuming – in effect – that there is no unemployment to cure'. According to Keynes inflation would only occur when full employment had been achieved. Consequently he dismissed the Treasury View as 'the natural result of standing half-way between common sense and sound theory; it is the result of having abandoned the one without having reached the other'.[317]

The Treasury view was that wages and prices were both flexible and that the adjustment would not therefore pose a problem. Keynes' view was that there would be a choice between forcing down wages and prices by deflationary methods, the route the Treasury had taken, or by devaluing the value of the currency by inflation and hence reducing the real value of money wages and prices. Keynes regarded the inflationary route as being the preferable one as it could be achieved and was less painful.[318]

The Treasury view regarding the flexibility of wages was not unfounded. The average money wage fell by roughly 5% between

1900 and 1904, before rising by about 5% more than the 1900 level by 1913. WWI intervened and wages rose. Taking 1900 as the base (1900 = 100) then wages had risen to 280 by 1920, before falling to 194 by 1923, a drop of nearly a third. At this time wages clearly were flexible and a substantial cut had been incurred without major discord in society. By 1933, wages had fallen by roughly 5% from their mid-twenties rates and by 1937 wages had once again recovered their mid-twenties level. The fall of wages in the slump, 1926 to 1933, was the same as that between 1900 to 1904. The slump had failed to push down wages further despite the number of unemployed. The fall in wages between 1930 to 1933 was accompanied by a fall in prices which was even greater, which meant that there was a real increase in living standards for those still in work. A fall was reasonably easier to achieve in 1921 to 1923 as this was a period just after a very significant wage increase and the wage fall was accompanied by a fall in prices, which meant that people were no worse off. The fall in 1930 to 1933 came after a long period of wage stability and people were naturally more used to that particular level of wages and therefore reluctant to see those wages cut.[319]

Given that the aim of government economic policy was to help get Britain back onto the Gold Standard, the recession which started in 1920 was not regarded as a problem. Wages and prices did fall. The government was confident that Britain could make a success of the pre-war parity level, despite the fact that British exports remained uncompetitive after the cuts in wages and prices that had been achieved so far. The Treasury view was that there was only likely to be a 'small additional strain' that would be required to get prices and costs down to hold sterling at its pre-war parity compared with its then value.[320]

Keynes pointed out that the fall in wages had stopped in 1923 and that any further fall would require a deflationary policy. Given that unemployment was already running at more than 10% then a deflationary policy would only push up an already high unemployment rate to even higher levels and that the goal of pre-war parity was not worth the hardship this would entail.

Re-joining the Gold Standard choked off Britain's recovery from the 1920/21 recession as sterling was revalued at pre-war parity of £4.86 even though its market value was £4.40.[321] There was an 11% appreciation in the value of sterling between 1924 and 1925.[322]

Among the industries struggling to enforce further wage reductions was the coal industry. British coal exports fell from 113million tons to 71million tons between 1923 and 1925.[323] The mine owners proposed wage cuts of up to 25%.[324] The miners refused to agree to this and, to avoid a clash, the government agreed to grant the coal industry a subsidy until May 1926 and set up a Royal Commission to investigate. The Commission reported in March 1926 and recommended that the subsidy end in May. The government accepted the Commission's report and ended the subsidy. The mine owners renewed the proposed wage cuts. The miners went on strike and the struggle culminated in the general strike of 1926.

Although the strike failed and the miners returned to work on significantly reduced wages, the government and employers were reluctant to impose wage cuts in other industries. Wages remained at the 1925 level for the rest of the decade.[325] Consequently, export industries remained uncompetitive and unemployment remained high. Export competitiveness worsened when other countries, such as France, also re-joined the Gold Standard but at a much lower rate than pre-war party, and therefore ensured that their exports were significantly cheaper than Britain's. The French rate was so low that they did not need to cut wages or costs at all.

Between 1920 and 1929, industrial production grew at an annual rate of 2.8% and industrial productivity by 3.8%. Between 1924 and 1929 GDP grew by 3.1% per annum measured by income. This healthy picture, as set against the years 1899 to 1913, is alongside the poor export performance, especially in the staple industries of cotton, shipbuilding and coal. Despite an increase in world exports of manufactures of 37.5% between 1913 and 1929, the British share of world manufactured exports fell from 30.2% in 1913 to 20.4% in 1929, the year in which British exports reached their highest level between the wars. Even so, due to the fall in the share of world manufactured exports, British manufactured exports in 1929 were almost one fifth below the volume in 1913. This has been attributed in part to Britain's reliance on primary producing countries and also its reliance on semi-industrial countries, such as India, South Africa, Australia, and New Zealand, where import substitution drove out British goods.[326]

Britain experienced a deteriorating trade position. In 1924, export volume was only 75.8% of the 1913 level, whilst retained imports had increased by 9%. This poor performance was covered by an improvement in the terms of trade and by invisible earnings, which turned a trade deficit in 1924 of £214million into a current account surplus of £58million after a net invisible income of £272million. The current account was further influenced by the depressed state of the British economy and thus a weakened demand for imports. Even so, the current account surplus was insufficient to fund the level of overseas lending, which was generally unregulated as government controls had been curtailed partly in pursuit of re-establishing the City to its pre-war international position. Britain was lending long term substantially more than the current account surplus could fund and was financing the difference by short-term borrowing. The situation was not helped by Britain's relatively puny currency reserves (in 1929 sterling balances were in excess of £275million while reserves were only £146million).[327]

Between 1925 and 1929 world manufacturing output increased by more than 25% and world trade increased by 19%. British industrial output increased by 9%. With the re-emergence of Germany as a competitor, strong competition from France and Belgium both of which had undervalued currencies, and crippled with sterling at pre-war parity on the Gold Standard, British exports fared badly, being worth less in 1929 than in 1925, and were still well below the 1913 levels in volume.[328]

Tariff Reform, or safeguarding being the then option to help industry, remained a contentious issue in government. In June 1925, the Iron and Steel industry applied for protection. This was supported by Amery and opposed by Churchill who argued that it would amount to a general tariff. Baldwin announced to parliament that although the Iron and Steel industry had proved its case under the safeguarding rules, such action would contradict his election pledges and so the industry was refused help for the lifetime of the present Parliament.[329] By April 1927 Amery was so disenchanted with the government's economic policy that he even suggested that he follow Chamberlain's example and leave the government to campaign for tariff reform. Like Chamberlain, Amery went on a tour of the Dominions only to return to find that, like Chamberlain, his absence had diminished his influence in Cabinet. Churchill had successfully persuaded the Cabinet that the best way to help industry was by derating and not safeguarding.

The 1927 Tory Party conference witnessed open dissent about the lack of safeguarding and Baldwin's promise that things would be different after the next general election did not placate critics. In the Budget of 1929, following on from Ritchie's past exploits, Churchill even went so far as to abolish the Tea Duty and hence the preference that went with it.[330] With increasing economic woes the Government lost the 1929 general election with a campaign slogan of 'Safety First'. Labour won 287 seats; Tories 260; and the Liberals 59. MacDonald was appointed Prime Minister on the 5th June 1929.

On the 30th June 1929, Lord Beaverbrook (1879-1964), newspaper owner and politician, published an article entitled *Who is for the Empire?*, and followed this up with the formation of the Empire Free Trade Movement, with the support of several prominent businessmen and Tories. After ten weeks the organization claimed to have 200,000 members.[331] Although it was pointed out to Beaverbrook that the Dominions were not in favour of free trade, but only preference (i.e. lower tariffs) towards Britain, Beaverbrook held that the appeal of the slogan was important, not its accuracy. In February 1930 this organization was transformed into the United Empire Party, with Beaverbrook as leader. In the spring a by-election was won by the United Empire Party and the Tories were beaten.[332] Baldwin reacted by appointing Neville Chamberlain (Chamberlain's son) as Party Chairman to placate the Tariff Reformers, but announced he would not be dictated to by press barons.

While most industrialised countries had fared reasonably well during the 1920s, the Wall Street Crash precipitated a worldwide economic slump. Unemployment became a widespread problem. Up until 1929, the USA had enjoyed a booming economy, with low unemployment, steady growth and rising wages – accompanied by stable prices overall. Profits also steadily increased and there was a confidence that this economic success would continue, which led to bullish stock market speculation. People even borrowed money in order to buy shares. One observer commented: 'The present level of stock prices discounts not just the future but the hereafter'.[333] Although the crash had not been foreseen – in 1927, Keynes himself had pronounced that 'we will not have any more crashes in our time'[334] – there was a sense of growing unease that the stock market was out of control and overvalued. One problem was that those who predicted the end of the apparent never-ending rise in the market, often, momentarily, appeared to be correct when there were temporary breaks in the soaring share prices. In early 1928, in June and again in December and in February and March 1929, there were a seeming end in the bull market before the normality of soaring prices returned, which discredited the sceptics.[335] There was also a robust view that the dealings on the Stock Exchange was not a matter for government. The newspaper editor and journalist Arthur Brisbane asserted: 'If buying and selling stocks is wrong the government should close the Stock Exchange. If not, the Federal Reserve should mind its own business'.[336]

Speculation was made worse by market manipulation, which by the summer of 1929 was open with not only predictions as to which stock was anticipated would rise but also bold comments that certain stocks would be 'taken in hand' at a particular time that day. More than one hundred issues on Wall Street were influenced by market manipulation in 1929 with members of the exchange on occasion pooling their resources to force up a particular stock; a pool manager might even be appointed. That stock were predicted to rise and with others being made aware that certain parties were determined to intervene to ensure that that rise did in fact occur bred confidence amongst the wider public, who would then buy the target stock merely on the strength of the predictions of those in the know.[337]

US industrial production was falling before the Wall Street Crash of October 1929. Although house building had been falling for several years, other output reached a peak in the summer of 1929 before starting to fall.[338] It has been alleged that the stock market crash was but a catching up with the other economic trends and reflected a decline in the economy. This line was attractive to those who wished to diminish responsibility of the conduct of those active in the stock market for the crash. However the economic slowdown was modest and might well have reversed itself as had been the case before. It was not the case that the market suddenly realised the looming downturn and suddenly all confidence was lost. Any serious blame attached to Wall Street for the Depression might have led to an attack on the role and importance attached to it and was thus most unwelcome. It suited the powers-that-be to downplay the wider economic consequences of the Wall Street Crash.[339]

Nor was the Crash recognised as such when it began. Professor Fisher said that he believed the fall had been only a 'shaking out of the lunatic fringe'. Confidence did not disappear overnight. New issues in September 1929 were higher than in August. From

September and into October the level of trading was high and even if the overall trend in the market was downwards there were good days as well as bad. In September the brokers loans increased by $640million which reflected the high level of trading and the penchant for speculation. In October, the American economist Professor Irving Fisher pronounced: 'I expect to see the stock market a good deal higher than it is today within a few months'.[340]

In October 1929 the bubble burst. The New York Stock Exchange witnessed substantial selling which gathered pace as those who had borrowed money to buy shares themselves sold before the shares fell to being worth less than the borrowed money. The more shares people sold, the more their value plummeted, which induced more people to rush to sell. The anxiety of ordinary people was made worse by the ticker reporting the transactions falling behind. This meant that it was difficult to see what was happening. In the past when this problem occurred, people would only find out in the evening by how much the market had risen and hence how much richer they had become. Now, they discovered that they were poorer and could even face complete ruin were the market to continue falling.[341]

When the ticker eventually revealed the extent of the market collapse, more people were propelled to try and sell and get out while they could. Those who were unable to meet the margin calls were sold out. The atmosphere was one of panic. A workman who appeared on top of one nearby building to carry out some repairs was deemed to be a would-be suicide and the crowd awaited the expected leap. Extra police were dispatched to maintain law and order. Crowds gathered around the brokerage offices scattered around New York, and this also occurred elsewhere in the country. The uncertainty created by the lagging ticker fed a variety of rumours as to the number of suicides and the suicides of well-known market names; stocks were apparently selling for nothing; other exchanges had closed. The visitor's gallery to Wall Street was closed. One of those ejected was Winston Churchill.[342]

One reaction of the market crash was a growth in morbid humour as a means of coping. Rumours and jokes circulated that people were being asked if they wanted a hotel room to sleep in or to jump from. Two men supposedly jumped hand in hand – they had a joint account. Despite the legend of Wall Street speculators hurling themselves out of windows, in fact the suicide rate remained unchanged.

Informed opinion was that the worst was over and also that there would be 'organized support' should there be any further market weakness; further falls would not be allowed by the movers and shakers of the market.[343] When the market resumed its fall there was a meeting at the offices of JP Morgan and Company of the USA's most powerful financiers and they agreed to pool resources in order to support the market. A well-known market figure, Richard Whitney, attended the floor of Wall Street and placed a number of orders at above the then market price. This intervention worked and prices moved upwards.

One problem was the stop-loss orders which triggered sales whenever a predetermined price was reached. The purpose was to liquidate the stock of customers who had not responded to margin calls and so protect the brokers from further losses. As the stop-loss sales were triggered this only drove down the market even further even faster. The organized support was able to effectively check this automatic triggering of further sales and further losses. However, the effect was only temporary and when the market fell again Richard Whitney did not reappear. There was no organized support. There was another meeting at the offices of JP Morgan and Company and a statement subsequently issued said that the bankers were not in the business of sustaining the market at a particular price level nor of protecting other peoples' profits. Prices would now be allowed to fall.

The crash was driven by the margin calls which meant that those who had bought stock with borrowed money found that as the value of their collateral fell they had to pay more cash to cover the decline in the collateral. This led to more selling and a further fall in the stock market, which in turn created more margin calls.

Another problem stemmed were the investment trusts. In 1927, the investment trusts sold $400million worth of securities to the public. By 1929, the figure had reached $3billion and they had assets estimated at $8billion in total.[344] Shares in investment trusts were often sold at a premium and the profits were split between the dealers and the trust management.[345] There were high-leverage and low-leverage trusts.[346] High leverage trusts, with a large amount of preferred stock and debentures (which did not change in price as the value of the trust changed), enabled a disproportionate change in the value of common stock to movements in the values of the securities bought. This was highly attractive if the values were continually rising but was very dangerous if the values fell. This advantage of leverage was heightened by the creation of investment trusts which specialised in the purchase of shares in other investment trusts: 'There was a rush to sponsor investment trusts which would sponsor investment trusts, which would, in turn, sponsor investment trusts'.[347]

Now, as the market crashed, investment trusts did badly and some could not find buyers for their stock at all.[348] The much vaunted leverage, which had previously facilitated vast gains, now operated in reverse. As the market fell, the value of the common stock of many investment trusts was completely wiped out. That the value of investment trust stocks was now worthless meant that other stock had to be sold by those who were struggling to meet the margin calls. This in turn drove down the value of the other stock. That many investment trusts had been investing in one another exacerbated their plight. Some investment trusts tried to survive by buying their own stocks and continued to do so, with limited effect on the stock prices, until they ran out of cash in a form of 'fiscal self-immolation'.[349]

People and companies started defaulting on their debts; banks were less inclined to lend out new money again. As banks came under pressure bank customers, fearing that their money might not be safe or to meet the margin calls, started withdrawing their money. The banks could not cope and so bank failures began.[350]

The shares lost one third of their value within one month.[351] The value of shares continued to fall for the next two and a half years and by summer 1932 industrial shares were worth, on average, only one-sixth of their 1929 value. In the USA, by 1932, the production of capital goods was only a quarter of its 1929 level, and there was also a significant fall in the production of consumer goods. By 1932 industrial production had halved from its 1929 level and economic output as a whole had fallen by one-third. Unemployment increased from 1.5 million to more than 12 million between 1929 and 1932.[352] This slump in the USA affected the rest of the world, as imports into the USA fell sharply.

Germany had become dependent on foreign investment from the USA in order to fund reparation repayments following WWI. These US funds dried up initially as Americans wanted to invest in their own booming economy, then because of the slump. This led to a contraction of the German economy as investment fell. As Germany's economic position worsened she was unable to make the reparation payments to France, Britain and other countries.

This led to other countries running into further difficulties other than the contraction of the American market. As international debts were paid for in gold, the demand for payments in gold threatened the solvency of certain countries – in particular Britain. The British trade deficit might have been offset by invisible earnings from overseas, but British gold reserves were low. Due to the return to the gold standard at pre-war parity and consequent uncompetitiveness of British industry, building up the gold reserves proved difficult. Britain was further investing heavily overseas which constituted a large outflow of capital. These overseas investments were funded by short-term loans from abroad as the small current account surplus was unable to cover the outflow. That Britain had been funding long-term overseas investments by short-term borrowing, such as three-month Treasury Bills, left Britain very vulnerable. After 1929, the fall in world trade led to a fall in British exports and a fall in income from the invisible overseas earnings. This led to a significant outflow of gold from Britain.

The British government's financial position also worsened as the rise in unemployment from 10% in 1929 to 16% in 1930, and then to 21% in 1931, led to an increase in the cost of unemployment benefits and diminished tax receipts. The economic orthodoxy of the 19th century was that a government should not run a deficit except in times of war; government should cover its spending by taxation. WWI had led to a substantial rise in government spending and this had not been reduced back to its pre-war level after the war was over, with extra spending to cover the extra interest payments, payments to those injured and war pensions and also to fulfil election promises such as to build 'homes for heroes' as well as covering the higher unemployment.[353] The government had been running a small deficit despite higher taxes and despite being able to run a small budget surplus in the early 1920s. The government had been urged to cut taxes and the fall in tax income and the higher expenditure, despite government attempts to make cuts, had produced small annual deficits in the second half of the 1920s. This deficit started increasing rapidly in 1930 and there were concerns expressed about this and that the deficit should be eliminated.

The financial crisis meant that countries were trying to get hold of their own money. There was foreign disinvestment from Britain as countries withdrew their monies and demanded payment in gold. By July 1931, there was an outflow of gold of £12-15 million a week and there was only £133million of the British gold reserves left. A report into the state government expenditure from the Committee on National Expenditure warned that in the annual deficit was due to reach £120million in the year 1931/32 and recommended tax increases and substantial cuts in spending. Keynes described this report as 'the most foolish document I have ever had the misfortune to read'.[354]

The Tory Opposition finally hardened its stance. Churchill, who had threatened to resign from the Shadow Cabinet in response to move towards adopting a policy of Preference before relenting and telling his colleagues that he would 'stick to you with all the loyalty of a leech', split nonetheless over India. Baldwin, taking a more protectionist stance, not least to head off a threat to his leadership, managed a reconciliation with Beaverbrook and Neville Chamberlain confirmed that Tory policy now included protection for agriculture and industry as well as Empire Preference in March 1931.[355]

The Labour Government arranged for a £50million loan from American and French central banks at the beginning of August and likewise moved towards adopting a policy of protection. The Cabinet voted, 15 votes to 5, in favour of introducing a tariff on manufactures. Snowden, the Chancellor, threatened to resign; the decision was therefore reversed in favour of proposals to cut government spending and a policy of deflation. The Cabinet split and the Labour Government fell, to be replaced with a Tory-backed coalition National Government with Ramsay MacDonald still as Prime Minister. Another loan of £80million was borrowed from France and the USA later that August and there were proposals for tax increases and spending cuts. Even so, the outflow of gold continued. In the year after the Wall Street crash in October 1929, unemployment increased from 1.5million to 2.5million – approximately one fifth of all workers. British exports were almost halved between 1929 and 1931. In the first quarter of 1929 half of British shipbuilders had no orders at all. Meanwhile, the flow of imports continued. By the summer of 1931 the Bank of England was haemorrhaging £2million of gold each day.[356] The gold outflow in August and September 1931 left Britain with little option but to leave the Gold Standard, as it had almost run out of gold. On the 21st September 1931 Britain suspended gold payments and left the Gold Standard. 'They never told us we could do that,' was one Labour Party former minister's response to Britain's exit.[357]

The immediate consequence of leaving the Gold Standard was that the value of sterling, which was now floating freely, fell. Sterling fell sharply and continued falling; it fell by 30% within months. Other countries in Scandinavia, the British Empire as well as Japan also left the Gold Standard and the cumulative effect of the devaluations was to the disadvantage of those countries remaining on the Gold Standard.[358] By the summer of 1932, the price of sterling against the US dollar had fallen from $4.86 it had been on the Gold Standard to a value of $3.58. This made British exports cheaper and imports more expensive. However, those countries remaining on the Gold Standard took other measures to protect their own balance of payments position and their home markets from foreign goods. Tariffs were increased and import quotas extended and there were further exchange controls. Between 1929 and 1932 the value of international trade fell by two-thirds. In 1932, British unemployment reached 22% and unemployment was even higher in both Germany and the USA.[359]

Up until 1931/32 and the economic crisis forcing the government's hand, the economic establishment had remained firmly opposed to tariffs. The Economic Advisory Council (EAC), consisting of Keynes, Pigou, Stamp, Hubert Henderson, and Lionel Robbins, agreed that the normal effect of a tariff 'must mainly be to divert the productive forces of the community from one occupation to another, and not to increase their total activity ... tariffs will tend to divert production from the channels where we are relatively more efficient into channels where we are relatively less efficient; that is to say, the play of natural forces will be more successful in discovering the occupations in which we can employ ourselves most profitably, than any system of tariffs will be'.[360] In reference to car imports, Keynes explained:

> 'From that point onwards the free trade argument would be, that would lead to a loss of gold, the loss of gold would lead to an increase in Bank rate, the increase of Bank rate would lead to unemployment, the increase of unemployment would lead to pressure for a reduction of wages; when wages had been reduced we should be able to produce cars in competition or to make some other article which we now import. When the final position had been

reached, while money wages would be lower than before, real wages would not be lower, in fact they would be higher than under protection, because we should be producing those articles for which we are distinctly better suited.'[361]

Keynes' view was that the government should try to boost demand in the economy by reducing interest rates and increase government spending to fund public investment by increasing the budget deficit. However, there was a fundamental shift in the political landscape regarding free trade in 1930, with the TUC, the Conservative Party, and a 'bankers' manifesto' all moving away from free trade. Keynes was a part of this shift and wrote to the Prime Minister in July 1930 stating that he had 'become reluctantly convinced that some protectionist measures should be introduced'.[362] In the period 1930/31 Keynes was in favour of import tariffs and an export bounty to offset the overvaluation of sterling. Keynes's conversion to issue of tariff reform was based on the plight of the British economy in 1931, so that dramatic measures were called for, and because the unfairness of the unilateral free trade stance that Britain had uniquely adopted in contrast to the substantial tariff protection adopted by other leading countries and Britain's competitors meant that British exporters were seriously disadvantaged in selling in those countries' markets, assuming they were able to effectively compete at all; moreover, his own favoured option of dealing with the rising unemployment was a programme of government investment in public works.[363] This programme was aimed at not only creating jobs directly by taking on unemployed people onto the various public works projects, but also by the extra demand pumped into the economy that such a public works programme would inject via the multiplier. Yet this would be compromised were Britain to remain on the Gold Standard (and so had to gear economic policy to trying to maintain the pre-war parity), and also would be compromised if a large part of the extra demand created were to disappear into foreign pockets due to a surge in imports. It therefore suited Keynes' argument for a public works programme that there be an introduction of tariffs to ensure that the extra demand was directed towards British firms. In March 1931, Keynes had an article in the *New Statesman* in which he argued for expansionary policies to be accompanied by tariffs to protect industry and raise taxes.[364]

Keynes' acceptance that there was a case for tariffs was not deterred by the often cited counter-arguments. He welcomed any increase in profits for businessmen as being what was desired, and likewise welcomed the prospect of a fall in real wages and price increases. To Keynes there was a problem of the economic system of getting jammed; it was not a question of a bad allocation of resources, making something for which we did not have a comparative advantage instead of something in which we did have a comparative advantage, but a question of making something, albeit inefficiently, or making nothing as people were unemployed. However, his preferred remedy was for there to be an increase in 'government investment which will break the vicious circle'.[365]

Keynes at one point stated that he preferred protectionism to exchange rate movements as protectionism was more certain and less disruptive to the economy. As a pragmatist Keynes accepted a need for tariffs in the period 1930-31 due to the exchange rate constraint.[366]

This support from tariff reform was short-lived, and Keynes dropped that support the moment Britain left the Gold Standard in September 1931.[367] Immediately following the exit from the Gold Standard, Keynes wrote a letter to *The Times* on the 28th September 1931 withdrawing his support for a protective tariff as he believed that monetary policy was no longer constrained by the need to defend the value of sterling.[368] Other economists took a similar view and rejected the notion that full employment could be restored simply by cutting wages. The government did cut interest rates and did cut public sector wages in 1931 and 1932, but did not push for other wages cuts. However, the government did not embark upon a large-scale public investment programme. In reference to the demands for an increase in government spending and public investment, the Chancellor from 1931 to 1937, Neville Chamberlain, said:

> 'There may be circumstances when it is right and sound to follow a policy of that kind, but not for the purpose of providing employment, because the whole experience of the past shows that, for the purpose of providing employment, this policy of public works is always disappointing ... The conclusion I draw ... is that the quickest and most effective contribution which any government can make towards an increase of employment

is to create conditions which will encourage and facilitate improvement in ordinary trade.'[369]

Once off the Gold Standard, lower interest rates prevailed, which helped British industry grow. However, by 1932, either by leaving the Gold Standard or by deliberately aligning their currencies in relation to sterling, many countries had currencies that fell as sterling fell, which undermined any positive effect from a British perspective from depreciation – either with a fall in imports or a rise in exports.[370]

In October 1931, the National Government won a general election which gave it the legitimacy it needed. Despite the inclusion of several Free Traders in the Cabinet (Churchill was not in the Cabinet given his rift with Baldwin, and nor was Amery to placate the Free Traders, including MacDonald) the economic crisis required desperate measures. In addition to abandoning the Gold Standard, the other measure the British government could take to help the economy, was to resort to that which successive governments had steadfastly resisted over the previous 50 years – to introduce a policy of tariff reform.

The slump heightened the concern that without a more protectionist stance then Britain would become a dumping ground for other countries' goods to the disadvantage of domestic producers.[371] During the 1931 election, the campaign for free trade was feeble. The Liberal Free Trade Defence Group only managed to distribute 100,000 pamphlets. The National Government parties won a landslide with the Tories winning 470 seats out of 615. Labour was reduced to 52 seats from its previous 287 seats. MacDonald's National Labour won 13 seats. The two main Liberal groups were reduced to only 30 seats each, and Lloyd George's group retained only four seats.[372]

In the late 1920s there was a steady erosion in the support for free trade. In January 1930, there was strong opposition in the Manchester Chamber of Commerce to Britain signing an international tariff truce and the lack of retaliatory powers, and in March a resolution was passed in favour of British tariffs. In May the Chamber held a referendum of its members in which 1,736 voted in favour of some form of tariff and only 607 opposed. In June the Bradford Chamber of Commerce voted almost seven to one in favour of protection as did the Leeds Chamber of Commerce (497 to 37) and in October Kidderminster likewise did so (28 to two). In July a poll of the membership of the British Engineers' Association showed 96% of those voting favoured protection. Even the City itself slowly moved towards the support for tariffs.[373]

Sir Robert Horne MP (1871-1940), contrasted the experience of the USA with Puerto Rico with that of Britain and Jamaica. In 1901, Puerto Rico, an American possession, sent 65% of its exports to the USA and the USA supplied 75% of Puerto Rico's imports. By 1928, 94% of Puerto Rico's exports were sent to the USA, which in turn supplied 86% of Puerto Rico's imports; those exports and imports had grown from £1.7million to £20million and from £1.8million to £19million respectively. By contrast, at the start of the 20th century exports and imports of Jamaica were both approximately £1.9million with Britain accounting for one-fifth of the exports and supplying half of Jamaica's imports. By 1928, Jamaica's exports had grown to only £4.75million with Britain accounting for 18%, and imports had grown to £6million only 28% of which were supplied by Britain.[374] This was typical of the dilemma facing Britain: its dependence on Empire markets at a time when it was struggling to hold its share of those markets which were comparatively slow growing.

The Government resolved to act. In November 1931 the Abnormal Importations Act was passed, which allowed import duties of up to 100% on certain goods. In practice, the maximum imposed was a duty of 50%. Within a month an order was made for 50% on a range of goods including pottery, sanitary ware, tiles, domestic glassware, metal furniture, cutlery, typewriters, woollen manufactures and linen goods, and another order adding glass bottles and jars, woollen cloth and metal utensils. In December items including cotton manufactures, cameras, wireless components and electric lamps were also added.[375]

In February 1932, decisively, the Import Duties Act was passed, which placed a 10% tariff on all imported goods apart from those specifically exempted (mainly raw materials, food and Empire primary produce). The Import Duties Advisory Committee made recommendations to parliament for revisions, most of which were introduced by the end of 1932. Beginning in April 1932 the nominal rate was doubled to 20% on all items apart from some specifically omitted. By the end of April 1932, only 30% of imports were free of any duty. By the end of 1932 most manufactured and semi-manufactured goods were subject to a 20%

tariff with some at a 33⅓% tariff. In 1935, the tariff on iron and steel was increased to 50% to force the European cartel to agree to a quota to be imported into Britain, and the measure was reversed back to the original level of 33⅓% within a few months as agreement was reached.[376] There were emotional scenes in the Commons when Neville Chamberlain presented the 1932 tariff legislation and that he was fulfilling the dreams of his father Joseph.[377]

Even so, the Free Traders in the Cabinet threatened to resign and had to be granted special exemption from the usual rule of collective responsibility to allow them to criticize the Government publicly. This concession was sufficient to keep them in the Government. More problems were experienced when a delegation was sent to Ottawa to negotiate with the Dominions for the introduction of an Imperial Preference scheme – now possible due to the General Tariff. The Dominions were protectionist, were far less concerned about the reaction of foreigners, and thought higher tariffs were desirable with preference given to Britain and other Empire countries by means of lower tariffs; they wanted to give Preference by increasing tariffs against foreign goods and wanted to redirect demand away from foreign goods to British and Empire goods and not increase the total amount of their imports. Britain however wanted to see lower tariffs within the Empire and were averse to higher tariffs against foreign countries. Many of the British delegation, led by Baldwin, were Free Traders and Ramsey MacDonald, who was still Prime Minister, was hankering after an International Economic Conference. Despite the problems agreement was reached allowing Dominion products free access to the British market in return for increased Preferences from the Dominions. Britain further agreed not to reduce tariffs on foreign goods without Dominion agreement.[378] The reaction of Snowden and the other Free Traders was to resign and, as MacDonald wrote to Baldwin, they argued:

> 'that the bargaining method adopted will soon break the Empire: that the five and seven years fiscal commitments are thoroughly unconstitutional and improper; that the bargain from the point of view of business is all against us, and from the point of view of politics is irredeemably bad; that it destroys the chances of a successful International Economic Conference; that it continues the influences

which have brought this distress upon the world; that it is so contrary, not only in its immediate contents but in its inevitable far reaching and more continuing results, to Free Trade and low Tariffs that they cannot support it.'[379]

As Britain grappled with its economic recovery, a far more evil threat was stirring in Germany than the Kaiser's naval ambitions of 1900. As the world's leading power, the economic incompetence of the 1920s was to leave Britain seriously weakened at a time when strength would soon be required. Although the combination of the exit from the Gold Standard, allowing sterling to depreciate and the freeing up of monetary policy to suit the domestic economy, and the introduction of import duties facilitated a return to growth and rapid recovery, Britain struggled to maintain its balance of payments, which went into deficit in 1931 and remained in deficit for the decade.[380] This was in part due to the fall in demand for British products due to the world depression. For example, the decline in British coal exports accounted by itself for the total fall in the whole of Europe between 1929 and 1931, falling by one-third. Britain's share of world manufactured exports amounted to 21.7% in 1929, when Britain was still the leading exporter of manufactures, and amounted to 20.7% in 1937. This fall was modest given the persistent lack of British competitiveness, with a serious lack of competitiveness between 1929 and 1931, then a rapid recovery up to 1935 before falling back again in the run up to WWII. Government attempts to hold down the value of sterling allowed an exchange rate advantage against major competitors; but the prices of British exports nevertheless remained high compared to the competition, declining by 10% measured in gold dollars while competitor export prices fell by 18%.[381] This underlying lack of competitiveness was another reason for the balance of payments deficit. Before 1931 the current account of the balance of payments had remained in surplus as the surplus from invisible earnings more than compensated for the deficit in the trade of goods. However, after 1931, lower earnings from shipping, financial services, and a fall in investment from abroad (as a result of defaults, loan conversions and lower rates of interest) meant this was no longer the case.[382]

The devaluation of sterling has been held by some to be the decisive factor in Britain's recovery, not so much because of the movement in prices and hence gains in competitiveness resulting from a lower value of sterling, but because of the freedom in monetary policy arising from a floating exchange rate.[383] Derek Aldcroft stated: 'the advantages [of devaluation] *such as they were*, were very soon whittled away by similar action abroad ... effectively the British advantages from devaluation lasted only a short time, probably less than two years'.[384] Some have been dismissive of the role played by tariffs. It has been pointed out that the fall in imports for the newly protected industries between 1930 and 1935 were less than for the older protected industries, and that therefore there were other reasons for the high growth rates of the new industries.[385] One study has focused on the impact of the tariffs on particular industries and concluded that tariffs played a minor role; for example, construction was found to be adversely affected by the tariffs due to the increased costs for timber, window frames etc., and yet the housing boom played a significant role in the economic recovery.[386] Assumptions made, such as that industries raised prices by the same amount as the tariff, have been challenged as false (e.g. by J Foreman-Peck, The British Tariff and Industrial Protection in the 1930s: an alternative model, *Economic History Review*, 34, 1981) and so the conclusions drawn wrong. Foreman-Peck estimated that the tariffs increased output by 4.1% between 1930 and 1935 which, given that GNP increased by 9.6% in those years, was a significant contribution to growth. TJ Hatton (Perspectives on the Economic Recovery of the 1930s, *Royal Bank of Scotland Review*, 158, 1988) estimated that between 1931 and 1937 the tariff increased aggregate demand by 7.2%, the greater part of that increase being in the years 1931 to 1933.[387]

A study by Kitson and Solomou (Protectionism and Economic Revival: the British inter-war economy, Cambridge 1990) concluded that there were four major routes by which the tariffs increased domestic demand. Firstly, import substitution due to the relative increase in competitiveness of the domestic industry. Secondly, the increased income spreads beyond the newly protected industry (this is consistent with Keynes' multiplier effect). Thirdly, increased output leads to economies of scale and so raised incomes. Fourthly, increased confidence and demand boosts the level of investment. Kitson and Solomou cite evidence of a noticeable acceleration in the 1930s of the newly protected industries which experienced the sharpest reductions in import penetration.[388]

An increase in British exports following the Ottawa agreements, which established Imperial Preference tariffs on the principle of 'home producers first, Empire producers second, and foreign producers last', was significant when the contraction of the world economy is taken into account. Retaliation was limited, in part due to the Ottawa agreements and in part due to the fact that Britain was merely catching up with other countries which had already adopted protectionist measures against Britain, in many cases for a very long time. The British home market was a large and important one and it was not in the interests of competitors to risk being shut out of it. British tariffs were also comparatively modest. British imports of manufactures were falling sharply and exports increasing at a faster rate than world trade through to 1935, despite the lack of competitiveness.[389] Between 1931 and 1937 industrial production increased by 70%. The chancellor, Neville Chamberlain, stewarded the British economy well, being, arguably, one of the better chancellors of the 20th century.[390]

In the period 1920 to 1929, Britain's per capita incomes had risen by 21%. By contrast, they had risen by 45% in Germany, 46% in France, and 24% in the USA.[391] In 1932, Britain's per capita incomes increased by 0.2%, and by 2.5% in 1933, and by 6.3% in 1934. By contrast, the US economy shrank, falling by 13.8% in 1932.[392] In the 1929-32 slump, output fell in Britain only in 1931, by 5.6%.[393]

Chamberlain quipped in the House of Commons in 1934: 'We have now finished the story of Bleak House and are sitting down this afternoon to enjoy the first chapter of Great Expectations'.[394] Chamberlain was an interventionist and, like his father, not a fervent free trader. He had run a manufacturing business in the Midlands, which had led Lloyd George to dismiss him as a 'provincial manufacturer of iron bedsteads' (Lloyd George being a provincial solicitor).[395] Chamberlain gave a state subsidy to Cunard to help fund the building of the *Queen Mary*, encouraged the formation of a cartel in the iron and steel industry, introduced measures to protect agriculture which led to a 50% increase in the acreage of wheat grown, and gave a grant to enable the creation of the London Passenger Transport Board, which created the most advanced underground systems of its time in the world.[396]

Even so, the main engine of the economic recovery was a housing boom which accounted for one-sixth of the increase in activity between 1932 and 1934, despite housing accounting for only 3% of the economy. British share of world trade in manufactured goods fell in both the 1920s and 1930s, and in 1937, the last year before rearmament commenced, exports were still only 70% of their pre-WWI level.[397]

The Ottawa Agreements were also a success. Between 1932 and 1937, British exports to foreign countries increased by 35% from £200million to £260million. By comparison exports to the Empire in the same period increased by 52% from £166million to £252million – and reached almost half of the export trade. In the same period, Britain's imports from foreign countries increased by 27% from £454million to £624million; the imports from the Empire increased by 64% from £248million to £405million – and reached more than 39% of total imports. Of this increase in imports £142million was accounted for by raw materials, £65million of which came from the Empire. This increase in imports of raw materials reflected the 51% increase in manufacturing production over the period. Only £14million of the increase in imports was due to an increase in imported manufactures. Meanwhile unemployment which had been nearly three million in mid-1932 fell to less than two million by 1935 and down to around one million by 1938.[398] Thus all the dire predictions of the Free Traders were proved totally wrong and the British economy staged a strong recovery even if underlying difficulties remained. Also the increase in total trade between the Empire countries, excluding Britain, increased by 124% in the same period from £70million to £157million.[399]

Keynes was not without influence, but it would be a mistake to believe that his thinking determined government economic policy and thus ended the Slump. It did not. He was almost totally irrelevant and on the wrong side of the argument more often than not. His views were rejected by the British establishment. Lloyd George referred to Keynes as being 'an entertaining economist whose bright but shallow dissertations on finance and political economy, when not taken too seriously, always provide a source of innocent merriment to his readers'.[400] The influence of Keynes' thinking in Britain was subsequently reflected in the contents of the Report on Social Insurance and Allied Services by Sir William Beveridge (1879-1963), the Beveridge Report, submitted to the government in November 1942.[401]

President Roosevelt, who rejected the 'old fetishes of so-called international bankers' was someone in whom Keynes found favour, and Keynes was identified with the Roosevelt New Deal programme. In an open letter to the President published in the *New York Times*, Keynes wrote:

> 'You have made yourself the trustee for those in every country who seek to mend the evils of our condition by reasoned experiment within the framework of the existing social system. If you fail, rational change will be gravely prejudiced throughout the world, leaving orthodoxy and revolution to fight it out.'[402]

Keynes was consulted by the USA government and his ideas were reflected in the New Deal programme.[403] The influence of Keynes on the US New Deal programme may be debated, but the USA under Roosevelt was more open to monetary manipulation and even embarked on an attempt to raise prices by buying gold, although Keynes dismissed this as 'the gold standard on the booze'.[404] Rather than devalue the dollar against other currencies, Roosevelt resolved to devalue against gold. Since this would involve and increase in the price of gold in $US, and thus making those holding gold more wealthy (and hence create an incentive to hoard gold), Roosevelt decided to confiscate peoples' gold under threat of huge fines by declaring a national emergency. In return for gold people were offered paper currency at a rate of $20.67 per ounce.[405] Export of gold was banned unless it had permission from the secretary to the Treasury. Gold mines were forced to sell their gold to the government for a fixed price.[406] Roosevelt further bought more gold on the open market and steadily forced up its price. By the time Roosevelt's various schemes were over the US dollar had been devalued by 70% against the value of gold, whose increased price was a profit for the government and not the ordinary people who had already been forced to sell.[407] Roosevelt exited the gold standard and committed his administration to deliberately causing inflation in an attempt to correct the consequences of deflation:

> 'The Administration has the definite objective of raising commodity prices to such an extent that those who have borrowed money will, on the average, be able to repay that money in the same kind of dollar which they borrowed. We do not seek to let them get such a cheap dollar that they will

be able to pay back a great deal less than they borrowed. In other words, we seek to correct a wrong and not to create another wrong in the opposite direction. That is why powers are being given to the Administration to provide, if necessary, for an enlargement of credit, in order to correct the existing wrong. These powers will be used when, as, and if it may be necessary to accomplish the purpose.'[408]

In Roosevelt's first term output rose 39% and prices rose by 13%. Between 1932 and 1934, total government spending rose from 5.6% of national income to 12.2%. The budget deficit increased from 2.2% of national income to 9%.[409]

Although Keynes was more involved in the economic debate in the USA than in Britain, many of the US economists were far from reverential regarding Keynes' output and did not regard Keynes' thinking as being the rationale for the New Deal. Dr Nabiel said:

'I do not accept that the New Deal can be considered as a type of Keynesian policy if by this we understand a certain governmental strategy in managing the economy. The New Deal was not seen as such an instrument but rather as an enlarged programme of public works intended to alleviate the burden of unemployment in expectation of the recovery which was considered to come in the normal course of events. If we look at the criticism which at the time was directed against the New Deal by its opponents, it was not from the position of overall economic policy but rather on the grounds that essentially it was ineffective and that to a large extent it was competing with private enterprise and private investment, and therefore by increasing employment in one sector it reduced employment in another.'[410]

JK Galbraith subsequently remarked about the *General Theory* that: 'As with the Bible and Marx, obscurity stimulated abstract debate'. This abstract debate and the revolutionary, as they were deemed, ideas within the *General Theory* gave it a strong following and attention beyond that afforded other economic works.[411] By comparison, in Britain, Neville Chamberlain was not a devotee of Keynes or his ideas and it was not until WWII that Keynes was embraced by the British establishment and taken into the Treasury and ennobled as Lord Keynes of Tilton in 1942.

The Austrian economist Joseph Schumpeter (1883-1950) regarded Keynesianism as basically applicable to Britain and not the USA. He saw it as a justification for Britain's economic decline, unlike the raw capitalism of the USA and its 'creative destruction': 'Practical Keynesianism is a seedling which cannot be transplanted into foreign soil: it dies there and becomes poisonous before it dies'.[412]

SUMMARY

WWI compelled Britain to defend the national interest and adopt protectionist measures to support industry as a necessity of fighting the war. At the time there was a sentiment that never again would Britain allow its industry to be so depleted. However, once the war was over the instinct was to try and recreate the free trade economy – whatever the cost. This reversion included a foolhardy attempt to rejoin the Gold Standard at pre-war parity, and rely upon cuts in wages to bring export industries back to competitiveness. This damaging policy was a failure and Britain was forced out of the Gold Standard when it ran out of gold. The management of the crisis was compounded by the rise of the Labour Party, which was fervently in favour of Free Trade.

The exit from the Gold Standard prompted a reassessment of economic policy. Even though a small number of tariff restrictions had survived following WWI, most imports were tariff free. When industries applied for safeguarding their applications were rejected by the government, even if their applications met the criteria. Meanwhile, Britain's rivals and competitors were using high tariffs to advantage their own industries.

The Free Traders may have won the elections, but they were wrong and were proven to be wrong by the wreckage of the British economy. Despite the defeats of the Tariff Reform campaign and the almost religious zeal in favour of Free Trade, with rising pressure in favour of protection from across the country, as the British establishment viewed the desperate economic plight in 1931 and 1932 they found the resolve to act and act decisively. Britain introduced tariffs to protect British industry. The new protectionist policy, and Preference, was successful and the British economy enjoyed substantial growth, although the underlying problems of uncompetitiveness remained. Keynes was consistently wrong and his advice was consistently ignored. His *General Theory* played no part in economic policy before WWII and it was only after WWII that his theories were influential.

A lot of rhetoric is uttered about the 1930s, with a background assumption that Keynes was in some way the lone voice arguing for a new progressive policy against the fuddy-duddy classical economics that favoured balancing the books rather than deficit spending to produce jobs and economic recovery. That rhetoric and the background assumption are wrong. The real battle (perhaps war is a more appropriate term) was between the Free Traders and the Tariff Reformers. Ultimately, the Tariff Reformers won and were proved to be correct in their analysis and in the effectiveness of their solutions.

So far as Britain was concerned, of the three competing economic ideologies – Keynesianism, classical laissez-faire free trade economics, and protectionism – the first was irrelevant, the second proved wrong and the third, protectionism, proved correct. The cack-handed implementation of classical, laissez-faire, free trade economics caused the Slump. It was protectionism, in the form of Tariff Reform and Preference, that was responsible for lifting Britain out of slump and back into growth.

It should be noted that no matter the scale of the economic crises or of the unemployment levels, there was a hardcore of fanatical Free Traders who remained committed to free trade come what may. Even after the Wall Street Crash, the exit from the Gold Standard, the levels of tariffs imposed by other countries and even after the successful introduction of British tariffs and Preference, there were still resignations by Free Traders. They were bigots in the true meaning of the word. They were impervious to reality. That bigotry remains to this day.

7 POST 1945 BOOM AND COLLAPSE

Britain emerged victorious from WWII and with a sense of optimism. Britain's European competitors lay in the ruins of war, with Germany defeated. Britain looked forward to a new prosperous era as Marshall Aid flowed to Europe to rebuild the shattered continent. Yet things turned out not quite as rosy as might have been expected and Britain's European competitors quickly overtook Britain's economic performance. There were reasons for this. The damage done to German industry, and that of other countries, was not as great as had been estimated. Germany and other countries retained the skilled personnel with which to rebuild their industries. Perversely, the destruction of the societies of most of Europe swept away the established order that might have acted as an impediment to change. That was not as true to the same extent in Britain, which had neither been conquered by Nazi Germany, nor by the triumphant allies. Germany benefited from the inward flow of monies as a consequence of the allied occupation and the military expenditure that that brought to within Germany.

Britain, meanwhile, had lost many of its overseas investments as a result of the USA insisting that the British be stripped of those possessions in return for US support in the war.

That support had been substantial as Britain, despite staging an economic and industrial recovery in the 1930s, was still too weak to wage prolonged all-out war, and had not yet, in 1939 and 1940, sufficiently rearmed to match German military might, which meant that further expenditure on rearmaments were needed. This was made worse by Britain's industrial weakness, particularly in steel production, and so was heavily dependent upon imports. In February 1940, an assessment of Britain's ability to pay for the war effort concluded that Britain would exhaust its gold and dollar reserves paying for imports within 12 months, even after selling off overseas assets and investments. The Chancellor of the Exchequer wrote that: 'It is obvious that we are in great danger of our gold reserves being exhausted at a rate that will render us incapable of waging war if it is prolonged'.[413] The Treasury believed that with careful management Britain could wage war for two years at the then present rate of dollar expenditure. This economic weakness helps explain Neville Chamberlain's caution in confronting Hitler in 1938 and 1939, and of his reluctance to take aggressive military action against Germany in 1939 once war had been declared. Churchill could demand rearmament from the backbenches in the 1930s without taking account of state of the weakened British industry that was unable to produce the necessary weapons and munitions – a weakness for which he was, arguably, more responsible than any other politician.

With the fall of France, the Dunkirk evacuation in early 1940 with the loss of equipment that entailed, and with Churchill taking over as Prime Minister, caution was thrown to the wind, economic difficulties ignored, and Britain embarked on a rapid military expansion with commitments to create an army of 55 divisions, 10 of which were to be armoured, and a major expansion of the air force. This required machine tools and steel. In April 1940 it had been estimated that Britain would need to import £12.6million of iron and steel from the USA in the year; by July that estimate had been increased to £100million.[414] In August 1940, the Chancellor wrote to the Cabinet that the total expenditure on North American imports (munitions, raw materials and industrial equipment) for the next 12 months would be $3,200million compared to total resources of foreign exchange and American securities amounting to £400million and another £200million of American securities being 'virtually unsaleable at present and could only be slowly realised'.[415] It was expected that Britain, given the new ambitious military expansion programme, would no longer be able to pay for the war for two years, but would in fact run out of foreign currency and hence be unable to pay for the necessary imports by December 1940. It was only credit from the USA, in particular Lend-Lease, that enabled Britain to keep fighting.

While the Dominion countries had given Britain almost unlimited credit, the USA most definitely had not and demanded a price for assisting Britain; the USA had pushed Britain into liquidating American investments and also to restrict exports, essentially handing over export markets to US producers. British exports at the end of WWII were roughly one third of their level in 1939.[416] Churchill resisted US pressure to end the Ottawa Preferences during the war. However, Britain lost the Imperial Preference trading area after WWII not only as the Empire started to break up, with India decolonised in 1948, but also, under pressure from the USA, had embraced free trade once again.

By 1945 Keynes had firmly embraced free trade and international institutions. In part this was a matter of expediency as he was trying to negotiate a loan from the USA to bail out the bankrupt British economy after WWII (the USA cut off Lend-Lease one week after the end of the war with Japan), and partly it was a genuine return to his own internationalist instincts. That he died in 1946 meant that he did not have time to object to the Left from taking his anti-capitalist pronouncements and adopting his demand management theories and use them for their own purposes. He did not see the true development of Keynesianism or how his theories were practised or what the outcome was. The Keynesians were free to do that themselves.

The Attlee Labour Government elected in 1945 calculated that it could not manage to bring the balance of trade back into equilibrium (the balance of trade deficit had been running at more than £2billion a year during the war) without lowering living standards, controlling imports and without borrowing from abroad – with Canada and the USA being the expected lenders – and this period of adjustment would optimistically take until 1949.[417] The USA was unsympathetic and the US Congress demanded that Britain should agree to 'the removal of discriminatory treatment, of quotas, exchange controls, and Tariff Preferences'; other members of the US Administration were concerned that should the USA not grant Britain the loan she needed, then Britain would retreat into its Preference area behind tariffs and that in the medium to long term the US exporters would lose out.[418] The USA granted the loan Britain needed (with a shortfall being borrowed from Canada) in return for a commitment to 'the substantial reduction of tariffs and for the elimination of Tariff Preferences' as well as other barriers to world trade.[419] The Labour Government accepted the loan and its conditions, and the Tories did not oppose this.

The Labour Government, as per the loan terms, made sterling fully convertible in July 1947. This led to a six-week run on sterling which cost Britain a large part of the loan, half of which had already been spent. With little of the money remaining, the Government introduced exchange controls and quotas were imposed on all imports outside the Sterling Area. Despite the experience the Labour Government signed the General Agreements on Tariffs and Trade (GATT).

In 1947, there had been strict controls on all manufactured imports. By 1955 only 34% of manufactured imports were subject to import control and by 1958 only 13% were so controlled. Restrictions on the convertibility of sterling were reduced before being abolished altogether in 1958.[420]

The successors to Keynes at the Treasury were free traders.[421] One of the perceived lessons of the 1930s was the need to avoid a resort to protectionism as each country resorted to tariffs and other import controls to try and prevent unemployment and loss of output in their own economies. This so-called beggar-thy-neighbour episode was held to be exporting unemployment to other countries and damaging the world economy as a whole as the volume of international trade collapsed (as can be seen from earlier chapters, this is a re-writing of history). Keynes played a leading role in the setting up of international financial institutions after WWII. He was instrumental in the creation of the Bretton Woods fixed exchange rate system and the creation of GATT, which was responsible for a series of treaties leading to cuts in tariffs and removal of trade barriers to international trade. The International Monetary Fund (IMF) was created in 1944, along with the World Bank, which was to concentrate on long-term loans to help Third World development. The IMF was to police the management of international trade and assist, with conditions, those countries in difficult straits. Countries were not allowed to devalue their currencies unless their balance of payments were in 'fundamental disequilibrium'. By the early 1970s, most countries had reverted to floating exchange rates when the Bretton Woods system collapsed. The IMF was also charged with ensuring international liquidity in order to avoid undue financial difficulties for countries with temporary balance of payments problems and to help them avoid undue deflationary policies in an attempt to cut imports. The IMF attaches tough conditions along with the granting of loans and these conditions can be described as Monetarist: reduce government spending, balance the budget and control the money supply, focusing on the deficiencies of the deficit country with a balance of payments problem and nothing is done to address the surplus countries who are under no obligation to reduce their surpluses.

The Tories became a part of the shift back to free trade. Although the Tory conferences of 1948, 1949 and 1950 passed motions opposing GATT and advocating the retention of the freedom for

Britain to set its own tariffs and Preferences; although the Tory election manifestos of 1950 and 1951 embodied such a policy; and although the Tory conferences of 1952 and 1953 passed motions calling for withdrawal from GATT; the Tory Government elected in 1951, the Tory Party containing many refugees from the former Liberal Party now that it had been superseded by the Labour Party, with Churchill as leader and Prime Minister, at first accepted the mood of the ordinary members but did nothing before, in 1954 with yet another motion against GATT, resolutely rejecting the election manifestos and the previous resolutions. In the debate which followed Amery set out the traditional tariff reform arguments and the then Peter Thorneycroft (1909-1994) advanced the free trade arguments; the result of the vote was that the free traders won.[422] The Tories thenceforward advocated free trade.

The post war boom allowed Britain to enjoy growth and prosperity to such an extent that the British people were told that they had never had it so good; nevertheless Britain's growth rate was lower than her major competitors as Britain gradually lost market share in world trade. The loss was unremitting. In 1899 Britain had a 39% of world trade in metal and engineering goods. In 1937 that share had declined to 20%. In 1950 it had climbed to 27% before falling to 24% by 1954, with West Germany gaining share at Britain's expense. Post-WWII there was a brief surge and by 1950 British exports had increased by 50% from their pre-war level and more than half of global car exports were made in Britain.[423] Part of the reason for difficulties was the struggle to maintain the balance of payments and the need to export. This led successive governments to discourage investment. For example, in 1955, the Chancellor, RA Butler, said: 'Business firms should endeavour to slow down investment not of the greatest national urgency'.[424] This had its effect. By 1950, investment as measured by total fixed capital formation in Britain was 12% of GDP. It was 14% in France and 18% in Germany. By 1980, the figure in Britain was 18%, in France it was 21%, in Germany it was 24% and it was 32% in Japan. The problem of curtailing investment, whether it be to export or as the consequence of a deflationary policy in response to a balance of payments problem, is that it leaves British industry reliant on less modern machinery and so reduces the growth in productivity and so undermines the long-term competitiveness of British industry. The less competitive British industry is, then the more easily balance of trade difficulties occur again and the more market share is lost – both in international markets and in the home market. Britain's overall share in world trade in manufactures fell from 18.5% in 1954 to less than 7% in 1980.[425] The share of Britain's home market taken by imports grew from 5% in 1955 to 26% in 1980. Imports even kept rising during the recession of 1975. The Thatcher government in the 1980s was lucky in that it had the oil revenues from the North Sea to help sustain the economy and provide the tax revenues that the decimated British industry was less able to produce. Another problem was that the proportion of R&D spent on Britain's world role and attempts to remain a world power. The military took up a high share which was only matched by the USA.[426]

Keynes' *General Theory* was highly influential after WWII and its deficiencies in its explanation or failure to convince doubters did not detract from its impact:

> 'Probably no other book has ever produced in so little time a comparable effect. It has tinctured, modified and conditioned economic thinking in the whole world. Upon it has been founded a new economic church, completely furnished with all the properties proper to a church, such as a revelation of its own, a rigid doctrine, a symbolic language, a propaganda, a priestcraft and a demonology. The revelation, although brilliantly written, was nevertheless obscure and hard to read, but where one might have expressed this fact to hinder the spread of the doctrine, it had a contrary result and served the ends of publicity by giving rise to schools of exegesis and to controversies that were interminable because nothing could be settled.'[427]

It received widespread support from across the political spectrum:

> 'Just at this historic crisis of experimental politics, with the Socialists lost in a wilderness lying somewhere between Utopia and totalitarianism, and with governments adrift on a sea of managed currency, afraid to go on and unable to turn back, the appearance of the Keynes theory was like an answer to a prayer. Its feat was twofold. To the Socialist planners it offered a set of algebraic tools, which, if used

> according to the manual of instructions, were guaranteed to produce full employment, economic equilibrium, and a redistribution of wealth with justice, all three at once and with a kind of slide-rule precision – provided only that society really wanted to be saved. And the same theory by virtue of its logical implications delivered welfare government from the threat of insolvency. That word – insolvency – was to have no longer any meaning for a sovereign government. The balanced budget was a capitalist bogey. Deficit spending was not what it seemed. It was in fact *investment*; and the use of it was to fill an investment void – a void created by the chronic and incorrigible propensity of people to save too much.'[428]

Keynesianism after WWII 'was a polite way of being a socialist' due to its advocacy of more government spending and involvement in the running of the economy. True socialists saw it as being an attempt to reform and hence be the saviour of capitalism.[429]

The outcome of WWII was that there was a national mood for change away from the economic plight of the 1930s, with high unemployment, and towards a new economic order. This was reflected by the election of a Labour government, which quickly introduced the NHS, secondary education, nationalised several industries, and made a commitment to full employment. The government had willed the means to win the war and now it was felt that they should will the means to maintain a New Jerusalem and full employment. Pre-WWII orthodox economics held, with only 'cranks' dissenting, that Say's Law was true and that money was neutral.[430] This had been the Treasury View. Keynes' *General Theory* rejected this orthodoxy and its influence was such that in 1944 the government published its *White Paper on Full Employment* based upon Keynes' reasoning. This is a triumph for a new theory, a paradigm change. The time for the Keynesian experiment had come. The government was to take responsibility for the maintenance of full employment by demand management:

> 'The government accept as one of their primary aims and responsibilities the maintenance of a high and stable level of employment after the war ... Total expenditure on goods and services must be prevented from falling to a level where general unemployment appears.'[431]

Sir William Beveridge was a devotee of Keynes as was evident in his book: *Full Employment in a Free Society*. He advocated full employment as being 'having always more vacant jobs than unemployed men, not slightly fewer jobs'.[432] The aim of the government should be to plan for 'continuous steady expansion'. He took a moral view regarding unemployment:

> 'A person who has difficulty in buying the labour that he wants suffers inconvenience or reduction in profits. A person who cannot sell his labour is in effect told that he is of no use. The first difficulty causes annoyance or loss. The other is a personal catastrophe.'[433]

Beveridge also described a system of gaining employment 'which relies mainly on personal application, that is to say on the hawking of labour from door to door' as 'an anachronism which is socially indefensible'.[434] Beveridge described the goal of full employment as 'an adventure because it has never been accomplished in the past' although it is 'an adventure which can be undertaken with confidence of ultimate success. Success, however, will come not by following any rigid formula but by adapting action to circumstances which may change continually ... It is a voyage among shifting and dangerous currents'.[435]

Beveridge set out the history, supported by statistical data, of the trade cycle in Britain going back as far as 1785. Beveridge denied that he was a socialist, although he did say to a Conservative party conference:

> 'If ... it should be shown by experience or by argument that abolition of private property in the means of production was necessary for full employment, this abolition would have to be undertaken.'[436]

Regarding Keynes' *General Theory*, Beveridge viewed it as an 'analysis (that) is probably now accepted by all persons qualified to judge' and as the start of a 'new era'.[437] Having adopted Keynes's hypothesis as fact, ignoring any opinion to the contrary, Beveridge warmly approved the concept of an ever-expanding government debt in the belief that government is different and not subject to the same constraints as the private borrower as 'it is able to control money in place of being controlled by it', and cited the assertion of the economist Nicholas Kaldor, 1908-1986, that [italics my own emphasis]:

> '... taking into account prospective changes in population, in productivity, and in working hours, as well as foreseeable changes of Government expenditure on pensions, education, etc., and assuming an average rate of interest of 2 per cent, the National Debt could be expanded at the rate of *not less* than £775 millions a year from 1948 (taken as the beginning of the reconstruction period) to 1970, without involving on that account any increase of tax rates to meet the additional charge for Interest. This is a rate of borrowing far in excess of anything that would be needed to sustain full employment in peace time. A policy of continuous borrowing, on a more reasonable scale adequate for all possible requirements, is consistent with a steady reduction of the burden of the debt on the taxpayer.'[438]

Beveridge, however, preferred taxation to borrowing primarily to avoid increasing the number of rentiers who, he believed, should be squeezed out of existence by high taxes and low interest payments until the 'euthanasia of the rentier' [Beveridge quoting Keynes] had been achieved. Beveridge also contemplated the practice of simply printing money:

> 'It might well be asked why the Government should not decide right away that the best rate of interest is a zero rate and proceed to finance all its deficits by the "creation" of new cash or bank money through "Ways and Means Advances". This question is a pertinent one. It does not raise, as many of the so-called monetary reformers seem to think it raises, an issue of principle. The difference between printing paper which is a claim to cash in ten years and carries an appreciable rate of interest and printing paper which is a claim to cash on demand and carries an insignificant rate of interest is merely a difference of degree, not one of substance. Equally, there is no difference of substance between "creating" cash and printing, say, short term bills carrying 1 per cent interest. If it is demanded, therefore, that the Government should cease to

borrow at interest and simply cover its deficits by creating cash, this, in effect, amounts to demanding that governmental monetary policy should reduce the basic rate of interests, that is, the rate on paper, which carries no private risk, not gradually, but suddenly and to zero. It would have to be shown that a sudden reduction is preferable to a gradual one. Can this be shown?

There are at least two objections against it. First, a sudden reduction in the rate of interest produces a sudden appreciation in the capital value of all outstanding long-term money claims and all durable capital assets, such as land, houses, industrial property and so forth. An appreciation of these values – particularly a sudden one – which means windfall profits to their owners, may induce them to increase their luxury expenditure on an appreciable scale. While this, of course, would create additional employment, it would do so for purposes of small social value and might create social tensions that are wholly undesirable. Second, there are innumerable financial and other institutions, whose activities depend upon their being able to convert cash into interest-bearing paper that carries no appreciable private risk. If there is no further supply of gilt-edged Government paper, an important foundation of their activity crumbles away, and special arrangements are necessary to maintain them in being. This applies not only to insurance companies and banks, but also to pension funds, charitable organizations, research endowments and so forth. These two objections lose their force when applied to a gradual and long-term policy of reducing the rate of interest; but they would appear to have considerable weight against a policy of sudden changes.

A policy of gradual reduction gives time for adjustment. The speed with which it proceeds can be adjusted to circumstances. If the long term rate of interest is reduced by one-tenth of 1 per cent every two years, a total reduction from the present level of 3 per cent to a new level of 2 per cent is effected in twenty years. This rate of reduction may be considered too slow; it can hardly be considered too fast. If through conversions of the existing national debt, it could be spread over the total of that debt, it would allow the annual amount of interest payable on the national debt to remain stationary in spite of an annual budget deficit of £400 millions. This calculation alone should dispose of the argument of those who claim that annual budget deficits would impose an unmanageable "transfer burden" upon society.

The method that might be applied for the gradual reduction in the rate of interest on long-term bonds is the following: the length of the bonds offered "on tap" is increased every month at a stable rate of interest. After a while, the length of the bond is reduced, and the rate of interest offered on the shorter bond is also reduced. This can be repeated over and over again, giving a perfectly smooth transition. As long as the method of issuing bills and bonds "on tap" is maintained, the rate of interest is controllable without any difficulty whatsoever.'[439]

The American author and vice president of JP Morgan & Co, R. Gordon Wasson, 1898-1986, did not beat about the bush in analysing this logic of Beveridge:

'One cannot lay at Beveridge's door any cheap-jack "semantic" evasions. This high-minded man is here proposing, without a trace of self-consciousness, a programme and technique by which the state would gradually cheat its creditors. As with the sharpster's thimble trick, one gasps with admiration at the smoothness of it all. If the managers of a private enterprise engaged in such plottings, imagine the outcry from "liberals"! In private business, schemings against creditors of this kind might bring a man into court, and one recalls with uneasiness the sentence of Beveridge's ... in which he says that "the State in matters of finance is in a different position from any private citizen". It is disturbing to see a liberal expounding the philosophy of a double moral standard for the state.'[440]

Keynes himself was alert to the danger posed by the desire to spend money on a better life after the war. In a memo to the Cabinet Keynes warned: 'Our own habits are the greatest obstacle in the way of carrying out almost every one of the above recommendations. All our reflex actions are those of a rich man, so that we promise others too much. Our longings for relaxation from the war are so intense that we promise ourselves too much'.[441] Regarding the Beveridge Report, the Chancellor of the Exchequer, Sir Kingsley Wood, wrote to Churchill:

> 'Whether the report is valuable will be the subject of much argument. But it is certainly premature ... Many in this country have persuaded themselves that the cessation of hostilities will mark the opening of the Golden Age (many were so persuaded last time also). However this may be, the time for declaring a dividend on the profits of the Golden Age is the time when those profits have been realised in fact, not merely in the imagination.'[442]

In assessing the validity of Keynes and the validity and relevance of Keynesianism in the 21st century, it is first necessary to define what is meant by Keynesianism and what was the purpose of Keynes's arguments. Kaldor summarised Keynesiansim thus:

> 'In a market economy the total amount of goods and services produced is not (or not normally) determined by the amount of scarce resources at its disposal, and the efficiency with which they are utilised, but on certain features of the process of income generation which will tend to establish an equilibrium level of effective demand which will limit the amount produced, irrespective of potential supply. Keynes' theory has shown how the economy can be managed so as to secure the full utilisation of resources, in particular the full employment of labour, mainly by government action in the fiscal and monetary field, without any radical change in the framework of institutions of a market economy.'[443]

The objective, according to Kaldor, was to achieve full employment by using fiscal and monetary policy to control effective demand at an equilibrium level of output consistent with full employment. Kaldor considered the *General Theory* to be the most influential book on economics of the 20th century, and that this would be agreed to by both supporters and adversaries alike.[444] Kaldor described Keynes's *General Theory* as being 'best analysed as a development or refinement of Say's Law, rather than a complete rejection of the ideas behind that law'.[445]

It should be noted that although Keynes' *General Theory* contained a lot of loose prose and that Kaldor's definition of Keynesianism is not inconsistent with the *General Theory*, nevertheless it is an extrapolation from it. Keynes' analysis for the reasons for the high unemployment of the inter-war years and how to boost demand to eliminate that unemployment is ignored. Instead, Kaldor is presenting Keynesianism, in line with Beveridge's rationale, as an ongoing overarching technique for economic management – fine-tuning. As Keynes readily acknowledged, in agreement with the classical economists, higher government spending would only be a short-term solution to unemployment. Yet Kaldor is advocating a short-term policy for the long-term management of the economy. This neatly side-steps any underlying economic problems, and ignores the issues and lessons of the inter-war years. Keynesianism thus becomes a dodge for avoiding difficult issues such as a lack of competitiveness or the need for tariff reform, and instead inserts more fine-tuning as a solution to unemployment. This was not what Keynes himself advocated. Keynesianism is the economic equivalent of treating a serious illness with painkillers. The painkillers might make the patient feel better for a while, and might be desirable, but they are not a cure for an underlying illness that needs to be treated. Kaldor's definition is an accurate reflection of what Keynesianism was understood to be, and the Keynesians readily embraced the policy of fine-tuning.

Although many economists were worried that the end of WWII would follow the same pattern of the end of WWI – a short boom followed by a slump – the next 25 years were ones of continuing economic growth and prosperity. Unemployment between 1945 and 1970 averaged only 1.8%; by comparison, in the inter-war period unemployment had averaged 13%.[446] Full employment was also enjoyed by other leading countries, in particular Germany and the USA which had suffered so badly during the inter-war years.

Not all of this success can be attributed to Keynesian demand management, which, for example, the Germans did not adopt. Germany benefited from a competitive exchange rate under the Bretton Woods fixed exchange rate system and had benefited, as did other West European countries, from Marshall Aid to help with reconstruction after the war. Germany enjoyed an export-led boom and low inflation. Also Germany benefited from the inward expenditure provided by the substantial military presence from the

USA in particular as well as other NATO countries (Japan, another economic success story, likewise benefited from a large military presence of the USA, as did South Korea). Effective demand in Germany was strong without the need for recourse to Keynesian demand management and private investment poured into Germany's export industries.[447] Obviously the economic growth experienced by Germany's export markets helped the German export-led economic growth.

After WWII, in the USA Keynesians had argued that government spending be maintained at its wartime level. In the event military spending was cut from $95billion to $15billion in the year following the war. The Truman administration ran a large budgetary surplus with no ill effects.[448] Far from a Keynesian predicted recession there was a boom. The USA enjoyed full employment, not least due to the high military expenditure due to the Korean War in the 1950s, but this petered out. President Eisenhower did not pursue Keynesian policies and unemployment reached 7% by 1960. President Kennedy took a more expansionist approach with policies to boost both private investment and government expenditure as well as introducing tax cuts, which ran foul of opposition in Congress. President Lyndon Johnson continued this policy and finally managed to get Congress to agree to the proposed tax cuts. The result was that higher consumption which led to more investment and higher growth, not least due to the multiplier effect upon which Keynes had stressed such importance. Unemployment fell as a consequence.

Britain embraced a Keynesian approach. The immediate problem after WWII was too much demand and inflationary pressures. The government ran budget surpluses in an attempt to reduce demand and also maintained rationing. Once the economy had adjusted to peacetime, the difficulties of maintaining full employment emerged and successive governments resorted to Keynesian demand management to help combat unemployment. Although it might be too simplistic to assign all the credit for this growth to Keynesian demand management, the fact that the government had committed itself to full employment and was prepared to boost demand to maintain growth and full employment can only have contributed to the sense of confidence that helped investment that made the economic growth possible. Full employment almost seemed to be taken for granted.

British growth was running at a rate of 3% per annum. This was a good achievement compared to historical growth rates, but it was not as good as other European countries. In the 1960s many were concerned at Britain's lower rate of growth and were advocating a target of an annual growth rate of 4%. One difficulty in achieving this was the rising level of inflation – a problem of which Keynes had himself been aware. Inflation had been chronic since 1935 and although there had been inflationary periods in the past, such periods were succeeded by periods of stable if not falling prices. In the one hundred years to the beginning of the 18th century prices had only risen by roughly 25%; in 1914 and the start of WWI prices were generally lower than they had been at the Battle of Waterloo in 1815. In the 650 years to 1935 prices rose by roughly 14-fold; however, in the fifty years following 1935 prices rose 28-fold. This inflation did not stifle the growth and the rise in living standards and GDP per capita more than doubled in the fifty years following 1935.[449]

Between 1945 and 1970 inflation averaged around 4%. This continuing rate impoverished those whose incomes were not inflation-proofed (in particular pensioners dependent upon private pensions that were not index-linked to inflation and others on fixed incomes); it further eroded the real worth of those holding money in bank and building society accounts; again this affected pensioners. Another problem was that the 4% inflation was higher than many of Britain's competitors. This led to a loss of competitiveness of British exports and this loss was compounded by being a member of the Bretton Woods fixed exchange rate system, the terms of which the USA virtually dictated following the outcome of WWII, when other countries were weakened and US strength at its height. Sterling was vulnerable under Bretton Woods due to there being four times as many external sterling reserves outside Britain compared to the dollar and gold reserves available to match, in addition to which Britain was struggling to keep its trade in balance.[450]

The central policy of the Harold Wilson's 1960s Labour government, set out in the National Plan produced by the new (and short-lived) Department of Economic Affairs, was to achieve a 5.5% annual increase in exports in order to boost economic growth to 4%. Unfortunately, Harold Wilson and the Labour government overlooked the French practice of 'devalue early and devalue often'.[451] Wilson by contrast set himself against any devaluation of sterling and was locked into a policy of saving the pound, which led to deflationary policies and the Stop-Go era, where an expansionist 'Go' economic policy was rapidly followed by a deflationary 'Stop' policy as imports soared and sterling came under pressure in the fixed exchange rate system. The National Plan was therefore doomed to fail. The French system of indicative planning produced a growth rate of 4.5% per annum in the three decades following WWII; Britain's growth rate being only 3%.[452] There were four sterling crises between 1964 and 1967, the final of which forced Britain to devalue by 14.3%.[453] Imports became more and more competitive in the British home market. This led to a loss of confidence in the value of sterling and consequent balance of payments difficulties. The government response of implementing deflationary policies clobbered demand, growth and investment. Britain was further forced to devalue sterling to try and regain export competitiveness, and reduce the competitiveness of imports, and hence relieve pressure on the balance of payments.

However, the surplus then achieved was gradually shrinking despite continued sluggish growth (and hence a weaker demand for imports).[454] Eventually the Bretton Woods system collapsed in 1973 and sterling was allowed to float and find its own value. Bretton Woods had crucially differed from the pre-WWI Gold Standard in that it was up to each individual country to correct a deficit, by initiating deflationary policies. This expectation was not always fulfilled as countries – apart from Britain in particular – preferred to devalue rather than go through the pain of deflation. The collapse of Bretton Woods occurred for two main reasons. Firstly, the differing inflation rates between countries rendered the rates of exchange increasingly unrealistic, and countries were unwilling to adjust domestic demand or their exchange rates. This led to market speculation against currencies. Secondly and more immediately, the US 'Vietnam inflation', which first led to the suspension of the dollar's convertibility into gold in August 1971, and then to a huge supply of dollars onto the exchange markets, which other countries had to absorb. Ottmer Emminger of the Bundesbank pointed out that from the 'beginning of 1970 to March 1973, European money stock increased by no less than 54%, while the main deficit country, the United States, the money supply, far from slowing down, had also experienced a record expansion'. This expansion of the money supply showed that Bretton Woods no longer exercised any discipline at all, and had become, in the words of Karl Bessing, the former governor of the Bundesbank, a 'perfect inflation machine'. The decision was taken to shield the German monetary system against further inflationary foreign exchange inflows after the Bundesbank had to absorb a dollar inflow worth more than DM20billion within five weeks, and first Germany, then other countries floated their exchange rates.

The introduction of floating exchange rates freed the British economy from the choke of having to defend the balance of payments. The introduction of prices and incomes policies freed, it was hoped, the economy from the problem of inflation and so allowed an expansionary economic policy be pursued to achieve growth.

The growth was deemed necessary due to the upward movement in the rate of unemployment. The then Heath government's growth strategy was deemed to be working with growth forecast at 4% and unemployment expected to fall to 900,000 by the end of 1972. Despite this, the calls for even faster levels of growth were still being made as an unemployment level of 700,000 by the end of 1973 was still pronounced to be too high. The government adopted a growth target of 5%, in what became known as the Barber Boom.

The so-called Barber Boom of the early 1970s was an example of fine-tuning going wrong. In March 1971 with sluggish economic growth and rising unemployment, the Tory Chancellor, Barber, responded with an expansionist Budget. Four months later when unemployment was still rising and it had been estimated that the real GDP in the first half of the year had been 1% lower than had been assumed back in March. This compelled Barber to introduce further expansionary measures which included a cut of 20% in the purchase tax and all hire purchase controls were abolished. Even so, unemployment continued to increase and it was forecast that it would reach 4% by the beginning of 1972 with a total of one million out of work, which was regarded as politically unacceptable. Therefore, during the remainder of 1971 and into 1972 Barber took further expansionist measures, including lower interest rates and a major increase in public spending. In the March 1972 Budget there was a substantial cut in income tax. While most economists and politicians were in favour of this policy, there was some criticism. The *London and Cambridge Economic Bulletin*, set out in *The Times*, forecast that the growth commitment and policies designed to achieve that would propel a balance of payments deficit of more than £1billion in 1973, and that the policy had the 'seeds of a classic inflation'.[455] Enoch Powell warned that Barber had lost control of the money supply and that economic disaster loomed.[456] However, at the time the main concern by most was that Barber may have acted too late and been insufficiently bold.[457]

The expansionary measures took time to work through and the earlier measures had not yet taken effect when the subsequent measures were introduced. Eventually all the measures took effect rapidly with the result of a very sharp rise in effective demand in 1972 and early 1973. Between 1971 and 1973 total expenditure rose by 12% in real terms, although output only rose by 8% as industry could not increase output fast enough to keep pace with demand. Consequently, there was a surge in inflation and a surge in imports. (This surge in imports created damage in addition to any inflationary consequences. For example, there was a surge in demand for TVs that the British producers could not meet. Japanese imports flooded in and when the boom turned to bust, the cheap imports threatened the existence of the industry. The government made an agreement with Japan that Japan would limit its exports to no more than 10% of the British market. However, Japanese firms circumvented this by setting up factories in Britain and labelling their TVs as being British if half of their components had been made in Britain.)[458]

The inflation rate peaked at 26% (as measured by the retail prices index) in June 1975. This came after the OPEC oil price hikes (the price of oil increased fourfold between 1973 and 1974)[459] and the large wage increases in 1974. The money supply had also expanded as a result of the Barber Boom and increased by 62% in two years.[460] The result was another housing bubble, followed by a surge in inflation and the three-day week during the miners' strike. Part of the problem of the Barber Boom was not only the simplistic and reckless implementation of Keynesian ideology, well beyond anything Keynes ever advocated, but the forecast outcome of the bold growth objective was dependent upon the accuracy of the forecast. In fact, the ability to accurately forecast the economic outcome of the ever finer tuning that the government of the day was now engaged in was increasingly in doubt, not least due to challenges being made to the accuracy of the computer models used. Peter Kenway wrote:

'The standard Keynesian models of the London Business School and the Treasury had been working towards the position where they modelled sectoral income and expenditure, but neither model had properly reached this point. The Business School had done so implicitly, with the public sector income in effect acting as the buffer that ensured equality between the income and expenditure measures of GDP. The Treasury model did not include such a sectoral disaggregation, explicitly or implicitly, but ... company sector profits played the role of the buffer to bring the two measures of GDP into equality with one another. Neild looked past these details to see how the sectoral financial balances should behave. This was the logical endpoint of the long development of the income-expenditure models, but the implausibilities that Neild uncovered indicated that that development contained significant and perhaps serious flaws. Indeed, to the extent that Neild traced the flaw in the official projections back to their implications for company sector profits, it is possible that the very structure of the Treasury model and the part played in it by profits (not as a "buffer" but also as a "sink") was one of the basic reasons for the implausibilities in those projections.'[461]

Not only was there a debate as to the accuracy of the computer models, but the outcome in the economy was not what the Keynesian doctrine predicted and the ideal of demand management smoothing the economic up and downs was not happening, as the economy was acting differently than expected. The Barber Boom of 1973 turned rapidly into a recession the following year. Further studies into the consequences of the attempted demand management which highlighted that changes in taxation and public expenditure would have an immediate impact on the level of income and output, but the ultimate effects would be entirely on the balance of payments; conversely, changes in import and export prices would have an immediate impact on balance of payments but the ultimate effects would be entirely on income and expenditure.[462]

In written evidence submitted to a House of Commons Select Committee Wynne Godley, Francis Cripps and Martin Fetherston, contributors to the *London and Cambridge Economic Bulletin*, pointed out that the 'record of demand management' over the previous twenty years 'had been extremely poor'. There had been a series of dramatic reversals in fiscal policy involving two years of an expansion of demand (1953-54, 1958-59, 1962-63 and 1971-72), followed by two years of demand deflation (1955-56, 1960-61 and 1973-74). Not only had these policy reversals been caused by changes in government policy aims, but also they were because: 'some of the outcomes were not properly foreseen – in particular that the conventional forecasting systems on which policy is based may underestimate the full effects of changes in policy'.[463] Cripps, Godley and Fetherston further stated that:

> 'It appears to have been the case that during the past twenty years or so, purely by chance, the fluctuations in UK exports, to the extent that these were induced by changes in world trade, have been roughly offset by changes in import prices attributable to the same cause. To the extent that this is true, fluctuations in world trade have generated very little disturbance either to the UK balance of payments or to real output in total, and the observed fluctuations in output have, to this extent, been *entirely* the consequences of the stabilisation measures!'[464]

This meant that the Keynesian demand management policies pursued by successive governments since WWII had had the opposite effects to that intended. They had not helped to stabilise the economy with counter-cyclical measures, but had in fact been *entirely* responsible for the economic instability. Cripps, Godley and Fetherston believed that greater stability might have been achieved 'had some simple rule been followed through thick and thin such as that a tax yield should be sought such as to cover, as nearly as possible, some fixed proportion of public expenditure'.[465] This is a complete condemnation of Keynesian demand management from those who would have happily described themselves as Keynesians.

One conclusion reached was that the standard Keynesian multiplier equation was wrong. That is because it was now believed that the government's current account expenditure would all be spent and none would be saved and so the marginal propensity to import was the only leakage from the domestic economy apart from the amount paid back to the government in tax. If true, then this meant that the multiplier was larger than the standard Keynesian one and the Keynesian multiplier therefore underestimated the multiplier effect of a change in fiscal policy on output. As the standard Keynesian multiplier equation was wrong, then a fiscal stimulus to the economy would lead to an overreaction of expansion, which in turn would lead to the government deflating the economy to dampen down the demand boost; this deflation, due to the same error in the multiplier equation, would lead to another overreaction in a downward direction, which in turn would lead the government to boost demand to correct the correction it had just made – and so on. The error in the multiplier would explain the exaggeration and counterproductive efforts of Keynesian demand management to stabilise the economy.[466] The opinions presented were rejected by most long-standing Keynesians and a lively debate ensued.

A further development was the shift to a longer-term outlook rather than the short-term of quarterly or even monthly analysis. This led to a focus on the underlying output trends of the economy rather than trying to predict the trade cycle and manage that. The underlying trend analysis was achieved by looking at past data and trying to accurately interpret it.[467] Although there remained a commitment to full employment, the issue debated between the old school of Keynesians and the new school, was over how to accurately predict the impact on the economy of demand management measures and which indicators to concentrate on. The move to trend analysis and not trade cycle prediction led to attention being focused on the determinants of the trend itself and how to manipulate them.

This debate came against a background of the failure of Keynesian economics. The failure to arrest Britain's long-term economic decline and the failure to match the growth rates of Britain's European competitors in particular; the failure to achieve full employment; the failure to control inflation; the failure to maintain a balance of payments; and the stagflation and civil strife that was a feature of Britain in the 1970s. In the same way that Keynes had himself questioned the economic orthodoxy of his day, now others were challenging the Keynesian orthodoxy. It may have worked in the 1940s, 1950s and 1960s to maintain full employment, but as time passed the orthodoxy was struggling to perform on its own criteria and in the 1970s, especially with the problems of stagflation and rapidly rising inflation, the orthodoxy was either wrong or out of date. That the response to these facts from various Keynesian parties was to embark on drawing up new computer models and arguing over the assumptions made demonstrates the grip that Keynesian demand management still had in that there was still an instinct to control the economy by demand management policies.

A further problem arose from the Cambridge Economic Policy Group in 1976 was that they forecast escalating levels of unemployment and yet concluded that the Keynesian solutions could not possibly work:

> 'The vital issue, both from the foreign and domestic standpoint, is how large a devaluation would be needed to secure an acceptable rate of growth of output and reduction of unemployment in Britain. As we shall now see, the scale of effective devaluation required is large and almost certainly impossible to implement.'[468]

The analysis was that British Labour costs would need to be reduced by up to 30% in foreign currency terms if a devaluation was to be a solution to the upward trend in unemployment by boosting the economy. This would require a 40% devaluation of sterling compared to its 1975 level. A devaluation on such a scale for a floating currency was unprecedented (there was only France in 1958) and the domestic implications on living standards would be serious. Import prices would increase by 30% and domestic prices were forecast to increase by 20% in the first twelve months after devaluation. Wages were assumed to increase by their then annual rate of 7.5%. There would therefore be a substantial cut in living standards if the gains from the devaluation were not to be wasted and the objective of cutting labour costs by 30% in foreign currency terms were to be achieved.[469] It was not believed that such a fall in wages was acceptable and this led to a dilemma in the viability of Keynesianism and the commitment to full employment by Keynesian methods.

The London Business School had also been examining the consequences of devaluation and concluded that the benefits in improved competitiveness were gradually eroded so that, after a 20% devaluation for example, by the end of the third year the export price competitive gain had been reduced to a mere 4% and the gain in home markets against imports was by the end of the third year reduced to only 7%; By the sixth year the export competitive gain had been completely eliminated as almost had the gains in the home market. The reason for this was that wage increases would catch up with the cost increases caused by devaluation. In terms of GDP, after a minor dip due to the fall in consumer real incomes the export competitiveness initially gained boosts GDP by 2% more than it would have been after two years, but the gain is eliminated after five years before becoming negative in the sixth year. So the benefit, if these predictions were correct, is short-lived although there is a long-lasting positive effect on the balance of payments.[470]

Further analysis of historical data revealed that in the long term, with fixed exchange rates, domestic price increases were the same as the rate of growth of increases in import prices. Therefore, in the long term, domestic inflation would equal the change in prices of imports – i.e. external inflation. If true, then the implication was that the British government cannot influence inflation as it is imported and cannot be independently controlled. Exchange rate stability is therefore a goal if there is to be a return to an inflation rate the same as the international average. The devaluations that Britain undertook, and the falls experienced by the floating exchange rate were therefore sources of inflation. By contrast if the exchange rate appreciated then the inflation rate would be lower than the international average.[471] Therefore the implication was that a floating exchange rate allowed Britain to pursue a rate of inflation that would be different than that of our competitors.

The London Business School's analysis, in a 1975 model, if true, showed that in the long run a devaluation of the currency would have no effects on output and therefore none on the level of employment. This was therefore a rejection of the suggested Keynesian response to the increasing unemployment levels – that what was needed was a major currency devaluation, and of course made redundant all the problems that the Keynesians themselves had identified with that. A later 1978 model from the London Businesses School showed that with floating exchange rates, increasing the government deficit, a traditional Keynesian response to rising unemployment, would also have no lasting effect on output or employment. If this analysis were true then Keynesian policy was thus debunked.

Not all Monetarists agreed with the London Business School. Milton Friedman wrote: 'Floating exchange rates are necessary in order for a monetary policy proper to be possible. They are a facilitating mechanism, not a "transmission mechanism".[472]

But the battle to control inflation was at odds with Keynesian demand management in the event of rising unemployment which called for policies likely to contribute to inflationary pressure. Wages were seen as a particular problem as the unions in the 1960s and 1970s became increasingly militant, bringing down the Heath government of the early 1970s, and they were very adept at demanding wage increases above the rate of inflation (Keynes had assumed that workers and unions would only focus on money wages and were not as sensitive to a below inflation rate increase in money wages as they would be to an outright cut in money wages). There was no need to restrict wage increases if the government was responsible for full employment, as any reckless wage increase would not result in unemployment but only more government inspired demand management. Businesses were more likely to grant reckless wage increases if they were confident of being able to pass the costs on in higher prices, which they could with a continuing inflation rate and with the government being willing to increase demand to combat any downturn which might be caused by falling sales due to a lack of competitiveness.

The government response to this was to introduce prices and incomes policies not only to allow demand management to continue without the inflationary response but also to try and tackle the 'cost-push' inflationary spiral. Prices and incomes policies were used by successive governments after WWII until the election of the Thatcher government in 1979.

The 1970s witnessed a collapse in the Keynesian consensus. The increased militancy of the unions began the decade by bringing down a Tory government as a result of a miner's strike and ended the decade by contributing to the election of a Tory government as a result of the Winter of Discontent, when people were even prevented from burying the dead. Economically the 1970s witnessed the condition of stagflation, where the trade-off between inflation and unemployment broke down and both were increasing at the same time. Also the rate of inflation accelerated, reaching more than 9% in 1971, 16% in 1974 and as much as 26% in 1975.[473] Although it might be arguable that a steady inflation rate of 4% is a price worth paying for full employment and can therefore be tolerated, an ever-increasing inflation rate cannot be tolerated as eventually the currency will become worthless.

A Keynesian solution to the inflation problem might be seen as to reduce demand as the economy was apparently at full capacity and the demand was too high and therefore was creating inflation rather than jobs. However, the rising unemployment indicated that the Keynesian response should have been to *increase* effective demand, which was obviously problematic, to put it no more strongly, when inflation was already so high and rising quickly. Unemployment had been 1.5% in 1966, between 2% and 2.5% in the years 1967 to 1970, 3.5% in 1971, 4% in 1972, and after falling sharply as a result of the Keynesian inspired Barber boom in 1973, it reached roughly 5% at the end of 1975.[474] The inverse relationship between inflation and unemployment had ended. There was no longer any trade off and both inflation and unemployment were rising at the same time.

Some Keynesian economists rejected any responsibility of Keynesian economics for the rising inflation and regarded inflation as a cost-push phenomena. To them, the problem was seen as a breakdown of the various prices and incomes policies which, had they been successful, would have prevented the rising inflation. The devaluation of sterling in November 1967 raised the prices of British imports by approximately 15%. There were the other rises in costs due to the poor harvests in both America and the USSR which led to a doubling of wheat prices between 1972 and 1973. World commodity prices generally rose by about 50%. The quadrupling of the oil price by the OPEC countries further pushed up costs.

Another problem was the inflationary economic policies pursued in the USA both to pay for the Vietnam War and also President Johnson's 'Great Society' programme. Because of the way the fixed currency system of Bretton Woods operated, this inflation was spread to other membership countries. The system's collapse and the floating of sterling led to another 15% depreciation in the value of the currency between June 1972 and autumn 1973. There were therefore a variety of cost-push factors present at the time of the birth of stagflation.

Other economists did not blame cost-push factors. They blamed Keynesianism itself. Many of the economists accepted the Monetarist analysis particularly of Milton Friedman and the University of Chicago. Monetarism won favour increasingly in both the USA and Britain and was the major influence on the economic thinking of both Margaret Thatcher and Ronald Reagan when they were elected (whether the policies actually pursued, especially by Reagan, were monetarist or not is open to debate). In the same way that Keynesianism had been the analysis of the moment, to secure full employment after the experience of the inter-war slump and the desire to build a New Jerusalem in Britain, so Monetarism was the analysis of the moment when it offered an alternative explanation for the inflationary surge and offered a cure: control the money supply.

Monetarism asserted once again that markets were self-correcting. This meant that full employment is the natural state of the economy, as classical economists had always asserted. The price mechanism would work to regulate the supply and demand and ensure the optimal distribution of resources and goods. Demand would equal supply and there would be full employment. The economy was self-stabilising. There could be no excess demand or excess supply. Say's Law was true and Keynesianism was wrong.

With Monetarist analysis, the government should allow the economy to work and allow markets to allocate resources. Government interference would only disrupt the market and disrupt the economy. As monetarists believe that a market economy will ensure the optimal distribution of resources and goods and that output will be optimised given the resources available, then an increase in effective demand will not increase output but merely increase prices.[475] Due to increases in output and productivity, then there is a need for a responsive growth in the money supply to match the growth in productive potential. This may be around 3% per annum.[476] Monetarists would regard a 3% growth in the money supply to be appropriate and not inflationary. To monetarists, an increase in the money supply beyond this will lead to rising prices and inflation. Monetarists reject the attempt to boost demand to solve involuntary unemployment. They assert that there is a time lag between increases in the money supply and increases in output and the relationship is therefore unreliable and unpredictable. Even in the event of unemployment and unused productive capacity, the increase in money supply might take time to feed through by which time the market may have already self-corrected and hence the surge in money would only result in inflation.

Monetarists believe that the labour market works like any other market and that the demand for labour and supply of labour is determined by the wage rate. If higher wages are offered then more people will offer themselves for work. If there is unemployment, then the wage rate will fall as more people will be willing to work for less in order to price themselves back into work. The market wage rate is the natural rate that all those who wish to work will have a job. This is the full employment level where the economy and labour market are in equilibrium at what Milton Friedman described as 'the natural rate of unemployment'. This natural rate of unemployment will involve some frictional and structural unemployment and the level will vary. Involuntary employment does not exist and all employment is voluntary. People are unemployed because they do not wish to work for the market wage being offered. The higher the real wage then the more tempting it is for people to work and the higher the unemployment benefit then the more tempting it is to remain on unemployment benefit. For those who want to work, if they offer to work for a lower wage, then this lower wage will increase the demand for labour and so unemployment will fall as the numbers in work increases.

For Monetarists, to attempt to reduce unemployment below its natural level by demand management will only lead to an increase in inflation. At the natural level of unemployment the inflation rate will be stable. If unemployment falls below its natural rate then inflation will increase and if unemployment rises above its natural rate then the inflation rate will fall. Milton Friedman believed that at the natural rate of unemployment inflation would be governed by people's expectations as to the level of inflation. If inflation was nil and people expected it to remain nil, then it would do so due to the decisions people themselves took (e.g. whether or not to demand an increase in wages or whether or not to pay higher prices).[477]

It therefore follows that Monetarists reject the Keynesian approach of demand management. Demand management to try to reduce unemployment, which would find its own natural level anyway, would only lead to inflation; there was no trade-off between unemployment and inflation. The problem from a Monetarist perspective was to ensure the sound working of the labour market and to reduce the natural rate of unemployment itself by providing incentives to work and tackling impediments such as militant trades unions that may be operating restrictive practices and forcing up wage rates. Monetarists believe that it is supply-side measures which are needed to increase the flexibility of the labour market.

Monetarists would regard a Keynesian demand management response to a higher than desired level of unemployment as inflationary come what may; that if a government stimulated demand then the boost in consumer demand would lead employers to increase wages to attract more workers; this might be successful in tempting those voluntarily unemployed to accept the new higher wages; but as the higher wages and prices work through then all the prices increase which will negate the original higher wage offered and once this is rumbled then the previous unemployed will desert their employment and voluntarily become unemployed again; meanwhile as the whole economy has experienced higher prices, all workers will seek wage increases to protect their standards of living, and employers will seek to push up prices to cover their extra costs and maintain their profits; there will now be an expectation of inflation which would become a self-fulfilling prophesy; any fall in unemployment below its natural rate would only be temporary. As far as monetarists are concerned to control inflation it is necessary to control the money supply and expanding the money supply will not create employment.

Although many Keynesians rejected Monetarism outright, others did not and sought to modify their own stance and commitment to a Keynesian approach without embracing Monetarism in its entirety. One such modification related to fine-tuning, when there was an attempt to control demand on an annual basis, if not over a shorter timespan, so that the effective demand was in line with the long-term productive potential of the economy. Forecasting effective demand was difficult and although the forecasting techniques became more sophisticated as the understanding of the economy grew, economists were not able to as accurately predict things as they believed they could do or were able to. The government and economists believed that they could monitor the economy quarterly or even monthly and make minor adjustments to the demand management polices with precision to ensure that the economy stayed on its projected course. Government believed that it could tweak taxes, government spending and interest rates in response to the latest economic indicators and control the economy.

However, such fine-tuning is dependent upon the accuracy of the data upon which decisions are based. Some economic data can take time to collect and evaluate. The statistics of private investment, for example, are many months out of date and are historical figures which tell us what has happened, not what is happening. The Monetarist point that the measures taken in response took time to work through compounded the problem. There was also the problem of the accuracy of the tweaking in response to the data when it was purely a prediction, possibly a forecast in the middle of a range of outcomes, any of which might in fact be the outcome.

The Keynesian position was still untenable given the failure of Keynesian policies to achieve the necessary growth to maintain full employment, in particular the requirement for a very dramatic fall in the exchange rate accompanied by a dramatic fall in real wages. The dilemma posed to the rationale of Keynesianism was set out in 1978 by the Cambridge Economic Policy Group:

> 'While during the past 25 years the changes in the direction of policy, at the time they were made, had come to seem inevitable, there were underlying trends of a most disturbing kind continuously at work which should have been apparent … Since 1960, exports have risen at 4-8% *per annum*, whereas imports have risen at 8-12% *per annum*. Exports were so much higher than imports that for many years the absolute gap between the two was roughly constant. But the continuation of past trends of imports of manufactures relative to exports would more recently have meant that the gap would close and that imports would come to exceed exports by a large margin. The necessary consequence is that growth of GDP has had to be sacrificed to hold down growth of imports and protect the balance of payments … So far as unemployment goes the picture is a clear one: after remaining nearly stable and very low until about 1965 there has been a marked, indeed sensational, turn for the worse.'[478]

The importance of the above analysis cannot be overstated. It proves the correctness of Joseph Chamberlain's and the Tariff Reform's campaign. Free Trade had remained Britain's policy and the result was the industrial and economic decline that was warned of. Keynesianism, being focused on unemployment, was not a policy capable of addressing Britain's inability to compete (Keynes was an ardent Free Trader), and its implementation exacerbated the underlying problem leading ultimately to rising unemployment and lower living standards that economic failure must produce.

Despite its attractions as a panacea for solving the problem of unemployment and ensuring, through demand management, that society would always enjoy full employment, and the justification of government spending increases as being a good thing, in the right circumstances, and so removing a constraint of the need for balancing the budget or restricting the government sector to a small part of the economy, Keynesianism gradually fell out of favour with British governments. Even though it was accepted by nearly all as received wisdom in the good times in the growth years after WWII, the increasingly unstable nature of the British economy meant that Keynesainism was bound to come under scrutiny. It no longer performed as expected, it no longer was relevant to the kind of problems (e.g. inflation and balance of payments) that Britain was bedevilled with, and to many it was even responsible for those problems. Keynes had written *General Theory* in the 1930s to deal with the problems at the time. The *General Theory* spawned an economic philosophy that dominated thinking in Britain, and many other countries, up until the 1970s. The changing world and changing problems compelled Keynesians to react to try and tailor Keynesianism to take account of this new environment. They failed to do so successfully.

Kaldor, in studying the Western economies since WWII, concluded that a modern economy's rate of growth was determined by the rate of growth of output per worker in manufacturing, which in turn is determined by the rate of growth of the demand for manufactures. The growth of demand includes both exports and the sale of goods on the home market, with the home market being more important as normally 80% of manufacturing output is sold to the home market;[479] foreign markets are more risky involving factors such as exchange rate movements, different culture, different political factors and instability, and local resistance to buying goods from another country. To depend for export demand for the increase in growth is risky for all these reasons and the economy may become vulnerable to foreign upheavals as well as cultural and policy changes. It further makes the strategy dependent on the smaller part of output, exports, responsible for lifting the entire economy out of recession.

To depend upon export-led growth, a mantra used often by governments, amounted to a mutation of the original Keynesian idea, which was to create jobs by increasing demand in the economy. Now what was being proposed was devaluation to make British exports more competitive in overseas markets. Yet it was the growth in imports which was causing the problem – not a shortage of exports (although it is true that Britain was losing its share of the world export market). It further subjected the policy to the consequences of the actions of other governments and the economic policies pursued in other countries, which may not be compatible with the strategy of increasing export sales (those governments may be pursuing deflationary policies or have put up protectionist measures, for example). Moreover, with a fixed rate exchange rate system the government might be able to devalue, subject to the rules of the system and the potential need to secure the agreement of other countries, but with a floating exchange rate system it is questionable as to the extent that the government can actually manipulate the exchange rate in a particular direction. The policy of devaluation with a floating exchange rate may be virtually impossible in the medium to long term without capital controls. A study by two IMF economists, Mundell and Fleming, in the 1960s concluded that a country could not both control its exchange rate and its interest rates *without using exchange and capital controls*, which would prevent capital being moved into and out of a country and so affecting the exchange rate or interest rate. Without capital and exchange controls it was only possible to control *either* the exchange rate or the interest rate.

The plight of manufacturing was dire and the British economy was unable to match the growth rates of its competitors. In Britain, manufacturing output *fell* by 3% between 1970 and 1980; in the same period it increased by 23% in West Germany, 37% in the USA, 35% in France, 38% in Italy and 56% in Japan. British GDP increased by 20% between 1970 and 1980; in the same period it increased by 32% in West Germany, 32% in the USA, 44% in France, 48% in Italy and 68% in Japan. In the years 1979-81, Britain lost 1.6million jobs.[480]

A number of economic thinkers deserted Keynes and even attacked Keynesianism itself. Friedman commented that: 'Keynesian economics doesn't work. But nothing is harder for men than to face facts that threaten to undermine strongly held beliefs'.[481] James Buchanan's and Robert Wagner's produced *Democracy in Deficit: The Political Legacy of Lord Keynes* in 1977, which painted Keynes as an elitist, anti-democrat, with a naïve understanding of politics, who had been seriously mistaken in rejecting the ethos of balanced budgets and had initiated a defective economic creed.[482] Margaret Thatcher herself said to an interviewer in 1979: 'No, no, no. I am afraid Keynesianism has gone mad and it wasn't in the least little bit what Keynes thought'.[483] In the British press and in political circles the turn against Keynes was widespread. Keynesianism had become the economic orthodoxy, yet it was failing and its adherents were unable to offer a solution to the stagflation, mass unemployment and conflict that now blighted the country. Denis Healey remarked that he was exasperated at the culture of the Treasury: 'In 1974 the Treasury was the slave of the greatest of all academic scribblers, Maynard Keynes himself'.[484] Nigel Lawson explained the Tory economic philosophy: 'At the macroeconomic level our approach is what has come to be known as monetarism, in contradistinction to what has come to be known as Keynesianism, although the latter doctrine is a perversion of what Keynes actually preached himself'.[485] For Hayek, the problem of rising inflation combined with rising unemployment was predictable: 'The economy will have become geared to the expectation of further inflation and much of the existing employment will depend on continued monetary expansion, the attempt to stop it will rapidly produce substantial unemployment. This will bring a renewed and irresistible pressure for more inflation'.[486]

Prime Minister Jim Callaghan told the Labour Party conference in 1976:

> 'We used to think that you could spend your way out of a recession and increase employment by cutting taxes and boosting government spending. I tell you in all candour that that option no longer exists, and in so far as it ever did exist, it only worked on each occasion since the war by injecting a bigger dose of inflation into the economy, followed by a higher level of unemployment as the next step.'[487]

The Labour government of Jim Callaghan implemented both a prices and incomes policy combined with tight fiscal and monetary policies. Inflation fell to 8% in May 1979 when the general election swept Margaret Thatcher and the Tories into office.

SUMMARY

Keynesianism triumphed after WWII. The long boom that followed the war allowed an increase in living standards and a reduction in the burden of government debt. This long boom was not necessarily the consequence of Keynesianism, as countries such as West Germany were very successful despite not adopting Keynesian thinking. For Britain, the boom hid the fact that imports were steadily increasing and export markets were being lost. Britain struggled to maintain the value of sterling in the Bretton Woods fixed exchange rate system and, foolishly, gave priority to 'saving the pound' in various sterling crises in the Stop-Go era, rather than devaluing as other countries were happy to do.

In assessing the success or otherwise of Keynesianism and the danger posed by government spending, one can compare the period post-WWI with what happened post-WWII. In 1914 the British national debt was 29% of GDP; by 1920 it had reached 148%, primarily as a consequence of WWI; the policy response was to try and balance the Budget and the outcome of this strategy was that the national debt was reduced to 136% of GDP by 1940. By contrast, the British funding of WWII, managed largely by Keynes himself, resulted in a national debt of 240% of GDP in 1945, an 80% increase rather than the 520% increase during WWI – although one needs not to overlook the US largess during WWII and not to overlook the dramatic reduction in British overseas assets which had to be sold to fund WWII and from which the Britain never recovered. Even though Britain was left teetering on the brink of national bankruptcy in 1945, the pursuit of economic growth meant that by 1965 the national debt had fallen to 96% of GDP, and by 1980 it had fallen to 48% of GDP and remained at around that figure until the end of the century. The reason for the fall in the burden of the debt was not that the debt itself was reduced (in fact the debt was twenty times greater in 2000 than it was in 1945), but because of the growth which resulted in a hundred fold increase in GDP which meant that the burden of debt had been reduced by roughly 80%.[488]

A difference between post-WWII and pre-WWI is that pre-WWI in the boom wages rose and in a recession they fell back. Post WWII wages rise in a boom but are less likely to fall back in a recession. Wages became much more 'sticky'. Furthermore, wage movements pre-WWI were much more confined to particular industries and other occupations were less affected. Post-WWII other workers also gain wage rate increases in the name of comparability and fairness and those workers are likewise less willing to accept wage cuts in a recession.[489]

Another problem post-WWII is that there is a social pressure for wages to increase. The surplus or scarcity of labour is less influential regarding wage rates. Wages are likely to rise irrespective of a scarcity or a surplus of potential workers and continue to rise even in a recession.[490] Due to comparability, there is a pressure for workers to keep up with one another.

The pressure on wages to keep pace is aggravated when there is depreciation of the currency as the result is to push up prices. This means that there will be a cut in living standards unless there is a corresponding wage increase to match the rise in prices.[491] If the deprecation is accompanied by a deflationary government policy, perhaps to try and stem the inflow of imports due to a balance of payments problem, then the economy may experience rising unemployment, rising inflation and rising wages all at the same time.

By the middle of the 1960s British GDP was growing more slowly than other leading industrialised nations and too slowly to maintain full employment. An attempt to increase the rate of growth of GDP foundered on balance of trade difficulties, which would force the government to tighten economic policy to slow down growth and restrict incomes in order to curtail the demand for imports. Devaluation was seen as a solution, but any gains had only a temporary effect. Devaluation was seen by Keynesians as means of achieving export-led growth rather than internal consumer demand-led growth. Consumption-led growth involved a delay between the boost in demand and an increase in investment and this delay meant that the increase in investment lagged the surge in imports (investment may not even occur if it is expected that the demand boost will only be short-lived and a deflationary policy will soon be introduced). What investment did occur tended to be in the services sector, which was not subject to the same import competition for obvious reasons, and so did not help the beleaguered manufacturing sector, which faced that import competition and was the sector responsible for both the increasing unemployment and the balance of trade difficulties. Manufacturing was also seen as the key to increasing productivity per capita.

However, since the focus was on short-term Keynesian fine-tuning and demand management, then manufacturing did not receive the attention it needed. As the Cambridge Economic Policy Group highlighted, with imports increasing at 8-12% per annum and exports increasing at only 4-8% per annum, then a balance of payments problem was inevitable. Free trade, now the economic orthodoxy along with Keynesianism, could not address this. Free trade did not ensure that Britain could compete. It was not a solution to Britain's economic decline. Deflationary policies were implemented to try and check the growth of imports, which in turn damaged industry and crippled Britain's growth rate and people's living standards. The import penetration of the home market was damaging.

The lessons of the inter-war years were ignored. Joseph Chamberlain and the Tariff Reformers were proved correct in their assertion that it was necessary to use tariffs to help British industry. It was Keynesian and free trade bigotry that closed the British ruling class's mind to that. Continued economic decline was the result.

Another problem, which manifested itself in the 1960s and 1970s, was that devaluation involved a cut in the standard of living for ordinary wage earners; import prices would increase as a consequence of devaluation. The purpose was to boost exports and cut imports by increasing import prices while making exports cheaper. The 1960s and 1970s were a period of increasing industrial unrest. Strikes were common and the unions were militant. The increase in the price of imports would affect the cost of living and therefore act as a spur for higher wage increases. Yet for the policy to be successful, it was necessary for ordinary workers to accept a cut in their standard of living, at least in the short term. Wage increases would simply increase the costs to employers and so push up the price of goods and exports – thus negating the rationale of the devaluation. This problem was made worse by the sheer scale of devaluation that was ultimately required to bring about full employment. The policy was not only impossible but, given the long-term failure of the Keynesian policy to maintain full employment, meant that ever more dramatic measures to boost demand, in this case the demand for exports, that the scale of the boost required was no longer feasible. The policy could not be implemented successfully as it would merely provoke demands for increased wages and strikes. The monetarist response to Keynesianism had the exact opposite policy for the exchange rate. They believed that an increase in the exchange rate was counter inflationary and would, along with a reduction in the public sector debt, reduce the rate of inflation.

Although Keynes believed that rising prices would only occur when full employment was reached, that belief was proved wrong by the 1970s stagflation, with rising prices at the same time as rising unemployment. Keynesian reliance on the Phillips Curve (which held that there was an inverse relationship between unemployment and inflation where higher inflation would lower unemployment) to explain the trade-off between inflation and employment was discredited. Keynesians were unable to produce a convincing explanation of why stagflation became so entrenched and were unable to tackle the ever-increasing rate of inflation without accepting that a rise in unemployment was inevitable.

One of the flaws in the arguments of the Keynesians, is that they demand that the government boost demand almost as a cure for any economic difficulty. Despite Keynes establishing his theory as a response to a particular situation, that restriction is widely ignored. As David McCord Wright wrote:

> 'Now the real cause of a depression can sometimes be not a lack of consumption but a maladjustment of cost and prices. Wages can be rising faster than productivity, and hence the prospect of profit is reduced. Or taxes may be so heavy as to have the same effect and leave little incentive. Under these circumstances, just putting in more money will not help the basic problem. And there is one further problem that can never be forgotten. The extra money put in during depression to stimulate the economy may not *at first* cause inflation, but that money will not just die. As after World War II in the United States, the piled-up accumulations of years of deficits may later on suddenly explode, plunging the nation into severe inflation.'[492]

The long boom came to a crashing halt in the 1970s – especially for Britain. Keynesian demand management failed to produce growth or jobs. The 1970s were a period of stagflation. In Britain there was large-scale industrial unrest and political instability. Whereas other countries experienced strong manufacturing growth between 1970 and 1980, in Britain manufacturing output fell by 3%. Monetarism replaced Keynesianism.

8 THE MONETARIST EXPERIMENT

The election of the Thatcher government heralded a Monetarist economic policy. Although the previous Labour government had embraced a Monetarist policy to tackle the surging inflation legacy bequeathed by Ted Heath and the Barber Boom, Margaret Thatcher sought to drive down inflation, put an end to the previous era of consensus politics and Keynesian demand management. The implementation of the policy was difficult, as controlling the money supply was easier said than done and there were arguments as to which measure of money should be controlled. The result was a deep recession with a fall in output of 2.5% in 1980 and another 1.5% in 1981. By 1983, output had recovered and was now 3.5% higher than it had been in 1979, although much of this was accounted for by the advent of North Sea oil. In 1984 manufacturing output was still 10% less than it had been in 1979. In 1984, gross fixed investment was just 3% higher than it had been in 1979, after falls in both 1980 and 1981. Manufacturing investment in 1984 was 30% less than it had been in 1979 and was less than necessary to match the depreciation of manufacturing capital plant and equipment. Throughout the 1980s British manufacturing firms prioritised dividend payments in preference to R&D; with profits rising 6% a year, dividends rising by 12% a year, while investment rising by 2% a year.[493] Unemployment increased from 1.3million (5%) in 1979 to around 3.2million in 1985 (13%), even after the method of counting had been changed (thus lowering it further).[494]

A major problem with controlling the money supply is the definition of money and exactly how to control it. The bulk of the money supply is actually the liabilities of the various financial institutions and not the physical notes.[495] The process of creating credit is restrained by the requirement of commercial financial institutions to hold reserves of money to meet demands for cash payments. The monetary base consists of the nominal liabilities of the central bank. The reserves/deposits ratio is fixed either by government or the banking system itself. Friedman believed that to control the money supply it was best to control the monetary base.[496]

In the USA there was an attempt to control the monetary base, limiting the ability of banks to create money to lend to their customers. Controlling the monetary base is something the central back can do but it can lead to large swings in interest rates and this happened in the USA in October 1979;[497] it would also lead to a position in which the central bank might refuse liquidity to the banks (this could cause extreme difficulties particularly in circumstances such as in the credit crunch recession which started in 2008). Other measures to control the money supply can be used, such as pushing up interest rates to discourage people from borrowing money. Monetarists concede that there is a lag between a tighter monetary policy and a fall in inflation (up to two years) as it takes time for the new tighter regime to take effect and for people's expectations and behaviour to change.

The difficulty of maintaining that there might be an excess of money supply is that the demand for money in part determines the supply of money. A central bank can control the monetary base but this will not of itself determine the total money supply. Banks are able to grant overdraft facilities and are able to increase the money supply of their own accord. A central bank is also lender of last resort and is therefore compelled to increase the money supply in the event of a banking crisis. In a downturn the money supply will automatically contract as firms repay their borrowings and as their need for working capital to fund a smaller turnover is reflected in the repayment of overdrafts.

The certainties expressed by monetarists were not always reflected in the economy. By the summer of 1980 inflation in Britain had increased to a rate of 22%. The second OPEC oil price hike in 1979/80 as well as large wage increases in 1979, contributed to this figure, as did the government's doubling the rate of Value Added Tax (VAT). The Thatcher government tried to control the demand for money by using interest rates, as well as a strong pound on the foreign exchange markets, rather than relying upon restricting the monetary base. The inflation rate fell to about 5% in 1984, despite an increase in the money supply. This was achieved by monetary policy (even if the increase in money supply was well ahead of what the government wanted) rather than prices and incomes policies – which the government refused to implement – and was accompanied with a large increase in unemployment from around 5% to more than 13% of the labour force. This increase in unemployment had a dampening effect on inflation. Worse, the unemployment was the result of and accompanied by a large number of business failures and a policy of de-stocking among large businesses. Furthermore, world commodity prices fell by 30% as a result of a world recession following the oil price increases.

The incoming Thatcher government's monetarist policy was in line with the thinking of the London Business School. The fight against inflation was the cornerstone of economic policy, rather than demand management to create jobs and maintain full employment. With the incoming policies the London Business School forecast a 2% fall in GDP in 1980 and nil growth in 1981. Unemployment was forecast to rise towards two million. In the event, this forecast was wrong. The increase in the exchange rate resulted in a loss of competitiveness of British industry, much of which never recovered and unemployment rose above three million. There *were* lasting adverse effects of the exchange rate appreciation.[498] Part of the reason for the London Business School's inaccuracy is that they ignored the short-term consequences of an appreciation of the exchange rate and focused entirely on the long term, ignoring their own previous forecasting models in their eagerness to devise a new one and also to turn away from the Keynesian policies that were now failing.[499] The model they now used was also designed to reflect the ideological preferences of those constructing it:

> 'The crucial individual equations were all designed so as to exhibit the desired long-run property. This was done either through the use of a suitable functional form (notably the error-correction form) or by the imposition of coefficients. Of the six equations, one was of the error-correction form while four of the other five can be interpreted as having had the necessary long-run properties built in to them through the imposition of coefficients reflected in the choice of independent variable. It is also possible to influence the speed with which the long-run arrives in an individual equation; *in extremis*, by the use of static equations (which imply an instantaneous long-run). Two of the equations were unambiguously of this form: the one for the exchange-rate and the one for nominal wages.
>
> Yet after all this attention, the model still failed to give a very convincing rendition of the Monetarist line. The

simulations from the model ... were by no means robust, being sensitive to specific assumptions about the details of fiscal policy. In the case of the government spending simulation, the results produced were ones that Ball and his colleagues preferred to discount. The problem that the simulations reveal is the difficulty of specifying equations one at a time. Individual equations – even sub-systems of equations – can be designed to behave as required, but this behaviour is always conditional on "all else being equal". In a complete model, however, all else is not equal but is instead determined somewhere in the rest of the model. In this case, the main "else" was GDP; when this was determined simultaneously, the fragility of the Monetarist propositions became apparent.'[500]

What is flawed in this computer model affects the validity of a particular brand of Monetarism and not Monetarism in its entirety. Milton Friedman, arguably the world's leading Monetarist at the time, himself criticised both the arguments being put forward by the London Business School and also of the economic policies of the Thatcher government. What is demonstrated is the dangers of relying on computer models as a means of economic management; it also shows that such difficulties are not confined to Keynesian fine-tuning.

Unlike with Heath, neither the economic problems generally nor even the depth of the recession of 1980-81 led to a U-turn. Thatcher stuck to her guns. She dismissed her Tory opponents as 'Wets'. This derogatory term personified the reason for their failure, along with their lack of unity and lack of a real ideological alternative. The Wet manifesto, entitled *Changing Gear*, stated: 'One job of the Conservative Party is to protect our citizens from experiments by theorists whose beliefs can never be scientifically proved'.[501] This veiled critique fell short of outright opposition to Monetarism and was insufficient to stop the Thatcher bulldozer.

The experience in Britain can be compared to the Reagan administration in the USA. In the USA, the Federal Reserve Board adopted a hard-line monetarist policy in 1979 and Reagan was elected president in 1980. Although output fell by 2% in 1982 it rose by more than 10% between 1982 and 1984. Unemployment steadily increased from 1981 and peaked at roughly 10% of the labour force by the end of 1982. However, by the summer of 1985 unemployment had fallen to 7% (roughly half the British level). Inflation fell from 12% in 1980 to roughly 4-5% by 1985. Reagan had cut taxes and had embarked on a major increase in military spending, which was greater than the other public spending cuts that he made. The result was a substantial fiscal stimulus and an increase in the US budget deficit from around $60billion (2% of GDP) in 1980 to around $200billion (5% of GDP) in 1985. This could be as much described as a Keynesian policy as a Monetarist one and the result was in tune with Keynes' own thinking and predictions. Between the years 1983 to 1985 the USA achieved a cumulative real growth in GDP of 16.6%. This has not been matched since.[502] Employment rose and unemployment fell. The tight monetary policy and a loose fiscal policy was combined with a very flexible labour market. There were high real rates of interest which in turn attracted a large inflow of capital to fund the budget deficit and a rising dollar as a result, which made imports cheaper and helped bring down the rate of inflation. The obvious drawback of the Reagan policy, which has been continued by his successors, is that the US government is sinking into debt, which is being funded from abroad, and is dependent upon a high dollar to keep inflation down, which in turn disadvantages US exports and the danger that a fall in the dollar will lead to price increases. Also it can be argued that a rise in military spending will make those jobs created dependent upon the sustenance of that military expenditure.

The experience in Britain of monetarism was also more complicated than the theory. The incoming Thatcher government targeted the money supply, and discovered that whichever measure of the money supply was targeted immediately acted erratically. Within a year of taking office the economy entered a deep recession, with massive falls in industrial output and unemployment reaching at first two million and then three million by the autumn of 1982. The depth and speed of the recession was unprecedented and was caused by a combination of factors. The Iranian revolution led to a sharp increase in the price of oil; the price of Saudi light crude increased from $12.98 to $35.40 between October 1978 and June 1979. As Britain was an oil producer, sterling increased from $2 to the pound when the Tories took office to $2.45 by the end of 1980. Meanwhile Geoffrey Howe, the chancellor, was struggling to keep sterling M3 within its target range and had pushed up interest rates to 17%. Such an interest rate level not only reinforced the rise in the exchange rate but also became a crippling cost to British industry. Companies in financial difficulties started to borrow more, which defeated the government's objective. Another important factor was that many companies attempted to cut current costs by de-stocking, which further cut demand and output. Firms supplied finished goods not by producing them, but by running down their stocks of such goods, which rapidly and inevitably led to reductions in the workforce. The object was to cut costs and reduce bank borrowings, but the effect was to help create a recession. Eventually and after great pressure, the government conceded that monetary policy was too tight and that sterling M3 was not an accurate measure of the money supply. Interest rates were steadily lowered.

Gradually and quietly, The Thatcher government's commitment to monetarism waned; not only due to the experience of 1980 and 1981, but also because the floating exchange rates moved, at times, sharply in response to movements in interest rates. Rising exchange rates damaged competitiveness of exports while making imports cheaper. Exchange rates tended to dictate interest rates. Furthermore, high levels of growth of the money supply were accompanied by falling inflation, which was not consistent with monetarist theory (although monetarists had always said that there would be a time lag between movements in the money supply and movements in inflation). There were strong reasons for a fall in inflation: the higher exchange rate made imports cheaper, the depressing effects of the recession, and the 20-30% fall in world commodity prices. As inflation was falling anyway, there was little compulsion for the government to try and control the money supply when it could not. There were even arguments that inflation caused increases in the money supply and not the other way around. Sterling M0 was focused upon rather than M3 – or any other measure.

However, Nigel Lawson, who succeeded Howe as chancellor, became convinced that it was in Britain's interests to join the European Exchange Rate Mechanism (ERM), and although he could not persuade Mrs Thatcher of the wisdom of this he started to covertly try and manage sterling to shadow the German DM. Lawson was not alone in his vision and his views coincided with those of other members of the government, the Foreign Office, The Treasury, both main opposition parties, a large number of Tory

MPs, a whole variety of economic academics and experts, as well as the Bank of England.

In the spring 1988, Lawson reduced interest rates sharply to try and prevent further rises in sterling (which led to an open row with the Prime Minister, Mrs Thatcher). This downward trend had been boosted by the stock market drama of 'Black Monday' in 1987 when Lawson, in consultation with US and European governments, had responded by cutting interest rates. The booming economy attracted inward investment which in turn pushed up the value of the exchange rate. This increase was a reflection of the British economy, yet Lawson was trying to control the economy by controlling the exchange rate.

It was not to be. By the summer Lawson concluded that the economy was 'overheating': a large and growing balance of payments deficit, large increases in borrowing and both sterling M3 and M0 (although he had previously being ignoring this), large increases in high street sales, pay rises in 1987 increasing at a rate of almost 8%, and, worse, a growing inflation rate. The response, which many were arguing was long overdue, was large increases in interest rates. Thus the tightening of monetary policy came in response not to money supply growth, nor even exchange rate movements, but to general inflationary pressures. Yet Lawson increased interest rates again in response to increases by Germany and other ERM countries. Interest rates were increased from a low of 7.5% in May 1988 to 15% in 1989, where they remained until October 1990. Yet again Lawson was shadowing the DM and was holding interest rates high even though the danger was now one of overkill and recession. Mrs Thatcher, for all her reputation for bossiness and 'handbagging', was in a minority in the cabinet and lacked the will to replace Lawson, even though she was keen to revert to a more monetarist policy. Eventually Lawson resigned in indignation over the appointment of an adviser and John Major was appointed chancellor.

Major turned a looming disaster into complete catastrophe. After leaving interest rates at a crucifying 15% for a full year, he proudly took Britain into the ERM in October 1990. On joining, Robin Leigh-Pemberton, the Governor of the Bank of England, speaking in Tokyo, said: 'This is a great event in our economic life. It is something that I have looked forward to for a very long time'. Britain's Great and the Good were fully in agreement with the governor. There was, however, some disquiet about the level of exchange rate chosen, and concerns that Britain had joined 'at the wrong rate, at the wrong time, for the wrong reason'. There was a danger that Britain was about to embark on a rerun of the decision to re-join the Gold Standard at a too high a rate.

There were three factors which would decide the success or failure of ERM membership: the sustainability of sterling at the chosen rate of 2.95DM even allowing for the 6% band within which sterling was allowed to fluctuate; the level of determination to defend this exchange rate *and the ability to do so*; and the stability of the ERM itself. In 1985, the euro currency market amounted to $3trillion, which was almost twice as large as the outstanding Federal Reserve Board debt, and exceeded by more than 50% the total value of world trade. Furthermore, of the $150billion or so daily turnover in foreign exchange in London, New York and Tokyo, only 10% or so represented trade related transactions. The other 90% was accounted for by capital flows. All that could be achieved is that short-term day-to-day movements in exchange rates could be prevented. In the long term, especially if the level of exchange rate was unrealistic, the central banks would be swamped. In the six months preceding ERM entry, sterling had risen by about 6% against the DM and by about 16% against the US$. The Bank of England held the view that: 'Our central rate against the other Community currencies was not abnormally high'. Mrs Thatcher, after she had been forced out as prime minister, let it be known that she had not intended an all out battle to defend sterling, but to devalue if necessary instead. However, Mrs Thatcher was replaced as Prime Minister by John Major himself and Norman Lamont was appointed chancellor. Both were fully committed to defend the 2.95DM exchange rate. The Bank of England's view was that 'we would still have wanted a strong exchange rate and high interest rates in order to bear down on inflation,' and that 'the ERM mechanism will require high interest rates of us until it is clear to the markets that we are determined to succeed and that the rates can be safely lowered'.[503] The British establishment, ignoring the lessons which should have been learnt from the débâcle of re-joining the Gold Standard at an overvalued rate, was 100% committed to the defence of the exchange rate at 2.95DM, and 100% opposed to devaluation or the resumption of floating exchange rates. This commitment proved fatal.

At the time Britain joined the ERM, German reunification posed a clear threat to the system's stability. The experience of the collapse of Bretton Woods due to the USA's Vietnam inflation demonstrated the danger posed when a system's anchor currency becomes a liability. Having joined despite the looming danger, flexibility and pragmatism were called for and not blind rigidity.

Initially, Britain's membership did not seem too bad and interest rates fell to 11% by July 1991, which ERM enthusiasts attributed entirely due to membership. Yet the interest rates did not fall far enough or fast enough. The economy was being squeezed and the growth of M0 was actually nil in the second half of 1990; house prices were now falling as was inflation. Britain sank into recession with company failures and rising unemployment. Meanwhile, sterling was struggling to hold its exchange rate value in the ERM, which prevented the interest rate cuts necessary to revive the economy. The ERM started to fall apart due to the inflationary effects of German reunification, with Germany keeping its interest rates high to tackle that inflation and ignoring the consequences on the other ERM members, who were likewise forced to adopt high interest rates to defend their exchange rates. Devaluation, a route which Italy took, was ruled out by Britain as being 'the soft option, the inflationary option' and the government sought to talk its way out of the recession by trying to convince the public that the recession, if it ever existed, was over and that the 'green shoots of recovery' were now visible. Despite pronouncing that they would defend sterling whatever the cost, in fact they did nothing; they did not increase interest rates. Even so, Major even went so far as to declare that he had 'embarked on an economic strategy designed to see the British pound replace the German mark as the hardest and most trusted currency in the European Community'. This delusion meant that the needs of the real economy were no longer a consideration.

Monetarists weighed in heavily, demanding leaving the ERM or at least devaluing within it, and savage cuts in interest rates – which were stuck at 10% even though inflation had fallen to 2%. The economist Tim Congdon asserted that: 'We should base monetary policy on the needs of our own country, not on another'. Even the Bundesbank, which suddenly acquired a capacity for indiscretion, pointed out that sterling was overvalued and claimed that they had offered Britain the option to devalue when Italy had done. Major had rejected this offer; not for him the 'the soft option, the inflationary option' – he was tough. Instead, Britain tried to defend sterling by intervening on the foreign exchange markets and borrowed a large sum of foreign currency with which to do so. Nevertheless, sterling fell through its lower limit and the government responded by increasing interest rates ultimately to a level of 15%, before Lamont announced that Britain was suspending its ERM membership.

Freed of the exchange rate constraint, the interest rate increases were reversed, bringing the rate back down to 10%, and sterling fell by almost 20% against the DM before steadily climbing back up again now that Britain was on a sounder footing. There were four further cuts in interest rates of 1% a time. Monetarists criticized the perceived dithering – if a 6% interest rate was the correct one then the government should have cut the levels of interest to that at once. Real interest rates of almost 5% were still considered too high in a recession. Even so, the interest rate cuts were what was needed and the economy steadily returned to growth. The ERM enthusiasts were proved wrong in that inflation did not take off and remained at less than 2%.

Although monetarism was perceived as a failure, it should be given its due credence. The target growth rate for M3 in the year to April 1981 was 7-11% and the outcome was an actual growth of 18.5%; in the year to April 1982 the target was 6-10% with an outcome of 14.5%; the year to April 1983 the target was 8-12% with an outcome of 11%; the year to April 1984 the target was 7-11% with an outcome of 9.7%; the year to April 1985 the target was 6-10% with an outcome of 12.2%; and in the year to April 1986 the target was 5-9% with an outcome of 16.6%. This clearly shows that the growth of sterling M3 was virtually halved in the four years to April 1984 and this was accompanied by a fall in inflation. In the following two years to April 1986, the rate of growth accelerated to 16.6% and inflation started to accelerate, forcing the government to increase interest rates in 1988. Despite the difficulties in controlling the money supply, monetarism was broadly proved to be right in that the falls in the money supply were linked to falls in inflation.

But this monetarist approach was muddied by other free market reforms that might be consistent with free market, even with monetarist theory, but which nevertheless negated the monetarist squeeze on inflation. The incoming Tory government of 1979 could look forward to a surge in North Sea oil revenues and the value of sterling soared as the markets looked forward to the oil revenues and the confidence given by the more market-friendly administration. The government was keen to deregulate and quickly abolished exchange controls, believing that such would lessen the demand for sterling. The government, in response to demands from the City as well as their own free market beliefs, abolished the so-called 'corset' which allowed the Bank of England to restrict bank lending. Bank reserve requirements were likewise abolished two months later.[504] In 1981, the banks were allowed to provide mortgages in competition with the building societies, which in turn were allowed to borrow long-term from the money markets.[505] The monetarist experiment therefore coincided with a lax control on credit, leading to a large consumer credit boom throughout the 1980s, alongside the mortgage boom to fund the increase in home ownership. The banks were allowed to create credit not to fund government spending, as Keynes had advocated, but to fund consumer spending, which was entirely consistent with Keynes' thinking. The high value of sterling, by pricing imports low, helped keep down the rate of inflation and the tax revenues from North Sea oil, alongside substantial sale of state assets such as the various nationalised entities, helped fund the government expenditure and pay for tax cuts. The high value of sterling likewise damaged British exports. Between 1980 and 1990 private levels of debt doubled, with mortgage debts increasing six-fold.[506] House prices more than doubled and many used mortgages as a means of equity withdrawal to fund consumer spending. Although the money supply was growing strongly, the doubling of cheap imports kept the level of inflation down, although the balance of payments went sharply into deficit, reaching 5% of GDP in 1989. Exports, meanwhile, only increased by 40%.[507] Those firms facing the most international competition had the lowest levels of investment.[508]

One controversy is the Monetarist goal of reducing wages to price the unemployed back into work, or to reduce unemployment benefits so that they are more compelled to look for work. This amounts to reducing the living standards of those who are already the poorest in society. Of course, were the government to cut the cost of employing people and the low paid in particular, by measures to cut taxes and National Insurance contributions, then this would reduce the cost to employers and so make employing people cheaper and therefore more attractive; such measures would fit in with the theory that cutting the wage rate would increase the demand for labour and would not be objected to by Keynesians. To cut the wages actually paid to workers, especially low-paid workers, would cause hardship and, as they would have less money to spend, would further reduce consumptive demand in the economy and would therefore reduce demand for goods; the multiplier effect also needs to be considered in assessing this. Although Keynesians would be able to compensate for this loss of demand by government measures to stimulate that demand, Monetarists believe that the fall in wages will be itself be sufficient to create employment and reduce unemployment.

In Britain, between 1979 and 1983 real wages of adult manual workers rose by 10%; at the same time the employment of those workers fell by 8%.[509] In the same period real wages paid to non-manual workers rose by 19% and the employment of such workers rose by 12%. The real hourly earnings of the top 10% of workers increased by 19% between 1979 and 1984, while the real hourly earnings of the bottom 10% of earners, and who bore the brunt of the rise in unemployment, fell slightly.[510] In practice therefore the drive to cut real wages as a route to reduce unemployment, as with controlling the money supply, is problematic as the behaviour of employers is not consistent. There are different labour markets between different sectors of the economy, between the public and private sector, and for any demand management response to work, then it must be able to target those sectors which are experiencing the unemployment without fuelling demand for those sectors which are already experiencing high demand and rising wages alongside secure employment.

Following the Reagan boom years, the USA has had problems of its own. It has failed to get to grips with its deficit and the aim of President Obama to introduce health and other social reforms is incompatible with a reduction in the deficit without a major increase in tax revenues – either through higher taxes or more growth.

A flat US economy led the Keynesians under both Bush and Obama to implement four stimulus packages of government spending between 2008 and 2010, which failed to create the hoped for new jobs and galvanised the US Tea Party to mount its challenge to what it saw as wasteful government spending.[511]

James Rickards wrote: 'In the case of monetarism, the flaw was the volatility of velocity as expressed in consumer choice. In

Keynesianism, the flaw is the famous "multiplier".[512] A problem arises over the measurement of the multiplier. A report written by two of Obama's advisers, Christina Romer and Jared Bernstein, estimated the multiplier to be about 1.54 once the new spending was underway. The entire Obama programme amounted to $787billion, which would mean that the extra output should have been about $425billion. Obama ran deficits totalling $5.4trillion in the four years to 2012.[513]

Meanwhile another report of the programme produced by John Taylor and John Cogan concluded that the multiplier effect is less than one! This meant that the output of the private sector declined for every extra dollar spent and estimated that the multiplier was only 0.96 in the early stages and would fall to 0.48. For every extra dollar spent private sector output would fall by 60cents. The extra government spending was damaging the private sector upon which the government was dependent for tax revenues to pay for its spending. Other earlier studies have suggested that the Keynes multiplier only works as Keynes expected in certain limited circumstances and worked only in the short term (e.g. studies by Michael Woodford of Columbia University, Robert Barro of Harvard, and Michael Kumhof of Stanford). This should not be seen as surprising as Keynes was open that he was only considering the short term and was dealing with a particular situation in the 1930s. It is now the 21st century. One 1960s study by Professor Carl Christ concluded that both Keynesian and monetarist policies worked most effectively for those economies which *started with a balanced budget.*[514]

Two years after the commencement of the Obama programme the Romer and Bernstein forecasts were proven to be wrong. They had estimated that total employment would be 137million, in fact it was 130million; they had estimated that GDP would increase by 3.7% by the end of 2010, when in fact there was hardly any increase; and unemployment reached 10.1% rather than the forecast of 8%.[515]

Despite North Sea oil, Britain enjoyed no industrial revival. The oil was used to pay for imports. In 1983, Britain's trade in manufactures went into deficit and has stayed in an ever-growing deficit ever since, apart from a brief rally following Black Wednesday and Britain's ejection from the ERM.[516] Blair's governments merely used growth to fund higher public spending and tax credits.

SUMMARY

The incoming Thatcher administration, elected in 1979, did not reverse manufacturing's decline, but merely relied on North Sea oil revenues, privatisation proceeds and increased consumer borrowing to fuel growth. Manufacturing output in 1984 was 10% less than it had been in 1979, with manufacturing investment being 30% less than it had been in 1979. While monetarism checked the inflationary surge that Keynesianism had contributed to, Britain experienced yet another recession in 1980 as the Tories tried to adhere to the monetarist theory of controlling the money supply, ignoring the impact of a high exchange rate and the strong deflationary squeeze. A large part of British manufacturing was wiped out as a result and unemployment reached 13%. Despite the government's best efforts, controlling the money supply was more difficult than expected and could not be done with precision. Inflation fell partly due to the fall in the money supply and partly due to the fall in world commodity prices as well as cheaper imports due to a high exchange rate.

The clamp down on the money supply was accompanied with a lax control of credit and a deregulation of building societies, banks, and the City. As with the USA, monetarism was sullied by credit growth pulling in the opposite direction. The economy boomed as did consumer debt. British manufacturing scrimped on investment, which was rising at 2% a year, while dividends were rising at 12% a year. North Sea oil paid the bills, as did the proceeds of privatisation.

By the late eighties monetarism fell by the wayside. The government was not fussed about controlling the money supply when doing so was so difficult and when inflation was low anyway. Meanwhile, Lawson was fixated with shadowing the German DM and firstly allowed an inflationary boom to take hold, then a recession, as he was gearing economic policy towards the ERM and the German DM rather than the needs of the British economy. Major, firstly as chancellor then as Prime Minister, made matters many times worse. Major ignored the lessons of history, ignored the problems of German reunification, and took Britain into the ERM with the intention of defending the value of sterling rigidly – when pragmatism and flexibility were vital. Major's willingness to sacrifice the health of the British economy, including the standards of living of ordinary people, in pursuit of his ambition of replacing the German DM as the ERM's strongest currency failed and Britain was forced out and forced to resume a floating exchange rate.

The fixation with fiddling about with the exchange rate doomed the legacy of the Tories and propelled Labour into office up until 2010. The Tories lost their credibility. The 1980s may well have been a boom time, but there were two serious recessions, consumer debt mushroomed and manufacturing declined. In 1983 Britain's balance of payments sank into deficit and has stayed there since. Britain's decline was not reversed. Overall, the Thatcher and Major years were a failure masked by North Sea oil.

9 ASPECTS OF THE 2008/13 SLUMP

'Just a year ago, American delegates speaking from this rostrum emphasized the US economy's fundamental stability and its cloudless prospects. Today, investment banks, the pride of Wall Street, have virtually ceased to exist. In just twelve months, they have posted losses exceeding the profits they made in the last twenty-five years.'[517] - Mr Putin, the Russian president, speaking at the World Economic Forum in Davos, January 2009

As with the Wall Street crash, the credit crunch was not foreseen and started in the USA. The real economies of the West were enjoying healthy growth and were free of the more routine problems of rising unemployment, inflation or both. But the underlying problems of large debts within the economies as a whole was steadily looming. As the banking sector lurched towards its apocalypse, there were attempts to quietly bail out the struggling banks. Sovereign Wealth Funds (SWFs) invested more than $58billion to prop up Citigroup, Merrill Lynch, UBS and Morgan Stanley in early 2008. The SWFs sustained large losses on this investment and the bailouts continued with large sums from the US government.[518] The scale of the government bailouts was awesome. By April 2011 the Fed had a net worth of approximately $60billion and assets (i.e. loans) of nearly $3trillion. A mere 2% decline in the value of the assets would be sufficient to wipe out the Fed's net worth and a decline of more than 2% would render the Fed's balance sheet insolvent. The response to this crisis has been to allow the Fed to suspend actual payments to the Treasury in relation to the interest it receives on bonds.[519] James Rickards wrote:

'The United States now has a system in which the Treasury runs non-sustainable deficits and sells bonds to keep from going broke. The Fed prints money to buy those bonds and incurs losses by owning them. Then the Treasury takes IOU's back from the Fed to keep the Fed from going broke. It is quite the high-wire act, and amazing to behold. The

Treasury and the Fed resemble two drunks leaning on each other so neither one falls down.'[520]

A similar situation exists in Britain, with the Bank of England using the Quantitative Easing (QE) programme to print money to buy government debt. Following an announcement in November 2012, the government agreed with the Bank of England that the interest earned by the bank would be handed over to the Treasury. The effect was to reduce the budget deficit by around £11billion per year. The chancellor had said it was economically inefficient for the Treasury to have to borrow money to make interest payments on the £375billionn of gilts acquired by the Bank of England in the QE programme.

Part of the reason for the lack of foresight for the credit crunch was that the banks relied upon VaR. Value at Risk (VaR) is a measurement of risk used by Wall Street to estimate risk. The problem with VaR is that it was simply a guess based on assumptions and it created a false reality that risk had been accurately calculated and managed.[521] It was not. The financial sector was booming as never before in the run up to the crisis – but was the boom genuine or was it a façade? For example, in Britain, between 1948 and 1978, one sector of financial services, financial intermediation, accounted for 1.5% of the profits of the total economy. By 2008, this ratio had increased to 15%. This tenfold increase is unprecedented and highly unlikely.[522]

The exuberance of the financial sector led to remuneration packages that were extravagant irrespective of performance. For example, Northern Rock was badly managed in that it lent out long-term but was financing that with short-term borrowings that it assumed would be continuously available.[523] Northern Rock chairman, Matt Ridley, was paid £300,000 a year in the run up to the collapse.

All these 'profits' and vast salaries were against a background of rising consumer debt. In 1964 household debt amounted to 14% of annual output and the aggregate balance sheets of the banks amounted to 46% of the annual output. In 1967, rules were changed to allow 'extended credit' facilities for consumers; this meant that it was no longer necessary to pay off card bills each month. This enabled the launch of first Barclaycard, then Access, then a whole host of other credit cards. Consumers now spend £500billion each year on credit cards. The 1971 Competition and

Credit Control Act reduced the amount that needed to be held by banks in reserves, and redefined what constituted reserves. Up until 1971 banks were required to hold a minimum of 28% in reserves. Restrictions on lending were relaxed in the early 1970s and discontinued altogether amidst the financial deregulation and Big Bang of the 1980s. Banks' reserves fell as they extended ever more credit. By 2007, the banks were required to hold virtually no reserves. New rules to be phased in between 2015 and 2018 (or even 2019) would require bank reserves to be increased to more than 4%, with the possibility of a buffer of another 2.5% in addition. Angela Knight, the chief executive of the British Bankers' Association, emphasised the need for a transition period, warned that the new rules would 'take money out of the economy' and said that: 'The consequence is that invariably the cost of credit – the price the borrower pays for money – will rise. The era of cheap money is over'.

By 2009 the aggregate balance sheets of the British banking system amounted to 497% of GDP. Household debt had risen to 80% of GDP, and the private sector as a whole had debts amounting to more than 150% of GDP. One study concluded that 70% of Britain's growth had been dependent on the increase in debt.[524] The British economy increased by £300billion in the five years before the crash, which was slightly less than the equity withdrawal during the same period. Had people not been able to spend equity of their homes then there would have been no growth. Mortgage debt reached £1.2trillion, overdrafts and credit card debts etc. reached another £200million, government debt reached £1trillion with at least another £1.5trillion in unfunded liabilities in addition.[525]

The losses caused by the banking crisis have been estimated as between £1.8trillion and up to £7.4trillion for the British economy.[526] Up until the 1990s a 1% increase in GDP would lead to a 0.89% increase in pay; but between 2000 and 2012 this increase in pay fell to only 0.43% – unless you were a senior banker or other privileged member of the ruling class.[527] In 2009 and 2010 the British government borrowed £1 for every £10 produced by the economy.[528] Bank of England research in 2012 held the collapse of the housing bubble as being responsible for 25% of the 2008-09 drop in output.[529]

By 2013, gross government debt was £1.4trillion and rising, business debts were £1.7trillion, household debts (including mortgages) £1.5trillion and banking debts £2.5trillion – giving a total of in excess of £7trillion against a GDP of approximately £1.5trillion.[530] In March 2015 household non-mortgage borrowing (i.e. unsecured debt such as credit cards) had reached an all time high to £239billion, the accountants PwC revealed.

The exposure to new weapons of mass financial destruction is vast. The notional principal outstanding of 'over-the-counter' derivatives alone amounts to $600trillion, which is forty times the US GDP.[531] The notional principal outstanding on the world's derivatives market is equivalent to fifteen times global GDP, and because derivatives are contingent liabilities, they are off balance sheet.[532] Lehman's collapse owing $129billion net brought down a system with a core capital of $3,500billion. Lehman's total creditors were $768billion, with derivatives liabilities in addition. The system which was supposed to disperse risk in fact multiplied it.[533]

Due to the increased market complexity and tradability of loans, rules were introduced that required banks to value these loans at market value. In spring 2009, these rules were scrapped and banks were allowed to resort to the previous loss provisioning system. For example, in 2012 Greek debt was trading at 40 cents on the dollar – i.e. Greek debt is worth only 40% of its book value. Only about 5% of the banks' Greek debt was valued at market level, the remainder was not adjusted to market values.[534]

The IMF calculated that Europe's banks had unrecognised losses amounting to a total of 200billion euros. Another study calculated that the banks needed 1trillion euros of new capital.[535] The European Financial Stability Facility (EFSF) does not have the resources (only 440billion euros in 2012) to bailout the troubled euro countries. According to the IMF in April 2011, Greece's government debt was 345billion euros, Portugal's was 156billion euros, Spain's was 693billion euros, Ireland's was 177billion euros, and Italy's was 1,916billion euros.[536]

Japan has its own problems. Its total government debt is 229% of GDP and is forecast to reach 250% of GDP by 2016.[537] Japan's economy has been stagnant, its GDP growing by just 0.7% per head per annum between 1991 and 2011, and it has teetered on the brink of deflation.[538]

In 2011, the US, Eurozone, British and Japanese banks have assets (i.e. loans) worth $66.6trillion and a net worth of $3.3trillion.[539] A 5% fall in the value of the assets will wipe out the banks, and a fall bigger than that will render them collectively insolvent.

One problem is that the velocity of circulation, contrary to the assumptions of many economic theories, is not constant. In the USA the velocity has been slowing ever since 1997. In 2008 the velocity slowed by 7% in one year alone. When consumers repay debts and increase their savings, this has the effect of slowing the velocity as well as lowering GDP. The effect of the Fed's QE programme has been to sustain nominal GDP in the face of declining money velocity.[540] The effect was to increase the monetary base by 242% between January 2008 to January 2011, but because the banks were lending less and because the monetary base accounts for only a fraction of the total money supply (80% of which is created by banks) the broader money supply only increased by 34%.

The QE programme has been without precedent. Since the start of the 2008 economic depression, Britain borrowed more in seven years than in all its previous history – and to little effect as the economy stagnated.[541] QE has involved the Bank of England printing money to buy up roughly one third of the entire government debt by August 2013.

The banks have largely emerged unreformed from the crisis, buttressed by QE which has allowed them to speculate in emerging markets, property and commodities. Nor have they cleaned up their act and continue to be dogged by revelations of shady dealings and even outright criminality. Even so, they remain weak not only due to the difficulties of many of the private customers they have lent to, but also due to the extent of the loans they have made to Eurozone governments. In the event of a major default in the Eurozone, the banks will struggle to stay afloat and there is no money left for a bailout on the scale that has already occurred. Mitch Feirerstein wrote: 'Worldwide, governments have chosen to respond by running huge deficits bailing out failed investors and lousy investments, adding to the pile of debt, and printing money. You might just as well seek to fight a fire by hosing it with gasoline'.[542]

Short-term lending can help bridge a liquidity crisis by providing the banks with the liquidity they need, but the crisis in 2008 was a solvency crisis where the banks liabilities exceeded their assets – primarily because the assets, the loans they had made, in many cases were worth less than their book value or were worthless.[543]

The authorities lent to insolvent banks irrespective of their ability to repay the debts and it was simply assumed that it was in the public interest that banks must be saved.

Banks bought sovereign debts in the belief that no country would be allowed to default. Countries, dazzled by the new euro currency and the cheap interest rates, took on debts that were unsustainable happy to take advantage of the low rates of interest and not considering what would happen in the future and pleased to get support from various public interest groups for their largess. Eurocrats were keen to expand the EU project and did not care if rules were bent or if countries ran into difficulty as such would justify yet further integration and more power for them.[544] The American Keynesian economist Paul Krugman wrote: 'European elites were so enthralled with the idea of creating a powerful symbol of unity that they played up the gains from a single currency and brushed aside warnings of a significant downside'.[545]

Greece's problems were well known. For example, their railway system incurred losses of in excess of $1billion on a turnover of $253million; and, for example, hairdressers could retire at fifty as it was a 'dangerous occupation'.[546] Once inside the Eurozone, Greece's only way out is default and not devaluation.

Greek government debt in 2011 was 152% of GDP. The Greek deficit has averaged 9.6% of GDP between 2009 and 2012, and average annual growth has averaged -2.2%.[547] That a variety of institutions were involved, including pension funds, was a reason for the Fed's secret bailout of the EU in 2008.[548] James Rickards wrote:

> 'By 2010, European sovereign finance was a complex web composed of cross-holdings of debt. Of the $236billion of Greek debt, $15billion was owed to UK entities, $75billion was owed to French entities and $45billion was owed to German entities. Of the $867billion of Irish debt, $60billion was owed to French entities, $188billion was owed to UK entities and $184billion was owed to German entities. Of the $1.1trillion of Spanish debt, $114billion was owed to UK entities, $220billion was owed to French entities and $238billion was owed to German entities. The same pattern prevailed in Italy, Portugal and the other heavily indebted members of the euro system. The mother of all inter-

European debts was the $511billion that Italy owed to France.'⁵⁴⁹

There was a flow of capital from northern Europe to the GIPSI countries (Greece, Ireland, Portugal, Spain, and Italy). This fed a housing boom and rising wages. Unit labour costs increased 35% in southern Europe compared with only a 9% rise in Germany. Germany's current account surplus was matched by the deficits of the GIPSI economies.⁵⁵⁰

In the last decade, Spain's unit labour costs increased by 30%; Ireland, Greece, Italy and Portugal had even higher increases; they increased by only 5% in Germany.⁵⁵¹ If the weaker countries leave the Eurozone, then the euro will reflect the stronger economies and increase in value and thus German exports will fall. The creation of the Eurozone carried the danger of its own destruction from the outset, as the German surpluses must, as an arithmetical certainty, be matched by deficits somewhere else – in southern Europe. It was after the euro was created that the struggling countries witnessed an explosion in their deficits. Before the euro's creation, Italy, Spain, France, Greece and Portugal between them only showed up among the top ten deficit countries 14 times during the decade of the 1990s, and they also showed up 14 times among the top ten surplus countries in the same period. Since 2000, they have never appeared among the top ten surplus countries and have appeared among the top ten deficit countries 42 times.⁵⁵²

Not to be overlooked is the impact on Britain of the euro, and its undervaluation so far as the North European countries are concerned. It is not simply that the harm done by the euro to the Southern EU countries damages markets that Britain is trying to export to, but the North European countries are able to exploit the euro's undervaluation, to them, in order to enlarge their trade surpluses with Britain. Germany, it was disclosed in August 2015, had further reaped a £70billion benefit from the Greek crisis by the savings made on interest payments on borrowings, being able to do so as the Greek crisis pushed investors to buy safe German bonds that in turn could be offered with a lower rate of interest payable. Thus far, Britain is ignoring all this and ignoring the ballooning trade deficit.

Problems following the credit crunch centre on the plight of the Eurozone countries, especially Greece, and the soaring US government deficit that is being funded by overseas sources, especially China. The USA has changed from being the world's biggest creditor to being the world's biggest debtor. The USA has not yet experienced the difficulties that the Eurozone has in financing its borrowing. However, the USA has yet to find the political resolve to address the issue and the government remains split between the President and the House of Representatives.

The Eurozone is focused on trying to save the euro as its new currency and is dependent upon Germany to bail out those countries which are now struggling for economic survival. Germany, because of the euro single currency, enjoys a very competitive exchange rate that is held down by the poorer performing countries along the Mediterranean in particular. Nevertheless, Germany has shown great reluctance to bail out its struggling partners and Greece has only received more money on condition that it implements savage cuts in government spending and increases taxes. Very real hardship and poverty has been the result and the Greek economy has contracted sharply. Italy and Spain have also encountered difficulties and both of these countries are considered to be too big to fail and too big to bail out. They could drag down the entire euro project if they encounter the same problems as Greece. Unemployment in Spain is very high. However, the Eurozone countries, even those which are having to implement austerity measures remain committed to Eurozone membership – even when their democratic government has been replaced by a technocrat. There remains a strong determination to make the euro project work.

Krugman wrote regarding Europe: 'Both private and public debt are somewhat lower than in the United States, suggesting that there should be more room for manoeuvre; inflation numbers look similar to ours, with no hint of an inflationary outbreak; and, for what it's worth, Europe as a whole has a roughly balanced current account, meaning that it has no need to attract capital from elsewhere'.[553] He goes on to point out that Europe is not the USA, it is a collection of different countries and labour mobility is low. There is friction between what the GIPSI countries need and what Germany is prepared to countenance. Stephen King (author and Group Chief Economist of HSBC Bank) wrote:

> 'How should monetary unions ideally work? Labour should be able to move to where the jobs are. Capital should be able to move to where the labour is cheap. A strong fiscal

authority would both encourage such mobility and stand ready to offer support in the event that factors of production temporarily became immobile.'[554]

Labour mobility is low in the EU compared to the USA or Canada. The immigration policy is for the benefit of the EU and not the benefit of Britain. Stephen King therefore advocates that:

> 'A central fiscal authority would pursue a regional policy based on "contingent redistribution" – in effect, offering succour to those in temporary difficulty funded via centrally collected taxes. It would also, at the very least, fund infrastructure projects that linked the various parts of the union together to create a binding economic and financial community: these would be the Eurozone's *grands projets*.'[555]

Stephen King's solution is either to 'pool financial sovereignty' or reintroduce capital controls. He is against the reintroduction of capital controls and favours the role of the European Central Bank and a widening of the Eurozone to include not only Turkey but beyond: 'It wouldn't be so difficult imagining euro membership extending eastwards to Central Asia and to the Levant and southwards to North Africa'.[556] He does not stop there: 'Why not, for example, have a single North American currency extending across Canada, the US and Mexico? Eventually, this new currency could spread further south, with countries in Central and Southern America also taking part and, in the process, receiving voting rights. After all, Panama and Ecuador are already 'dollarized', but, unlike my suggested new arrangement, they currently have no voting rights over US dollar monetary policy'.[557] Nor does he stop there: 'Why not go one step further and create an Asian monetary union? Could China and Japan, for example, bury their differences and end up with a common currency? Might India also want to take part? If these countries did so, would South Korea still hang on to its won? Would the Thai baht, the Philippine peso and the Indonesian rupiah then survive?'[558] In fairness, he does concede that 'many of these ideas are no more than flights of fancy'. Subsequently Stephen King rowed back hard regarding the euro: 'In the absence of a well-defined fiscal union built on democratic principles, the risk of eventual Eurozone break-up is considerable.

It's not so much that the project was, in itself, a bad idea but rather that it currently lacks the political glue to hold it together in the wake of the extreme economic shocks'. That Stephen King was so wrong regarding the desirability of the euro and was even keen to replicate it across the world with yet more single currency areas, demonstrates that experts from the financial sector are not to be fawned over. He took no account of the long history of failed fixed currencies. His political acumen is non-existent. He is advocating that which is in his own self-interest – namely an unreformed, unfettered banking sector that owes no loyalty to the host country and yet can expect unlimited financial support from the local taxpayers to cover any losses, no matter how vast they might be. Stephen King wrote:

> 'The US and Europe will need to come to terms with their diminished role in the world economy. No longer will their economies determine the price of raw materials. Their workers will be unable to determine the market price for their labour. Their people will not be able to pursue so easily the rent-seeking agendas that allowed returns on all factors of production in the US and Europe to rise far beyond those seen elsewhere in the world. Their pensioners will not be able to look forward to a guaranteed real income. And they will no longer so easily be able to manage their economic destinies.'[559]

Stephen King hopes that, 'It is surely better for the West to lose relatively than it is for the world as a whole to lose absolutely. As its population ages, I hope the West gains the wisdom to make the right choice'.[560] He adds that: 'Given the deafening demand for more, as opposed to better, regulation, the obvious risk is the re-establishment of a – self-defeating – home bias in financial market activity'.[561] One needs to be alert to what is being advocated. Stephen King is advocating that the West should simply accept its decline and lower living standards rather than resort to measures that might halt it – such as a more protectionist outlook – and Britain should continue a policy of mass immigration as an attempt to fund future pensions. For the reasons set out in chapter 11 below, this is Ponzi economics.

The current situation facing Britain is grim. In the 100 years since the outbreak of WWI Britain has changed from being the world's greatest power into being a de-industrializing offshore province of the EU undergoing a process of decay and de-civilization, both economically and politically. The triumph of Thatcherism in the 1980s may have galvanised a period of economic growth and wrestled the running of the country from union power, but it nevertheless failed to halt Britain's long-term decline, which continued apace albeit masked by North Sea oil revenues, cheap imports and rising debt.

The cost of living in 1914 was lower than it had been in 1815.[562] Defence accounted for almost half of government spending, yet only 3.1% of national output (half its level in the 1960s). Government debt was falling as a share of GDP despite the introduction of new welfare provisions, being only 27.6% of GDP in 1913, and was lower in nominal terms than it had been in 1815.[563] Whereas in 1914 Britain had the beginnings of welfare provision and the greatest navy in the world with a fleet of modern Dreadnoughts, today the Welfare State is collapsing as provisions are cut back or abolished, and the navy has only 19 warships and an order for aircraft carriers with only a handful of aircraft to put on them. Due to the scale of mass immigration and a stagnant economy with declining productivity, then falling living standards are inevitable. Downward mobility for many is the future.

In 1950 Britain had 37.9% of the world's shipbuilding orders as measured by tonnage.[564] By 1965 Britain's share had fallen to 13.62% compared to Japan's 51.9%.[565] The QE2 was the last liner to be built in Britain.[566]

In 1950, Britain was the world's second largest car producer, after the USA, and had 52% of the world's automotive exports.[567] In the seven years to 1979, British car production halved. Imports of cars increased from 14.4% to 56.7% in the 1970s.[568] By the year of the Diamond Jubilee, British car production amounted to 1.8% of global production.[569] Upon taking over Rover, the Phoenix Four quickly arranged salary and pension pots for themselves totalling £42million.[570] An attempt to sell MG Rover to the Shanghai Automotive Industry Corporation (SAIC) was vetoed by China's National Development and Reform Commission. SAIC did acquire the design rights for the Rover 25 and 75. Ford bought the rights to the Rover marque.[571] Rover went bust.

Unemployment was negligible between 1950 and 1966 and even fell below 2% in 1954. Labour shortages arose, particularly in transport, the NHS and the textile industry. Even so, there were rampant overmanning and restrictive practices. For example, the firm Bowater discovered in the early 1960s that its Mersey paper mill had 50% more workers than its mill in Newfoundland to do an identical job. For example, Britain had 14 separate craft unions in the steel industry, each of which was guarding its own craft and hostile to the concept of multitasking.[572] In the 1970s at British Leyland, overmanning was such that there were twice as many workers as required in some sections so that half the workers spent their time playing cards before swapping over with their colleagues mid-shift.[573] Immigration from the Commonwealth was seen as the solution, rather than to modernize working practices and increase productivity through more investment.

By comparison, West Germany experienced a two and a half times increase in industrial production in the 1950s with only a 1.2% unemployment rate. West German share of steel exports rose from 11% to 20% in the 1950s, while Britain's share fell from 15.1% to 7.9%.[574]

Germany's share of world trade rose from 8.9% to 9.3% in the first decade of the 21st century; Britain's share fell from 5.3% to 4.1%, including financial services. Britain's share of world goods exports is only 3%, down from 4.4% in 2000. Britain is a net importer of industrial goods, food and energy.[575]

By 1961, Britain's share of world trade in manufactures had fallen to 16.2% – a decline of one-third in 11 years.[576] By 1966 the share had fallen to 12.1%.[577] In 2009, Britain's share of world trade in manufactured goods had fallen to 2.9%.[578] Manufacturing accounts for only 12% of GDP in 2012.[579] By 1979 there were 6.16million employed in manufacturing – half the numbers employed in 1952; the number of apprenticeships had almost halved.[580] Between 1997 and 2010, the number of people employed in manufacturing fell from 4,278,000 to 2,494,000. There had been 1.6million new jobs created between 2000 and 2010, 80% of which were taken by immigrants.[581]

In 2012, of Britain's 20 largest companies by market capitalisation, only five are manufacturers and only eight have a British-born chairman.[582] When companies are doing well, their profits flow overseas and when they are doing badly there is a danger that they will be closed, with production being transferred to a cheaper overseas location.

In the decade to 1997, Germany produced three to four times as many engineers per year as Britain.[583] In 1997, Germany was subsidising industry to the tune of €11.7billion, Italy €9.4billion, France €5.7billion, Spain €1.9billion against €2billion in Britain.[584] Britain has lost two million manufacturing jobs per decade.[585]

In 2007, investment in research and development increased among British-owned firms while it declined in foreign-owned ones. In 2008, according to the ONS, only £3.4billion of the £25.6billion invested in research and development was funded by overseas businesses. Foreign-owned businesses control 39% of British patents; for the rest of the EU the figure is 13.7%, in the USA the figure is 11.8% and in Japan 3.7%.[586]

British annual growth averaged 2.36% between 1955 and 2010. Average global GDP growth averaged 3.1% between 1971 and 2009. In 1971, exports accounted for 22.5% of Britain's GDP as opposed to a global average of 13.7%. In 2004, Britain's exports amounted to 25.3% of GDP against a global average of 25.8%.[587]

In 1950, Britain had a trade surplus in manufactured goods amounting to 10% of GDP, and Britain was also a net exporter of energy due to coal production.[588] Despite an overvalued currency, from 1947 to 1971 the current account of the balance of payments was either in balance or in surplus in 17 of the 25 years. Between 1973 and 1980, world industrial output rose by 13%, in Britain it fell by 10%.[589] The last time the current account of the balance of payments was in surplus was in 1983 and it has been in deficit ever since. In 1952 Britain's share of world's manufactured exports was 25%; by 2013 it had fallen to less than 3%. By 2014, Britain had not had a surplus in manufactured goods for more than 30 years, and the trade deficit was running at around £120billion per annum, about 8% of national output. This deficit has been funded by a steady sale of assets and foreign ownership of British assets exceeded Britain's ownership of foreign assets by £200billion.[590] Approximately one third of this trade deficit, £42billion, is accounted for by China and Germany (£21billion each in 2012).

More than 70% of German firms are involved in technological innovation compared to only 40% of British firms. Only 20% of German workers are low-skilled, and only 30% of French workers; in Britain the number is 60%.[591] Even those companies that are held to be world class are increasingly transferring production overseas. For example, in 1979 96% of a JCB digger was sourced from within Britain, but by 2010 that figure had fallen to 36%. James Dyson makes his vacuum cleaners in Malaysia.[592] Britain's hope in the computer industry, ICL, was ultimately sold to Fujitsu and is now a shadow of its former hoped for potential.[593] The 25% devaluation after the financial crisis did not lead to an increase in the growth rate of British exports.[594] Instead of investing North Sea oil revenues in rebuilding British manufacturing, it was squandered on tax cuts and unemployment benefits. Norway, unlike Britain, put aside oil revenues to save for the future and has now built up a £300billion pension investment fund.[595]

Based on the estimates of oil reserves remaining (750 million cubic tonnes) and the current rate of extraction (63 million tonnes in 2010), it is likely that North Sea oil will be exhausted within 20 years. This will leave Britain once again having to import all its oil at a time when prices will be rising due to increased demand and falling production.[596]

The creation of the NHS doubled the proportion of national income spent on health to 2% of national income. By the 1960s, it had doubled again to 4% of national income. By 1979 it had reached 5% of national income. By 2010 it had reached 8% of national income.[597] The NHS employs nearly 1.4million people. Its spending tripled between 1997 and 2007, yet 10% of trusts were teetering on insolvency. Between 2003-04 and 2005-06 trust deficits increased from £50million to £547million.[598] Social Security spending has also increased dramatically, from 4% of national income in the early 1950s to almost 14% by 2010.[599] Between 1997 and 2007 the number drawing some form of welfare benefit increased from 17million to 21million.[600] Education spending increased in real terms by 68% between 1997-98 and 2007-08. There were 40,000 extra teachers and another 100,000 classroom assistants.[601] No matter how worthy, all of these things have to be paid for and spending on them cannot continue to grow at a faster rate than the economy indefinitely. During the May 2015 general election, all the three main political parties were focused on spending taxpayers' money and focused on vying with each other as to the new spending commitments made. None of them prioritized increasing economic growth or of reversing the decline in manufacturing.

Attempts to raise tax revenues are compromised by the extent to which much of Britain's firms are owned by foreigners and so can manipulate their affairs to minimize their tax bills both generally and in this country. If needs be these firms can relocate overseas and do not hesitate to threaten to do so.

Between 1997 and 2010, the public sector payroll increased by 600,000. This has been accompanied by an increase in private sector jobs dependent on the public sector.[602] Between 1979 and 2011, the numbers classed as too disabled to work has increased fourfold to 2.1million people. The numbers in employment who were not British citizens were 2.5million.[603] According to the ONS, in 2010 net migration increased by 21% when 239,000 more immigrants arrived in the UK than people emigrating.[604] Nigel Lawson expressed the opinion in September 1984, that in future many of the jobs would not even be low-tech but 'no-tech'.[605]

There has been the establishment and growth of a pseudo-private sector. Railways, water, gas and electricity operate as state-backed monopolies and cartels, mostly foreign owned, ratcheting up prices irrespective of the economic depression. In December 2012, it was reported that Britain's largest companies have reduced their corporation tax payments by 20% since 2000 despite increased profits of 65%. This is a fall of £5billion from £26billion to less than £21billion. In the same period, the amount paid by small businesses has almost trebled from £4.4billion to £12.1billion. On sales of £2.6billion in Britain in 2011, Google paid only £6million in corporation tax. Foreign takeovers of firms such as Cadburys and Boots has led to their headquarters and tax base moving overseas. In November 2013, Ofgem reported that the energy companies had increased their profits per household by 76% to £53 profit in 2012. Research by the consumer group 'Which?' revealed that, allowing for inflation, the average household energy bill (gas and electricity) had increased by £410 in a decade, despite consumption falling by 17%. Ofgem further reported in January 2015 that the energy firms had enjoyed an increase in profit per household of 52%, from £77 to £114 within 13 months, while 'Which?' calculated in February 2015 that the average household was paying £145 more than they should due to the energy firms' refusal to pass on the dramatic fall in wholesale prices. British Gas defiantly announced that it would make no significant cuts in energy prices until 2016, despite a halving of the price of oil since the summer of 2013 and a 29% fall in the price of gas (the incoming new British Gas chief executive was awarded £12million in shares and a remuneration package of £13million a year). There had been a five-fold increase in profits from supplying households between 2009 and 2014, from £221million to £1.19billion. NPower admitted paying no corporation tax over the last three years, despite making £766million in profits. This is in addition to other companies such as Amazon, Google, Starbucks who are likewise paying little if any corporation tax; Amazon, it was revealed in May 2014, had sales of £4.3billion in Britain and yet had only paid £4.2million in corporation tax (by contrast, in February 2014 France demanded a tax payment of £830million from Google, notwithstanding its accounting manoeuvres). Npower is owned by the German company RWE, which divested itself of Thames Water after the outcry when people were banned from watering their gardens while the front lawn of the RWE chief executive was benefiting from sprinklers in the Netherlands.

In June 2013 it was reported that of Britain's ten regional water companies, only three remain publicly-quoted companies with their headquarters in Britain. One of those three, Severn Trent, was subsequently a takeover target of a Kuwaiti SWF-led consortium. The other seven companies are largely foreign-owned and have their headquarters abroad. Thames Water, having been privatised in 1989 for a price of £922million,[606] was taken over by private equity investors led by the Australian investment bank Macquarie in 2006. Since then it has increased bills by 35.6% and pocketed profits of £1.7billion, and £1.4billion has been distributed in dividends to a variety of – mostly foreign – investors including the governments of China and Abu Dhabi as well as Australian, Canadian and Dutch pension funds. Thames Water has paid no corporation tax. Thames Water, which made £549million profit in 2012 after an above-inflation price increase and a 6% increase in sales, paid no corporation tax at all. Pre-tax profits in 2013 were £550million, and in November 2013, Thames Water announced that it will not pay any corporation tax for the next seven to ten years. A Chinese SWF owns 8% of the company. Thames Water's debts have increased from £1.8billion to £8billion within ten years under foreign ownership.[607]

The British railway network is a similar story. The various rail companies are dominated by foreign ownership with foreign firms profiteering at Britain's expense. For example, it was disclosed that the rail firm Keolis, 70% owned by the French state firm SNCF and 30% by a Canadian pension fund, paid out £37.9million in dividends over two years. A railways expert, Christian Wolmar said: 'Why should these companies be making a profit out of our railways to help their railways? It is clear they operate in their own national interest, and that is to be expected'. Despite the negligible inflation rate (it was only 0.5% and subsequently fell to zero), in January 2015 fares increased, yet again, by an average of 2.2%. Rail fares have rocketed since privatization – as have the salaries, perks and bonuses of the various rail executives. The highest-paid chief executive, who was being paid £2.23million, was responsible for running Britain's most crowded commuter trains in the South West and East Midlands. In the period from January 2010 to December 2014, fares had increased by up to 22% and average salaries by 6.9%.

In June 2013 it was revealed that Starbucks had increased the remuneration of three senior executives from £590,000 to £1.1million. This is despite claiming to make losses in Britain, even though sales are surging, and despite paying no corporation tax. The losses arose after a payment of £26.5million in royalties to overseas subsidiaries, as well as another £1.8 million in interest and other payments to various other Starbucks companies. Over 14 years of trading in Britain it has only paid £8.4million in corporation tax on sales of £3billion. In February 2015, it was announced that Starbucks UK would finally pay some corporation tax – they announced their first profit in years of £1.1million, refused to disclosed their sales figure (sales were £300million the previous year), and that they would therefore be liable for £232,363 in tax.

Apple caused outrage in July 2014 when it was disclosed that the American giant had been funnelling sales through Ireland, a trick used by Google and others, which had enabled it to limit its British corporation tax to only £11.4miilion on sales of £10.5billion. Apple had been called before the US Senate to explain itself after its own shareholders had been complaining about the £87billion held in offshore accounts to avoid tax. In February 2015, President Obama announced plans for a one-off 14% tax on overseas profits of large US firms, such as Apple, Microsoft, Google and Starbucks; the intention is to raise up to £160billion.

In October 2015, it was revealed that Facebook had only paid £4,327 in taxes despite having made sales of around £105million. Although Facebook's 362 British employees had enjoyed an average salary and bonus package of £210,000 in the year, with Facebook paying out £35.4million in a share bonus scheme, it recorded an accounting loss of £28.5million. Facebook is believed to have transferred profits via Ireland to the Cayman Islands.

Although other countries, such as France and the USA, have been prepared to take action against these tax-dodging multinationals, Britain has done almost nothing. One solution would be to tax those sales booked as being received in low tax countries (i.e. impose a tariff) and to take a much tougher line on transfer pricing (making charges to transfer profits to low tax countries). But such measures would be inconsistent with free trade theories and EU single market agreements. Instead, matters simply plough on as they are with the result that there is a shortage of tax income to pay for public services.

According to ONS figures, average wages have increased by only 1% whereas house prices are increasing three times faster on average, with an increase in London of 8.1% over the 12 months to August 2013. The average family would have to spend an extra £730 simply to meet the cost of inflation, running at 2.9% in July 2013. In December 2013, Mark Carney, the governor of the Bank of England, warned that there would be no decent pay rises until 2015. In November 2013 it was revealed that the top 2,700 City workers were paid an average of £1.6million each in the last year as the bonus culture reasserted itself. Average workers saw their earnings increase by 0.8% by comparison. Interest payments on instant access savings accounts had fallen to 0.44% by October 2013. The government's Funding for Lending scheme was blamed for the recent falls as it enabled the banks to borrow cheaply from the Bank of England rather than having to pay reasonable interest rates to attract more savers. Banks are able to borrow at 0.25% under the scheme.

Meanwhile, Nationwide revealed that prices of the average home rose by 6.5% in the 12 months to November 2013. 67,701 mortgages were approved in October while SMEs struggled to get funding, with a fall of £1.2billion in business lending in October. Mark Carney announced that the Funding for Lending would now focus on lending to small firms. At a time when RBS has been found to be needlessly driving firms into insolvency via their GRG (Global Restructuring Group) division, RBS revealed that it had reduced its lending to small firms by £17billion since being bailed out by the taxpayer. In December 2013, RBS was fined £62million by the USA for breaching US sanctions against Iran. Lloyds Bank was fined £28million by the FCA for mis-selling. Salesmen had been bullied and enticed by champagne bonuses for hitting targets.

Apart from consistent government budget deficits run by the Attlee government in the late 1940s, most governments ran budget surpluses up until 1968. Since 1968, governments have been running budget deficits in most years. Even the Thatcher governments of the 1980s did so in every year except two. Since 1969 there has been a surplus only six times.[608] Government spending on welfare (including pensions), healthcare and education increased from 2% of GDP in 1900 to 30% in 2012.[609]

In 2001, the Labour government had a budget surplus. The increases in spending had been kept to within the increases in tax revenues. From 2002 onwards, the Labour government let spending rip and funded it by ever increasing deficits.[610]

Had there been a G7 of the world's richest countries in 1945, Argentina would have been a member.[611] Today, Britain, like Argentina, is heading towards becoming a relatively backward country. At the beginning of the 20th century Germany and Argentina had similar incomes per capita. In 1870, Argentina had had only 70% of the per capita income of Germany and yet had caught Germany up. After the inter-war years and post-WWII when Germany was struggling to recover from its defeats, Argentina sneaked ahead of Germany. It was only in the 1950s that Germany overtook Argentina and moved decisively ahead. By 2008, German standards of living were double those of Argentina.[612] In 2013 Angola, Botswana, Ethiopia, Nigeria, Rwanda, Uganda and Tanzania were all enjoying high growth rates – unlike Britain.[613]

There have been a series of efforts, of varying degrees of effectiveness, since WWII to try and arrest Britain's economic decline and grapple with the continuing economic difficulties. These efforts were dominated by Keynesian thinking and demand management rather than addressing the lack of manufacturing competitiveness directly. The Tory Party's commitment to free trade in 1954 ended any realistic consideration of tariff reform or other protectionist measures. After 1983, when Britain became a net immigration country and moved into a trade deficit, successive British governments chose to ignore the mounting problems; Britain's decline was to be orderly managed – if not welcomed – as being modernity and not decline at all. A balance of payments deficit was deemed acceptable; rising debts and debt fuelled consumption was welcomed; housing bubbles were not a problem; selling assets to pay for imports was perfectly normal; and gambling was the future. In fairness, Margaret Thatcher probably believed her own rhetoric about putting the 'Great' back into Britain even as she proceeded to hand over so much power to the EU. Free trade evolved and was corrupted into globalization and Britain embraced the concept of globalization more determinedly than any other nation, as with free trade.

Financial services is something that Britain is supposed to do well. Britain is the world's leading exporter of such services earning more than 10 times more than the USA in 2008. In 2010, financial services produced a trade surplus of £36billion. In 2009 financial services accounted for 10% of total economic output.[614] The City has benefited from public money, for example due to the large-scale privatizations. Likewise the legal profession benefits from legal aid. The BBC depends on the £3.6billion per annum licence fee. Much of Britain's 'successful' sectors are dependent on taxpayer's money.[615] In 1950, the financial sector accounted for 4% of total corporation tax paid; in 2006, at the peak of the boom, that figure had increased to 40%.[616]

In the period 1997 to 2007, financial services share of GDP increased from 6.5% to 8.5%, while manufacturing's contribution fell from more than 20% to 12.5%; the numbers employed in manufacturing fell from 4.5million to three million.[617] In 2011, a typical year, the balance of trade current account was in deficit to the sum of £37billion.[618] The total deficit in manufactured goods increased from £33.03billion in 2000 to £98.46billion in 2010. Sterling was 25% lower in 2012 than in 2007. Even so, the trade deficit continued.[619] Manufacturing accounted for 28% of national income in the 1930s, and only 10% in 2012.[620]

In Britain, in the second half of the 20th century, living standards doubled approximately every 30 years. At the turn of the millennium this growth slowed, stagnated and then living standards began to fall.[621] In the credit crunch, peak to trough, Britain's national income fell 7.1%.[622] Real incomes fell by more than 7% between 2009 and 2012 – the largest three-year fall on record. In 2011, household income fell by 3%; a fall on this scale was last experienced in the 1980s and that was followed by a period of strong growth with earnings growing at 7.5% by the mid-1980s.[623]

The period 1960 to 2000 witnessed an approximate tripling of per capita incomes. The period from 2000 to 2013 has seen, roughly, a mere 4% increase in per capita incomes.[624] In the run up to the credit crunch and subprime crisis in 2007, it was clear that investment was being allocated to housing, financial services and public spending, rather than in more productive, manufacturing, investment.[625] Manufacturing is important as it has the potential for far greater productivity growth than other sectors of the economy. What recovery there has been since the 2008 downturn has not been accompanied by a recovery in productivity growth. This has been referred to as the productivity puzzle:

> 'The fall in labour productivity during the recent recession has been larger than in any other post-war recession. And the recovery has been more protracted than previous experiences. Even six years after the initial downturn, the level of productivity lies around 4% below its pre-crisis peak, in contrast to the level of output, which has broadly recovered to its pre-crisis level.
>
> The weakness in labour productivity is even more pronounced if one compares the current level with a simple continuation of its pre-crisis trend: this shortfall in productivity is currently 16%. And the shortfall is large whether one measures it as output per hour or output per worker, across the whole economy or only within the private sector.'[626]

In every recession since 1970, after the initial crash, productivity returned to its trend growth and to its pre-recession level within 18 months. For the 2008 recession it has not.[627] The OBR has produced forecasts on the assumption that there will be a return to real wage growth of 1.8% per annum by 2019, based upon an annual increase in productivity by that year of 2% (it was increasing by only 0.5% in January 2015), without explaining why there should be such a recovery, without which the public sector net debt increases rather than decreases.[628]

Between 2007 and 2013, the gross debt almost tripled from £490billion to £1,354billion.[629] One-fifth of households have no savings at all. Despite the proclamation of the aim to create a property owning democracy, in 1988 58% of people under 35 of middle and low incomes were mortgage payers, 30% were in social housing and 14% were renting from private landlords; in 2008, before the housing bubble burst, only 29% of those under 35 of middle and low income groups were mortgage payers, and 41%

were renting from private landlords. Just under one-third of those buying their homes needed a 100% mortgage.[630] One study revealed the growth of a new class in the 21st century of people moved from one low-paid job to another, interspersed with periods of unemployment and borrowing to make ends meet.[631] More recently there has been the growth of unpaid interns and zero-hours contracts, the number of which have doubled between 2010 and 2015 to an estimated 1.4million.[632]

In addition to the government debt, there are those liabilities which the government keeps off balance sheet, such as PFI contracts. By 2009, at the end of the Labour government's period in office, despite years of growth, the off-balance sheet debts were astronomical. The future cost of schools and hospitals were estimated to be £148billion (£5,619 per household); guarantees to Network Rail totalled £28billion (£1,054 per household); there was the £73billion cost of the decommissioning of nuclear power stations (£2,779 per household); then there was the cost of public sector pensions estimated to be £1,261billion (£47,998 per household) as well as the state pension totalling £2,191billion (£83,397 per household).[633] By June 2015, it was reported that the government debt had exceeded £1.5trillion, amounting to £23,000 for every adult and child, and the interest upon which had reached £46billion per annum – even with the low interest rates then prevailing. Despite all the talk of austerity, according to figures from Eurostat, it was revealed in April 2015 that British government deficit in 2014, at 5.7% of GDP, was higher than that of Greece (3.5%), Italy (3%), or Ireland (4.1%); only Spain and Cyprus had a larger deficit.

In 1997 there were 97,900 work based-pension schemes. In 2009 that number had dropped to 53,801, of which 18,900 no longer accept new members, 4,354 are frozen, and 1,779 are being wound up.[634] Gordon Brown and his Treasury team are responsible for the collapse of Britain's private pensions. Brown's budget speech in 1997, having just taken office, included an announcement that there would be an end of dividend credits on advance corporation tax. This technical-sounding change had a major impact for pension schemes as they had previously not been paying tax. £5billion was stealthily taxed in the first year and by 2009 £175billion had been taken out of the pension schemes in tax.[635]

A report from Civitas revealed that over the last 25 years employers have cut their contributions to the pensions of their employees by two-thirds.[636] A £100,000 pension pot that would have bought an annuity of £17,000 in 1980, would only buy an annuity of £6,700 per annum in June 2008, £6,000 in 2011, and a measly £4,800 in April 2013;[637] this is due to longevity and lower returns on savings as well as high charges by the pensions industry.[638] One consequence of the government Funding for Lending Scheme is that banks can get cheap money from the government and so do not have to bother to attract savers, which means that interest rates on savings remains pitiful.

The trend is clear: debts are massive and increasing whilst assets are falling. Ordinary people have fewer assets, be they houses or pensions. Living standards are falling.

The method of calculating the GDP has been adjusted. For government expenditure the GDP calculation includes 'estimates from volume measures such as the number of operations, pupil numbers and the like' rather than using RPI or CPI as are used for household items, and in 2012 the ONS ceased using RPI and adopted CPI. The effects of these adjustments is to increase the apparent growth rate. Pete Comley states that, 'it is likely that we now appear to have significantly higher economic growth than the country is really experiencing. Indeed, if RPI was used instead of the GDP deflator, the UK would have remained in recession since 2010, i.e., during the whole period of the current government'.[639] In September 2014 it was announced that the growth figure would now include an estimate for such items as drug-dealing, prostitution and charities.

There has been no bounce back following the recession. The growth has been anaemic. Importantly, GDP *per capita* was still below the 2008 level even in 2014. The growth has been achieved by expanding the size of the labour force by mass immigration and also by forcing women out to work. This expansion means that provided the extra workers do something or other, no matter how little or inefficiently, then there is additional output and hence 'growth'. It is therefore to be expected that productivity is so low. This is not genuine growth, but growth brought about by cramming more immigrants into Britain and ignoring the costs of that immigration. This policy can only result in a lower standard of living for ordinary English people.

Hyman Minsky (1919-1996), an American economist, argued that after a financial crisis there was always a period when it would be asserted that the errors should have been spotted and institutional flaws corrected and that these were responsible for the disaster. But, no matter how plausible these assertions might be, they miss the point that any financial system will tend towards instability and this instability caused by underlying monetary and balance sheet conditions.[640] Charles Kindleberger (1910-2003), an American economist, cited the causes of these monetary conditions as being potentially a shock to the system caused by new gold discoveries, financial innovation, or capital recycling.[641] The challenge facing any government is how to control the financial system and minimize the likelihood of the entire economy being dragged down by the consequences of banking failures, and yet at the same time allow a genuinely profitable financial sector to flourish.

In Britain the aim was to use taxpayers' monies and borrow to shield a bunch of crooked bankers from the consequences of their own actions. Had the banks been allowed to fail, then there would be no need to try and change their reckless, crooked and greedy culture as they would not exist any more and neither therefore would their culture. Smaller and more honest banks would have emerged and their culture would have prevailed.

SUMMARY

The scale of the losses suffered by the banks in 2008 and the slump was vast. The financial sector had been reporting substantial profits which proved to be illusionary. Bonus payments had been made out of profits that did not exist. The scale of the losses and the credit crunch dragged down the real economy, which had been growing well, into a deep and prolonged slump. Various national governments resorted to printing money to give to the financial institutions to save them from insolvency. QE was a banking policy that destroyed the true worth of private pensions. QE was a means of transferring wealth from ordinary pensioners and savers to bankers.

The crisis resurrected Keynesian sentiments and Keynes was again held up to be some economist genius. 'Crass Keynesianism' is how the German Finance Minister described the aim for 'credit-financed growth'.

Meanwhile, the euro single currency hit the buffers. The economic downturn brought to a head a looming debt crisis in the

Eurozone that could not be alleviated by currency devaluation. The south European countries were overburdened with debt and uncompetitive due to the single currency. One size did not fit all. The single currency likewise made Germany more competitive and allowed its exports to boom. Unlike the Bank of England with the pre-WWI Gold Standard, Germany has not been willing to smooth the operation of the euro by making loans to countries in difficulties; any monies have had to be dragged out of Germany at the last moment.

Britain's economic decline continued apace. The economy is unbalanced with a persistent, substantial and escalating balance of payments deficit, a substantial government spending deficit, and an anaemic growth rate dependent upon consumer borrowing and spending. There has been no bounce-back from the recession and there has been no rebalancing of the economy. Productivity growth is negligible. Consequently, wage growth has been negligible. Immigrants take up a large portion of the jobs available, and such immigration places a further strain on public services. Foreign firms are launching takeovers of the best of British industry. Britain is being asset stripped and the government is keen to encourage this with a view to paying for the imports by selling off British assets, and funding the deficit by yet another raid on private pensions. Assets are consumed as consumption. Long-term tax revenues are lost as foreign-owned firms relocate overseas and various monopolies, cartels and oligarchies are imposing inflation-busting charges on captive consumers. British banks remain unreformed and crooked, with a flow of a variety of scandals hitting the headlines. The incomes for ordinary people following the 2008 slump have either fallen or remained stagnant; the bonus culture of both the City and the public sector has, however, continued uninterrupted.

The policy of Free Trade has evolved into the policy of globalization. As Free Trade was responsible for the difficulties of the 1930s, both with the return to the Gold Standard as well as unilateral free trade, globalization was responsible for the 2008 slump, both due to the eagerness to encourage reckless bank lending to all and sundry from wherever, as well as the mind-set that the banks had to be bailed out, using *national* monies, no matter the cost. The determination to re-join the Gold Standard at pre-war parity was as ruinous as it was stupid, and the same applies to the creation of the euro. Britain was forced to leave the

Gold Standard, it has yet to be forced to confront the problems caused by the euro.

10 INFLATIONISM

Churchill's close friend, Brendan Bracken MP commented that it was Keynes 'who made inflation respectable'.[642] The economist Melchior Palyi, referring the Keynes' *General Theory*, commented: 'Stripped of crypto-scientific semantics, the Keynesian's medicine is inflation'.[643] The opposite view was expressed by the economist Sir Alec Cairncross who remarked that Keynes had a 'horror of inflation'.[644] Was Keynes an inflationist, and does this matter? *The Times* wrote:

> 'As Professor Hayek has argued ever since his pre-war disputes with Keynes, the price of maintaining full employment by more and more inflationary public finance is not only accelerating inflation but also a progressive diversion of economic resources into activities favoured by or dependent on inflation. If inflation is to be checked, that structural distortion has to be reversed, which must be painful'.[645]

Professor Neil Carothers of Lehigh University, in reference to the New Deal and the attempt by the US government to lower the gold value of the dollar:

> 'Inflation is not a desperate remedy for a desperate situation. On the contrary, it is an arbitrary and unnecessary interference with a recovery already well begun. Its purpose is not to end depression, but to relieve certain groups of people of their obligations and to permit the government to spread money recklessly without balancing its budget. Peace-time inflation in all history is the device of a government unwilling to pay its debts but quite willing to dishonour its promises in order to give subsidies to clamouring elements in the population.
> The bloated prices of 1929 caused the collapse. The morbidly low prices of 1933 are the painful but necessary condition of restoration ... They deflate the swollen and unearned profits of industry and finance. They reduce the

salaries and wages of certain parasitic groups. They wipe out the waste and the incompetence in business. Until this purging process is complete there can be no recovery. Four years of the Hoover administration proved the futility of attempt to stop the process.'[646]

Keynes himself wrote: 'Lenin was certainly right. There is no subtler, no surer means of overturning the existing basis of society than to debauch the currency. The process engages all the hidden forces of economic law on the side of destruction, and does it in a manner which not one man in a million is able to diagnose'.[647] Keynes commented: 'A government can live for a long time, even the German government or the Russian government, by printing paper money. That is to say, it can by this means secure the command over real resources, resources just as real as those obtained by taxation ... It is the form of taxation which the public find hardest to evade and even the weakest government can enforce, when it can enforce nothing else'.[648] Keynes began to see the danger of the union-backed wage demands that would be the result of a rise in prices:

> '... a demand on the part of the trade unions for an increase in money rates of wages to compensate for every increase in his cost of living is futile, and greatly to the disadvantage of the working class. Like the dog in the fable, they lose the substance in grasping at the shadow. It is true that the better organised might benefit at the expense of other consumers. But except as an effort at group selfishness, as a means of hustling someone else out of the queue, it is a mug's game ...'[649]

Ultimately inflation, if it gets out of control, can soar to become hyperinflation. For example, during the French revolution, the French increased the size of their army from under 100,000 to roughly 800,000 men. This was from a labour force of an estimated 7.2million – a major reallocation of manpower. The reduction in the labour force was estimated to be around 10% and led to a fall in output despite rhetoric about women and older men being brought into employment. There was therefore an increase in demand for military equipment and supplies at a time that the available workforce was falling significantly. The funding of this was inefficient with a disorganized tax system, and there was no effective measures taken to dampen down private sector demand. There was, in consequence, a strong demand for both products and labour, resulting in a large rise in both prices and wages. Income distribution remained unchanged. As prices rose, the government, determined to achieve the military mobilization it deemed to be vital, spent ever-larger sums trying to outbid the private sector for resources. Prices and wages soared and led to hyperinflation.[650]

A similar situation occurred in both the Hungarian and Chinese episodes of hyperinflation in the mid-1940s – a reduced labour force accompanied by an increased demand for output. In Hungary, following the siege of Budapest, the city's entire adult population was employed and generously paid to build temporary shelters and clear up the rubble. In China, the casualties of the civil war removed millions of people from the workforce.[651]

In Germany, in 1923, the entire workforce of the Ruhr went on strike. The Ruhr being the industrial heartland of Germany. The strike was encouraged and financed by the German government to protest against the occupation of the Ruhr by the French.[652] The Weimar hyperinflation is notorious to this day.

These cases of hyperinflation have in common an excess demand for products and an excess demand for labour. The excess demand for both the product and labour markets simultaneously is a factor in how the inflation arose, accelerated rapidly and rose to astronomic levels. Hyperinflation, if defined as a ten-fold or greater annual increase in the general level of prices, is a product of the exceptional circumstances of a general shortage of the workforce and a rapidly rising level of demand for products.[653]

However, another factor must be the willingness of the government to increase expenditure in order to fund its own activities and to achieve its own intended objectives. Demand can only increase if there are resources to fund the demand increases.

The value of several European currencies collapsed after WWI. Austrian prices increased by 14,000 times their pre-war level (Joseph Schumpeter was the Finance Minister of the Austrian Republic); Hungarian prices increased 23,000 times, those in Poland increased 2,500,000 times and those in Russia by even more. Ultimately one trillion German marks had the same value as one gold mark.[654] To prevent inflation, Keynes argued that: 'Some means must be found for withdrawing purchasing power from the market; or prices must rise until the available goods are selling at figures which absorb the increased quantity of expenditure – in other words the method of inflation'.[655]

In *Treatise*, Keynes distinguished between income inflation and profit inflation. Income inflation is described as a rise in the rate of efficiency earnings. Profit inflation is described as a rise in the level of profits to abnormal levels. The WWI and the following post-war boom were essentially profit inflation, but with the post-war boom income inflation emerged also and continued after the profit inflation faded in 1920. This was then followed by a profit deflation in the 1921-24 period.[656]

In *General Theory*, Keynes defined 'true inflation' as being when an increase in effective demands results in an increase in costs 'fully proportionate to the increase in effective demand' rather than an increase in output,[657] that is to say the entire impact of an increase in effective demand is to increase prices; this is deemed to occur once full employment has been achieved.[658] Keynes was also aware that prices may rise as bottlenecks occur before full employment is reached. Up until this point it is a matter of judgement as to the extent to which the monetary expansion is inflationary, as some increase in output will have been achieved alongside any increase in prices.

Keynes had been tolerant of inflation as a price to be paid for full employment and even a means of cutting real wages rather than adopting the more confrontational method of directly cutting money wages. He, and others, saw a trade-off between unemployment and inflation. If an economy is already at full capacity, including full employment, then any further increase in demand can only be met by an increase in prices, or more imports. This raises the difficulty in identifying involuntary unemployment as opposed to voluntary unemployment, and the further issue of an underlying natural rate of unemployment which demand management will not eradicate but merely increase inflation. The trade-off between inflation and unemployment as demonstrated by the Phillips curve, an inverse relationship between unemployment and inflation, with higher unemployment being the result of lower inflation and higher inflation being a cost of lower unemployment.

Therefore there was a necessity to tolerate an increase in unemployment in order to combat inflation. This led to concern that an unemployment rate of 1.8% was too low and that there was excess demand in the economy and that a higher rate of unemployment should be the target if inflation is to be reduced if not eradicated. This led to a debate as to the causes of inflation and the difference between 'demand-pull' inflation and 'cost-push' inflation. Dampening down demand might combat 'demand-pull' inflation but is less effective in dealing with 'cost-push' inflation, such as wage increases.

Some Keynesians responded to the Monetarist concept of a natural rate of unemployment with their own concept. These neo-Keynesians did not accept that there is a natural rate of unemployment and remained committed to demand management as a means of creating employment and reducing unemployment. However, they did accept that there is a non-accelerating inflation rate of unemployment (NAIRU). This NAIRU is the level of unemployment below which, were unemployment to drop below that level, inflation will tend to increase; and conversely, if unemployment rises above that NAIRU level then inflation will tend to fall. Those neo-Keynesians who adhere to this view still believe that the government needs to implement demand management policies in order to ensure that the unemployment level does not rise above the NAIRU level. Other neo-Keynesians do not accept the NAIRU argument. They argued that estimating the correct NAIRU level is problematic and would argue that the level itself changes due to circumstances and from time to time. These neo-Keynesians would deny that there is any one such unique level at which inflation is stable. They believe that inflation is caused by many factors and that the level of unemployment is only one such contributory factor. However, many Keynesians and neo-Keynesians would accept that in addition to demand management economics supply-side measures, such as training and re-training, are also necessary to help reduce unemployment.

When there is prolonged price stability, then money values tend to be treated as real values. The gold parity of sterling had been maintained up until WWI, save for the Napoleonic Wars and for a time after, since Sir Isaac Newton had established that parity in 1717. The level of prices in Britain was the same in 1844 as in 1881 and in 1914. From 1826 to 1914, prices never rose above or fell below more than 30% the level of 1844, 1881 and 1914.[659]

Britain's GDP increased by more than seven-fold during the Victorian era following the Napoleonic wars and at the same time prices actually declined by a quarter.[660] In the 67 years since WWII, prices have risen by an average of 5.4% per annum; in the 67 years before WWII they increased by an average of only 1.5%

per annum, most of that increase being in the years 1916 to 1920. An item that cost £1 in 1946 would cost £32 in 2013.[661] By comparison, according to the ONS, prices as measured by RPI have increased by 50% between 2000 and 2013.[662] Prices have even continued to increase despite the slump, whereas household income has been stagnant. According to the ONS average gross weekly income was £713 in 2008 and was still £713 in 2011. Over the same period RPI increased by 12.5%.[663]

Since 1913, the US dollar has lost more than 95% of its value. By contrast the denarius of the Roman Republic maintained its value for two centuries until the reign of Augustus. The Byzantine Empire maintained the value of its currency for more than 500 years from AD 498 to 1030.[664]

In Britain, national debt as a proportion of GDP peaked at 260% in 1819 following the Napoleonic wars. It was reduced to only 25% as a proportion of GDP by 1914. This reduction was achieved mainly by keeping the gross debt level while the economy grew. Little debt was actually repaid.[665] The debt was not inflated away as prices were stable and even fell during this period. The growth achieved was genuine growth and not money growth.

In 1940 inflation in Britain reached 17.2%, partly as a result of a 17% devaluation of sterling against the dollar, and partly as a result of the shortages following the outbreak of war. At the end of WWII the national debt had reached 237% of GDP and Britain faced what Keynes described as a 'financial Dunkirk'.[666] The Labour government's Chancellor after WWII was Hugh Dalton, who had written in 1922:

> 'The comparative acquiescence of a public opinion in taxation by inflation is a measure of public ignorance of economic principles and of the inability of wage earners, and still more the recipients of fixed money incomes, to safeguard their economic interests. Thus persons who would certainly vote against a government which added one shilling in the pound to their income tax, have been found to tolerate a government which, by doubling the price level through inflation, has in effect, imposed upon them an additional income tax of ten shillings in the pound.'[667]

Dalton fixed interest rates at a low level, which reduced the interest payable on the government's debts.[668] Dalton also rapidly increased the money supply, which expanded by 16% in 1947.[669] A tolerance of inflation accompanied a commitment to Keynesian economics by both Labour and Tory governments up until the 1970s. By 1973, British government debt had been reduced from its WWII peak down to below 50% of GDP, which had increased 7.5 times in the period 1946 to 1973.[670] However, much of this reduction had been because of inflation. It has been estimated that as much as 80% of the post-WWII government debt had been inflated away by 1969.[671] There is now open acceptance of inflation as means of reducing the debts of both the governments and the banks.

A current problem is that there is an excess of world savings looking for investment. This pushes down interest rates. Much of that investment is in US (as well as other countries') government debt. So long as the government borrows so much the savings will be available. It can therefore by arguable that to increase the government debt even further would be possible without crowding out the private sector, due to the amount of savings available.[672] This is a rationale that is very attractive to Keynesians.

Investing in government debt is an attractive option for savers, not only because of the perceived safety. According to Simon Lack's *The Hedge Fund Mirage*, over the last decade the average hedge fund investor would have enjoyed a better return if he had invested his money in Treasury bills. Many hedge fund investors have made no money at all.[673] It is the hedge fund managers who make a lot of money, for they not only get paid fees but also a percentage of the profits. This encourages risk taking to achieve paper profits, generating incomes for the managers that are not handed back if the fund eventually incurs a loss. There is a case for governments to attract more of savers' monies as the returns on stock market investments are, arguably, so poor. Similar analysis applies to Britain, where £10,000 invested in a FTSE 100 tracker between 2000 and 2015, with all dividends reinvested, will have seen growth lower than inflation once fees are deducted, according to analysis by Axa Wealth; by comparison those who had invested in the best fixed rate bonds or tax-free Isas would have enjoyed a profit. Stephen King pointed out:

> 'In the ten years ending in 2008 (a year in which equities collapsed) or 2009 (when equities rebounded), investors would have been better off investing in safe, boring, US

Treasuries – simple claims on future US taxpayers – than in US equities or, indeed, in the equities of many emerging markets. Given that many profit-hungry US companies chose to invest all over the world – including its emerging parts – this is a remarkable and historically unprecedented result.'[674]

This analysis merely shows that the benefit to the wider economy of the stock market is overstated. To put the interests of stock market speculation ahead of the interests of manufacturing is a serious mistake that will lead to lower growth rates and living standards in the long term.

Calls for more government spending to cure economic woes should nevertheless be treated with extreme caution. Krugman, his supporters, and other Keynesians, have a depression fixation in that they are continuously arguing for more government spending to solve alleged economic problems. Krugman asserted:

> 'The basic point is that the recession ... wasn't a typical postwar slump, brought on when an inflation-fighting Fed raises interest rates and easily ended by a snapback in housing and consumer spending when the Fed brings rates back down again. This was a pre-war-style recession, a morning after brought on by irrational exuberance. To fight this recession the Fed needs more than a snapback; it needs soaring household spending to offset moribund business investment ... I just don't understand the grounds for optimism. Who, exactly, is about to start spending a lot more? At this point it's a lot easier to tell a story about how the recovery will stall than about how it will speed up.'[675]

However, Krugman made his claim in 2002, long before the crash and as the subprime boom was getting under way.[676] Krugman attributes the cause of the depression as being a lack of demand:

> 'Why is unemployment so high, and economic output so low? Because we – where by "we" I mean consumers, businesses and governments combined – aren't spending enough. Spending on house construction and consumer goods plunged when the twin housing bubbles in America

and Europe burst. Business investment soon followed, because there's no point in expanding capacity when sales are shrinking, and a lot of government spending has also fallen as local, state, and some national governments have found themselves starved for revenue. Low spending, in turn, means low employment, because businesses won't produce what they can't sell, and they won't hire workers if they don't need them for production. We are suffering from a severe overall lack of demand.'[677]

Therefore, because there is a supposed lack of demand, Krugman believed: 'The case for fiscal policy is precisely that by spending more, the government can keep the economy from being deeply depressed while indebted families restore their own financial health'.[678] For Krugman:

> 'At a time when many debtors are trying to save more and pay down debt, it's important that *someone* do the opposite, spending more and borrowing – with the obvious someone being the government. So this is just another way of arriving at the Keynesian argument for government spending as a necessary answer to the kind of depression we find ourselves facing.
> What about the argument that falling wages and prices make the situation worse; does that mean that rising wages and prices would make things better, that inflation would actually be helpful? Yes, it does, because inflation would reduce the burden of debt (as well as having some other useful effects ...). More broadly, policies to reduce the burden of debt one way or another, such as mortgage relief, could and should be a part of achieving a lasting exit from depression.'[679]

Krugman might be citing Keynes, but his rationale harks back to the glut theorists of the early 19th century. He is solely focused on the demand for goods. He does not explain but simply assumes that Keynes' theory applies without taking account of the different circumstances or that Keynes was dealing with a particular problem at a particular point in time. The Western economies were growing well until the banking credit crunch. The Slump was not caused by a lack of demand.

Krugman argued: 'Ignoring the foreign component, of looking at the world as a whole, we see that the overall level of debt makes no difference to aggregate net worth – one person's liability is another person's asset'.[680] He went on: 'The plausible-sounding argument that debt can't cure debt is just wrong. On the contrary, it can – and the alternative is a prolonged period of economic weakness that actually makes the debt problem harder to resolve'.[681] This reasoning is wrong on many levels. It is impossible to ignore the 'foreign component' and look 'at the world as a whole'. The world is not whole, but made up of a variety of economic and political systems at different stages of development. The government of Britain is supposed to be governing on behalf of Britain and to protect British interests. Running up debts to foreign countries is not in British interests. The liabilities of Britain are not OK if they are assets to another country. Selling assets and running up debts to pay for imported goods is damaging. This is a corruption of Keynes' thinking. At no stage does Krugman take into account that Keynes was irrelevant to solving the economic crisis of the inter-war years. At no stage does Krugman acknowledge those policies which *did* actually extricate Britain from its 1930s quagmire.

Krugman argued that the threat of a boom if not inflation will not happen because of the liquidity trap and that the banks are hoarding money.[682] Krugman asserted:

> 'All that inflation fearmongering has been about a non-existent threat. Underlying inflation is low and, given the depressed state of the economy, likely to go even lower in the years ahead. And that's not a good thing. Falling inflation, and even worse, possible deflation, will make recovery from this depression much harder. What we should be aiming for is the opposite: moderately higher inflation, say core inflation of around 4 percent. (This was, by the way, the rate that prevailed during Ronald Reagan's second term.)'[683]

This is a view also expressed by Oliver Blanchard, for example, in his paper for the IMF, where he criticized both the Fed and the European Central Bank for aiming for a 2% inflation rate and that a 4% inflation rate might be preferable.[684]   Krugman wrote: 'The reality is that inflation is actually too low'.[685]

Krugman sees inflation as a means of solving the Eurozone crisis, which he believes should be between 3% and 4%, and which he believes should be achieved by an expansionary monetary policy from the ECB and a fiscal stimulus from Germany.[686] A *MoneyWeek* item stated in May 2013: 'The war between inflation and deflation ... may well be over. As far as central bankers go, it's inflation or bust!'[687]

Krugman has been proved correct in his analysis that inflation was unlikely to take off. It has remained low and stable, despite the scale of the QE programmes on both sides of the Atlantic, and in Britain inflation fell away to deflation as the oil price cuts worked through to affect prices in 2015. Before WWI, a recession would lead to a fall in prices, yet that has not happened in the 2008 slump. It is only afterwards and due to the fall in oil prices that ultimately produced a fall in prices – even though wages fell. Therefore, it may well be that the QE programme has maintained the inflation rate when otherwise it would have fallen, with the result that living standards for the majority have been reduced. Krugman is looking at inflation from a *government* viewpoint and assumes that it is *government* interests that inflation is higher – he does not take account of the interests of ordinary people, whose interests are not automatically the same as the government's.

In the May 2013 Inflation Report, Mervyn King pointed out that 1%, almost half, of the inflation rate as measured by CPI, was accounted for by government administered or regulated prices.[688] The British government has been more than willing to endorse annual inflation plus increases in prices for a number of state-backed multinational cartels and monopolies (rail fares, electricity, gas, water, etc.) – as their beleaguered customers are well aware.

SUMMARY

For all his intellectual gymnastics, Keynes was an inflationist. Inflation was his solution. He believed that he could engineer a one-off reduction in the value of the currency as a means of cutting the real value of money wages. His definition of unemployment lends itself to his inflationist strategy as does his definition of inflation by linking it to the consequences of an increase in demand. He convinced himself that he could manipulate the value of money to remedy a problem created by the definition of unemployment he chose. He then convinced a very large number of others, including the major part of the British establishment.

Keynes did not explain, or perhaps not even realise, that it would not be possible to artificially cut the value of the currency so precisely and so quickly. He did see the looming union demands for higher wage increases, but did not live long enough to see the final outcome of stagflation that occurred in the 1970s, with the attendant industrial and civil strife. Keynesianism *is* an inflationist theory which is attractive as it enables governments to inflate away their huge and increasing debts.

Prices may have been stable in the Victorian era of the Gold Standard, but they have not been in the Keynesian era post-WWII. Inflation has been a persistent problem and it eventually got out of control in the 1970s – due to a number of factors such as increased oil prices, the Vietnam inflation and the Barber Boom.

Following the 2008 Slump, Keynesians, such as Krugman, have been open in their advocacy that inflation is too low and needed to be stoked up. Given the scale of the QE programme, one might have expected inflation to take off. It has not. Prices, despite the profiteering by the banks and cosy inflation plus pricing arrangements of key monopolies etc., by 2014 had stabilized, not least due to the fall in oil prices. Given the scale of the Slump, perhaps they should have stabilized sooner as they would surely have done pre-WWII before falling. Had they done so, then living standards for ordinary people would be much higher.

11 TRADE POLICY AND THE TRADE DEFICIT

'Kindness, tolerance and love of order become snobbery, woolliness and love of the past. Effortless ease becomes the ease of not making an effort to do anything. Gentlemanly intuitive wisdom becomes the inability to make up one's mind. Doing the decent thing comes to mean that there should be no sharp clash of attitudes, no disagreeable new beliefs, that might disturb someone. The sense of fairness becomes the belief that competition is unfair: it might benefit some new person, but it might also harm some old person.' – Donald Horne (1921-2005), Australian writer and academic

By definition, every deficit must be matched with a surplus in trade between countries. This creates a problem where certain countries play the system and use protectionist measures themselves while having free access to other countries' markets. Japan has been adept at doing this and their strategy, which has been very successful from a Japanese viewpoint, triggered a belligerent response from the USA. Likewise the industrial revolution in China has been accompanied by protectionist measures. China remains a communist-party controlled state albeit one which has allowed significant capitalist free market activity. The trade surpluses that Japan and China enjoy are at the expense of the economic health of those countries which have balance of trade deficits, in part caused by the unfair trade practices used by China and Japan. It is not helpful for a country in deficit to be held responsible for that trade deficit, which is the product of the surpluses and the result of the protectionist policies of other countries. Nor is it fair on the population of the host country, which has to bear the loss of jobs and fall in living standards that a continued large scale trade deficit must entail. The negative impact of a trade deficit was illustrated by Britain in the 1960s, for example, when the Stop-Go era crippled growth and hence living standards.

No country has industrialized or developed a manufacturing industry by relying on free trade. *Every* country, including Britain, that has developed a manufacturing industry has done so by using tariffs and other protectionist measures. Post WWII, this particularly applied to the East Asian economies. Until the 1990s China's average tariff was more than 30%. China further has restrictions and ceilings on foreign ownership and local content requirements for foreign investment. India likewise has had manufacturing tariffs in excess of 30%.[689] Free markets are not a panacea. Chile adopted free-market policies under the influence of the Chicago Boys, who had been taught at the University of Chicago, until a financial crash which forced the government to nationalize the banks, and further introduced help for exporters and capital controls.[690]

New global corporations regard themselves as global and seek to remove any vestige of national identity from their image. Business and finance are borderless.[691] While globalization is the phenomenon of the 21st century, state capitalism is another, being the reincarnation of Mercantilism, which had dominated state policy in the 17th, 18th and 19th centuries. Mercantilism involves governments favouring national firms and industries, with the use of tariffs to advantage domestic producers and trade treaties with friendly countries and not so generous treaties to economic rivals.[692] Mercantilism is incompatible with a policy of globalization. A problem is that Western countries which fancy themselves as immersed in a globalized economy fail to grasp that others, in particular Japan, China and Russia, see things very differently and act very differently. For them, the Western policy of globalization is something to be exploited and not be a party to. For both Russia and China, state capitalism is the norm. A company such as Gazprom has no equivalent in the West. Gazprom is Russia's largest company and the world's largest natural gas company. It accounts for 10% of Russia's GDP, produces more than 85% of Russia's natural gas and accounts for more than 20% of the world's supply. It controls nearly 20% of global gas reserves and 60% of Russian reserves. It is vertically integrated with the energy market and has further interests in banking and operates as an international investment company. Russia's elected president in 2008 was Dmitry Medvedev, who had served as chairman of Gazprom twice. In 2013, the chairman was Viktor Zubkov, who was also Russia's deputy prime minister. Its CEO was a Putin crony. It even has its own security force. Although its stock is traded, it remains under state control.[693] In

2006, Russia/Gazprom used its monopolistic control of gas to cut off Ukraine's supply of natural gas and ultimately the supply to wider Europe.[694] The crisis in the Ukraine and the Crimea in 2014 is against the backdrop of Europe's dependency on Russian gas supplies and Russia's past willingness to cut off those supplies as an act of foreign policy.

In 2008, Russia accounted for 12.4% of global oil production, only just behind Saudi Arabia which accounted for 13.1%, and 19.6% of global natural gas production, slightly ahead of the USA which accounted for 19.3%.[695] Unlike the USA, Russia is an exporter of gas and has 23% of proved gas reserves whereas the USA has only 3.6%.[696] Germany relies on Russia for 50% of its gas consumption, Italy 30%, Austria 75% and Finland 80%.[697]

In addition to tariffs, countries can also use legal measures and subsidies to support their industries as well as setting up state owned enterprises (SOEs). Prussia used such methods in the 18th century for linen, iron and steel industries, and Japan used SOEs and subsidies to launch steel, shipbuilding and railway industries.[698] In Taiwan, SOEs accounted for more than 16% of national output in the 1960s and 1970s. Even though many were privatized in the 1980s, the government retained a significant shareholding, averaging 35%, and appoints 60% of the directors. Despite the move away from state communism in economic policy, the Chinese SOEs still account for 40% of industrial output. France, which had had experience of interventionism under Louis XIV's finance minister, Jean-Baptiste Colbert (1619-1683), developed a programme of indicative planning after WWII, and channelled investment into strategic industries via state-owned banks.[699] According to EDF's own annual report in 2008, 84.66% of its share capital is owned by the French state.[700] After WWII Japan's Ministry of International Trade and Industry (MITI) restricted imports by controlling foreign exchange and used both direct and indirect export subsidies. The government directed subsidized credit to key sectors and foreign investment was regulated, with ownership ceilings and local content requirements in addition.

Contrary to Ricardo's free trade rationale, in Japan government agencies promoted industrialisation. In 1950, income per capita in Japan was less than a quarter of the level per capita in Britain, and less than a sixth of the level per capita in the USA. Japan's industry was backward and Japan had few natural resources. 90% of Japan's energy requirements and all basic ores had to be imported. Even so, the Japanese successfully increased their share of the world's trade in manufactures from less than 4% in the early 1950s to 15% in 1980. Japan's manufactured exports overtook Britain's in the 1960s.

After WWII Japan adopted development policies that focused on newer industries of iron and steel, electronics, modern synthetic textiles, cars and industrial machinery. In 1970, MITI's vice minister, Y Ojimi said:

> 'After the war Japan's first exports consisted of such things as toys or other miscellaneous merchandise and low-quality textile products. Should Japan have entrusted its future according to the theory of comparative advantage, to these industries characterised by intensive use of labour? That would perhaps be a rational advice for a country with a small population of 5 or 10 million. But Japan has a large population. If the Japanese economy had adopted the simple doctrine of free trade and had chosen to specialise in this kind of industry, it would almost permanently have been unable to break away from the Asian pattern of stagnation and poverty, and would have remained the weakest link in the free world, thereby becoming a problem area in the Far East.
>
> The Ministry of International Trade and Industry decided to establish in Japan industries which require intensive employment of capital and technology, industries that in consideration of comparative cost should be the most inappropriate for Japan, industries such as steel, oil refining, petro-chemicals, automobiles, aircraft, industrial machinery of all sorts, and electronics, including electronic computers. From a short-run, static viewpoint, encouragement of such industries would seem to conflict with economic rationalism. But from a long-range viewpoint, these are precisely the industries where income elasticity of demand is high, technological progress is rapid and labour productivity rises fast. It was clear that without these industries it would be difficult to employ a population of 100 million and raise their standard of living to that of Europe and America ...'[701]

Japan's traditional industries of low-quality textiles and toys were ignored and left to their own devices. The newer industries were protected against foreign competitors by a range of tariffs, excise duties, controls on foreign investment and foreign exchange controls. The foreign exchange controls limited the amount of foreign exchange available to buy foreign goods and so limited the ability to pay for imports. For example, in 1954 there was only sufficient foreign exchange allocated to allow the import of 370 cars. In addition, MITI bought foreign patents to speed Japanese development. Krugman wrote:

> 'One by one, the Japanese government would target "strategic" industries that could serve as engines of growth. The private sector would be guided into those industries, helped along by an initial period of protection from foreign competition during which the industry could hone its skills in the domestic market. Then there would be a great export drive, during which firms would ignore profitability while building market share and driving their foreign competitors into the ground. Eventually, its dominance of the industry secured, Japan would move on to the next one. Steel, autos, VCRs, semi-conductors – soon it would be computers and aircraft.[702]

The Japanese strategy was very successful. Between 1955 and 1961 passenger car production increased from 50,000 to 250,000, of which only 11,500 were exported. Although the Japanese home market was protected from foreign competition, competition between the Japanese firms was fierce. The 50,000 cars produced in 1955 had cost two and a half times the equivalent European models.[703] By 1980, the Japanese cars were not necessarily cheaper but were competitive on non-price items such as quality and reliability. Despite the success of the Japanese car industry, both at home and on export markets, the production of cars is still aimed at the home market and the same applies to other industries. The import penetration of the home market has been greater in Britain than in other advanced industrial countries. The Japanese industrial strategy is clear, to protect the home market and support the newer growth industries to expand output and achieve international competitiveness before exporting to overseas markets. Despite Japanese export success, the Japanese home market remains by far the more important market for Japanese industry. Britain, by comparison, has been more reliant on free trade and exports and although the rate of growth of the world trade since WWII has led to a growth in the absolute level of exports, Britain has steadily lost competitiveness and market share. In 1978, Japanese exports accounted for only 9.3% of GDP as opposed to 17.8% in Britain. Imports accounted for only 2% of GDP as opposed to 15.3% in Britain. Imports accounted for only 4.9% of GDP in the USA, 9.7% in West Germany, 10.5% in France and 9.7% in Italy.[704]

Britain needs to decide how to react to the type of Japanese economic policies in which a protected Japanese home market is denied to British goods and yet Japan has unfettered access to the British market. The same problem arises with China and the threat posed by the Chinese industrial revolution. This is a dilemma that the USA has had to deal with both with Japan and, to a lesser extent, China. Japan has been an American ally but has also been an economic competitor. The USA has not relied upon free trade arguments to respond to Japanese competition and has also resorted to threats of and actual retaliation to defend its national interest. One striking example of this was the Japanese attempt to destroy the US semiconductor industry, using their traditional methods of closing their home market to foreign competition and dumping semiconductors on the US and world markets at well below the cost of production. The US semiconductor industry faced extinction. After repeated attempts to resolve this issue, including trade agreements which the Japanese did not honour, and after intense lobbying by the industry association and both houses of Congress, a sympathetic President Reagan acted decisively. He imposed 100% import tariffs on $300million of Japanese electrical goods, including televisions, laptop computers, disc drives, stereo equipment, electric motors and various other consumer goods.

There subsequently emerged a revisionist school of thought concerning Japan. The Revisionists were concerned that the US/Japan trade balance still favoured Japan even after Japan had stopped manipulating its currency and believed that the problem with Japan was more deep-seated. To the Revisionists, Japan could not be treated as just another Western democracy, as Japan was different. In 1989, Robert C. Neff, journalist and expert on Japan, wrote in a *Business Week* article that 'no less than a fundamental rethinking of Japan is now under way at the highest levels of US government, business, and academia. The standard rules of the free market, according to the new school, simply don't work with Japan'.

The Revisionists were able to alter the US thinking towards Japan away from its traditional approach. The goal finally pursued by the Revisionists after much debate, books and articles was that what was needed was a results orientated policy as the Japanese economic system was different to such an extent that it constituted a unique form of capitalism. They argued that the USA needed to respond aggressively to protect its interests. The traditionalist assumption that Japan was another capitalist economy was false; the whole of Japanese society operated in a different manner to the West. It was incorrect to assume that Japan had the same consumer-orientated objectives determined by market forces. Alan Blinder, an economist, put it an article, *There are Capitalists and Then There Are Japanese* in which he argued that 'market capitalism, Japanese-style, departs so much from conventional Western economic thought that it deserves to be considered a different system'.[705] The Revisionists focused on the nature of the Japanese state and its economic bureaucracy with its successful agenda of a nationalistic, Mercantalist industrial strategy geared to develop and protect strategic industries to enhance national strength. The central differences included the use of patent laws to prohibit foreign investments; *dango* – collusion between business organizations; predatory pricing; controls on mergers and acquisitions; and the restriction on free competition by *keiretsu*, which was described by Chalmers Johnson, co-founder of the Japan Policy Research Institute, as a 'form of industrial organization ... [which] makes a mockery of much of the economic theory that is predicated on the workings of "market forces"'.[706] (The *keiretsu* is a system which has a group of companies that have interdependent business relationships and have shareholdings in each other, with a bank at the core which provides funding for the group. During occupation after WWII, the USA's attempt to promote competition by breaking up large industrial organizations, such as Mitsui and Mitsubishi, failed as they recombined with the help of the unreformed banks.)[707]

The threat posed by Japan was described as 'adversarial trade', a term coined by the economist Peter Drucker who said: 'adversarial trade aims at dominating an industry ... [the objective] is to drive the competitor out of the market altogether rather than let it survive'.[708] The Revisionists tended to regard the Japanese economic policy as a form of economic warfare for the 21st century. Chalmers Johnson stated:

> '[If] Japan's foreign economic policy reflects genuine mercantilism – protecting its domestic market, overcharging domestic consumers, using the overcharges to subsidize exports, and predatory pricing abroad to destroy competitors – then GATT rules are irrelevant and policies tailor-made for Japan will be required'.[709]

The fear was that in an economic struggle between the USA with Japan and its 'acolytes' Taiwan and South Korea, the free-trading USA, and the West, will lose. Chalmers Johnson warned that 'the United States must either begin to compete with Japan or go the way of the USSR'.[710] The Revisionists therefore urged that the USA should treat the threat as a matter of importance; should develop its own industrial strategy to target high technology strategic industries; and should take specific action against Japan. Karel van Wolferen, writer and expert on Japan, pointed out that 'international trade legislation of the most general kind is unlikely to have enough effect on Japan. Only action that specifically singles out Japan will be effective'.[711] The type of results orientated approach being urged was that Japan should set aside a portion of their home market for some goods for foreign imports as this was the only way to ensure success.

The American political scientist Samual Huntington (1927-2008) argued that the USA's primacy was being undermined due to Japan 'waging an economic Cold War' and that 'since the 1950s Japan has pursued a strategy designed ... to maximize Japanese economic power ... Japanese strategy is a strategy of economic warfare'. Huntington also cited a statement made by Ishihara Shintaro, a Japanese politician, when he said that 'Economic warfare is the basis for existence in the free world ... the twenty-first century will be a century of economic warfare ... There is no hope for the United States'.[712] Huntington likened the threat posed by Japan to that posed by the Nazis and the Soviet Union:

> 'Japanese strategy, behaviour, and declarations all posit the existence of an economic cold war between Japan and the United States. In the 1930s Chamberlain and Daladier did not take seriously what Hitler said in *Mein Kampf*. Truman

and his successors did take it seriously when Stalin and Khrushchev said, "We will bury you".

Americans would do well to take equally seriously both Japanese declarations of their goal of achieving economic dominance and the strategy they are pursuing to achieve that goal.'[713]

The solution of a managed trade between the USA and Japan was urged even by Henry Kissinger, the former Secretary of State for both President Nixon and President Ford, and Cyrus Vance (1977-1980), the former Secretary of State for President Carter, who argued that there should be an agreement as to the acceptable level of the trade imbalance and then leave it to Japan to figure out how to achieve it. Congress, which in 1987 had been angry at the illegal sale by a Toshiba subsidiary of sensitive submarine technology to the Soviets, also found favour with the demands for a radical approach. The complaint was that hitherto dealing with Japan was 'like trying to peel an onion' and the results had been unimpressive. The relationship between businesses, with the Japanese government, and with each other, was such that the structural barriers, both informal and formal, would continue to defeat US attempts to sell to the Japanese home market. Instead of telling Japan how to run their economy or how to adopt a free market rules and procedures, the USA should come to an agreement to specific import results and leave Japan to introduce policies to achieve that result.

In 1988 Congress passed the Omnibus Trade Act which included the so-called 'Super 301' provision that required the President to take retaliatory action against those countries deemed to be 'unfair traders'. Congress had grown weary of the traditionalist approach to Japan as the attempts to remove trade barriers had been a failure, and was favourable to the Revisionist arguments. Congress had also been in receipt of a large volume of complaints from ordinary people and business interests detailing the horrors of the Japanese home market. The Revisionists were preaching to the converted. Richard Gephardt, the House majority leader, speaking on the anniversary of the attack on Pearl Harbour, said that 'the unrecognised incompatibility of our economic systems is at the root of our current tensions and frictions', particularly citing *keiretsu,* and continued: 'The United States has been handcuffed during the last ten years because of the Reagan and now Bush

Administration's blind ideological adherence to the principle of free trade'.[714] Michael Pettis, a Beijing-based economic theorist and financial strategist, has pointed out:

> 'Whenever foreign purchases of Japanese bonds accelerated, the Bank of Japan intervened heavily, buying US dollar assets as a way of pushing down the value of the yen – effectively converting foreign purchases of yen into foreign purchases of dollars, with the Bank of Japan acting as an intermediary.'[715]

In February 2012, for example, after upward pressure on the yen, Japan openly stated that it would act unilaterally to weaken the yen as necessary.[716] Some of this intervention was hidden as the Japanese Ministry of Finance only records purchases according to where they are made and not who is making them.[717] In the 1970s, Japan's current account surplus averaged 0.7% of GDP. In the 1980s, the surplus rose to 2% of GDP. From 2000 to 2008 the surplus averaged 3.5% of GDP. This is despite a rise in the yen from an exchange rate of one dollar to 300 yen in the early 1970s to a rate of one dollar to 114 yen in the 21st century.[718] A rise in the yen, or fall in the dollar, did not correct the trade surplus (as was the case with Britain in the 1931/32).

In the 1990s, Japan entered a phase of 'growth recession', when its growth was slower than the increase in production capacity potentially allowed. Thus plant and people were becoming idle.[719] Japan entered a decade of stagnation and deflation. Eventually, Japan benefited from rising export growth to both the USA and China, and this growth lifted the economy out of its torpor.[720]

China has been repeatedly accused of manipulating its currency to an artificially low value.[721] Up until 1983, the Chinese were happy for the yuan to be overvalued against the US dollar as it enabled China to import cheaply to develop its infrastructure. In the next 10 years to 1993, the Chinese devalued their currency six times. Next, on 1st January 1994, the Chinese announced a reform of the exchange system and massively devalued the yuan again. This move prompted the US Treasury to designate China a currency manipulator, pursuant to the 1988 Trade Act. China steadily revalued its currency upwards.[722]

The yuan does not trade freely on the currency markets and its usage is tightly controlled by the Peoples' Bank of China (PBOC).

Chinese exporters are required to exchange the foreign currencies for yuan from the PBOC at a rate determined by the PBOC. The PBOC restricts the amount of foreign currency available to pay for imports and further prints yuan to exchange for US dollars in particular. This had the effect of allowing the US to determine the supply of yuan.[723] By 2011 the Chinese foreign reserves were estimated at roughly $2.85trillion. Under pressure from the USA, China increased the value of the yuan.[724]

Despite the harm being done to the US economy, both presidents Bush and Obama have been prepared to take a tolerant view of the value of the Chinese currency for geopolitical reasons.[725] However, on 11th October 2011, the US Senate passed the Currency Exchange Rate Oversight Reform Act, which would allow any 'fundamentally misaligned' currency to be labelled a subsidy and therefore imports from that country would be subject to tariffs. The bill was revived in 2013 and in 2014 two senior American senators, Sherrod Brown and Jeff Sessions, urged President Obama to support the act and in a letter stated: 'China's currency manipulation weakens our economic recovery and makes US exports less competitive, which is why we must combat it with every tool in our toolbox'. In August 2015, to the anger of many Americans, China devalued the yuan to help its export drive in response to its less booming economy. China was, again, accused of not playing by the rules. Donald Trump, a republican presidential candidate, said: 'They're just destroying us. They keep devaluing their currency until they get it right. They're doing a big cut in the yuan, and that's going to be devastating for us'. The British government, yet again, stayed silent and was unmoved by Chinese economic aggression.

While China has low tariffs, it has generous subsidies for favoured domestic enterprises, discriminates against foreign firms and compels them to hand over technology, and further tolerates open intellectual-property theft. The yuan only floats in a particular direction when China is under pressure from the USA.[726]

In June 2009, China, despite its public utterances about supporting free trade and commitments to rebalance Chinese output towards the domestic economy, introduced larger tax rebates, more generous loans from state-owned banks and government-funded travel for exporters. Simultaneously, China banned all local, provincial and national government agencies from buying imported goods unless there was no domestic supplier.

China also restricted the export of raw materials, such as bauxite and zinc, of which China is the world's largest producer, in order to damage foreign firms and favour domestic ones. China further intervened heavily on the currency markets to halt the rise of the yuan. Provincial governments also cut back on the enforcement of counterfeiting laws.[727]

When China joined the WTO in November 2001, it gained full access to foreign markets, pledging that it would join the agreement on government procurement 'as soon as possible'. In fact it has continued to favour domestic firms for its vast state sector; this is important as China remains a communist state, and so the size and power of the state is substantial. The USA imports $4 worth of goods for every $1 of exports to China.[728] According to the ONS, Britain imports roughly three times the value it exports to China, and imports from Japan are roughly 170% the value of exports to Japan.

In September 2009, the European Chamber of Commerce in China drew up a report complaining of the extent of Chinese protectionism. Foreign companies were being 'excluded outright' from China's service sector. China was using an array of technical regulations and certification procedures to block foreign companies. China has not once permitted the takeover of a local firm by a foreign company. Two colonels in the Chinese Peoples' Liberation Army wrote in 1999:

> 'Financial warfare has now officially come to war's centre stage – a stage that for thousands of years has been occupied only by soldiers and weapons ... We believe that before long, "financial warfare" will undoubtedly be an entry in the ... dictionaries of official military jargon. Moreover, when people revise the history books on twentieth-century warfare ... the section on financial warfare will command the reader's utmost attention ... Today, when nuclear weapons have already become frightening mantelpiece decorations that are losing their real operational value ... financial war has become a "hyperstrategic" weapon that is attracting the attention of the world. This is because financial war is easily manipulated and allows for concealed actions, and is also highly destructive.'[729]

That China is prepared to use economic measures to exert pressure – or as a form of warfare – is not just idle chatter. In July 2010, China announced a cut of 72% in its export of rare earths, which are necessary for certain manufactured products such as electronics. Following a row with Japan over some disputed islands and the arrest of a Chinese trawler captain who had collided with a Japanese patrol vessel, China ceased all rare earth exports to Japan. Japan retaliated by forcing down the value of the yen against the Chinese currency. Eventually the trawler captain was released and Japan issued an apology.[730]

Between 2004 and 2009, China secretly doubled its stock of gold.[731] That stock increased again by 60% up to 2015.[732] The aim of this is to reduce China's dependence on the US dollar and to present the yuan as a reserve currency to the IMF.

The effect of China's trade policies are also impacting upon the Third World. China has become Iran's biggest trade partner, and is also happy to deal with any pariah state including Sudan, Burma and Zimbabwe. In November 2011, the journalist Damian Thompson wrote in the *Daily Telegraph*:

> 'There's a school of thought which says that China's *modus operandi*, however brutal, at least gets things built. In contrast, Western aid is tipped into dictator's pockets without anything to show for it. But the benefits of Beijing's "investment" are elusive, because the Chinese don't usually employ Africans to perform anything but menial tasks. Chinese construction engineers build motorways and hospitals without passing on the skills to maintain them. The result: everything falls into disrepair within a decade, by which time the copper is safely out of the ground.'[733]

China's looming superpower status renders it a major destabilizing influence. This is worsened by it being a continuing communist regime. China's share of global output has increased from 5% in 1950 to 15% by the start of the 21st century.[734] China's market reforms started in 1978, when its industrial production was $59billion; in 2003, industrial production was $844billion. Between 1982 and 2003, China's exports increased from $44billion to $428billion.[735] China is the second-biggest consumer of energy in the world. In the 21st century, China has accounted for almost all the increase in global demand for tin, nickel, lead and zinc. About half the increase in global demand for aluminium and copper is accounted for by China and China also accounted for 30% of the increase in global demand for oil.[736] China's GDP doubled between 1992 and 2000.[737] China's export growth and the cheapness of its goods due to low wages and production costs, exported low prices across the world.[738] As with many a newly developing country, China ran trade deficits up until 2004. The US trade deficit with China was less than $50billion in 1997, but it steadily increased, reaching $124billion in 2003 and then leapt to $234billion in 2006.[739] The British trade deficit with China was £21billion in 2012. If China maintains its current rate of growth, then in 30 years time its economy will be the same size as that of the USA and its oil consumption will be equivalent to all of today's global oil output (in practice this will not happen due to market forces, but the strain that will be placed on the world's resources is clear).[740] In October 2014, figures from the IMF, using purchasing power parity (PPP), put China as the world's largest economy being worth £11trillion compared to £10.8trillion for the USA. – without using PPP China's economy is still behind the USA's being worth £6.4trillion.

In October 2015, according to the magazine Hurun, China has the largest number of billionaires, with 596 compared to 537 in the USA. India has the third largest number, with 97, ahead of Russia, with 93, and Britain with 80.

Only 2.1% of Japan's exports went to China in 1990. By 1995, that figure had increased to around 5%. By 2001, the figure had increased to 7.7% and had reached 16% by 2008.[741] Since the early 1990s these rising exports have been dominated by capital goods, which China needs to develop its industry. FDI follows growth and is drawn to high-growth economies. It does not create high-growth economies unless the potential profits are identifiable. FDI prefers good infrastructure and a skilled, flexible workforce. FDI tends to bring short-run benefits, where development requires the long term. Being the world's biggest recipient, China is receiving about 10% of the world's FDI.[742] Japanese multinationals sought to buy cheaper supplies of industrial components from China rather than from more expensive Japanese ones, which is one reason why capital goods were being exported. In effect, these exports were an export of jobs for while Japanese exports were increasing, the Japanese economy stagnated. The Japanese economy's growth slowed from 4% per annum in the 1980s to only 1% per annum since.

The migration from the rural areas of China to the industrial complexes involves tens of millions of young workers living in overcrowded dormitories, working 70 hour weeks and having few if any amenities or leisure activities.[743] It is estimated that in the year 1000 Chinese per capita incomes were slightly higher than European ones. By 1820, Chinese per capita incomes were half European levels.[744] By the 1960s, Chinese per capita incomes had fallen to as low as 8% of European ones.[745] China's per capita incomes are now 5% those of the USA; Brazil's are 12%; Russia's are 15%; and India's are 2%.[746] When Ricardo was developing his theory of comparative advantage, such poor countries did not have access to Western capital. Now they do, and the transportation costs of goods is so low as to be negligible. This means that multinationals can take full advantage of low, if any, tariffs, export capital and production facilities to exploit the cheap labour and relatively unregulated industrial conditions of the developing world to maximise their profits. In effect they are transferring jobs from the West to the developing world. The G7 share of global GDP has fallen from 70.5% in 1971 to 61.1% in 2008, while the BRIC (Brazil, Russia, India and China) countries share has increased from 3.3% to 11.6%.[747] In December 2013, the Centre for Economics and Business Research (CEBR) forecast that China will become the world's largest economy in 2028, overtaking the USA. Currently, China's GDP is roughly half that of the USA's. India is set to overtake Japan within 15 years and will have the world's third largest GDP by 2028, overtaking Britain in 2023. Ricardo's assumptions of comparative advantage no longer apply. Stephen King wrote:

> 'As emerging economies have increasingly specialized in the activities that used to take place in the West, the developed world has struggled to work out what to do next. In Japan, the cost has been seen in economic stagnation. In the US and the UK, the costs can be seen in the form of inflated financial sectors operating in a global casino which, unlike Las Vegas, has no hard-and-fast rules.'[748]

The experience of Japan in relation to China may now be spreading to other Western countries. In 1988, 1.6% of US exports went to China. By 1998, 2.1% of US exports went to China. By 2008, 5.5% of US exports went to China. Yet China exports four times as much to the USA as USA exports to China. The USA's current account is $308billion in deficit with China in 2008.[749] The USA has been able to borrow cheaply, despite the size of its deficit and the consequent need to attract savings, because of the abundant savings available from China and others. It does not need to raise interest rates to attract internal savers and the low interest rates facilitate high levels of borrowing.

The high levels of Chinese savings are, in part at least, a consequence of the lack of sophistication of China's financial services. For example, China does not have the developed pensions industry that the West has, where pensions can take account of the different death rates with annuities being payable. In the absence of this, people can only save a capital sum in the bank and not insure themselves. China's liberalization meant that ordinary Chinese lost the work unit to which they belonged, and hence lost the employment, educational, medical and retirement support that the work unit used to provide. Now these costs have been transferred from the state to the households themselves, and thus household incomes have been reduced, and their need to save has been increased.[750] Nor does China have the social welfare provisions of a welfare state. They do not have an NHS and people can only provide for potential illnesses by saving a capital sum in the bank. Nor is it possible to buy on hire purchase or credit cards. This is a common situation in the Third World. In China, deposit savings rates have been negative for many years. Even so, household saving remains high.[751]

Countries can run trade deficits for many years, especially when they are developing and in the midst of major investment in the economy. This applied to the USA in the 19th century. It may be natural for a country that is developing to run trade deficits, yet these deficits will self-correct when the investment ultimately increases the country's productive capacity. At this time the country may begin to run trade surpluses as it repays the foreign capital. A country must have a trade surplus in order to repay foreign capital or to invest abroad.[752] However, when there are trade imbalances that are not caused by high levels of productive investment in the deficit country, but by policy distortions or institutional factors distorting the trade flows, then these policy distortions prevent the adjustment (such as a falling exchange rate) taking place. Michael Pettis wrote: 'Large and persistent trade imbalances, in other words, are almost always caused by distortions in financial, industrial, or trade polices'.[753] When these imbalances continue in the face of continued policy or institutional obstruction, then the ultimate adjustment may be dramatic and can take the form of a financial crisis. For Michael Pettis:

> 'The main imbalances of recent years were the very large trade surpluses during the past decade of China, Germany, and Japan and the very large trade deficits of the United States and peripheral Europe. There are many precedents to the global crisis through which we are living. In fact many, if not most, of the global and regional crises that preceded it during the past two hundred years were driven by the same kinds of imbalances, most famously the global crisis in the 1930s and the so-called LDC (less developed countries) crisis in the 1980s.'[754]

For Michael Pettis, the imbalances were due to policy distortions in both the surplus and deficit countries; 'the large deficits led to unsustainable increases in debt and, ultimately, to the deleveraging process necessary to restore balance. It is this deleveraging process that is at the heart of the global financial crisis'.[755] The historian Robin Blackburn, in *Age Shock*, wrote:

> 'The huge imbalances racked up during the boom years of the global economy (1992-2007) were the product of an ever widening US deficit and the ever-growing Chinese surplus. Chinese workers or farmers were not paid enough to become good customers for overseas products, while in the US the low paid and the poor (subprime) borrowers were taking on debt – especially housing debt – that they soon found impossible to service.
> The over-borrowing and asset bubbles that resulted were aggravated by financial deregulations, and by the greed and subterfuge of the banks. The heedless pursuit of short-term profit led to the largest destruction of value in world history. Huge public deficits had to be incurred to prevent collapse. Now those are to be paid for by slashing public spending and shrinking social protection for many decades to come. The welfare state is to be dismantled at a time

when higher unemployment and an ageing population make this a certain recipe for destitution and widening misery.'[756]

Stephen King took a similar line:

'The Bank of England's policy of raising interest rates more or less continuously from 2003 to 2007 triggered huge capital inflows from abroad. These were then invested by UK financial institutions in low-quality junk bonds, helping fuel a real-estate boom. While the inflows also pushed up the sterling exchange rate, thereby keeping a lid on inflation, the economy as a whole became increasingly unbalanced, paving the way for the credit crunch that followed later in the decade.'[757]

This blame on the Bank of England and the British government policy ignores the involvement of the British banks in the USA subprime mortgage calamity, their reckless lending to overseas entities, and their own flawed business models.

A 'country's current account surplus is by definition equal to the excess of domestic savings over domestic investment',[758] the excess savings not used for domestic investment are invested abroad. When a country has a net investment abroad, then it must run a trade surplus to create the foreign currency needed for the investment. Krugman explained: 'If a country is running a deficit on its current account – buying more goods than it sells – it must correspondingly be running an equal surplus on its capital account – selling more assets than it buys. And the converse is equally true: a country that runs a surplus on capital account must run a deficit on current account'.[759] Keynes had always warned that those countries with a trade surplus were just as much to blame as those with a trade deficit. Michael Pettis wrote: 'If foreign central banks increase their currency intervention by buying more US dollars, their current account surplus necessarily rises, along with the US current account deficit. This makes it very easy to determine which government receives the most "help" from foreign investors. The math is simple. The larger a country's current account deficit as a share of GDP, the more "help" that country's government gets from foreign investors to buy its bonds;'[760] and further: 'Rich countries like the United States (and Europe for that matter) do not need foreign help in funding domestic borrowing needs. Net foreign borrowing funds the debt or investment associated with the current account deficit – nothing more'.[761] Those countries which are struggling to fund their deficits have a problem with credibility and are feared to be in danger of default – it is not that they need to attract surplus countries to lend to them.

There are three accounting identities that must be true: firstly, 'for every country, the current account and the capital account must balance to zero. To put it another way, every dollar that enters a country, either in payment for that country's exports ... must leave that country, either in payment for imports ... or in the form of outward investment ... [because] it will use that dollar to purchase something from abroad or to make a foreign payment, or it will save the dollar by purchasing a US asset. There is nothing else it can do with the dollar ... one way or the other the dollar must leave the country through the current or capital account, so the sum of dollars entering the country and dollars leaving the country is always equal to zero';[762] secondly, 'for every country, the difference between total domestic savings and total domestic investment is equal to the net amount of capital imported or exported, and so is equal to the current account surplus or deficit';[763] thirdly, 'everything that a country produces must be either consumed or saved ... because the total of goods and services that a country produces is generally defined as its gross domestic product, or GDP, then a country's savings can be defined simply as its GDP less total household and other consumption'.[764]

By applying these accounting definitions, Michael Pettis asserts that: 'If China exports less capital, its trade surplus will decline. This is an arithmetical necessity'.[765] Michael Pettis further stated: 'Anything that affects the gap between production and consumption also affects the savings rate, it must also affect the gap between savings and investment'.[766]

For Michael Pettis, a tariff on foreign imports increases the cost of the imports and therefore reduces household incomes as more money is now needed to buy the imports. Consequently, on this logic, the amount of total goods and services bought must fall, as there is less money to buy them. Therefore, unless the government uses the tax revenues from the tariff to increase consumption, then savings must rise – savings being the difference between total production and total consumption. If there is no change in domestic investment, then the savings will be invested abroad. Therefore, 'the imposition of the tariff itself automatically forced up the national savings rate by reducing household consumption, and this forced down the trade deficit'.[767]

These accounting definitions may be true, but the logic is flawed in that it ignores cause and effect. Taken simply, the logic advanced is that China has a trade surplus because it invests overseas, which is obviously wrong. China may be able to *continue* its trade surplus because it invests overseas. To put it at its simplest and set it out in terms of a barter, China has offered to sell goods in return not for other goods, but for ownership of lucrative assets. A responsible country would refuse to deal with China on those terms. Michael Pettis's logic is also flawed regarding the effect of a tariff on imports. The flaw is the assumption that there would be no change in domestic investment. If a tariff is imposed, then there would be an increase in tax revenues to the government; demand would be redirected towards domestic producers who would then seek to expand output *by increased investment*; and the increased expenditure in the home economy, reinforced by the multiplier effect, would lead to an increase in consumption.

Michael Pettis explained the Asian growth model thus:

> 'Many Asian countries have followed the growth model established in the 1960s and 1970s by Japan, and this growth model includes crucially these three conditions:
> - Systematically undervalued currencies, in which the central bank intervenes in the currency to reduce its exchange value
> - Relatively low wage growth, in which wages grow more slowly than improvements in worker productivity
> - Financial repression, in which the state allocates credit and the central bank forces interest rates to below their natural or equilibrium rate.'[768]

Financial repression is at the heart of the Asian model, and of the imbalances of those countries. Carmen Reinhart, Jacob Kierkegaard and Belen Sbrancia in an article, defined financial repression thus:

> 'Financial repression occurs when governments implement policies to channel to themselves funds that in a deregulated market environment would go elsewhere. Policies include

directed lending to the government by captive domestic audiences (such as pension funds or domestic banks), explicit or implicit caps on interest rates, regulation of cross-border capital movements, and (generally) a tighter connection between government and banks, either explicitly through public ownership of some of the banks or through heavy "moral suasion".

Financial repression is also sometimes associated with relatively high reserve requirements (or liquidity requirements), securities transaction taxes, prohibition of gold purchases, or the placement of significant amounts of government debt that is nonmarketable. In the current policy discussion, financial repression issues come under the broad umbrella of "macro-prudential regulation", which refers to government efforts to ensure the health of an entire financial system.'[769]

Unlike the West, the more protectionist Asian countries, such as Japan and China, are openly manipulating their currency values and their financial sectors to their own advantage – even to the detriment of their own population. In China, where household savings are high, a cut in interest rates reduces household income and therefore reduces demand.[770] Higher interest rates can make people feel more wealthy and hence increase their consumption. Yet China is determined to manage the economy to the benefit of its manufacturing industry at the expense of the living standards of ordinary people. Michael Pettis pointed out:

> 'China in recent years has generated what is probably the largest trade surplus as a share of global GDP in history. Although many analysts describe this as evidence of a very successful growth model in which the trade surplus derives from good planning and fundamental strengths within the Chinese economy ... the Chinese trade surplus is actually a symptom of very distorted and unsustainable domestic policies, the reversal of which will be fraught with difficulty. It is a mistake to characterize China as an export-driven economy. China is an investment-driven economy. The trade surplus is a residual result of investment-related policies that force up the savings rate to levels above the investment rate.'

Although the high investment rate that China, as a developing country, would normally be matched by a deficit as foreign investment pours in, in fact the high investment is surpassed by the high savings. In the 1980s China's household savings fluctuated between 10% and 20% of disposable income; by 1990 they had reached 12% to 15% of disposable income; by 1998 they reached between 24% and 25%, and more recently even 26% of disposable income.[771] In 1990, investment was around 23% of GDP; it rose to 31% of GDP in the period 1992 to 1994 before climbing after 1997 to reach 50% by 2011.[772]

There are a variety of factors leading to the high savings: an undervalued currency, slow wage growth, a weakening of social safety nets, and financial repression:

> 'Growth strategies engineered by Beijing forced households to subsidize investment and production, thus generating rapid economic and employment growth at the expense of household income growth. It is the lagging growth in household income ... that has primarily constrained household consumption growth.'[773]

From 1990 to 2002 household income fluctuated between 64% to 72% of GDP. It peaked in 1992 before falling back to 66% of GDP in 2002. It has since fallen to less than 50% of GDP.[774] Since 2000, Chinese productivity has tripled while wages have doubled.[775] China's growth rate since 2000 has been between 10% and 11% annually, while household income, and hence household consumption, has increased between 7% and 9% annually.[776] This is taking place in a communist country.

China's financial system is comprehensively repressed. Nearly all household savings are in bank deposits and banks are controlled by the monetary authorities, who decide the direction of credit and set the interest rates. The PBOC, controlled by the State Council, sets the maximum deposit rate and minimum lending rate which banks are compelled to adhere to. Both rates are set very low and so resources are essentially transferred to borrowers, such as state-owned organizations, infrastructure investors and other favoured institutions. Because the difference between saving rate and lending rate is high, banks are guaranteed a high profit.[777] Depositors are unable to transfer capital out of the country. Local stock markets are primitive and rife with insider dealing. Depositors have little option but to accept the low savings rates. Despite China's large and low-paid workforce, the Chinese industrial revolution is very heavily capital intensive due to the low cost of capital – as fixed by the state.[778]

While investment can help develop an LDC's infrastructure, by transforming dirt tracks into roads, for example, there is an increasing danger that, as time passes and the country develops, that the quality of the investment declines; that roads are needlessly transformed into motorways, for example. Vanity projects creep in. With very low interest rates bad investment might be a waste, but its economic viability may be passable, provided low interest rates are maintained. But if interest rates increase, then firms with large borrowings will be forced into financial difficulties. Over-investment can destroy wealth.

China is exposed to being dependent upon export markets for too large a part of its output. If those export markets decline, or disappear, perhaps because the countries can no longer afford the goods, then China's growth model will be in difficulty. China needs to invest overseas due to its trade surpluses and its determination to stop its currency appreciating. China's potential problems are for China to sort out; what matters to Britain and other Western countries is the harm caused to them by China's policies and what they need to do about that. Krugman wrote: 'It's long past time to take a tougher line on China and other currency manipulators, and sanction them if necessary'.[779]

South Korea likewise has successfully industrialized by using protectionist measures. The Korean war resulted in four million deaths in three years, the destruction of 75% of South Korea's railways and half of its manufacturing base. Eight years after the conclusion of the war, in 1961, South Korean average income was less than half that of Ghana.[780] Since then, South Korean per capita income has risen roughly 14 times, an increase that took Britain two centuries to achieve and the USA one and a half centuries to achieve.[781] Despite, or because of, President Park's 'auto-coup' in the early 1970s, when parliament was dissolved and a rigged voting system introduced, between 1972 and 1979, there was a nine-fold increase in exports and a five-fold increase in per capita income.[782] In 1975, average wages in South Korea were only 5% of those in the USA; by 2006 they had increased to 62% of those in the USA.[783] This growth is against a background of the threat posed from North Korea and democratic instability.

The government put great emphasis on the need for foreign currency and the need to export; buying foreign cigarettes was not only a social stigma but also illegal, and those doing so were branded as 'traitors'.[784] Foreign currency was too important and needed for industrial development to be squandered on luxury items, including small cars, whisky and biscuits, which were subject to import bans, high tariffs and 'luxury consumption taxes'. Foreign travel was banned unless it was for business or studies and had government permission.[785] Violation of the foreign exchange controls ultimately carried the death penalty.[786]

Working conditions were grim. Girls from poor families in the countryside were often forced to work when they left primary school, aged 12. There were 12-hour working days in the textile and garment factories, and conditions in other factories were similar. The average working week was 53-54 hours.[787] There were urban slums where families of five or six lived in one room and hundreds of people had to share a toilet and a standpipe for water.[788] South Korea up until the late 1980s was one of the pirate capitals of the world, producing counterfeit goods such as Nike shoes and Louis Vuitton bags.[789] In 2007, South Korea's per capita income was similar to Portugal's.[790]

South Korea achieved this spectacular economic surge, not by liberal free trade economics, but by mercantalist policies, including protectionism and even by creating SOEs.[791] Foreign investment was not allowed unless it was in favoured sectors.[792] North Korea used to be richer than South Korea, mainly due to the Japanese development during Korea's period as a Japanese possession. It was not until the 1960s that the south overtook the north. South Korea is now in favour of free trade.[793]

Despite a lot of talk of there being an export-led recovery, manufacturing only accounts for 10% of Britain's national output and is too small for a depreciated currency to have a major effect. Britain exports as much to Ireland as it does to Brazil, Russia, India and China put together.[794]

Even the biggest creditor countries, China, Germany and Japan, are actively pursuing a policy of export-led growth.[795] Britain and the USA are pursuing export-led growth. In January 2010, President Obama announced the National Export Initiative, which had the aim of doubling US exports within five years. If successful, this would increase GDP by 1.3% and increase growth from 2.6% to 3.9%.[796] No country is prepared to allow a large rise in imports. It is an arithmetical impossibility for every country to have export-led growth. Someone, somewhere, has to allow a rise in net imports. In the face of other countries pursuing policies of export-led growth, and in the face of protectionist measures including undervalued currencies, then a British policy of export-led growth for its enfeebled manufacturing sector is doomed to failure. For Britain, talk of export-led growth is a cop-out to avoid facing the reality that the real problem is the import penetration of the home market, and hence a cop-out to avoid countenancing the need to reduce that import penetration – in other words the policy is a mechanism for avoiding the real lessons of the inter-war years; that it was tariff reform that extricated Britain from the 1930s Slump.

Despite the fall in the value of sterling in 2008-2009, Britain's export performance has remained poor. In 2012, for example, Germany, France, Italy, Spain and Greece all were better at producing exports than Britain. Angola is a more important trading partner to China than Britain.[797] Of the 194 items of the 2012 Olympics memorabilia (the Olympics being staged in Britain) only 9% were made in Britain whereas 62% were made in China.[798]

Britain's trade imbalance will not be helped by the fact that in the year to December 2013 Sterling had risen significantly against other major currencies. It had risen by 29.8% against the Indonesian Rupiah, 24.7% against the South African Rand, 2.4% against the Japanese Yen, 18.4% against the Turkish Lira, 18.2% against the Australian Dollar and only 1.7% against the US Dollar. The Bank of England warned that the 10% rise in the value of Sterling against the US Dollar since the summer, and more than 4% against the euro, is in danger of stifling the economic recovery. The consequence of a continuing weak recovery is serious. In July 2013 Robert Chote of The Office for Budget Responsibility claimed that: 'It is clear that longer-term spending pressures, if unaddressed, would put finances on an unsustainable path'. Britain's GDP is £1.6trillion. Government collects £600billion in tax, but spends £700billion. At 2.5% growth the economy grows by £40billion annually. A lower growth rate has a significant impact on tax revenues and hence the budget deficit.

The USA, despite its free trade rhetoric, has always been far more practical and pragmatic than Britain, and has always been far more ready to defend its economic interests. The Nixon shock and Reagan's reaction to Japanese dumping are but two examples. Another, also involving the Reagan administration, was the Plaza Accord of 1985, which was an agreement between France, West Germany, the USA, Britain and Japan to depreciate the US dollar against the Japanese and German currencies. The USA was running a trade deficit of 3.5% of GDP while Japan and West Germany had large surpluses. The US dollar had appreciated sharply. This policy agreement was announced and that the central banks would be intervening to carry it out. The immediate effect of the announcement was that the dollar depreciated by 4% against a basket of currencies and by slightly more against the Japanese and German currencies. The dollar continued to fall and the central banks spent $10billion to ensure this in the following months. The policy was a success in that the USA trade deficit fell and the USA staged a recovery from a recession, however the deficit with Japan continued – the reasons for which are dealt with above.

In contrast to the mercantalist policies of the BRIC countries, or the hard-headed approach adopted by the USA or Germany, Britain has remained blindly committed to a puritanical interpretation of Ricardo's theory in the face of a steadily deteriorating economic position. Far from helping British manufacturing the government, either Labour or the Tory/Liberal Democrat coalition or Tory, regard helping British manufacturing as being something beneath it – even in the depths of the 2008/13 depression. For example, there was the awarding of the largest-ever order for inter-city trains, worth £7.5billion, to the Japanese firm Hitachi instead of the British firm Bombardier in February 2009 – in the early stages of the credit crunch. The Labour government boasted that 12,500 new jobs would be created and safeguarded, omitting to mention that only 500 of these would be in Britain. Despite all the spin, it quickly emerged that of the first 10 trains, 70 vehicles, would be made in Japan and the outer shells and parts of the bogies of the other 1,330 vehicles would also be made in Japan. Bob Crow, the general secretary of the biggest rail union, the RMT, said: 'We have been campaigning long and hard to protect what is left of Britain's train-making capacity and skills base, and if the basic manufacture of these [train] sets is to be undertaken elsewhere today's announcement will have been a triumph of spin over substance. We need to know why the order was not placed with Bombardier, which has established train-building capacity and a skilled workforce in Derby'. Derby North Labour MP Bob Laxton said: 'This is a crass decision which gives the Japanese an opportunity of getting into the UK market. I don't believe for one moment the figure of 12,500 jobs because work will be brought into the UK from overseas'. The Department for Transport said that: 'Both bids were deliverable and substantially compliant, and so comprehensively evaluating and choosing between them was a lengthy process'.[799]

Unfortunately, this was not the end of the Bombardier saga, as the incoming Tory/Liberal Democrat coalition government was just as hostile to British manufacturing as Labour. In 2013, in preference to Bombardier, the German firm Siemens was given the contract to build 1,140 train carriages for the Thameslink route, worth £1.4billion, and this deal came two years after Bombardier had suffered 1,000 job losses and a suspension of its apprenticeship scheme as a result of yet another order for new rolling stock going to Siemens.[800] It subsequently emerged that one of the reasons why Bombardier lost the contract was because the government, by setting out requirements for private finance, unduly set the criteria in favour of Siemens, which is the richer company with greater financial resources.[801] It subsequently emerged that with orders from other countries, Siemens had undertaken to have the carriages assembled locally, but this had not been required with the Thameslink order.[802] This further kick in the teeth for a capable British firm put its existence at stake, leaving it dependent upon a £1billion Crossrail project for its survival. Fortunately, Bombardier won the Crossrail contract after strong lobbying from the local and national press and other interested parties. Yet the fact remains that foreign firms were awarded £8.9billion worth of contracts and the British based firm won only a £1billion contract – *and this was in an economic slump.*

A similar story can be told regarding the Royal Navy, which will now operate ships built in South Korea rather than built in England. In February 2012, the government awarded a contract to build four new fuel tankers, worth £452million, to Daewoo Shipbuilding and Marine Engineering, with all four ships being built at Daewoo's yard at Okpo-dong in south-east South Korea which produces 70 commercial and specialist ships (such as the South Korean Navy's destroyers) every year. This is despite the potential redundancies hanging over Portsmouth and despite the promise of one of the final bids, from the Italian firm Fincantieri, including an undertaking to build one of the vessels in Britain and that 35% of the work on all four vessels would take place in Britain – 15% more than Daewoo. Of the three final bids, two were from South Korea and one from Italy. That there was no final bid from a British firm speaks volumes.[803]

Another example of the failure of British business acumen is Jaguar Land Rover (JLR), which was taken over by the Indian firm Tata in 2008. JLR announced in 2013 that it would be forming a partnership in China with the Cherry Automobile Company to build a manufacturing plant at Changshu, and also that it would commence an investment of £240million to build a factory in Rio de Janeiro capable of producing 24,000 vehicles a year. One of the reasons cited was that it would enable JLR to avoid paying Brazil's high import tariffs. In February 2014, JLR announced that it would build its XJ saloon car in India. This means that there are now three Third World manufacturing bases for JLR vehicles. This overseas production can be beneficial, if it reduces tariffs for example, but it does mean that production which might have taken place in Britain is being transferred overseas, with the profits going to Tata. Furthermore, this cheaper overseas production could easily grow at the expense of the British.[804] Tata are quite open about this and describe it as their global strategy: 'The creation of new international plants allows Jaguar Land Rover to increase its presence in regions that have been identified as having growth potential, protect against currency fluctuations and achieve a more efficient, globally competitive business'. In August 2015, that strategy included a new plant to be opened in Slovakia to manufacture Land Rovers.

Far from defending British interests regarding Chinese trade measures, the Tory Government remains wedded to free trade theories and have convinced themselves that the Chinese think likewise. In a trip to China in December 2013, David Cameron said: 'I see China's rise as an opportunity not just for the people of this country but for Britain and the world. Britain wants China to realise its dream and I believe we can help each other succeed in the global race', and that: 'Some in Europe and elsewhere see the world changing and want to shut China off behind a bamboo curtain of trade barriers. Britain wants to tear these trade barriers down. An open Britain is the ideal partner for an opening China ... No country in the world is more open to Chinese investment than the UK'. Cameron promised to 'champion an EU-China trade deal with as much determination as I am championing the EU-US trade deal'. Cameron continued: 'Britain is uniquely placed to make the case for deepening the European Union's trade and investment relationship with China. Building on the recent launch of EU-China negotiations on investment, and on China's continued commitment to economic reform, I now want to set a new long term goal of an ambitious and comprehensive EU-China free trade agreement. And as I have on the EU-US deal, so I will put my full political weight behind such a deal, which could be worth tens of billions of dollars every year'. Cameron believed that eliminating tariffs in the 20 sectors where they are highest, such as vehicles, pharmaceuticals and electrical goods, could save UK exporters £600m a year. The £600million a year saving is paltry when set against the £21billion trade deficit that Britain has with China. Given that the Chinese have yet to honour their previous commitments to abide by free trade principles, a free trade deal with China is the exact opposite of what Britain needs. Britain needs measures to redress the trade imbalance and not just more measures to increase trade, when such trade is so heavily in China's favour. Cameron's statement that 'no country in the world is as open to Chinese investment' than Britain, means that he is happy for the trade deficit with China to continue; that the Chinese should buy British assets rather than British goods.

Another example of the British government's naiveté in dealing with China, is the announcement in October 2013 that Britain would enter into a generous deal with the Chinese to allow them ownership of British nuclear power plants. Chinese state owned companies CGN and CNNC would be allowed to take a 40% stake in the company planning to build the Hinkley C nuclear power station in Somerset. Furthermore, Mr Osborne announced that the Chinese firms could become 'majority owners of a British nuclear power plant subject to British safety rules and policed by the British' – this was in response to a condition set by the Chinese before they would agree for the Hinkley C investment to proceed.[805]

Tory MP Dr Phillip Lee said it was 'perverse' and 'Orwellian' to allow Chinese state owned firms a role in critical infrastructure projects like nuclear power at a time when questions over Chinese cyber-attacks on the West had not been resolved, and that future conflicts would not be about the 'physical possession of nations' but would involve 'control of information, control of infrastructure, water electricity and communication'. The CNNC website states:

> 'China National Nuclear Corporation (CNNC) is the large state-owned enterprise under the direct management of the central government. Historically, CNNC successfully developed the atomic bomb, hydrogen bomb and nuclear submarines and built the first nuclear plant in the main land of China. CNNC is the main body of the national nuclear technology industry, the core of the national strategic nuclear deterrence.'

Labour MP Dr Alan Whitehead called CNNC an 'arm of the state' and that 'there doesn't appear to be a clear distinction between the role of the Chinese National Nuclear Corporation in developing civil nuclear and developing and forwarding military nuclear'. He pointed out that 'Big corporations particularly national corporations in China are not companies in the way that we would see them in the UK,' and that the Chinese military – the People's Liberation Army – would be involved in some of the decisions made by the firm.

Peter Atherton of the City firm Liberum Capital said they were 'flabbergasted' by the deal. At £8bn per reactor, Hinkley Point is 'the most expensive power station in the world (excluding hydro schemes) on a per megawatt basis,' said Mr Atherton, and that the French and Chinese state-owned firms would earn between £65bn and £80bn in dividends from British consumers over the project's lifetime, being allowed to charge nearly double the current wholesale cost of electricity. Would any other leading country conduct its affairs in this way? The Chinese have a track record of gaining highly favourable deals from backward if not corrupt countries in Africa. Would any other country offer such a deal to Britain? The Tories are supposed to oppose nationalized industries although it would seem that opposition does not apply to foreign ones.

The Hinkley Point deal was followed in June 2014 with a deal signed during a visit by the Chinese prime minister, Li Keqiang, which enabled China to design, own and run British power stations outright. In addition, Mr Li expressed an interest in other infrastructure projects such as HS2 high speed rail project. The day following this deal, the Chinese Global Times, owned by the communist party, took issue to reports that Mr Li had demanded to meet the Queen, and stated: 'A rising country should understand the embarrassment of an old declining empire and at times the eccentric acts it takes to hide such embarrassment ... Britain's national strength cannot be placed in the same rank as China now, a truth difficult to accept for some Britons'.

Another example is Huawei. In October 2013 George Osborne said: 'Huawei and Rekoo's investment into the UK is a great testament to Britain's tech industry and I am here to make sure that relationship goes from strength to strength'. Huawei is building a £125million research and development centre in Britain. There are concerns expressed by MPs that Huawei, which a US Congressional Committee has called for American companies to blackball due to national security concerns, is monitoring peoples' internet usage via the infrastructure it provides to BT and O2. Huawei was founded by a former officer in the People's Liberation Army. One assumes that the government is not keen on Huawei as a means of stepping up its own eavesdropping activities.

The government's attitude towards China was demonstrated by David Cameron's trip to China in December 2013, when he wrote in a Chinese magazine:

> 'Last year China became the world's largest trading nation. Next year China is set to become the world's largest importer of goods and later this century it will become the world's biggest economy. We should be clear that there is a genuine choice for every country over how to respond to this growing openness and success. They can choose to see China's rise as a threat or an opportunity. They can protect their markets from China or open their markets to China. They can try and shut China out – or welcome China as a partner at the top table of global affairs. Britain's answer is clear. We want to see China succeed'.

David Cameron proposed a free trade deal between the EU and China, and undertook to be China's strongest advocate in the West. The Global Times, owned by the Communist Party People's Daily newspaper, immediately responded: 'The Cameron administration should acknowledge that the UK is not a big power in the eyes of the Chinese', and continued, 'We've discovered that Britain is easily replaceable in China's European foreign policy. Moreover,

Britain is no longer any kind of "big country", but merely a country of old Europe suitable for tourism and overseas study, with a few decent football teams', and concluded, 'We wish Prime Minister Cameron and his delegation a pleasant visit to China'. In a subsequent article, the newspaper said: 'China and the UK hold divergent views in terms of human rights, democracy and freedom because of different development phases, political systems and ideologies. But this should neither dominate bilateral ties nor overshadow the momentum for cooperation'.

The craven attitude of Britain to China is despite the comprehensive counterfeiting of British goods. In November 2014, a Chinese firm Landwind launched its X7 vehicle at the Guangzhou motor show which was identical to the Range Rover Evoque, costing in excess of £40,000; the X7 was priced at £14,000. China has further counterfeited the Mini Cooper and also the Rolls Royce Phantom (priced at £350,000 compared to the £30,000 Geely GE copy). A whole range of British goods are counterfeited and even exported back to the West, from Vivienne Westwood shoes (copies priced at £15 compared to £120 for the genuine item), menswear, cigarettes, Burberry cashmere coats, (copies priced at £60 compared to £2,500 for the genuine item), designer handbags (copies costing £150 compared to £700 for the genuine items), and a variety of high-street brands. China's patent laws are favourable to local firms and it is almost impossible to get the Chinese courts to uphold Western firms' patent rights. Even when British firms, and hence the wider economy, are damaged by these Chinese trade practices the British government is unwilling to defend British interests. For the British ruling class, globalization, encompassing free trade, is the new religion. Defending the national interest is so passé.

By March 2015 the USA had finally baulked at Britain's craven approach and 'constant accommodation' of China. The White House was angry at the British involvement with the launch of a new Chinese investment bank, Asian Infrastructure Investment Bank, about which there had been 'virtually no consultation' despite US concerns that it would be a vehicle for Chinese domination.

The British textile industry, once so prominent, has been decimated. In 1966 import quotas were imposed for textiles, which failed to halt the failure of British firms to compete, and in 1972 the Tory government imposed tariffs on Commonwealth textile imports.[806] The plight of British firms was not helped by the practices of overseas competitors. The Tory MP Peter Viggers visited a textile factory in Taiwan and found that half the output was labelled 'Made In Huddersfield'.[807]

M&S made a virtue of its 'Made in England' brand for clothes. However, it did not last. At first, suppliers were told that the clothes could be cut abroad and finished in Britain; then that they only had to have the 'Made in England' label sewn on in Britain. By the mid-1990s production was being transferred to Morocco and then China.[808] In 1998 M&S, after a poor performance and a bad press, decided to cut costs by switching its orders for clothing to overseas suppliers. Hitherto it had been supplied by four British companies which were now faced with a sudden loss of business. One of the companies, William Baird, lost 40% of its business overnight.[809] The British textile industry was devastated as production was transferred overseas. The M&S 'Made in England' fraud should never have been allowed. It merely facilitated the import penetration of the home market without the British consumer realising the fact, and ultimately made it far easier for M&S to deliver the fatal blow to its British textile suppliers.

Britain has been very relaxed about allowing foreign takeovers of British firms. In part this is seen as globalization and in part is because it is government policy to hawk British assets in order to pay for imports rather than paying for them by relying on exports. In the 1950s and 1960s, capital controls meant that it was difficult for foreign firms to take over British ones.[810] Nigel Lawson emphasized the importance of the removal of capital controls and that 'one of the consequences is that companies get taken over'.[811] Will Hutton wrote:

> 'No other economy is as open as ours with takeovers so easy. And, apart from the US, no other economy needs the inflow of overseas cash so acutely. Britain's industrial and financial jewels are being auctioned to pay for a record trade deficit ... with no end to the deficit in sight, the auction will go on until the cupboard is bare.'[812]

Between 1997 and 2007, foreign ownership of quoted British companies rose from 30% to 50% according to the Treasury.[813] In the 10 years to 2015 British companies worth £440billion were sold to foreigners.[814] 72% of City trading is done by hedge funds, high-frequency traders, or investment banks trading on their own account.[815] In 1991, 50% of British shares were held long-term by British pension funds and insurance companies; by 2015 that figure had fallen to less than 15%, with 41% of British shares held overseas.[816] Figures from HM Revenue and Customs show that those sectors most affected by takeovers are paying either lower or broadly the same tax revenues – and thus a declining share of the overall total. The takeover culture is reducing tax revenues and so is impacting on government services and forcing up taxes from other sources such as VAT, personal tax and national insurance.[817] For example, Boots transferred its headquarters to Zug in Switzerland to dodge British taxes.[818]

The willingness of the British to allow the takeover of Cadbury by Kraft in 2009 was not matched by the French when they discovered in 2005 that Danone, a dairy organization, was to be the target of a bid from Pepsico. The French rushed through a new law (dubbed 'Loi Danone') to protect companies in 'strategic industries' from takeover. Unlike Britain, France was not worried about possible EU interference.[819] The Dutch supervisory boards, a feature of both the British Steel/Hoogovens merger (to form Corus) and the Leyland DAF merger, had the effect of tilting the management decisions in favour of the Dutch side of the businesses. Spain has tax incentives relating to the cost of goodwill for the takeover by its companies of foreign firms – unmolested by the EU. Spain protects its energy companies from foreign takeover and the merger between British Airways and Iberia was allowed on condition that the board meetings would be held in Spain.[820] The French have Loi Danone and a list of companies which are shielded from foreign takeover.[821] Germany passed a law allowing the government to veto foreign investment of 25% or more in a company if the government considers national security to be under threat.[822] The USA does not allow its airlines to have more than 25% of their shares owned by foreigners and it also protects its oil companies.[823] France subsidises its railways to the tune of €58billion a year. The £5billion British railway subsidy is paid to foreign owned firms.[824]

The USA has a very determined approach to protecting its interests and the sale of British P&O to Dubai Ports World led to six US ports, owned by P&O, to be kept under US control, with even Hilary Clinton speaking out against Dubai Ports World being allowed to control US ports.[825] On one occasion they pushed the

British too far. In 1985, Boeing took the role of lead manufacturer for the Harrier – with BAe's agreement.[826] When a successor fighter was planned in collaboration with the USA, the Joint Strike Fighter (JSF), the transfer of technology was so complete that the Pentagon refused to allow Britain access to the vertical take-off technology which Britain had developed. It took a visit in 2006 by Lord Drayson, who threatened to withdraw Britain from the project, before the USA agreed that the RAF be allowed to operate and maintain the JSF independently and allowed access to Britain's own technology.[827]

By 2010, only 34% of energy provision remained in British hands, with Germany controlling 27%, France controlling 32% and Spain 7%.[828] In 2011, it was revealed that the Spanish owners of Scottish Power had used a cash surplus at Scottish Power to make a ten-year loan of £800million to a sister company in the USA.[829] According to the IFS, between 1987 and 1997 the profits of the electricity industry increased from £249million to £1.5billion. The water industry enjoyed a 147% increase in profits between 1990 to 1997, with the pay of company executives increasing by up to 200%. Meanwhile the British Gas chief executive in 1994 secured a 75% pay increase for himself reaching an income of £475,000.[830] Thames Water, taken over by Germany's RWE, enjoyed a 30% increase in profits to £346million in 2005, helped by a 21% increase in prices imposed on consumers which Ofwat, the supposed regulator, had agreed despite the very high leakage rate at Thames Water. In 2006, a water shortage led to bad publicity when British consumers had water restrictions enforced upon them while the executives of the RWE, who were pocketing £20million per annum in pay, were photographed watering their lush green lawns with sprinklers and having full swimming pools. Prices on the Continent were as little as half what British consumers were being charged.[831] The attendant bad publicity and eventual condemnation from Ofwat led RWE to sell off Thames Water to an Australian water company controlled by a private equity company (in its five years of ownership, RWE had paid out £1billion in dividends to its German shareholders).[832]

By comparison, for example, German power firms are protected from foreign takeover by a series of measures including legislative protection. Likewise, the USA has a series of rules, regulations and price controls that make profiteering within the energy industry very difficult; proposed price increases can be subject to public hearings and full disclosure of internal financial information, including the details of executive remuneration and benefits, which British firms have found very hard to comply with (the British firm National Grid was even found to be overcharging).[833]

David Cameron's government was even prepared to see BAe become controlled by EADS in a merger which would have given BAe shareholders only 40% of the combined enterprise. The government was not prepared to exercise its golden share voting right to veto the deal. In the event, with much controversy, after demanding the split be 70/30 and not 60/40, Germany vetoed the deal as being not in their national interest.[834]

The demise of British Steel is a sad testimony to the disaster of the takeover culture stemming from the City and successive British governments. British Steel was making good profits and was investing in new production methods. By contrast several European steel producers were dependent upon government subsidies and those governments were reluctant to reduce surplus capacity. The subsidies enabled those less efficient producers to undercut British Steel. Even so, by 1997 British Steel was the second largest producer in Europe with an output of 17million tonnes – only 0.5million tonnes less than Germany's Thyssen Krupp.[835]

In 1999, British Steel merged with the Dutch company Hoogovens to form the largest producing steel company, now called Corus, in Europe and the third largest in the world (behind POSCO of South Korea and Nippon Steel). The merger was a disaster with falling output and increasing losses. Despite the merger, the Dutch part of Corus had maintained its own supervisory board which vetoed decisions, demanded extra investment for the Dutch side of the business, and was accused by the British unions of trying to preserve Dutch jobs at the expense of British ones.[836]

Corus was taken over by Tata Steel in 2007. Half the cost of the takeover was a loan secured against the assets of Corus.[837] The capacity of 18.2million tonnes that Tata took over from Corus is a small part of the 120million tonnes that Tata aims to have worldwide by 2015.[838] That the plight of Britain's steel industry was of minor concern to Tata and of little concern to the Tory Government was shown by the demise of the Redcar steel plant, which had been sold by Tata to the Thai firm SSI in 2011. As a result of a number of factors, including electricity costs *on average*

82% higher than EU competitors, not least due to climate change levies, other green costs, the inclusion of plant and machinery in business rates, and the fact that China had been dumping surplus steel production onto the European market, led to the permanent closure of the Redcar plant in October 2015.

The steel industry's energy costs were so high because in order to comply with the Climate Change Act, which Britain unilaterally adopted, Britain must reduce the use of carbon-based energy and, due to the 'carbon price floor', cannot cut the price of carbon-based energy even if its costs fall – as they have. Consequently, along with the dash for unreliable and expensive green energy, accompanied by the closure of cheap electricity from coal-fired power stations, the energy costs for Britain's heavy industries is roughly twice that of other European countries such as France and Germany (which is currently building a number of new coal-fired power stations). Consequently, British industry cannot compete. The new nuclear power station at Hinkley will only make matters worse. The cost of the agreed 'strike price' of Hinkley's output is roughly twice the current wholesale cost of electricity, and this price is further index-linked to inflation for the next 35 years. Furthermore, Hinkley's 3,200 Megawatts of capacity will cost as much to build as 50,000 Megawatts of gas power station capacity.[839]

The Tories did not allow the fact that China was a communist state and therefore able to fix the costs of its steel production, nor the fact that other countries are supporting their steel industries, to interfere with their commitment to globalization. Chinese steel producers are heavily subsidized and are dumping surplus production onto world markets at less than *their own* cost of production. Chinese surplus capacity was 340million tonnes in 2014, which is more than double demand for steel in the entire EU.

The numbers employed in the steel industry has collapsed from 200,000 in the 1970s to less than 20,000 in 2015. Other steel plants, especially the Tata owned one at Scunthorpe, were also under threat of closure. The steel firm, Caparo, went into administration. Of the Redcar plant, Alexander Temerko, deputy chairman of the oil rig maker OGN and a major customer, said: 'The closure of SSI's Redcar plant is a damning indictment of the Government's ineptitude when it comes to supporting UK heavy industry. A business like ours can use more than 100,000 tons of steel per year, but the opportunities for synergy and collaboration have been wasted by successive energy ministers, who have turned their backs on UK oil and gas suppliers, pointing to EU regulations and claiming their hands are tied'. It was only after the closure of the Redcar pant that the Tory Government finally asked the EU for permission to assist the British steel industry meet the unnecessarily high energy costs. Other European countries have been willing and able to assist their own steel industries without EU obstruction. The Tories are simply using the EU as a cover for their true agenda, which is their policy of *unilateral* free trade and globalization. Gary Klesch, who had withdrawn from a deal to buy the Scunthorpe plant in the summer of 2015, said that Scunthorpe's 6,000 workers were 'being led to the slaughterhouse' by politicians.

The Tory Government was somewhat embarrassed when it was revealed, just after the Redcar plant had closed, that the Ministry of Defence had entered into a £3.8billion deal to use Swedish steel for an order for 589 Ajax armoured vehicles and three naval offshore patrol ships. Once again the British government put *unilateral* free trade theories ahead of the national interest and the livelihoods of ordinary people. That the British war effort at the outbreak of WWII was crippled by the inability to produce or buy the required amount of steel needs to be remembered, and that it was only US Lend-Lease that bailed Britain out.

Joseph Chamberlain's observations as to the plight of those who lose skilled employment also needs to be remembered. Presumably, the redundant steel workers will now receive government assistance to find jobs on zero-hours contracts, stacking shelves in a supermarket, or perhaps working at Costa.

There was a bruising takeover battle for the control of the pharmaceutical firm AstraZeneca, after the US firm Pfizer launched a hostile takeover in 2014 (which ultimately did not proceed). The bid was the largest ever takeover proposal in British history. Pfizer was open that thousands of jobs could be lost if they were successful and that AstraZeneca might even be broken up; these jobs lost would be skilled research jobs. Downing Street described the bid as 'a positive step' and the Tory chairman hailed the takeover as being 'a great Anglo-American tie-up'. Roughly 40% of Pfizer's subsidiaries were based in offshore tax havens and, despite British sales of £5billion over a three-year period, it claimed £184million in tax credits and paid only £118million in corporation tax. Pfizer admitted that it intended to exploit Britain's tax regime to try and save up to an estimated £1.4billion a year.

In the run up to the 2015 general election the foreign takeovers continued apace. The highly successful Domino Printing Sciences, responsible for producing bingo tickets and supermarket bar codes as well as much else, agreed to a £1billion takeover from the Japanese firm Brother. In response, a government spokesman said: 'Attracting investment to the UK from around the world is a vital element of the Government's strategy to ensure sustainable long-term economic growth'. Meanwhile Thomas Cook, which had successfully bounced back from serious troubles a few years previously, agreed a partnership with the Chinese firm, Fosun, which declared that it had spent almost £100million to acquire a 5% stake in Thomas Cook and intended to acquire another 5%. Then the Spanish bank Sabadell announced a takeover of the TSB, which had de-merged from Lloyds Bank Lloyds Bank declared that it was prepared to sell its remaining stake in the TSB to Sabadell. These takeovers demonstrate that it is success and potential success that makes them attractive to foreigners – understandably.

Cadbury's success, as other such companies have found, made it a takeover target. With this scenario the more successful a company is the less likely it is to survive as an independent organization. A crucial factor in Kraft's takeover of Cadbury in 2010 was the role played by short-term speculators such as hedge funds, which bought shares with a view to selling them to Kraft for a profit.[840] Almost one-third of Cadbury's shares would change hands. People who had owned 5% suddenly owned 30% and were looking for a quick sale for an easy profit.[841] At the time of Kraft's opening bid, 49% of Cadbury's shares were owned by North American investors, with British investors only owning 28%. 85% of the company's employees were based overseas and it was closing a British factory while simultaneously investing £100million in new facilities in Poland.[842] Kraft funded its takeover with £7billion of debt, including a £630million loan from RBS.[843] Even when this was known during the takeover battle, the government did not intervene.

The former chairman of Cadbury, Sir Roger Carr, said: 'In France the loss of a "Cadbury" would be out of the question. Germany believes that strength at home is the first step to success abroad. In Japan, selling a company over the heads of management is unthinkable. And in the United States, regulations exist to protect strategic assets'.[844]

Kraft's announcement that control of Cadbury would be moved to Kraft's Zurich headquarters signalled that Cadbury's tax bill would be at least halved. When Boots, which had been based in Nottingham for 161 years, had been taken over by a private equity firm moved its headquarters to Zug, its tax bill was reduced from £89million, payable in Britain, to only £9million, payable in Switzerland. This reduction was achieved by offsetting the debt used to buy the company against tax and by switching to a low tax regime.[845]

These profits are not generated by profit making by Cadbury, but by the size of the offers, funded by loans, made by Kraft – that is from the amount of money gleaned from other investors, as with a classic Ponzi scheme.

SUMMARY

All countries that have developed a significant manufacturing industry have done so using protectionist measures. Britain's commitment to unilateral free trade is an aberration and a commitment that has been a contributory factor in Britain's long-term economic decline. In the 21st century Britain and the West face growing competition from Asia, from countries which do not abide by the rules of free trade and are using protectionist policies to boost their own economic growth. The USA has been much more firm in its dealings with these countries, whereas the British position has been positively craven – even when China has been openly contemptuous.

A key aspect of the problem is that (apart from grandstanding when doling out overseas aid), as with the EU, British politicians simply assume that all countries are the same. All countries are not the same. In the EU, the Eastern European countries have a different political, cultural and standard of living background. There is no single European market. There is no global market as such, but simply a collection of national markets. Communist China is not the same as the West, nor is Japan. Western firms are not going to be able to sell goods and services to China as if they were selling to the domestic market – even if the Chinese government allows them to sell at all.

Britain has been foolish to allow foreign takeovers of so much of British industry and has been foolish to grovel to persuade

Communist China to buy up British assets, from housing to power stations. China is a quietly hostile power on the rise and its relationship with the USA (if not the West) is the same of that of Germany to Britain in the run up to WWI. It is an expansionist rival power.

In assessing the seriousness of Britain's plight, what matters is the combination of three aspects. Firstly, the seriousness of a particular set of figures; a large deficit is something to be treated seriously. Secondly, the cumulative effect; a large deficit may be serious, but it is even more so if it is merely one of a series of deficits – the larger the more dangerous – which add up together to make an even worse situation. Thirdly, there is the trend; that is to say that the deficit is getting bigger and bigger. Naturally, if all three aspects are seriously negative then the overall picture is grim.

Britain has been running balance of payments deficits, on the current account, since 1983 – despite the positive impact of North Sea oil. The size of the deficits increased noticeably in the years 1988-1990 when the deficit was 3.8%, 4.4% and 3.3% of GDP respectively. The deficit then shrank and fell to a paltry 0.1% of GDP in 1997. The reason for this can be attributed to the disastrous membership of the ERM and the recovery after ejection. The position then deteriorated to a deficit of 2.6% of GDP in 1999 before falling back again, and then rising to 2.7% in 2007, 3.7% in 2008, 2.8% in 2009, 2.6% in 2010, 1.7% in 2011, 3.7% in 2012, 4.5% in 2013 and reached 5.5% in 2014.[846] These latest figures are well above the deficit that the USA grappled with in the Plaza Accord.

A more detailed analysis of the figures reveals that the situation is likely to get much worse. Firstly, Britain has committed itself, in law, to hand over a greatly increased amount of foreign aid. Secondly, Britain is committed to handing over an ever increasing amount to the EU (net payments are currently roughly £12billion and rising). Thirdly immigrants are sending ever increasing amounts of monies back home and this figure is likely to increase as the size of the immigration population increases, and is estimated to be around £7billion per year,[847] and was as much as £16billion in 2014 according to the World Bank (£2,441million being remitted to Nigeria, £2,380million to India, £823million to Pakistan and £631million to China). Fourthly, whereas in bygone years Britain could rely upon investment income to help pay for the trade deficit, Britain has now sunk into deficit on investment income – not least due to the large-scale selling off of British companies, which means that dividend payments and other investment income flow out of Britain, and with the relocation of headquarters overseas, overseas income to a firm's headquarters no longer necessarily flows to Britain; the deficit in investment income more than doubled between 2013 and 2014 to £37,747billion from £14,964 billion,[848] last being in surplus in 2011 to the sum of £18,671billion (down from £30,150billion in 2005) before sinking into deficit in 2012 and 2013 to £4,841billion and £12,337billion respectively.[849] Fifthly, Britain, being unwilling to defend its interests, is certain to continue to suffer from the unfair trade practices of rivals and competitors. China is an obvious example and the trade deficit has reached no less than £22.347billion in 2014. By comparison, the deficit with Japan is a relatively modest £3.061billion. Another example is Germany, with whom the trade deficit has rocketed to a whopping £30.392billion in 2014, up from £20.225billion in 2012. Germany does of course benefit from, for it, an undervalued euro. Germany and the other northern EU countries, with whom Britain also has significant trade deficits, are exploiting the EU to fix a currency to their own advantage. For example, the 2014 deficit with Belgium & Luxembourg was £8.92billion up from £4.702billion in 2012; with France the figures were £5.967billion up from £1.871billion; Italy £7.982 up from £6.441billion; Netherlands £8.669billion up from £6.3billion; and Spain £4.378billion up from £3.224billion. The trade deficit with these EU countries alone totalled £66.308billion.[850] The total current account deficit with the EU in 2014 was £109.213billion, up from £89.080billion in 2013.[851] From a trade perspective, membership of the EU has been disastrous for Britain.

There are many pro-EU enthusiasts in Britain who eagerly proclaim that were Britain to leave the EU, then the EU would erect tariffs against British goods. This is despite the large number of non-EU countries from around the world that have happily negotiated a free trade relationship with the EU. Assuming that the EU were to so act, to the eager approval of its supporters, in the event of Britain's exit, and assuming that Britain were to likewise introduce tariffs on EU imports (ignoring those free trade puritans, of whom there are many, who argue that tariffs interfere with the purity of the market and create an inefficient distribution of resources, and therefore to introduce a retaliatory tariff would be undesirable as it would simply create yet another impurity and yet another inefficiency) then, at a rate of, say, 20% (the same rate as was introduced in 1932) assuming that the level of imports remained unchanged from 2014, there would be a flow of tax revenues to the government to the sum of £44.981billion (20% of £224.904billion). Also assuming that Britain, as did President Reagan with Japan, stops its craven attitude to China and imposes a 100% tariff on Chinese imports, then this would raise the sum of £36.199billion. Leaving the EU would mean that payments to the EU would cease, and a reduction of the overseas aid to humanitarian crises only might save at least another £22billion together. In other words the income from the tariffs and the saving in expenditure would amount to more than the government's deficit of roughly £95billion.

To look at the problem in a different way, the total deficit in the balance of payments in 2014 was £97.920billion, with the deficit in the trade in goods being £119.605billion.[852] If this deficit in the trade in goods was eliminated, by whatever means, that is Britain sold as much as it imported (heaven forbid that after running deficits for more than 30 years Britain actually had a surplus!) then, by definition, British output would increase to produce those extra goods now being sold either as exports or on the home market. Once again, combined with the saving in overseas aid and payments to the EU, then the extra demand that might be created within the British economy would amount to £141.605billion; then there is the multiplier effect; then there is taxation. If the multiplier is assumed to be 1.7 (as per a recent estimate by the IMF) and the tax rate of around 40% then the extra revenues flowing to the government would amount to £96.291billion – again, a sum more than the government deficit. An increase in manufacturing activity and the well-paid jobs that would entail would also decrease the demands for increased government spending (e.g. there would be fewer unemployed) In practice the deficit is unlikely to simply solve itself and if tariffs were used then there would be the additional monies raised by them.

In reality, the introduction of tariffs would reduce imports and so there would be a combination of extra tax revenues from the tariffs as well as the extra revenues flowing from the increased economic activity brought about by the elimination of the trade deficit. It is untrue, as has been claimed, that the government spending deficit can only be reduced by cuts (austerity) or by increased rates of taxes. It can be eliminated by tariffs and by bringing the balance of trade back into balance.

Another option is to address the currency manipulation by certain countries and the inflow of capital into Britain which in turn drives up the value of sterling and so undermines the export effort and makes imports cheaper. As has been explained above, the continued inflow of capital into a country does not necessarily do that country a favour as it merely funds the current account deficit (as Michael Pettis wrote: 'The math is simple. The larger a country's current account deficit as a share of GDP, the more "help" that country's government gets from foreign investors to buy its bonds'.)[853]

Studies have shown that there is a correlation between foreign exchange purchases and current account surpluses ('large current account imbalances ... probably would not have occurred, and certainly would not have persisted, without massive official net purchases of foreign assets'),[854] China being by far the worst offender and having by far the largest foreign exchange reserves at 45% of GDP at the end of 2011. This is compared to other currency manipulators: Switzerland 43%, Malaysia 46%, Azerbaijan 53%, Qatar 58%, Taiwan 83%, Saudi Arabia 91%, Algeria 95%, Norway 113%, Hong Kong 118%, Kuwait 133%, Singapore 187%, and the United Arab Emirates 216%.[855]

China claimed that its current account surplus had fallen to 2% of GDP in 2012, compared to other surpluses being: Taiwan 7%, Malaysia 8%, Switzerland 10%, Norway 15%, Singapore 21%, as well as the oil exporting countries Saudi Arabia 26%, and Qatar 30%, and Kuwait 44%. China's current account surplus amounted to $191billion in 2012, according to IMF estimates. However, the UN Comtrade programme reported that China has been significantly under-reporting its trade and current account surpluses for at least six years and that its real surpluses are double those claimed (this is known by examining the trade data from those countries China is trading with).

According to the IMF, China's total holdings of total reserves stood at $3,262billion at the end of 2011, nearly three times greater than Japan's total reserves of $1,225billion. After slowing in 2012, China's purchases of foreign exchange increased dramatically in 2013 and its total reserves reached $3,660billion by the end of September 2013. Also, the holdings of China's SWF, the China

Investment Corporation, increased from $200billion in 2007 to $575billion by the end of 2012.

Research has shown that if government buying of foreign assets is ended, then the currency exchange rates will realign, thus ending the large trade and current account imbalances and thereby create jobs and growth in countries like Britain, as well as lower import costs and therefore a higher standard of living for ordinary people in countries such as China, which will be more focused on their domestic economies for growth.

The USA has already shown compunction to challenge unfair trade practices to defend its interests, but Britain has so far shown none at all. The options include not only tariffs on imports, but also the idea of a withholding tax, possibly at a rate of 30%, that would be imposed on investment income on Chinese assets ('the U.S. government should tax the income (the interest payments) on Chinese holdings of U.S. financial assets'),[856] which would make it less attractive for China to hold US assets. This withholding tax would be very unpopular with China but would be allowable under international trade agreements whereas tariffs would be more controversial. Even so, tariffs worked in the 1930s, would be simpler, and would raise more monies in tax revenues.

Britain cannot forever pay for imports by selling assets. Eventually all the saleable assets will have been sold. Doing a sale and lease back on the Royal Navy, or having Buckingham Palace promote Oinky's Pork Sausages might fund the trade deficit for another few days. Nor should the loss of tax revenues due to the sale of businesses be overlooked. As stated above, small businesses are paying almost three times as much tax in 2012 as they were in 2000, despite the lending squeeze enforced by the banks. Meanwhile, large companies, whose profits have increased by 65% are paying 20% *less* tax. Had the tax revenues from large companies almost trebled as with small companies, then the tax revenues would be £50billion a year higher – that is more than enough to halve the size of the government's deficit in 2014. This corporate tax dodging is a major issue in itself.

Britain needs to face up to the consequences of unilateral free trade and its bastardized version in the form of globalization. Selling assets to pay for imported goods cannot continue indefinitely. Membership of the EU merely makes matters far worse. Action needs to be taken to bring the trade deficit back into balance. Whichever option is chosen, something has to be done if

Britain is to reverse its decline, resume genuine economic growth, and witness a continuing increase in living standards for ordinary people.

One can only imagine what Joseph Chamberlain and the Tariff Reformers would think if they could see Britain today, let alone what Lord Palmerston might make of China's counterfeiting and other trade practices. They might conclude 'the star of England has already set'.

12 PONZI ECONOMICS

Italian American Charles Ponzi made history in that he gave his name to a particular type of fraud. He founded the Securities Exchange Company, which made millions. He bought a bank. He lived the millionaire lifestyle. But he was headed for complete destruction, for his business model was not only fraudulent, but ruinous. He had given up any effort to invest peoples' monies as he had originally intended, instead he merely placed it on deposit earning 5% interest. Yet Ponzi was offering investors a 50% return on their investment every 45 days. He was funding these payments, and repayments of the capital invested, by using the monies from new investors. Given the 50% return promised, which means a 50% cost to Ponzi, every 45 days, this scheme could not last long and could only last at all provided there was an ever-increasing number of new investors.[857]

The laws of arithmetic are remorseless and Ponzi's scheme collapsed in a pile of debt. Investors lost their money. Some lost their life savings. Those who had re-mortgaged their houses to raise money to invest in Ponzi's scheme lost their homes too. Despite several other fraud schemes and jail terms, and ultimately dying in poverty in Rio de Janeiro, Ponzi became a footnote of history. Mitch Feierstein defines a Ponzi scheme thus: 'A Ponzi scheme is any financial adventure in which depositors can only be paid out by using the money of new investors'.[858]

We have witnessed the rise of the Ponzi class. People who have seen a dramatic rise in incomes well beyond the modest gains of ordinary people. This has been accompanied by a rise in lobbyists who tout for monies for their clients and pet projects. The Ponzi class pursue an economic policy which increases government debts and further dumps debts, including unpaid bills (this is often described as the strain on public services), onto the wider public. As with a classic Ponzi scheme, with Ponzi economics assets are consumed as income and the escalating debts are kept out of sight. In Britain assets are being sold off to foreigners, such as businesses, housing, power stations and government gilts; while vast debts are escalating and are unquantified, not just the government debt but also those unpaid bills and debts passed directly onto the general public which are not included in the government accounts, detailed below.

One needs to understand why a Ponzi scheme will always fail. To take the original scheme offered by Charles Ponzi, a 50% return every 45 days. To stick with the 50% return for whatever period, in order to speed up the inevitable collapse, let us assume that the scheme begins with a receipt of £1million of investors' monies. The scheme therefore now has £1million on deposit and the fund has plenty of cash for all sorts of things that the management might wish to spend it on – whether it be nice houses, yachts or other luxuries (or, on a larger scale and with far more monies, pet political projects such as overseas aid, the EU or on a variety of quangos etc.). However, the scheme is now liable for £1.5million, being the original capital and the 50% return promised on it – all of which is due for repayment at the end of the period.

But there is no problem, lured by the prospect of such a high return, the scheme is popular and people queue up to invest. At the end of the first period another £2million has been received in new monies. So, the scheme can repay the £1.5million it owes and has another £500,000 to put on deposit. For the ease of argument, we can assume that the luxuries are funded by the interest on the monies on deposit, leaving the actual cash available untouched. The scheme, with the extra £500,000 is now £1.5million in funds, with debts of £3million, being the £2million of new monies plus the 50% return. Net debts now stand at £1.5million. By the end of the second period, the scheme has proved so popular that it has attracted £4million of new monies. £3million of this is used to pay the outstanding debt that has fallen due for payment and the £1million spare is added to the monies on deposit, bringing the total on deposit to £2.5million; the debts outstanding are now £6million. However, by the time that that £6million is due for repayment, the scheme has proved so attractive that it has now received £8million in new funds. The £6million is duly repaid and another £2million is put on deposit. The total on deposit is now £4.5million. The outstanding debt is now £12million, being the £8million received and a 50% return.

The next period continues to see the scheme prove to be popular, with another £14million received, of which £12million is used to repay the outstanding debt and another £2million is added to that on deposit. The total on deposit is now £6.5million and the outstanding debt is £21million. The next period sees the scheme remain a favourite with an increase in funds coming in reach £18million. Even so, this is not enough to meet the £21million falling due for repayment. However, there is sufficient on deposit to cover the shortfall, so £3million of the deposit money is used to meet the £21million due for payment, leaving the amount on deposit at £3.5million. There is now a debt of £27million.

The scheme continues to attract new investors and no less than £24million is now received, all of which is used to pay the £27million falling due for payment, leaving a shortfall of £3million, which is covered by using £3million of the monies on deposit. The sum left on deposit is now only £500,000 and the outstanding debt is £36million. The next period sees the amount received increase by 25% to £30million. Both this amount and the £500,000 on deposit is wiped out trying to repay the outstanding debt of £36million, leaving an unpaid debt of £5.5million from the previous period and another £45million owing (the latest monies plus the 50% return). The unpaid debt causes bad publicity, there are no new monies, and the scheme collapses with total debts of £50.5million and no assets.

The collapse of a Ponzi scheme is inevitable, as *it is consuming capital as if it were income.* It is using new capital to meet outstanding debts, including costs, with the consequence that the capital is reduced and the total debt remorselessly increases. While the lucrative returns are seen and enjoyed, for a time, the scale of the outstanding debt is kept hidden. Of course, if the promised return is not 50% but some lower figure, then the scheme will last longer. But the result is the same: wealth is destroyed and the debts escalate.

The present economic policy is not Keynesian. The citing of Keynes to justify the various expansionist policies that have been implemented since WWII has been misleading. Keynesianism has evolved into something well beyond anything Keynes advocated. Keynes' theory was derived to solve a problem, as Keynes saw it, as a lack of demand and a malfunctioning of the economy in that there was continuing high levels of unemployment, which questioned the validity of the free market system and its ability to solve unemployment. Since WWII and up until the 1970s, Keynesianism had become a dodge that enabled spendthrift politicians the excuse to tax and spend and meddle with the running of the economy, regardless of the consequences, in the guise of achieving full employment – rather than to deal with the deteriorating British economic position and the causes of that deterioration. Britain's economic decline was managed, with increasing disorder, and not reversed. Problems such as the volatile industrial relations, lack of competitiveness, and the shrinking manufacturing sector could be ignored. All that was needed to deal with more unemployment was more printed money and greater controls on wages and prices to try and repress inflation.

The credit crunch and banking crisis of 2008 reignited Keynesian economics. There were similarities with the 1930s slump: a crisis in the financial sector (this time it was the banks rather than Wall Street), adverse consequences of trying to fix the exchange rate (this time it was the creation of the euro rather than the Gold Standard), and high unemployment (this time the problem was more in the Eurozone rather than in Britain, although Britain has a long standing unemployment problem with a large number of people tucked away on incapacity benefits).

One German politician dismissed the calls for an expansionist economic policy as 'crass Keynesianism'. Quack Keynesianism would have been a more accurate term. What is often overlooked is that Keynes, and even less Keynesianism, was not a factor in solving the economic problems of the 1930s. The *General Theory* was written *after* the British economy had returned to growth. It was only after WWII that Keynes' thinking and his *General Theory* was taken seriously by the government. Yet to Keynesians in 2008, the credit crunch and the bank bailouts were like manna from heaven: deficit spending and money printing beyond the wildest dreams of economists from a bygone age. To Keynesians, it was just like old times again – as if the 1970s had never happened. As for the bank bailouts, no amount was too much. Printing money to pay for government spending was back in fashion.

Despite what Keynes might have convinced himself in his ever-changing and convoluted thinking, he *was* an inflationist. Inflation was what he offered in the belief that he could bring about a one-off reduction in real wages by manipulating the value of the currency. From 2008 onwards, inflation was openly lauded as a means of reducing both bank and government debts. But what is really happening goes well beyond inflationism.

Mitch Feierstein has described the financial crisis as a Ponzi scheme. Like Kahn and those others who were grappling with the concept of the multiplier before him, Mitch Feierstein has hit on a concept that requires further development. The real Ponzi scheme lies in the government sector. The economic policy that is thrust upon us is not Keynesian, it is Ponzi economics. Assets are being consumed as income, financial commitments are being made and debts are being run up, not only in the government sector but also in the wider economy. The key to understanding the Ponzi scheme is to see where the debts are being hidden out of sight. In Britain, the debts are being imposed upon ordinary English families and comprise of both financial costs and also the costs of the diminution of the quality of life. Those running the Ponzi scheme, the ruling class, the political establishment and their supporters, might collectively be described as the Ponzi class. The Ponzi class hold the interests of the nation in contempt and their commitment to globalization is only matched by their political correctness.

Back in the mid-1980s, when Thatcherism was at its height, there was a surge in self-belief and national pride in Britain. The Falklands war victory showed that the British were no longer being run out of their own territory. The incoming North Sea oil revenues boosted the economy. The privatizations provided the City with lucrative earnings as well as demonstrating that socialism and state ownership was not inevitable and irreversible. Deregulation was seen as a way of ridding Britain of its stodgy business practices. The power of the unions had been broken, especially with the defeat of the miners' strike. Free markets and free trade were to be promoted. Yet this ethos already contained the seeds of its destruction. Large parts of manufacturing industry had been decimated by the early 1980s recession and never recovered, with Britain running continuous trade deficits from 1983 onwards. The free trade fixation propelled Margaret Thatcher to sign the Single European Act, which vastly expanded EU powers and rendered Britain subservient to Eurocrats.

Mrs Thatcher's vision of a future of a property-owning democracy was the spur which led to the sale of large part of the council housing stock being sold off with tenants gaining the right to buy, in the Housing Act of 1980. More than one million council houses were sold. Michael Heseltine, who as the minister responsible for implementing the scheme, stated that 'no single piece of legislation has enabled the transfer of so much capital wealth from the state to the people'. But what of the property-owning democracy in 2014? A typical family's fortunes have been adversely transformed. One change, the decline of marriage, was as much a legacy of the Thatcher years as what happened thereafter. The married couples' tax allowance was gradually chipped away by successive Tory governments, keen to get their fingers on monies that would otherwise have been used to buttress marriage. Far from respecting married couples' wishes to be treated as a singly legal entity, the Tories decided to tax marriage. In an interview in 2010, Kenneth Clarke had even gone so far as to boast: 'I abolished the married couples' tax allowance and I thought at the time, as I was raising revenue and cutting the main body of income tax, that was the better way to do it'. It was in fact left to Gordon Brown and the Labour government to finally kill off the allowance in 1999. This has left single wage, traditional families struggling to make ends meet and so has pushed young mothers back out into the labour market while their young children are assigned to childminders and nurseries at significant cost. Stay-at-home mothers are quietly denigrated.

In April 2013, it was revealed that the number of stay-at-home mothers had fallen to 2.06million, a fall of 850,000 since 1993 and the figure was falling by 500 a day. In September 2013, it was revealed that the number of working mothers has increased from 66.7% in 1996 to 72.2%. Lynne Burnham of Mothers at Home Matter said: 'It is a well-known fact that separating a small child from its primary carer (most often the mother) for long periods of time, causes a rise in the stress hormone cortisol in the child. Formal day care substitutes care by a parent who loves the child with care by someone who doesn't. By ignoring love, we diminish motherhood and fatherhood and discount one of their most precious strengths'. In March 2013 figures showed that nearly half of families have just one child, an increase of 700,000 in 15 years. If the trend continues then single child families will become the majority within 10 years. The cost of bringing up a child was a factor in the decline in the size of families.

Meanwhile the number of married couples with children has fallen to 4,017,793 in 2011. This is a fall of 15.2% compared to 2001. Nearly half of all teenagers aged 13 to 15 are not living with both of their parents. In May 2013, research by the Marriage Foundation discovered that only 9% of children born to cohabiting couples will still have their parents living together by the time they are 16 years old: 'With family breakdown costing an estimated £46billion a year – more than the entire defence budget – in addition to the immeasurable social damage, it is clearly in the interest of the Government and the taxpayer to work to counter this devastating trend'. 97% of those whose parents were still together were married. Almost 50% of children are born to single or unmarried parents. The number of lone parent families has more than doubled to 2million compared to 1980. Cohabiting couples account for 19% of all couples but 48% of all family breakups. 31% of cohabiting parents have split by the time their child is 7, whereas only 12% of married couples have split. Marriage Foundation research has shown that half of all babies born in 2012 will have their parents split up by the time they are 15.

According to research by the IPPR for the Joseph Rowntree Foundation in November 2013, 30% of those classed as poor are single earner families where the mother stays at home. 27% are lone parents on benefits, 8% are lone parent working, 20% are two parents on benefits and 15% are two parents working. In 2015 Treasury figures showed that households with both parents working had benefited most from the government tax reforms as the increases in personal allowances was maximised as each parent could claim the allowance. In June 2015, figures showed that single earner British families, where the mother stays at home, pay one-third more tax than the average for OECD Western countries. Nicola Leach, from the Charity CARE, said: 'Stay-at-home parents are making an important investment in their children and yet they end up being discriminated against by our tax system'.

In March 2013, a Treasury briefing document stated: 'Working families who are struggling with their childcare costs, or families where parents want to go to work but can't afford to are in greater need of state support for child care than families where one parent chooses to stay at home and look after their children full-time'. The Institute of Fiscal Studies revealed in October 2014 that a childcare subsidy (the part time pre-school places scheme) had cost the government £66,000 for every mother with young children lured back to work. Laura Perrins of Mothers at Home Matter, said: 'The policy is ineffective at getting women into work. It would be better to use the money to pay for a transferable tax allowance to help married families'. Anastasia de Waal of Civitas said: 'The main problem with the Government's support at the moment is that it gives a tax break to couples so long as they pay someone else to look after their children. It would be better – for both children and the economy – if the Government let parents keep more of the money they have earned so that they can decide whether to care for their own children or pay someone else'. In August 2013, George Osborne dismissed stay-at-home mothers as making a lifestyle choice as he pledged to give families with working mothers £1,200 towards the cost of childcare per child from 2015. The scheme is available for families with a total income of up to £300,000 per annum. In April 2013, the Education Minister, Elizabeth Truss, announced on Newsnight that two-earner families are now the norm and that the government was right to target them for more benefits and tax breaks. The academic, Dr Aric Sigman, has attacked the adverse comments regarding stay-at-home mothers as a new form of prejudice: 'motherism'.

In January 2013, it was calculated that mothers with full-time jobs need to work for four months (17 weeks) each year to pay for childcare costs, according to research by Family Investment. The costs are on average £7,127 per annum. A mother can get 15 hours of free care per week once their child reaches three. Research by the insurance group RIAS has found that 10million grandmothers are looking after their grandchildren while their mothers go out to work. This is an increase of 60% in five years. In January 2014, research by the Department of Education found that 57% of working mothers would cut back their working hours to be with their families if they could afford to. 37% of working mothers would prefer to be stay-at-home mums. In September 2015, figures showed the toll that the more stressful life was having on women when it was disclosed that their life expectancy had fallen to being only four years longer than men's, down from more than six years in the mid 20th century. These financial costs to families and the diminished quality of life is one cost of the British Ponzi scheme.

An aspiring couple might send their children to university. It was the goal of the Labour government to boost the numbers attending university. Tony Blair set a target to get 50% of young people into university. One result is that free university education can no longer be afforded. Hence, we now have university tuition fees of £9,000 per year. That is £27,000 for a three-year degree course, plus interest, plus living expenses. For a family with two children, that family is in debt to the tune of £54,000 to pay for something which in the 1980s was free. In the July 2015 Budget, the Tories announced that they would save £1.6billion by abolishing the means-tested student grants, to be replaced with yet more loans.

In December 2013 The Student Loan Company currently was owed £46billion in outstanding student loans. This sum is expected to increase to £200billion within the next 30 years. According to the National Audit Office, EU students are three times more likely to default on their loans than British ones. Of the 26,800 EU students who have completed their courses, around 7,000 have disappeared, owing £50million. Under the rules, these debts will be written off after 30 years. Last year 130,000 EU students applied for and were granted £100million to study in England and Wales. Although British students must supply a National Insurance number so that their loan repayments can be taken directly from their pay, no such system exists for EU students. The loans only become repayable when an earnings threshold has been reached. The Commons Public Accounts Committee has heard that in 2010 it was estimated that 28% of money loaned to students would not be repaid, but by 2013 that figure had leapt to 35% and could reach 40%. Meanwhile, universities are refusing to justify why the salaries of senior staff have risen by up to 10% in 2013. The average vice-chancellor's pay package, including salaries, benefits and pension, has reached £254,692. The new director of the London School of Economics has been awarded a pay package of £466,000, including £88,000 for relocation costs from the USA. This is another Ponzi scheme all by itself, with the Ponzi class being very generous with English taxpayers' money in order to demonstrate their own European credentials – there is no reason at all for English taxpayers to be paying for the university education of foreigners.

The Student Loan Company's treatment of EU students as if they were all the same is a prime example of the stupidity of pretending that the EU is one market. It is not. It is a collection of different countries, some of which are ex-communist states, with different political histories, different degrees of economic development, and different standards of living. It is wilful stupidity to expect EU students to repay loans based on their expected earnings when, for example, countries such as Poland have average wages only 28% of those in Britain; with Spain the figure is only 64%, Latvia only 22%, Hungary only 21%, and Greece only 37%.

Even crazier is the decision in July 2015 that an illegal immigrant was entitled to a student loan, inevitably, citing her human right to an education. Judges ruled that she could not be 'discriminated' against. This Supreme Court ruling is expected to open the floodgates, with the accompanying difficulties, if not impossibility, of recovering student loans from illegal immigrants.

At the other end of the generations, back in the 1980s those pensioners who needed to go into a care home could expect the state to pay for that – but not any more. The Tories introduced fees and also gave councils the right to seize peoples' homes to meet those fees. Homes that people have worked all their lives to own are taken away from them. A study by NFU Mutual has found that 75% of those whose parents go into a care home lose virtually all of their inheritance. Two million pensioners have had to use their savings to meet the costs of care in the five years to 2014 and one million homes have been sold. NFU Mutual also found, in 2015, that 100 pensioners per week were having their homes seized by the councils to pay for care home fees, and the numbers had increased by 10% between 2010 and 2015. The government has proposed £75,000 cap, to be introduced in 2016, which will not include assumed costs of £12,000 per year on accommodation and food costs. Contrary to John Major's desire to see 'wealth cascading down the generations', it does not. Children are deprived of their inheritance. A report by the Institute and Faculty of Actuaries calculated that on average pensioners would pay out £140,000 before they would reach the government's cap once hidden charges, not included in the cap, are taken into account.

The cost of accepting the Dilnot Commission proposals to reform care home charges, with the supposed intention of lessening the practice of seizing pensioners' homes, was estimated to be £1.7billion a year. This sum is a piddling amount when compared to the tens of £billions freely splashed out on overseas aid and the EU. The commission had recommended a cap of £35,000 and that the threshold below which people pay nothing be raised from £23,500 to £100,000. The proposed cap of £72,000 limit on care costs would only help one in eight pensioners, ministers admitted. The cap is double that recommended by the Dilnot Commission. Age UK pointed out that the £72,000 limit would be reached after four years in a care home, while the average stay is only two years. Ros Altmann, a pensions expert, said: 'By setting the cap so high, and not including accommodation costs, most people will not get anything near the cap. This means that any insurance system is hardly likely to get off the ground, because it is difficult to fund an insurance policy on the basis of something that people are unlikely to benefit from. Most people will have to save for the costs of their care rather than rely on the state. It simply will not pay for most people'.

The Tory manifesto for the 2015 general election included the commitment: 'We will cap the amount you can be charged for your residential care – so you can have the dignity and security you deserve in your old age. We will cap charges for residential social care from April 2016 and also allow deferred payment agreements, so no one has to sell their home. For the first time, individual liabilities will be limited, giving everyone the peace of mind that they will receive the care they need, and that they will be protected from unlimited costs if they develop very serious care needs – such as dementia'. Having won the election, the Tories promptly ratted on this pledge, with Alistair Burt, the social care minister, saying: 'A time of consolidation is not the right moment to be implementing expensive new commitments such as this'. The Tories now said they might get around to doing something after 2020 (i.e. after the next general election). The former minister responsible for care in the Coalition Government, the Liberal Democrat Norman Lamb, said: 'It is naïve to see this delay as anything other than an abandonment'. This brazen treachery shows the Tories for what they are.

Pensioners' ability to meet care home, or even care in their own home, charges is made even worse by the Thatcher government's removal of the state pension's automatic increase in line with earnings. The state pension in Britain is one of the most miserly in Europe. In Britain the state pension is 17% of average earnings as opposed to 57% for the EU.[859] The International Longevity Centre UK found that the British state pension is typically only one-third of the average wage, while the rest of the EU has a state pension equivalent to around half of the average wage (in Greece it is equal to the average wage and it is 60% of the average wage in Italy).

Private pensions have not escaped government attention either. Firstly, the Tories introduced personal pensions and stopped employers from forcing their workers to join an occupational pension scheme – a change which was promoted by the Department of Social Security in a series of advertisements. This change led to the mis-selling scandal in the 1990s, and the subsequent compensation payments totalling many billions of pounds. Pensions adviser Ros Altmann commented: "The principle was right, but the practice turned out to be problematic. Fees were too high, investment promises were too optimistic, reliance on annuities and inflexibility of products have all damaged DC pensions in practice. If expectations had been managed well and fees and charges had been more reasonable, without the lure of commission-induced hard-selling and transfers out, the retirement savings culture would not have been so badly damaged'. At the same time, the Finance Act of 1986 also included legislation to force those pension schemes with surpluses to reduce those surpluses in excess of a certain amount by making taxable payments to the employer, suspending employer or employee contributions, improving benefits or providing new benefits to scheme members. The reason for the change was that employers had started boasting that because they were able to pay money into a scheme tax free and then persuade the Inland Revenue to allow the scheme to repay the employer, tax free, that this was a good way of tax dodging and boosting company profits. However, the effect of the new rules was that many schemes refunded monies to the employer and many employers took contribution holidays for several years. Ros Altmann commented: 'The so-called "surpluses" were not really "surpluses" but were funds needed for future pensions and risk buffers against unexpectedly bad markets or rising longevity. While the schemes were immature, they should have been keeping those surpluses intact but, once they became taxable, there was an instant incentive for employers to ensure they were no longer there. If only we had had better funding buffers and risk margins, our pension system would be much stronger today'. The effect of cutting the investment into those schemes was the result that once times were bad there was no cushion to fall back on. But the coup-de-grace was delivered by the Labour government's raid on pensions by abolishing the dividend tax credit; pension schemes could no longer shield 100% of their investment dividends from the Inland Revenue. The raid is estimated to have raised £5billion per annum in tax, but this is correspondingly a cost to the pension schemes, whose values have been cut by in excess of £100billion as a result. Future generations of private sector workers have lost out in the defined pension and face a retirement in poverty. The number of private sector workers in a pension scheme has fallen to 11.2% from 81% in 1967 according to the ONS. However, 89.5% of state workers are in a defined benefit occupational pension scheme. Since 2000, the number of private sector workers in a defined benefit pension scheme has fallen from 4.6million to 1.7million, and the number continues to fall. In January 2014, pensions experts, Jardine Lloyd Thompson pointed out that the total pensions black hole for the private sector final salary schemes was £150billion. For the FTSE 100 companies, their pension schemes have swung from being in surplus of £14billion in 2008 to a deficit of £57billion at the end of 2013. Companies will therefore need to allocate funds to their pension schemes rather than investment.

In July 2013, an ONS report highlighted that 42% of adults have no pension scheme at all. These include the unemployed, stay-at-home mothers and carers, as well as many working in the private sector. The report showed that the average state worker earned £14.83 per hour compared to £11.41 per hour in the private sector, a 29.9% difference. 82% of state employees have contributions amounting to a typical retirement pot of £90,100, and only 38% of the private sector save to have a typical pot of £40,000.

The OBR calculated that the pensions liability for state workers totals around £960billion – £37,000 for every family. Unlike Norway which invested its oil revenues, for example, no money has been set aside to meet this expense, which has been likened to a Ponzi scheme. Financial advisers Hargreaves Lansdown have calculated that someone aged 26 years old, earning £30,000 increasing to £60,000 before retirement could expect to receive an annual pension of £40,310 were he a state employee and only £11,980 were he a private sector employee.

As if this was not bad enough, QE has decimated the annuity rates. The QE programme has pushed up the price of gilts as the Bank of England has been buying gilts to fund the government debt, and thereby decreased the annuity rates as pension funds, which rely on gilts to fund annuities, have to pay more to get the same income. Those retiring today are only getting a fraction of what they would have done back in the 1980s. Nevertheless, this has not stopped the management of the pension firms from living well. In April 2015 it was revealed that the Prudential had lavished £49million on its management in the previous year. The firm's chief executive, Tidjane Thiam, an Ivorian, had received a package totalling £11.8million. Prudential has been paying amongst the lowest annuity rates to its customers in recent years – just £3,899 per annum from a £100,000 pension pot.

It was announced in March 2014 that from 2015 an estimated 13million pensioners will be allowed to spend their pensions savings any way they like, rather than having to buy an annuity. Those with savings of £10,000 or less will benefit greatly as presently annuities for small amounts are for a pittance. As to the danger that many pensioners might spend their money rather than eke it out for their retirement, Steve Webb, the Liberal Democrat architect of the new policy, even went so far as to say: 'If people do get a Lamborghini, and end up on the state pension, the state is much less concerned about that, and that is their choice. Some people want their money perhaps early on, to spend it while they're more fit and able, and make a conscious choice to do that, knowing they'll have less income later. Annuities will still be a part of the mix, but people will have new choices as well'.

However, while pensions are excluded from the calculation of care home fees to be payable, cash assets are not. Cash withdrawn from pensions can be taken by the state if the pensioner goes into a care home. Steve Webb himself had previously told a House of Lords committee that people should be encouraged to downsize their homes in order to meet care costs.

In March 2015 George Osborne announced that the scheme would be extended to include existing pensioners who would be allowed to cash in their annuities, many of which provide poor returns. Osborne was dismissive of critics who raised concerns about the monies simply being spent, saying: 'I just think it is a very patronising attitude to take towards people who have shown responsibility, saved through their lives, saved for a pension. By changing the law we are trusting people who have worked hard and saved hard all their lives'. The prospect of pensioners cashing in their savings rather than buying an annuity would push up house prices as pensioners would move into the buy-to-let market. Forecasts revealed that as many as 50,000 pensioners could be planning to invest in property.

There is the problem of insurers imposing large fees for withdrawal of savings. Some schemes were planning to impose charges of 2.76% per annum in return for holding the savings and allowing ad hoc withdrawals. According to Which?, a 2.76% charge would gradually reduce the average pension pot by £13,600 compared to charges of less than £3,000 if the more usual charges of 0.5% applied. To take the money out in one lump sum poses the danger of a high tax bill amounting to thousands or tens of thousands of pounds, depending on the size of the lump sum and any other earnings. A lump sum withdrawal could turn the recipient into a higher rate taxpayer for that year. Only a quarter of a pension pot can be withdrawn tax free. Once withdrawn, then any of the sum which is spent will attract various tax charges including VAT. Any left unspent by someone who has to move into a care home will then be eligible to be taken to meet the care home fees. If any is left, then on death inheritance tax applies to an estate on everything in excess of £325,000 at a rate of 40%. Anyone who decides to spend their pensions instead, were threatened in March 2015 by the Department for Work and Pensions that: 'If it is decided you have deliberately deprived yourself, you will still be treated as having that money and it will be taken into account as income or capital when your benefit entitlement is worked out'; in other words, pensioners risk losing their benefits if they run out of money. In the July 2015 Budget, it was revealed that yet another raid on pensions was under consideration with a proposal to abolish tax relief on pension contributions (thus raking in £34billion for the government a year) in return for allowing subsequent tax-free withdrawals. The Ponzi class are circling around what remains of private pensions like vultures.

In December 2013, a report by the IFS revealed that those born in the 1960s and 1970s will be worse off than their parents, with low pay rises, low pensions, and high housing costs. Between 1974 and 2002, household income, both earnings and benefits, increased by an annual average of 1.5%; this had fallen to 0.1% since. Two thirds of Londoners born in the 1940s were on the property ladder by the time they reached their forties, but only half of those born in the 1970s now are. Meanwhile the collapse of defined salary pensions leave many of those born in the 1960s and 1970s facing a retirement in poverty.

In December 2013, the ONS annual Family Spending Report for 2012 showed that household spending had dropped by £18.40 per week since 2010. At the same time, there was higher spending on fuel and power. The IFS warned that a childless couple on a median income will have experienced a drop in income of 6.9% by 2015 compared to 2010, from £481 per week to £450 per week. The IFS further warned that there would have to be another £12billion cuts in welfare spending after the next general election to meet the government's deficit reduction programme. In January 2014, the IFS said that the income for typical families was lower than in 2001, mainly because take home pay has not matched the ongoing increases in prices. Since 2008, food prices have increased by 30% and energy prices by 60%. A couple with two young children had an average real income after tax of £33,253 in

2001/02 and an income of £32,488 in 2013/14. The ONS has revealed that real wages, adjusted for inflation, fell by a cumulative 6.1% in Britain compared to increases in Canada, France and Germany.

Another problem that Thatcher did not resolve is immigration, which is a problem that has gone from bad, to worse, to an unimaginable catastrophe. The scale of mass immigration to Britain is massive. David Goodhart, of Demos, wrote:

> 'From 1066 until 1950, immigration was almost non-existent (excluding Ireland) – a quarter of a million at the most, mainly Hugeunots and Jews. Post-World War II immigration has been on a completely different scale from anything that went before. These days, more people arrive on our shores as immigrants in a single year than did so in the entire period from 1066 to 1950, excluding wartime'.

By December 2012 13% of Britain's residents were born abroad. This figure takes no account of the offspring of those who were born to immigrant parents. 3.8million immigrants moved to Britain between 2001 and 2011. 1,079,000 immigrants from Eastern Europe now lived in Britain. ONS figures showed that there were 2.33million EU immigrants living in Britain. Eurostat revealed that 541,000 Poles had moved to Britain by 2011.

In September 2013 official figures showed that more than two million immigrants had been given British citizenship since 2000. 204,541 were given British citizenship in 2012, the top 10 originating countries being, India (28,352), Pakistan (18,445), Nigeria (8,881), Philippines (8,122), China (7,198), South Africa (6,924), Sri Lanka (6,163), Bangladesh (5,702), Zimbabwe (5,647), and Somalia (5,143). The figures also showed that the claim that more jobs are going to 'British' workers was because immigrants were being given British passports and hence were being reclassified as being British. The government claim that the number of British citizens in work increased by 208,000 and an increase in the foreign workforce of 98,000 was wrong when the place of birth was taken into account, which showed that only 98,000 new jobs had gone to people born in Britain and the rest, 204,000, had gone to immigrants. The coalition government gave British passports out at a faster rate than the previous Labour government (203,789 were given out in 2009).

According to census figures, the number of immigrants in England and Wales has doubled since 2001. More immigrants arrived between 2001 and 2011 than in the previous 50 years put together. There are now an estimated 7.5million immigrants, more than half, 3.8million, of whom arrived since 2001. The 2011 census uncovered 464,000 extra immigrants that the government did not know had entered Britain. ONS research has found that the majority came from Eastern Europe following the expansion of the EU in 2004. One of the greatest problems with immigration is that no one is sure just who has been let in. For example, in December 2014 John Vine, the Chief Inspector of Borders and Immigration, claimed that there were 89,000 missing immigrants in Britain, but the Home Affairs Select Committee said that there were a further 304,222 elsewhere in the system including asylum seekers and criminals. This is equivalent to the population of Cardiff. In November 2014, MigrationWatch UK highlighted that the ONS had underestimated the true scale of immigration as it did not include 1.3million children born to immigrants as being immigrants. Of the 4.6million population rise between 2001 and 2012, 3.8million was attributable to immigration once the children were included.

The 2011 census revealed that 4.2million people, 7.7% of the population, speak a first language that is not English. One in eight in Leicester speak Gujarati as their first language; 6% of those in Rushmoor speak Nepalese. In London, around 1.7million people, 22.1% of the population, speak a language other than English as their first language.

Mass immigration steadily increased under the Tory/Liberal Democrat coalition. ONS figures show that net migration into Britain increased to 182,000 in the year to June 2013, up from 167,000 in the year to June 2012. In the year to March 2014, net migration had increased to 243,000. A major factor in the upsurge was the increased number coming from the Eurozone. In February 2015, it was disclosed that the net inflow in the 12 months to September 2014 had reached 298,000. In May 2015, it was revealed that the net immigration figure for 2014 reached 318,000; in August it was revealed the annual figure for the year to March 2015 had reached 330,000. In 2011, 224,943 babies born had at least one parent who was born abroad. This is 31% of the total. In London, 64.9% of babies born had at least one parent who was born abroad. The ONS has disclosed that the number of babies born in Britain in 2012 is the highest since 1971, when the baby boom started to end. 25.9% of the 724,000 births were to mothers who were born abroad. In August 2015, the ONS revealed that there were 8.3million immigrants living in Britain; this is more than one in eight of the population.

In January 2013, a Home Office report said that there are an estimated 863,000 illegal immigrants in Britain. 70% were living in London. The report also said that 10,000 illegal immigrants had been granted permission to stay under the 14-year rule, where immigrants can stay if they have been in Britain that length of time. In November 2013, it was estimated that illegal immigrants were costing £3.7billion each year in health and education services. The per person cost was calculated to be £4,250. The total number of illegal immigrants was assumed to be 863,000. This is certainly a gross underestimate of the number of illegal immigrants given the previous reports of the scale of illegal immigration, even from the government itself. MigrationWatch UK reported in June 2014 that the total number of illegal immigrants was estimated to be as high as two million. Even David Cameron's favourite curry restaurant, The Shaan, has been found to be employing illegal immigrants. Three were arrested, two of which had entered the country illegally and one had overstayed his student visa. In May 2014, it was revealed that of the 155,000 students who enter Britain each year, only 50,000 were recorded as leaving – with the other 100,000 being regarded as missing, which in practice mean they are likely to have remained.

The attempts to reduce illegal immigration are not helped by rampant political correctness. In December 2014, in response to John Vine using the term 'irregular migrants', a Home Office spokesman said: 'If you say "illegal immigrants" there is a presumption and connotations that they have done something wrong. There are other reasons people come to this country by illegal methods, for instance because they are trafficked by organised crime groups'.

In March 2013 it was disclosed that more than 4,100 foreigners enter Britain each year without either a valid passport or a visa. It costs as much as £25,000 to deport each of these illegal immigrants, adding up to a £100million annual bill. Some of the illegal immigrants had flushed their documents down the lavatory on the flight to make it more difficult to deport them.

Ministers believe that up to one in four organised criminals are from overseas. The figure includes 7,400 'high-harm' criminals who are involved in fraud, drug-dealing and violence. In June 2013 the police have admitted that more than 40 'predatory' rapists had been allowed into Britain in a single year, and that 25% of those arrested for serious crimes and gang activities were foreigners. In January 2013, it was revealed that 3,980 foreign criminals, including murderers and rapists, remained in Britain as they had successfully avoided deportation. Many had used the Human Rights Act. Foreign criminals on immigration bail had committed three murders, three kidnappings, 14 sexual offences including rape, and there have also been 27 other violent crimes and 64 thefts. One example is Mustafa Abdi, a Somali child rapist, who Britain had been trying to deport for more than 10 years, at a cost of £600,000 in legal aid fees. He was awarded £7,000 and released after the European Court of Human Rights declared that his human rights had been breached by being 'wrongfully detained'. Abdi entered Britain in 1995 and claimed asylum. His claim was rejected but he was granted indefinite leave to remain. In 1998, he was convicted of the rape of a child and was sentenced to eight years in prison. In January 2014, a leaked Home Office document revealed that there were 10,779 foreign criminals in British prisons; there were another 1,430 detained pending removal; and another 4,238 had been freed as there was 'no reasonable expectation of removal in the short term'. Home Office figures in December 2014 showed that there were 11,719 foreign criminals in Britain, of whom 775 were murderers, 587 were rapists, 155 were child rapists and 15 were convicted terrorists. It was further revealed in December 2014 that thousands of criminals were being granted British citizenship each year (the number of immigrants gaining British citizenship had surged to 208,000 compared to 82,000 in 2000). Speaking to the Tory party conference in 1978, Mrs Thatcher said:

> 'Our civilisation has been built by generation after generation of men and women inspired by the will to excel. Without them we should still be living in the Stone Age. Without the strong who would provide for the weak? When you hold back the successful, you penalise those who need help.

Envy is dangerous, destructive, divisive – and revealing. It exposes the falsity of Labour's great claim that they're the party of care and compassion. It is the worst possible emotion to inspire a political party supposedly dedicated to improving the lot of ordinary working people.

From there it is but a short step to the doctrine of class warfare. The Marxists in the Labour Party preach that this is not only just, but necessary and inevitable.

But let me put this thought to you. If it is wrong to preach race hatred – and it is – why is it right to preach class hatred? If it's a crime to incite the public against a man simply because of the colour of his skin – and it is – why is it virtuous to do so just because of his position?

The political organization of hatred is wrong – always and everywhere. Class warfare is immoral, a poisonous relic of the past. Conservatives are as fallible, as human and therefore as given to making mistakes as the next man. But we don't preach hatred and we are not a party of envy.

Those who claim that we are a class party are standing the truth on its head. So, too, are those who claim that we are racists. Our determination to deal with the very real and difficult problems of immigration control has inspired Labour to a shameful attempt to frighten the coloured population of Britain.

Last month the Liberal leader (David Steel) added his voice to the chorus. No doubt in an effort to distract attention from his many deep and pressing problems, he too did his best – or worst – to pin the label of 'racialism' on the Conservative Party.

I realise that a drowning man will clutch at any straw. But let me remind young Mr Steel, millions of Conservatives were among those who spent five years of their lives fighting a war against racialism when he was still in short trousers.

It is true that Conservatives are going to cut the number of new immigrants coming into this country, and cut it substantially, because racial harmony is inseparable from control of the numbers coming in.

But let me say a word to those who are permanently and legally settled here, who have made their homes with us. Your responsibilities are the same as those of every other

British citizen, and your opportunities ought to be. Compulsory repatriation is not, and never will be, our policy and anyone who tells you differently is deliberately misrepresenting us for his own ends.'

Mrs Thatcher's moral certainly stands out in this quote. She had no doubt who was right and who was wrong; who was moral and who was immoral; and she gave no quarter to those she considered to be the enemy. She did not react to name-calling by trying to be a Trendy Leftie in the hope that she might be considered nice and not nasty. She did not regard political correctness as the basis of morality. And she won elections.

But despite indicating that they would bring mass immigration to an end, the incoming 1979 Tory government did not. Immigration was allowed to continue and it was under the Thatcher government that Britain became a net immigration country from 1983 onwards (apart from the years 1988, 1992 and 1993). The John Major government of the early 1990s lost control of the asylum system and immigration really started to take off. Under the Labour governments from 1997 onwards, any pretence at controlling immigration was abandoned, with *net* immigration breaking the 100,000 number in 1998. Labour wanted mass immigration to be maximised and demonized anyone who disagreed with them as racist. Andrew Neather, a former adviser to Tony Blair, Jack Straw and David Blunkett admitted that: 'I remember coming away from some discussions with the clear sense that the policy [of mass immigration] was intended – even if this wasn't its main purpose – to rub the Right's nose in diversity and render their arguments out of date'.

Now, the Ponzi class, be they Tories, Liberal Democrats, Labour or other members of it, are forcefully insisting that mass immigration is a good thing, that it increases growth, that Britain needs a higher population to pay for pensions, and even that it reduces the government deficit (according to the so-called Office for Budget Responsibility, for example). Stephen King, for example, even relies on the Ponzi arguments about an ageing population:

> 'If governments can control cross-border migration, they might, for a while, protect workers' incomes in the West. Tough controls over migration ultimately, however, may

be self-defeating. As the West ages, its greying population will increasingly depend on the support of immigrant workers. To turn them away will eventually leave the West weaker, not stronger. The demographic clock is ticking and alarm bells should be ringing for Western nations.'[860]

This is baloney. To deal with the allegation that we need ever more immigrants to pay for pensions (a Ponzi argument if ever there were one), figures produced by the ONS state that with net migration of 225,000 per annum then the dependency ratio (the number people aged over 65 per 100 people aged between 15 and 64) would increase to 50.5% by 2087 and the population would increase to 92.9million. By comparison, with net migration of 50,000 per annum, the dependency ration in 2087 would be 54.0% and the population would only increase to 74.2 million. Therefore, the extra immigration required to reduce the 2087 dependency ratio by 3.5 percentage points (from 54.0% to 50.5%) increases the population by an extra 18.7million, and this minor reduction in the dependency ratio requires continued net migration at the higher rate indefinitely.[861] Therefore, even the argument advanced by the Ponzi class, that ever more immigrants are needed to pay for pensions, does not justify the scale of immigration that has been thrust upon Britain against the wishes of ordinary people. The minor benefit of a minor reduction in the dependency ratio has to be set against the very significant costs of a very much higher population (it should be noted that in advocating this argument the Ponzi class, in true Ponzi fashion, completely ignore all the present and future costs of that immigration to the wider economy). In any event, the argument is specious. Pensions are not funded by taxing numbers of people. People may have to pay taxes, but to be exact, it is their *incomes* which are taxed. What is needed is an increase in *incomes*. One person earning £50,000 per annum will pay more tax than two people earning £25,000 each. What is needed is genuine growth.

Immigration is a Ponzi scheme all by itself and one could write a book on the damage done by it. A proper cost-benefit analysis of immigration would include not only a calculation of the likely net cost or extra tax revenue impact on government *in the short term*, but also the extra costs-benefit implications for ordinary people. There would be a *national*, not just a government, cost-benefit *balance sheet*. To begin with, there is the cost of processing the immigrants, especially so-called asylum seekers; this must include not only the cost to officialdom (e.g. the issuing of visas), but also the cost of legal aid, for example, incurred by the various immigrant groups as they fight to stay in the country. Then there is the cost to the criminal justice system for those immigrants who break the law. Then there is the cost, mostly ignored, to the victims of crime and their families. Then there is the cost in terms of housing. Not only do the immigrants have to be housed but, due to the housing shortage, there is also the cost to the quality of life of those English people who are denied social housing who would otherwise have got it were not so much of it being allocated to immigrants. Then there are the wider housing costs. It might be true that the housing shortage pushes up house prices, and so those who own property might benefit. But this has to be set against the extra financial burden of raising the finance and paying interest on mortgages to buy those properties. Many people today have been priced out of the housing market and can no longer afford, as a previous generation could afford, to own their own home. This trend has been worsened by the large-scale buying of properties by foreigners as an investment. Not only have the Chinese and Russians embarked on a property buying spree, but even wealthy Africans were reportedly spending nearly £4million per week on London properties. Investors from Hong Kong, China, Malaysia, Australia, Singapore and Sweden own sites in London earmarked for in excess of 30,000 properties. Major property developers, including Barrett Homes and Berkely Group, have opened offices in Bejing and Shanghai to sell direct to Chinese buyers. In Birmingham one prestige development has seen 30% of its flats sold to the Chinese. The Bank of China is offering mortgages to help Chinese buy British properties. Paula Higgins of the Homeowners Alliance said: 'The money from these buyers should be invested in businesses or the manufacturing industry not in family homes. This pushes up prices out of reach of families. How are first time buyers supposed to ... compete with a foreign investor who can pay for a home up front with cash?' In July 2015, £140million of flats of Maine Tower at Canary Wharf in London were sold in only five hours, even though they were not due to be built until 2019, with half of the flats being bought by foreigners including buyers from China, Greece, India and the Middle East.

A third of homeowners are now pensioners, due to the collapse in young people being able to buy their own homes. According to the

English Housing Survey, in 2003 71% of householders were owner occupiers. By 2014 it was 65.3% and falling. It has been forecast that by 2041 on present trends that only half the population will own their own homes. A record one in three men are still living with their parents. The figure for women is one in five. The increase is attributed to high house prices, low wages, high unemployment and increased numbers of university students. In 1996 there were 2.7million boomerang children who had had to return to their parents' home. That figure increased to 3.4million by 2014. The average cost of a first home has increased from £50,000 in 1996 to £190,000 in 2014. Under Mrs Thatcher the average age of the first-time buyer fell to around 25. It has since climbed to 37 and the National Housing Federation are forecasting that it will increase to 43 in the near future. Only 3% of house sales in June 2014 were to those aged between 18 and 30. For those affected, this loss in their quality of life and their future wealth is a real cost to them and is a cost of mass immigration – and the Ponzi scheme.

In December 2013 Nick Boles, the housing minister, announced that we need to build on more Green Belt land to accommodate the 100,000 immigrant families each year. Up to two million acres of green fields may have to be built upon to deal with the housing shortage. Nick Boles said: 'The population of England has gone up by two million in the last 10 years. These people now live here, these people are now British and they need homes just like other British people. The fact is, 43% of the new households which want a home, is accounted for by immigration. We can't go on like this. We need to have less immigration and more housebuilding'. Nick Clegg said: 'There's only one way out of this housing crisis: We have to build our way out'. In May 2014, it was estimated by the ONS that there would be a need for one million more houses in the South East alone. One in ten of those given social housing in 2012 were foreign. A count by the Department of Communities and Local Government showed that foreigners made up 10% of those newly given social housing, up from 9% the previous year and 6.5% in 2008. This equates to 23,000 homes, at an estimated cost to the taxpayer for those homes over their useful life of £1.5billion. The figures exclude those immigrants who have been given a British passport. The number of families waiting for social housing has reached 1.8million. Of the four million immigrants who entered Britain between 2001 and 2011, 469,843 had council or housing association properties. Melanie Phillips wrote: 'Last week it emerged that, between 2001 and 2011, almost 500,000 immigrants were given social housing at a cost to the taxpayer of up to £8billion. And this when a record 1.8million British families are on the social housing waiting list'. Around 1.2million foreigners now live in social housing, one in eight of the total. In London the figure is about one in five. A Home Office report, entitled Social and Public Service Impacts of International Migration at Local Level, highlighted that large numbers of immigrants were driving up the cost of rented accommodation, warning of 'inflated rents, unregistered houses of multiple occupation, exploitation by unscrupulous landlords, waste management and pest control issues that can quickly spread'. Then there was the problem of 'beds in sheds'. In July 2013 Slough Borough Council has had to hire a spy plane with a thermal imaging camera to identify those outbuildings being used as 'beds in sheds' to house immigrants. One two-hour night flight highlighted 6,350 suspicious dwellings. In June 2013, Police and immigration officials had to clear a 'shanty town' built by a group of mainly Romanian immigrants in Hendon, London. Out of 68 people, only five were discovered to have a right to be in Britain. The remainder were told to leave Britain before being released back into the community.

Those immigrants who have children, or who give birth to children after they enter the country, will need those children educating. There is therefore an increased burden on nurseries, primary and secondary schools. In 2013, a total of 1,061,000 schoolchildren have English as a second language. This is an increase of more than 5% in one year. 28.5% of primary schoolchildren and 24.2% of secondary schoolchildren are from ethnic minority families.

Five Primary schools in England do not have a single pupil who has English as their first language. Another 240 schools have at least 90% of pupils who grew up learning another language as their first language. Such schools receive extra funding from the Department for Education, which revealed in February 2014 that one in nine English schools now have a majority of pupils for whom English is a second language. There are now more Muslim children in Birmingham than Christian.

Children are being crammed into Primary schools, some with classes of more than 30, due to the shortage in places brought about by immigration, the baby boom and parents being priced out of the private sector. Due to limited places, one in ten children were going to a school that was not their parents' first choice. Some schools were using bulge classes – a one-off reception class that continues until spaces becomes available. Many schools were being expanded with extensive building work. The National Audit Office warned that an extra 240,000 places would be needed. In January 2015, the Local Government Association complained that the local council taxpayers could not meet the £12billion cost of the estimated extra 900,000 school places that would be needed over the next ten years. This has now become a real problem as the surge in immigration under Labour and hence the surge in immigrant children is now working through the system. All of this has to be paid for. But there is also the cost of the impact on the lives of the English who find that their children are in school classes which are far larger than would otherwise be, and even where they are in a minority with the majority perhaps not even speaking English as a first language if at all.

Immigrants and their families have to be cared for. They become entitled to benefits, use roads, and make demands on the NHS. At a time of austerity when the government is trying to reduce the benefits bill, these extra benefit payments to immigrants needlessly increases the benefits bill and/or reallocates monies away from the host nation (as well as the existing immigrant communities). This is a cost. Increased road usage places a strain on that infrastructure and is detrimental to existing road users. This is a cost to those road users in their quality of life, as well as the cost of maintaining and expanding the road network. The same applies to railways and airports. Then there is the cost to the affected local residents of the extra infrastructure construction, and adverse environmental considerations.

It is routinely alleged that the NHS is completely dependent upon immigrant labour for its continued functioning – from doctors, to nurses, to cleaners. That a supposedly leading country cannot train sufficient doctors and nurses to staff its own hospitals rather than draining such badly needed medical personnel from LDCs is as shameful as it is patently unnecessary. The NHS is recruiting thousands of doctors from abroad, from countries whose training is substandard by British standards, such as Egypt, Nigeria, Sri Lanka, Sudan, Libya, Burma, Syria, Kazakhstan, Liberia, and even four came from Haiti. India provides the most doctors, 25,336. In fact the government is restricting the training of doctors and now requires that nurses take university degrees (and thus incur all the expense of doing so). In 2005, as a result of the new system of training doctors, Modernizing Medical Careers, there was a fall in the number of places in the middle training grade of 50%, at the same time as the number of places in medical schools increased. This led to around 5,300 newly trained doctors emerging every year who were seeking middle training grade positions, and up to 2,000 of these were unemployed while the NHS continued to recruit from abroad. These junior doctors had cost £237,000 to train over a period of six years, and many still had substantial debts. In 2005, the impact of poaching of LDC health staff was highlighted by both the British Medical Association and the Royal College of Nursing in a press release:

> 'BMA chairman Mr James Johnson and RCN General Secretary Dr Beverly Malone warn that the migration of healthcare workers from developing nations is not only claiming millions of lives, but also preventing the world's poorest people from escaping poverty.'

The reliance on foreign medical staff has been exacerbated by the reduction in the numbers of medical staff trained in Britain. It was disclosed in December 2014 that between 2010 and 2014 the numbers of nurses trained was cut by 10,000. Up to 80,000 British students were not allowed to train as nurses as the training numbers were restricted to 20,000 (the number applying being 100,000), according to the RCN. Even older nurses wanting to return to work were unable to find places. Having made cuts to training and the staffing levels, hospitals resorted to an easy quick fix of importing nurses from abroad, irrespective of language difficulties. It was reported in December 2014 that of the 7,111 nurses who were recruited by the NHS in the last year, 5,778 had been recruited from abroad. In March 2015 it was revealed that Gloucestershire Hospitals, comprising of Gloucestershire Royal and Cheltenham General hospitals, alone recruited 200 overseas nurses. It costs £70,000 to train a nurse over three years, whereas a qualified nurse can by hired from abroad for an average of £23,000.

Meanwhile, hospitals have become more reliant upon less skilled staff such as nursing assistants – in other words there is a de-skilling of those tending to patients. Even so, the management of the NHS cannot be an excuse for mass immigration, whereby the immigrants are bound to increase demand on health services, in particular, presently, upon maternity facilities due to the immigrant baby boom. In 2013, more than half of maternity units admitted that they had had to send away mothers to other hospitals due to a shortage of midwives. One in four of mothers giving birth were left alone by midwives, the NHS watchdog, the Care Quality Commission, has disclosed. Some were forced to give birth on the floor in waiting rooms. Thousands of new midwives are needed according to The Royal College of Midwives (RCM). Cathy Warwick, chief executive of RCM, said: 'Maternity units are under intense strain, with many midwives really at the end of their tether. We are reaching a crucial tipping point for maternity services'. It is claimed that up to another 5,000 midwives are needed – a 25% increase. Those English mothers who find themselves struggling in a substandard service are paying a cost for this in that they are receiving substandard care.

The bill for health tourism has been calculated as costing the NHS £2billion per annum, and only 16% of the money is recovered, according to official figures. A Home Office report, entitled Social and Public Service Impacts of International Migration at Local Level, highlighted that those born abroad accounted for 73% of TB cases, 60% of HIV cases, and 80% of Hepatitis B-infected blood donors. As the immigrant communities age then so the demands they make on the NHS will increase. This is a cost that may not yet be imposing demands on current taxation, as is the case with a Ponzi scheme, but will certainly do so in the future.

As Say has set out, supply will equal demand. The law of supply and demand affects the jobs market like any other – albeit there are greater difficulties as Keynes pointed out and it may take longer for the market to clear. The increased numbers of immigrants looking for work not only displaces the indigenous population (as well as those immigrant communities already settled in Britain) but also forces down wages and living standards (this is unavoidable). For example, agricultural worker's wages fell by 6.6% in 2013 as a result of cheap labour from Eastern Europe, whose workers are prepared to work for the minimum wage. In May 2015, even the governor of the Bank of England, Mark Carney, admitted that 'strong population growth partly driven up by net migration' had 'contained wage growth in the face of robust employment growth'.

Sir Stuart Rose, the former Marks and Spencer boss, said: 'I'm a free market economist – we operate in a free market. If these people want to come here, and work the hours they are prepared to work for the wages they are prepared to work for, then so be it'. This free market argument needs to be qualified, as the government hands out £5billion in tax credits to immigrants, it emerged in July 2014.

The Migration Advisory Committee found that for every 100 non-EU workers employed in Britain, the number of British workers fell by 23. In August 2015 the total immigrant workforce had reached 4.9million, of whom more than two million were from other EU countries, amounting to roughly one in six of all workers. It is often alleged that immigrants will do work that the English will not and that they have a better work ethic. Apart from the insulting nature of such comments, the standards of conditions at work, such as the working conditions, holidays, and length of hours, are a part of the standard of living. Immigrants have pushed British people out of work. They have forced down wage rates.

It should be noted, that despite their supposed differences, the Ponzi class – the three main political parties, the banks, multinationals, the corporate sector, the unions, most charities, the media, senior civil servants and an array of quangos – have no complaints about the impact of immigration on the host nation, nor on the depressed living standards it causes. Not even the unions object or try to defend their members' interests. Despite a supposed 'progressive' outlook, the extra profits gained by large businesses by cutting wages is seen as acceptable, even if the costs of immigration are dumped onto the general public. Self-appointed 'progressive' opinion is so keen on immigration that it is impervious to the damage it causes.

In April 2013 it was discovered that Britain was advertising 250,000 jobs in the EU. Over half the jobs on the EU website were in Britain, compared to France which had only 14,000. In July 2013, the EU, under a scheme known as EURES, was offering British firms up to £870 for every foreign EU citizen they employed, up to a maximum of 20 per year. The scheme was being run with the assistance of JobCentres. Also, jobless youngsters across the EU could get a grant of £260 to travel to Britain for an interview and a further £870 grant if they get a job. More than 800,000 British jobs were being advertised under the scheme – more than half of the EU total.

There were 30.09million people in work in Britain in 2014. This included a record 1.1million pensioners. The numbers unemployed for more than 12 months was 866,000. 1.47million were working part-time. 1.2million more were in work than in 2010. The number of British people in work early 2014 was still below its 2005 peak (the number falling by 700,000 between 2008 and 2010), meanwhile the number of foreign-born workers in employment had increased by roughly 1.5million. Given the difference in living standards and the economic disaster of the Eurozone, it is scarcely surprising that many choose to immigrate to Britain. Incomes per capita in Eastern Europe are very low, Bulgaria's being only 39% of those of the Britain in 2013, Romania's being only 36%, Hungary's being only 54% and Poland's being only 57%. This is compounded by the unemployment levels, with 40% of Italians between 15 and 24 being unemployed in 2013, with the corresponding numbers unemployed in Portugal being 37.7%, Spain 55.5% and Greece 58.3%.[862]

The argument that immigrants are needed to fill supposed skills shortages is a fallacy and a deviation from genuine free market economics. Joseph Chamberlain highlighted the difficulties faced by those skilled workers who are made redundant and end up doing low-paid unskilled work. Free market theory is that workers in declining sectors move to thriving sectors of the economy. The price mechanism, the wage rate, is the facilitator of this. However, if those sectors which are booming and would otherwise have to offer better wages to attract workers can instead import immigrants, then where are those workers in declining sectors supposed to go? Those better paid jobs that would otherwise have been open to them are filled, and since the wage rate is not adjusted to attract new workers then the labour market does not function properly. Lower wages and living standards are the result.

In November 2013, Rachel Sawford, a single mother who attended University of Portsmouth as a mature student, was told not to mention her honours degree in her CV by JobCentre staff. Her experience is similar to Liza Fitzpatrick in Hull, who was likewise told not to mention her Honours Degree in her CV. The ONS has revealed that half of all graduates find work in a job not requiring a degree. Frances O'Grady from the TUC said: 'Nearly half of recent graduates are doing lower-skilled jobs. This is pushing young people who don't have a degree out of work altogether'. In June 2014 the Institute for Public Policy Research revealed that 20% of low-skilled jobs are taken by graduates. In January 2014, Esther McVey has advised young people to take low-paid jobs in coffee shops: 'You could be working at Costa. But in a couple of year's time you might say, "I'd like to manage the area" or might even want to run a hotel in Dubai'. Words fail. In 2013, 1,700 people applied for eight jobs at a new Costa coffee shop in Nottingham.

Those businessmen who say that they have a better workforce, one that does not have to be trained either, only measure the cost in terms of what they actually pay in wages. They do not pay those costs mentioned above which are ultimately born by the very taxpayers that the businessmen are denigrating. To be blunt, the businessmen concerned are freeloading. It should be noted that the Tory Government announcement in the July 2015 budget that they might get around to introducing a 'living wage' guarantee by 2020 was met with quiet dismay by big business, with John Cridland, head of the CBI, complaining that the move would put 'businesses under pressure'. That many British people are either jobless or else getting a lower wage than they otherwise would is a cost of immigration to them, in addition to the cost of extra unemployment benefit and more means-tested in work benefits paid for by the government. Let those businessmen, or government institutions, be it the NHS or universities (for example), pay those costs.

Such costs can be very high. Training and skilled occupations have to be nurtured. The apprentice system, which had originated in the Middle Ages, having benefited from ongoing government support across the centuries, had grown to 240,000 places by the 1960s. It had largely collapsed to a figure of 53,000 by 1990 (Germany had two million apprenticeships in 1993).[863] The government has since tried to revive it and there were 279,700 apprenticeships starting and 171,500 completing their courses in 2009/10. Many young people today have to work for free as an intern to get the relevant experience. Even then, there is no guarantee of employment and using free interns is a good way of cutting the wage bill. There is also the growth in zero-hours contracts, where workers have no certainty as to their hours worked or their income. A survey by the Chartered Institute of Personnel and Development of 1,000 companies found that at least 20% had at least one person on a zero-hours contract. If this applied across the country then up to one million workers are on such contracts. Another report estimated that the number of zero-hours contracts had doubled over five years to 1.4million.[864] Dave Prentis of Unison said: 'The vast majority of workers are only on these contracts because they have no choice'. Companies using them include JD Weatherspoon, Sports Direct and even Buckingham Palace. Sports Direct has 23,000 employees of whom 20,000 are on zero-hours contracts with no holiday or pension entitlements – while the pay and bonuses of the executives soared to such an extent that even the shareholders revolted at one point.[865] Amazon, which has been criticized for its tax avoidance, tags its zero-hours workers to monitor their activity.

Another hidden away cost of the British Ponzi scheme are the various PFI contracts. These commit the government, and hence the taxpayer, to make payments, often very lavish ones, to private sector companies who have built public assets, such as hospitals, which would formerly have been funded using taxpayers' money. By 2015, the NHS owed £121.4billion cumulatively for assets valued at £52.9billion.[866] The Labour government simply pocketed the tax income and then ran up large bills of unspecified amounts under their PFI contracts. The present coalition government is executing a similar scheme with Britain's power stations, where foreign companies are to be guaranteed lavish profits to construct nuclear power stations. These guaranteed payments are yet another hidden cost of Ponzi economics.

There is the further example of the 2014 floods, where, despite all the chatter about global warming – or climate change (being the preferred term given that the climate is not currently warming) – Britain has actually cut back on its flood defences and hence has suffered the worst flooding for a very long time. Dredging of key rivers was stopped, not only to save money but also out of environmental considerations such as protecting birds and other wildlife. The hapless householders who have been flooded are paying the price and the full cost is not simply the cost to the government, but the wider cost to the national community.

As with a commercial Ponzi scheme, the British Ponzi class are able to enjoy the trappings that the income stream of tax revenues allow, while the costs and debts pile up elsewhere. These trappings not only include remuneration and pensions (and also houses, chauffeur driven cars, generous expenses, overseas junkets etc.), but also the funds for various pet projects.

An expensive Ponzi class pet project is the EU. The original rationale for joining this organization was economic, although the organization itself was always political with the goal of an 'ever closer union'. The costs of joining were high, with Britain agreeing to make substantial payments towards the EU and made significant sacrifices such as discriminating against the farming produce of Australia and New Zealand (British kith and kin) and allowing British fishing waters to become open to all, and also the very high cost of complying with a vast array of EU directives, regulations and laws. The trade benefits Britain was so desperate to enjoy have turned out to be illusionary. According to a 2014 report from Civitas, using OECD figures, the EU states accounted for 63.9% of British exports in 1973 and only 61.9% in 2012. This fall is despite EU enlargement and despite North Sea Oil. Meanwhile British exports to Iceland, Norway and Switzerland, which are not EU members, more than doubled from 5.1% to 10.7%. According to the ONS British exports to the EU were 11.2% lower in the quarter period ending September 2014 compared to the same period in 2013. Only 5% of British firms directly export to the EU, and yet EU rules and regulations are enforced on all British businesses. The *net* cost of the EU payments was £11.3billion in 2013, according to the ONS.

A report from UKIP, written by Tim Congdon in September 2014, puts the total annual cost of the EU to Britain at no less than £185billion. Taking Britain's GDP to be just over £1,600billion in 2013, then the report estimates the costs to be: direct costs 1.25% of GDP; costs of regulation 6% of GDP; costs of resource misallocation 3.25% of GDP; costs of lost jobs 0.375% of GDP; costs of waste, fraud and corruption 0.375% of GDP; potential costs of contingent liabilities 0.25% of GDP. This totals 11.5% of GDP – roughly 185billion.[867] This is an enormous annual cost for membership of an organization which is presented as a necessity for economic prosperity, which it patently is not given the euro crisis if nothing else, and presented as benevolent. An alternative view is that the EU is a predatory, German-dominated, trade organization which is asset stripping Britain and dumping millions of continental unemployed and Third World immigrants onto British streets for good measure.

Another expensive pet project is overseas aid. This is very damaging to the giving nation from a Keynesian perspective as it constitutes an outflow of demand. The West has spent more than $2.3trillion in foreign aid over the last five decades.[868] By 2014, more money had been spent on Afghanistan, £62billion, than was spent reconstructing Europe after WWII under the Marshall Plan. Since 1960, more than $1trillion has been given to sub-Saharan Africa, while GDP in the region has fallen. In Palestinian territories, aid was doubled between 1996 and 2006, yet GDP halved. In the period 1950-2001, those poor countries with less than average levels of aid had the same growth rate as those with above average levels of aid. Botswana, for example, was one of the poorest countries in 1950 and yet enjoyed a 13-fold increase in income by 2001.[869] William Easterly, an American economist specialising in economic development, wrote:

> 'There is now a regular cycle in the literature on foreign aid and growth. Someone will survey the evidence and find that foreign aid does not produce growth. There will be some to-and-fro in the literature, in the course of which a few studies will find a positive effect of aid on growth. Foreign aid agencies will then seize upon the positive effect, usually focusing on only one study, and will publicize it widely. Researchers will examine the one positive result more carefully and find that it is spurious. Then there will be more to-and-fro in the literature, and a new twist will be discovered under which aid has a positive effect on growth. Aid agencies will seize on this result again, and the cycle will begin all over again.'[870]

One of the recent ideas is that what is needed is a big push on aid to break a poverty trap. However, a typical African country has already had what might be considered a big push, having received more than 15% of its income from foreign donors during the 1990s.[871] As aid surged growth fell, despite the fact that African growth had been 2% up to the mid-1970s. Even if the increased aid did not cause the slowing of the growth rate, it definitely did not halt that slowdown and per capita growth fell to almost zero.[872] Research by the LSE economist Peter Boone discovered that aid had a zero effect on investment and a zero effect on growth; what aid did do was boost consumption. Another study by World Bank economists Craig Burnside and David Dollar found that 'aid has a positive impact on growth in developing countries with good fiscal, monetary, and trade policies but has little effect in the presence of poor policies'.[873]

The White House website was keen to promote the idea that 'economic development assistance can be successful only if it is linked to sound policies in developing countries'. The Millennium Challenge Corporation (MCC), which the USA launched, was created to identify those countries which were deemed well governed and deserving of its aid programme, with Madagascar being the first country to be awarded aid.[874]

However, a subsequent study using additional data to that used by Burnside and Dollar, and conducting the same statistical analysis, found no evidence that aid increased growth even in those countries deemed to be well governed.[875] Once again a following study from the Centre for Global Development (CRB) took a different slant, this time focusing only on that aid which was deemed to have an impact on growth in the short term as opposed to that which had a long-term impact or humanitarian aid. This study concluded that there was a strong growth effect for aid with a short-term impact – even in those countries not designated as being well governed. This CRB study was subsequently cited as being evidence of the need for more aid by the UN Millennium Project Report in January 2005.[876] However, this CRB study revealed that there was a zero effect on growth when the aid reached 8% of the developing country's GDP and even higher rates of aid produced a negative effect on growth.[877] This finding contradicts the whole big push argument for aid that what is needed is a critical mass of aid to solve all a country's problems simultaneously.

Of only eight countries which have experience take-off into self-sustained growth in the 1950-1975 period all were in South East Asia: China, Hong Kong, India, Indonesia, Singapore, South Korea, Taiwan and Thailand. Only three, Indonesia, South Korea and Taiwan, had an above average level of aid. Other countries which received above average levels of aid did not take off into self-sustained growth.[878] Statistically those countries with high levels of aid are no more likely to take off than those with low levels of aid – which is contrary to the whole concept of an aid Big Push.

The British overseas aid budget reached £12.6billion per annum in 2014, more than the £12.1billion spent on policing. 60% of this aid is given to agencies such as the World Bank, the UN and the EU. In order to meet its spending target, in December 2013 the government was spending almost £60million per day (one report put the figure as high as £100million per day) on something or other, with the Department for International Development spending a quarter of its annual budget in one month. The Permanent Secretary for the department received a £20,000 bonus in addition to his salary of £165,000, presumably to reward him for the scale of the department's expenditure. Andrew Mitchell, the Tory overseas development minister, even boasted that Britain was to become 'a development superpower'. The mind boggles. The Commons International Development Committee has warned that the government has no checks on how this money is spent. Despite a supposed crackdown, the amount spent on foreign aid consultants leapt by 45% in October 2012 to £45.9million. The 'poverty barons' in receipt of monies include PriceWaterhouseCoopers, £4million in October 2012, and Adam Smith International, £5.8million, as well as foreign consultants such as ABT Associates which received £2.1million. The Big Six accountancy firms were major recipients of foreign aid for Eastern Europe, and they drafted laws, with little if any input from local people, to impose Western standards on the recipient countries to enable them to qualify for Western aid. The imposition failed. Likewise the attempts to impose Western standards failed in Africa.[879] One lesson being that England's development of common law, where the law develops in response to precedents, rather than civil law where theoretical solutions are imposed from above is a more successful route as it responds to local culture and is derived from practical issues.[880]

The attempt to impose a market economy on Russia, via top-down reforms and shock therapy, did not work. Far from forcing Russian firms to make profits and become competitive, shock therapy increased the number making a loss – up to 40% of the total and holding – and they survived via a network of bartering and back-scratching to secure orders. Russian per capita income fell 17% between 1989 and 2004.[881] William Easterly wrote:

> 'In one illustrative example, the Middle Volga Chemicals Plant in Samara Oblast managed to find a "market" for ten tons of toxic chemicals. It passed these along to Samara Oblast government in lieu of obligations to pay into the unemployment fund. The Samara government in turn used these chemicals to satisfy its obligation as a relatively rich region to make transfer payments to poor regions. It did so by agreeing with the Russian Ministry of Labour that Samara would ship goods to the unemployment

compensation fund in the poor republic of Mari-El. So the ten tons of toxic chemicals wound up in Yoshkar-Ola, the capital of Mari-El. What the unemployed workers in Mari-El did with ten tons of toxic chemicals is not known.'[882]

Britain spends more on overseas aid than any other G8 country, spending 0.56% of national income in 2011/2012, compared to 0.19% for the USA and 0.03% for Russia. Japan spends 0.17% of national income on overseas aid. Britain gives more in aid than Germany. Britain further has the expense of military commitments which those countries spending a similar percentage in overseas aid (Sweden, Norway, Denmark and the Netherlands) do not.

Transparency International has highlighted that Britain sends overseas aid to virtually all those countries with serious corruption in 2012. Somalia, branded by Transparency International as the most corrupt country in the world and described by the World Bank as the worst governed, received £86.8million; North Korea received £756,000; Afghanistan received £200.4million; Sudan received £50.5million; South Sudan £107.6million; Libya, despite its oil reserves, £6.7million; Iraq £5million; Uzbekistan £1.6million; Turkmenistan £416,000; Syria £38.5million; Zimbabwe £139million; and the Democratic Republic of Congo also £139million. Britain gives more than £2million to Argentina, a hostile country with designs on the Falklands Islands and a member of G20, in overseas aid and a further £7million via the EU. In 2013, Britain spent in excess of £1billion on the most corrupt regimes, according to Transparency International, with spending increasing by almost a quarter in 2013 compared to 2012. All but one of the 20 most corrupt regimes received aid from Britain. In Somalia aid monies are reportedly being used to fund Al Qaeda-backed terrorists.

Ethiopia received the most aid of £261.5million in 2012, followed by Pakistan £203million and India £197million. Commons International Development Committee has complained that Pakistani corruption is rife and that wealthy Pakistanis pay little tax (less than 1% of Pakistanis pay tax), while Pakistan is set to become the largest recipient of British aid, reaching £446million in 2014/2015. A report from the Indian government, in May 2011, found that £70million from the DfED's £388million budget for the Education for All programme was either lost or stolen. Much of the money was allocated to schools that did not even exist, and amounts were spent on private cars for officials. School attendances by both children and teachers was found to be dismally low. Britain suspended £11million in aid to Uganda due to fraud. Only aid that is funded through non-governmental agencies will continue following allegations of Ugandan government theft of aid monies. In Uganda, the road network funded by aid is so extensive that the country cannot afford the maintenance costs, a report from the Independent Commission on Aid Impact found. Auditors have discovered that more than half of the £1.6billion funding in aid to the Congo has been wasted, failing to deliver any results – £240million of which was from Britain. In one example, 1,000 police officers trained in 2005 have 'vanished without trace'. British taxpayers funded the Congolese police even after reports of their involvement in summary executions. Congo's MP's salaries were increased tenfold – although this did not come from EU funds.

In 2010/2011 the DfID spent £900million on climate change projects, many of which were 'awareness-raising' exercises involving well-paid consultants. For example, in Indonesia grants were allocated to help the government with 'effective leadership and management of climate change programming'. South Africa, Ghana, Uganda and Kenya, all of which are receiving British aid (totalling £1.5billion over the next five years – Kenya £596million, Uganda £480million, Ghana £460million and South Africa £112million), each have their own space programme. Aid to South Africa is due to end in 2015. India has its own overseas aid programme, amounting to £328million per annum. In 2010, India was the largest recipient of British overseas aid at £421million in that year. India has spent £600million on its space programme and has even put a spacecraft into orbit around Mars. It has a large defence budget, including nuclear weapons, and in February 2015 announced a £10billion expansion of its navy with orders for new frigates and nuclear-powered submarines. Andrew Mitchell granted another £1.1billion in aid in 2010. Aid is due to end in 2015.

Britain will increase aid to Nigeria to £275million in 2014. Nigeria is one of the MINT economies (Mexico, Indonesia, Nigeria and Turkey) and is expected to become a major power. All of Britain's aid is funnelled through agencies, such as UNICEF, and private contractors. Nigeria is spending millions in a space programme and expects to have astronauts ready within two years.

Nigeria is due to receive £1.14billion in aid over the next five years. Nigeria has three satellites in orbit and expects to construct its own spacecraft by 2028. Professor Seidu Onailo Mohammed announced: 'By our road map we are supposed to have astronauts prepared by 2015. Before the end of the year, the recruitment of astronauts will begin so that we have them handy and as soon as we get the nod we can pick from that number'. Despite its poverty, Nigeria has oil revenues of £40billion per annum and spends £31million per annum on champagne. Nigeria's population is 170million. Nigeria has oil reserves amounting to 35billion barrels – enough to supply the entire planet for one year – and also 100trillion cubic feet of natural gas. It produces more crude oil than Texas. Its legislators are paid £122,000 – more than double the salary of a British MP. 70% of Nigerians live below £1.29 per day.

Since independence in 1960, Nigeria has received £257billion in aid – six times more than the USA spent on the Marshall Plan for Europe after WWII. 136million barrels, worth $11billion, were skimmed off in corruption in 2009 to 2011. Millions in subsidies were paid for petrol that was never supplied. It is estimated that roughly £245billion of government money has been stolen since 1960. Almost 100,000 barrels of oil are being stolen in Nigeria every day, from pipelines, ports and storage tanks with the connivance of officials, politicians and the military. This amounts to £2billion every year. A Chatham House report has stated: 'Nigerian crude oil is being stolen on an industrial scale. Proceeds are laundered through world financial centres. In Nigeria, politicians, military officers, militants, oil industry personnel, oil traders and communities profit, as do organised criminal groups'. Britain is highlighted as a 'hotspot' where profits are laundered, involving 'bulk cash smuggling ... heavy use of middlemen, shell companies and tax havens, bribery of bank officials, cycling cash through legitimate businesses and cash purchases of luxury goods'. Justine Greening, the International Development Secretary, said on Radio 4: 'I believe it [the aid to Nigeria] is well spent ... We do expect them to invest in their country as well. The so-called space programme was in fact investment in satellites, weather satellites and for communication. So actually this investment that they're making in the so-called "space programme" which is actually satellite technology, some of which actually has been provided by UK companies based in Surrey, is a sensible investment and actually one that we would be expecting them to be making alongside the investment that we make'.

The extent of the aid farce is such that an Ethiopian farmer has been granted British legal aid to sue Britain for sending aid to Ethiopia! He has been granted anonymity, and is arguing that his human rights have been breached because Britain has been giving money to a brutal regime that drove thousands of farmers off their land. Amnesty International has accused the Ethiopian security services of murder, rape and torture. The judiciary have ruled in the High Court, citing human rights legislation, that to ban foreigners from claiming legal aid, even to sue Britain itself, would be 'unlawful and discriminatory' and its justification would be 'little more than reliance on public prejudice'. Britain even granted £4million in aid to an Ethiopian equivalent of the Spice Girls, with further aid to follow under a Girl Hub project supposedly to 'empower' African girls.

An EU fund, the European Development Fund, in receipt of £400million a year from Britain has funded trapeze, acrobatic and juggling lessons in Tanzania, a study of coconuts in the Pacific, a study into 'youth perceptions, attitudes and views towards EU development policy' as well as 'media and communication' support for EU delegates in Jamaica. Directly, Britain has funded Hamlet workshops in Ecuador, paying for Haitian schoolchildren to see Hamlet, an anti-litter campaign in Jordan, and a campaign to promote 'safe and responsible' use of Facebook in Laos. While half the 28 industrialized nations cut their overseas aid spending, Britain's was increased with foreign aid staff being paid up to £1,000 a day.

Despite the abuses, the British government has passed legislation to enshrine the 0.7% of GDP aid target into a legal requirement. Only six MPs voted against with 164 voting in favour. By comparison there is no legal commitment to maintain Britain's defence spending at the NATO target of 2% of GDP, despite the increasing international instability – whether it be the descent of the so-called Arab Spring into chaos and civil war across many countries, the increasingly assertive China, or the incursions into British airspace and territorial waters by an expansionist Russia. In the face of such threats, Britain's military capability continues to be run down to the point of being puny (the Royal Navy, for example, once the largest in the world, now has only 19 surface warships). After the May 2015 election the Tory Government did promise to keep defence spending at the NATO target of 2%, although it emerged that this was to be achieved by fiddling the figures to include items such as war pensions, UN peacekeeping missions, pay-outs to retired civil servants, and switching some of the intelligence and security services budget to defence – thus increasing the 'defence' spending by 14% by 2020 according to the Royal United Services Institute.

Another pet project is climate change. In May 2013 The Renewable Energy Foundation reported that: 'Shifting to current renewables for the bulk of our energy would result in a reversal of the long-run economic trend since the Industrial Revolution. More people would be working for lower wages in the energy sector, energy costs would rise, the economy would stagnate and there would also be a significant decline in people's standard of living ... The annual additional cost to consumers will be upwards of £16billion a year in 2020, which is over 1% of current GDP. One-third of this cost would hit households directly through their electricity bills, regardless of income, making it an intensely repressive measure. The remainder of the cost would be passed through from industrial and commercial customers and eventually be met by households from increases in the cost of living. The total impact would be in the order of £600 per household per year'. A new £1billion offshore wind farm off the Lincolnshire coast, opened on the 1st August 2013 by Nick Clegg, has been largely constructed by foreign firms, employing foreign workers and the site will be maintained by foreign workers flown in from Scandinavia. So the taxes raised to pay for this are to be used to create jobs abroad – yet again. Meanwhile, Japan abandoned its commitment to the Kyoto protocol to cut greenhouse gas emissions. Instead greenhouse emissions would increase by 3% by 2020. Britain has further spent at least £1.6billion on so-called green projects in the Third World, including countries such as Brazil, India and South Africa, and including expenditure on flood defences while back in Britain, Somerset and other areas suffered severe flooding due to a lack of flood defences and a failure to dredge the rivers. Britain even spent £27million fighting global warming in China even though the Chinese are building two coal-fired power stations per week. According to the Treasury's own figures, the burden of so-called Green taxes is estimated to amount to £4.6billion on businesses in 2015.

The Ponzi class dispenses austerity on the wider economy, but pet projects and the living standards of the state sector remain protected. In October 2013, Sir Gus O'Donnell, the former Cabinet Secretary from 2005 to 2011, writing in *The Political Quarterly*, condemned 'the ludicrous bias whereby the old are subsidised by the young' as being 'bad economics and bad social policy'. He further opined that the government's determination to bring down net migration may lower future potential output. While pensioners might be deemed a target for cuts, yet again, the state sector bureaucracy is not. In July 2013 researchers at Birmingham and Sheffield universities revealed despite all the talk of cuts, that out of around 900 quangos, only 199 were no longer a public body. Of the 199, only 80 have been completely abolished whereas the remainder have been had their functions transferred to other state entities. Government spending in 2015 will be the same in real terms as it was in 2010. Meanwhile the government debt will have increased from £1trillion in 2010 to almost £1.5trillion in 2015. Despite their dismal failure to govern effectively, MPs received an 11% increase in their salaries to £74,000 from 2015 with an accompanying increase in their pensions. The increase has been made by the Independent Parliamentary Standards Authority, whose own management are paid more than MPs.

The special treatment is not confined to the government. For example, a review by PricewaterhouseCoopers for the BBC Trust, which discovered that the BBC's senior managers were being paid up to three times more than other public sector counterparts, was suppressed. The BBC lavished £369million in severance payments in an eight-year period, the National Audit Office revealed. £61million had been given to senior managers. In a quarter of the cases, the payments were in excess of what the staff were entitled to. In November 2014 it was revealed that 286 full time staff had been made redundant over a 12-year period, receiving £10million in redundancy payments, before being rehired. Some had been re-employed despite receiving redundancy payments of up to £365,000. A report from the BBC independent trustees states that the BBC intends to allocate £740million of licence fee monies over four years towards its pension scheme black hole which has almost doubled to £2billion from £1.1billion in 2010. The BBC's commitment to stop paying its presenters off-payroll via personal service companies in order to reduce their tax, ran into difficulty as those affected refused to cooperate, even though by becoming

BBC employees they would qualify for pensions and other benefits. It is estimated that they would have to have pay cuts of 25%. More than 6,000 freelances are involved. In June 2015, it was disclosed that of the licence-fee funded BBC's annual budget of £5.1billion only £2.4billion is actually spent on programmes. Fearful that the government might not increase the licence fee, the BBC orchestrated a lobbying exercise by a number of sympathetic luvvies, which backfired when the lavish salaries of those luvvies was highlighted. By September 2015, the BBC had hit on another idea. Its director general, Tony Hall, said that the BBC needed more money and that the licence fee was no longer sufficient. He thought that 'a household fee merits further consideration, because it could bring new investment and safeguard the BBC's support for the creative economy for the long term'.

The BBC is not the only public sector organization where certain employees benefit from high salaries and generous payments. In May 2014 it was disclosed by the Intergenerational Foundation that more than 12,000 retired public sector workers were in receipt of pensions 'in excess of £50,000 a year', with 150 people getting more than £100,000 per year. A Department of Health investigation showed, in May 2014, that more than 2,400 NHS staff were using off-payroll arrangements to reduce their taxes. Most of these were bureaucrats. One NHS executive, aged 58, at a time that her trust was declaring losses of £15.7million, pocketed £155,000 tax free by 'retiring' for 24 hours before being rehired on her previous salary of £190,000 a year plus expenses. In May 2015, it was revealed that more than 14,000 NHS had retired in the previous year on £50,000 per year pensions.

Not only are public sector employees or multinationals tax dodging. A whole host of celebrities including footballers, TV presenters, actors, actresses and singers have been exposed for using a variety of schemes to minimize their tax liabilities. All of which might be acceptable were it not for the high percentage of such people continuously demanding that more taxpayers' monies are used on a number of politically correct worthy causes. In February 2015 one such scheme was revealed to have had 141 stars and wealthy people who were believed to have jointly saved £28million in tax. In February 2014 one Radio 1 DJ claimed to have been a second-hand car dealer in an attempt to save £1million in tax. In May 2014, one scheme, Icebreaker LLP, was revealed to have had as much as £336million invested in it from a variety of people including a football club manager and a former Olympic athlete. In July 2014, one scheme, called Liberty, had 1,600 investors including celebrities, lawyers and doctors who were trying to shield an estimated £1.2billion from tax in a network of offshore companies; HMRC missed a 12-month deadline for reclaiming much of the money and so many were able to benefit from the intended tax avoidance. However, also in July 2014, HMRC acted more decisively and published a list of 1,200 schemes and given the investors 90 days to pay their taxes. It was believed that up to 33,000 individuals and 10,000 companies were involved, with an estimated £4.9billion owed. Notoriously, the HSBC bank was exposed as helping 7,000 people avoid tax via its own private banking operation and schemes in Switzerland. One senior BBC figure was revealed in September 2014 as being sued for her involvement in HSBC cash laundering.

In the corporate sector, while business managers and executives firmly believe in cheap immigrant labour, such parsimony does not extend to their own remuneration packages. It was revealed in August 2015 that, despite the flat economy, the chief executives of Britain's top 100 firms pocketed around £5million each – 183 times the average worker's annual salary.

On top of all this, not to be left out, in February 2015 the judiciary started complaining that they were not being paid enough; Appeal judges being on £200,661 per year and High Court judges being on £176,226 a year. 90% of all judges considered themselves to be deserving of higher pay. In May 2015, 190 judges even went so far as to take legal action against government regarding allegedly 'discriminatory and unlawful' proposals to amend their pensions, condemning the changes as being motivated by cost considerations. The judges are noted as having a very generous pension scheme. Britain has been spending £2billion a year on legal aid, which is 20 times the European average and seven times the amount spent by France or Germany. Lawyers have been receiving millions of pounds representing foreigners, such as Iraqis, who have made claims of abuses in order to sue British institutions. Public Interest Lawyers, one firm, was revealed in December 2014 to be representing 1,500 Iraqis who were claiming damages from Britain. These cases stem from judges using so-called human rights laws to in effect help themselves to taxpayers' monies to pursue a variety of politically correct causes.

Rather than introducing a rough and ready means of calculating a divorce settlement, lawyers continue to pocket tens of thousands, if not hundreds of thousands of pounds representing divorcing couples – and thus pocketing a large part of the marriage assets. In December 2014, Judge Mostyn described as 'madness' a divorce case where the couple had spent nearly one-third of their assets on legal and expert fees. Of £2.9m in assets the wife will receive 38.9%, the husband will receive 29.2% and lawyers and experts will be paid 31.9%. The same applies to small businesses in financial difficulties where a large part of the assets are pocketed by lawyers and accountants.

The concept of actually acting in the national interest is considered vulgar to many of the Ponzi class. David Goodhart wrote: 'When dining at an Oxford college and the eminent person next to me, a very senior civil servant said: "When I was at the Treasury, I argued for the most open door possible to immigration (because) I saw it as my job to maximise global welfare not national welfare"'. This view was endorsed by a powerful TV executive who felt that global welfare was paramount. Such people can carry on in this way because they are able to offload the costs of their actions onto the long-suffering English taxpayer.

Another internationalist visionary is Thomas Piketty, a Marxist, who has been hailed by the *New York* magazine and his supporters as 'the rock star economist'. Piketty has produced his own magnum opus, which has been lauded by the Left almost as if it were the New Testament, dealing with not mere national economic issues – but *global* inequality and how to solve it.

Piketty, to pick up on two of his ideas, advocates mass immigration as a means of reducing *global* inequality and also a *global* tax to redistribute wealth. In some ways Piketty prefers mass immigration as being a 'more peaceful form of redistribution and regulation of global wealth inequality ... Rather than move capital, which poses all sorts of difficulties, it is sometimes simpler to allow labour to move to places where wages are higher'.[883] In this Piketty is in agreement with free traders such as Stephen King: 'If, then, capital mobility is to be reduced, it makes perfect sense actively to encourage the enhanced mobility of labour both within and between countries'.[884] The hard left are in agreement with Free Traders.

Piketty asserts that mass immigration has been of great benefit to the United States, where those immigrants on low incomes are settled as they are still better off than they otherwise would be in the countries of origin, and that Europe is increasingly experiencing the US phenomena although:

> 'It bears emphasizing, however, that redistribution through immigration, as desirable as it may be, resolves only part of the problem of inequality. Even after average per capita output and income are equalized between countries by way of immigration and, even more, by poor countries catching up with rich ones in terms of productivity, the problem of inequality – and in particular the dynamics of global wealth concentration – remains ... One might hope, moreover, that immigration will be more readily accepted by the less advantaged members of the wealthier societies if such institutions are in place to ensure that the economic benefits of globalization are shared by everyone. If you have free trade and free circulation of capital and people but destroy the social state and all forms of progressive taxation, the temptation of defensive nationalism and identity politics will very likely grow stronger than ever in both Europe and the United States.'[885]

Piketty recognises that his idea of 'a progressive global tax on capital' is 'a utopian idea' that will not be implemented 'anytime soon', not least due to the lack of the necessary international level of cooperation, but nevertheless it is an idea that should be pushed as a useful benchmark against which other activities can be judged.

What is worth noting is that Piketty is openly advocating greater national wealth inequality, and presumes that those immigrants benefiting from their higher incomes than they would otherwise have in their own countries will be grateful and not restive. This is the precise opposite of politically correctness, where immigrants are seen as a means of bringing about revolution, and the precise opposite of the experience of the host countries across Europe that are having to deal with increased ghettoisation and terrorism by disaffected immigrant communities.

Arguably, the most damaging legacy of Keynes' thinking, is the notion that there is no such thing as finite resources. That the government can just borrow and spend, and that money sort of circulates around and so it all pays for itself. It does not. Resources must come from somewhere. If the government suddenly borrows large sums of monies, then those monies must come from somewhere. If they are to be found by attracting existing savings then interest rates will go up, thus imposing extra borrowing charges on businesses and ordinary people, and competing with businesses for funds. If the monies are to be attracted from abroad, then funds will be used to invest in government debt and not used to buy British goods. If the money is simply printed then that creates inflation and/or, as with the QE programme, it will destroy much of the value of annuities. Resources are finite. Someone somewhere ends up out of pocket.

Britain, as with the rest of Europe, is a developed country. In 1862, the USA passed the Homestead Act giving people 160 acres to farm provided they farmed it for five years. The USA was sparsely populated and was able to exploit untapped resources. Britain cannot. In its natural state, Britain is an emigrant country not an immigrant country.

The commitment to the policy of mass immigration is not only a consequence of the policy of Ponzi economics, that ever more immigrants are needed to pay for an ageing population; or of the hegemony of the ideology of political correctness with its attendant multiculturalism, that mass immigration is good as it dilutes and will eventually replace Western culture and opposition to this is politically incorrect and must therefore be demonized as being a dislike of immigrants (this is beyond the scope of this book); but is also a consequence of the corruption of free trade into the policy of globalization, that national boundaries should be ignored for Western countries and a flow of immigrants to the West, as Piketty openly advocates, is desirable, and that immigration control is a form of protectionism.

Lord Mandelson advanced the protectionist argument regarding immigration in 2009, in the depths of the slump, when workers went on strike at the Lindsey Oil Refinery in protest at the use of foreign workers by an Italian company at the site. Lord Mandelson said: 'It would be a huge mistake to retreat from a policy where, within the rules, UK companies can operate in Europe and European companies can operate here. Protectionism would be a sure-fire way of turning recession into a depression'.

More recently the protectionist argument has been advanced on the conservativehome website by Stephen Tall, co-editor of LibDem Voice, who argued that the Tories 'have form' regarding free trade and claimed that the free trade Liberals defeated Joseph

Chamberlain's attempt at tariff reform and that: 'wind the clock forward a hundred years and – once more into the breach, dear friends!' The Liberals were allegedly 'standing up for free and open trade' unlike the Tories and 'those latter-day protectionists, UKIP'.[886] In advancing this fiction Tall opposed what he described as 'anti-immigration protectionism'. It is untrue that either the Tories or UKIP are protectionist, or even that they oppose mass immigration. Tall's fiction regarding Joseph Chamberlain and the Tariff Reform campaign ignores the fact that there was no free trade in the early part of the 20th century; what there was, given that all other countries apart from Britain were protectionist, was only a British policy of tariff free imports, and ignores the fact that tariff reform ultimately triumphed in 1932 when Britain successfully implemented policies that were responsible for the dramatic return to growth. Tall dismissed the Tory net immigration policy as being trying to 'hit an entirely arbitrary target' 'no matter what the cost to business'.[887] Tall totally ignored the cost of immigration to ordinary people, in the form of overstretched public services, higher taxes, lower wages and a lower quality of life due to the housing shortage etc., and was only concerned with the saving in wages that business might make. In support of his attack Tall cited both *The Economist* and the Institute of Directors. *The Economist* 18 months previously had condemned the Tory attempt to limit mass immigration as 'barmy' and as 'crippling business and the economy'. Simon Walker, the Director General of the Institute of Directors, had said: 'The UK is an open, trading economy that benefits from the skills and ideas of migrants. We will not become more prosperous by closing our borders to talented individuals and entrepreneurs from across the world'.[888] Once again, the costs of mass immigration are totally ignored, in true Ponzi fashion.

In the *Daily Telegraph*, a Tory supporting newspaper, James Kirkup wrote: 'For some time, the populists have held the upper hand on immigration. But perhaps, just perhaps, something is stirring. The free marketeers are stepping up the fight for the free movement of people'.[889] Kirkup was particularly excited by a diatribe from, of all places, the Adam Smith Institute:

> 'UKIP's line on immigration is intellectually and morally bankrupt. Despite what UKIP claims, immigration is good for virtually everyone in society, rich and poor alike. The evidence is clear that even low-skilled immigration only

hurts low-skilled native wages temporarily, and does not affect the number of jobs available to natives at all. The reason for this is that immigrants demand services as well as supplying them; every job taken by an immigrant also means a new job will be created to supply him or her with their needs.

Opposing immigration is economically no different to 19th Century-style trade protectionism – the only difference is where the people we're trading with are. Economists left and right, agree that trade makes everyone richer, and immigration just allows us to trade with more people more often at home. One of the best things about the EU has been the guarantee of free movement between member states; to throw that away would be an economic catastrophe. If UKIP's priority is to leave the EU, it is vital that they maintain open borders with the EU.

Immigrants are a huge boon to the welfare state. Because they are usually young and motivated to find work, they pay more in taxes overall than they cost the state in services. As Britain gets older, with more and more retirees to provide for with pensions and healthcare, we will need more immigrants to avoid a massive debt crisis by 2050. Far from being a cost to the state, immigrants may be the only way to fulfil our obligations to the older generation.'[890]

The Adam Smith Institute has not only embraced globalization, a corrupted evolution of free trade, but also Ponzi economics proper, a corrupted version of Keynesianism – both of which are reinforced by the ideology of political correctness. This is an apparently free market organization advocating irresponsible, hard-left politics with a scant regard for the interests of ordinary people. The idea that economic development requires manufacturing, which in turn requires investment and product development, does not enter the Adam Smith Institute's considerations at all; they completely ignore historical facts. If the resources to meet the demands made by immigrants were as unlimited and freely available as the Adam Smith Institute assumes, then the strain on public services or the housing shortage, for example, would not have occurred. The argument about the need for ever more immigrants to provide for pensioners is a pure Ponzi argument and is economically illiterate.

One might marvel at the remark that low-skilled immigration 'only hurts low-skilled native wages (i.e. the poor) temporarily'. On the Adam Smith Institute's own logic, since mass immigration is ongoing, open ended, and escalating, then this means that the damage to the living standards that 'only' the poor suffer is not temporary but likewise ongoing, open ended and escalating – i.e. the hurt is *permanent*. Adam Smith's original idealistic analysis of the economy has been replaced with a casual malevolence spouted by zealots using his name.

Keynes warned of 'madmen in authority, who hear voices in the air, are distilling their frenzy from some academic scribbler of a few years back'. Now those madmen are mindlessly chanting slogans from the last century and chant the slogans ever louder as the evidence mounts that the slogans are not capable of resolving the economic ruin to which Britain has been subjected.

SUMMARY

In run up to the May 2015 general election in Britain, much noise was made as to the Tories' long term economic plan and how they had reduced the government spending deficit – that is they were still borrowing vast sums of money each year but that the scale of the borrowing was lower than it had been at the end of the rule of the previous Labour government. There had now been growth and the nation should be humbly grateful to the Tories for its return. There had been under the Tory/Liberal Democrat coalition government a number of changes as to how the statistics measuring growth had been compiled. For example, the inclusion of prostitution and drug-dealing in the growth figures.

That there was growth and a more positive economic outlook should not be taken as being a government achievement. Apart from fiddling the statistics, the massive fall in oil prices was bound to help the economies of all countries. Between June 2014 and December 2014, the oil price fell by no less than 45%. The price continued to fall in 2015. This helped reduce inflation to virtually nothing and then to actually reduce prices – or deflation. Given its causes, this deflation can only be a good thing and has a beneficial impact on the standard of living given that wages were by 2015 mildly increasing.

Even so, government borrowing continued with the size of the national debt, and hence the interest payments on it, increasing remorselessly – although the interest payments were less than originally anticipated due to interest rates being kept so low. British workers remained far less productive than their other G7 counterparts, being 19% below the G7 average according to the ONS in October 2014. Unemployment fell sharply under the Tory/Liberal Democrat coalition, but much of this was due to a surge in part-time jobs and workers being willing to work for lower pay. The unemployment rate was down to 6% by October 2014. Nevertheless, the increase in income tax receipts was only a measly 0.8% and not the 6.5% forecast by the OBR. Consequently the large government deficit continued and the national debt continued to mushroom. The low-paid part-time jobs created were not only insufficient to increase living standards but also were insufficient to seriously increase tax receipts. The real poverty of poor families cannot but help contribute to the numbers of mothers who find that they have to return to work to help make ends meet.

Despite the talk of an export-led recovery, there was no such thing. The recovery was dependent upon consumer and government spending. Export performance was weak. In the third quarter of 2014, household spending increased by 0.8% and government spending increased by 1.1%; exports fell by 0.4% and business investment fell by 0.7%. The National Institute of Economic and Social Research revealed in December 2014 that in the three months to November 2014 GDP had increased by 0.7% while manufacturing output had fallen by 0.7% (despite the fall in oil prices); manufacturing output had increased by a modest 1.7% in the year to October. There had been no rebalancing of the economy. In the first half of 2015, manufacturing output fell again – hence falling back into recession; in the third quarter it fell again, by 0.3%. This poor manufacturing performance is during an economic recovery. Whereas output for the whole economy was 8% higher in the second quarter of 2015 compared with the first quarter of 2007, for manufacturing output was 5% *lower*.[891] In 2014, manufacturing productivity grew by 3.4% compared with growth of 0.2% for the whole economy,[892] once again demonstrating the importance of manufacturing. In 2014, manufactured goods amounted to 44% of total exports (£224.3billion), and 56% of all imports (£305.6billion). In 1998, the figures were 60% of all exports and 65% of all imports.[893]

The slow growth, low tax receipts and continuing lavish government spending on pet projects as well as those areas ring-fenced, such as the NHS and foreign aid, means that it has been forecast by the Financial Times and by the OBR in November 2014 that unprotected areas of government spending face savage cuts after the general election and that the promised tax cuts are unaffordable. Unprotected departments face cuts of 33% compared with cuts so far of only 21% since 2009-10. The Institute for Fiscal Studies predicted in December 2014 that welfare spending would need to cut by £21billion after the general election. That further cuts were necessary was not in dispute. George Osborne openly boasted in December 2014 that: 'We are going to have to make savings ... but the prize is economic stability, growth, jobs in the future, brighter future, I think that's a price that works for our country'. Osborne promised cuts for at least another four years, which merely confirmed what David Cameron had told the House of Commons in November 2014: 'We have made clear that after the next election there will be further reductions in spending. The alternative of simply putting up taxes would destroy the recovery'.

It is of course very easy for bureaucrats and politicians to make cuts in services, overlooking that there is much to be cut from the bloated budgets of their own administrations and pet projects. Showing off as to the amount of taxpayers' monies gifted to a variety of crooks, gangsters and terrorists in a vast array of LDCs is sacrosanct, yet having a bedroom too many in rented accommodation is intolerable and cuts to home helps to care for the elderly in their own homes is deemed necessary. The seizure of the homes of those taken into care homes is to continue apace.

In February 2014, the Taxpayers' Alliance had calculated that the government was wasting as much as £120billion per year, and alleged that the government had 'squandered' as much as £1 of every £6 it spent – £4,560 per household: 'the amount of waste revealed is greater than the UK deficit and is bigger than the Gross Domestic Product of New Zealand'. The report recommended that public sector wages, pensions and sick pay should be brought into line with those of the private sector; and further recommended that the Department for Culture, Media and Sport be abolished. Jonathan Isaby, the chief executive of the Taxpayers' Alliance, said: 'Politicians and bureaucrats are still squandering our cash while families struggle with punishing levels of taxation'.

In March 2014, Save Our Savers, a campaign organization, claimed that savers had lost £326billion due to the low interest rates compared to the pre-credit crunch rates of interest. This loss, as well as the other losses of the wider economy, caused by the banks should be set against the announcement in December 2014 by George Osborne, in all seriousness, that the banks would have to pay £3.85billion over five years as part of their contribution to meet the bill of recovery. Osborne had decided that the banks would only be able to set off half of their profits against past losses. Bonuses for bankers and traders are running at around £14billion per annum. Meanwhile, the banks not only continued to starve small businesses of loans, but also continued to call in loans and hence plunging the firms affected into insolvency. The most high profile example of which was the RBS GRG division whose activities were disreputable if not criminal, as was highlighted by the Tomlinson Report. RBS was not an aberration. During a Westminster Hall debate in September 2015, Jo Stevens MP set out the dishonesty of Lloyds Bank:

> 'During the financial crisis, it is alleged that Lloyds and other banks adopted a mechanism known as down-valuation, to engineer a shortfall. Again, that practice has been recognised in the Tomlinson report, and it has two consequences in this case. First, Lloyds was able to secure a larger bail-out from the taxpayer. Secondly, individual customers were held to be in breach of their loan conditions. That enabled Lloyds either to renegotiate more favourable terms for itself or to eliminate its customers altogether, by triggering receivership proceedings and then the sale of those businesses. It was that second engineered consequence—of being in breach of loan conditions—that brought about the unjustified failure of many successful companies and individuals.'

Jo Stevens summed up:

> 'In conclusion, we are left with a situation in which it is alleged that a partly nationalised bank, having found itself in unfavourable business arrangements, has been able to manipulate matters to its advantage, steering successful companies into receivership while depressing the valuation

of those companies and individuals' assets to augment the emergency funding it would receive from the taxpayer. The bank has been assisted by supposedly independent professional advisers who are embedded in the bank and financially benefit from receivership appointments engineered in conjunction with the bank. An obvious and significant conflict of interest has been allowed to operate, unfettered by any regulator.'

The lack of any kind of regulation of the banks' treatment of businesses is an issue that even the police raised. After receiving a large number of complaints about Lloyds Bank, Dr Kristie Cogram (Manager – Financial Investigation and Economic Crime) of the Avon & Somerset Constabulary, after speaking to 'other regulatory agencies' about Lloyds Bank, wrote: 'It is of concern to us that the members of the public that we aim to protect are vulnerable to business practices and the law appears powerless and we are willing to brief those interested Members of Parliament in respect of our conclusion'. During the Westminster Hall debate, Huw Irranca-Davies MP highlighted the fury of Lloyds Bank and its agents when a client's father tried to buy that property in receivership:

> '[The] father bought all the lots, but Bristol Recoveries [and the agents] were furious and used an opt-out clause in the small print to cancel the sale. They then sold the farmland on a "first come, first served" basis at a knockdown price ... [the customer] had started out with a portfolio valued at £5 million and a successful business, with borrowings of £1.3 million; he has ended up bankrupt and with nothing.'

This kind of crookedness is typical and made far worse by the fact that the judges have ruled that banks do not owe their business customers a duty of care; *consequently, banks cannot be sued for negligence*; judges manipulate the interpretation of what duties *in theory* the banks are supposed to owe and ensure that the banks (and their lawyers, receivers and other agents – all of whom earn substantial fees and commissions from a receivership) remain, in practice, above the law. Banks are not even required to act fairly; for example, in a case also involving Lloyds Bank, a judge ruled: 'I have ... no doubt in concluding that for me to find either that there is on mortgagees some general duty to be fair or some more specific duty ... would be wrong in law'; this ruling was upheld at the Court of Appeal, which regarded the idea that banks should act fairly so utterly outrageous that permission to appeal was refused. The above examples concerning Lloyds Bank cited by Huw Irranca-Davies and Jo Stevens should not come as a surprise; banks do not have to act fairly, they cannot be sued for negligence, the regulatory system is deficient, and the police refuse to investigate let alone prosecute. Were this to be happening in any other country, it would be described as organized crime. Catherine McKinnell MP, the Shadow Attorney General, pointed out in the Westminster Hall debate the scale of the matter:

> 'As many of us know from our constituency postbags and surgeries, there are many more cases such as those we have heard about today throughout the country. Since the financial crisis, small, medium and even large firms have been brought to their knees by the banking system, with serious allegations of malpractice being made. Good and credible businesspeople ... have seen their credit ratings destroyed, after having worked hard for years and decades to build up their businesses. We only need to look at the [pressure group] Bully Banks campaign to see just how many firms and individuals have been affected by allegations of malpractice over the past few years.
>
> Indeed, I have a constituency case involving the now acknowledged mis-selling of interest rate hedging products, or swaps; my constituent's family, and the many who rely on them for good, skilled employment, have been reeling from the consequences of that ever since. We are not discussing the swap mis-selling scandal today, but the activities alleged and the consequences of those activities, bear a striking resemblance to the situation suffered by my constituent. I have a real fear that that indicates a systemic failure in our banking system across the country.'

Far from sorting out the banks, the Tories are determined to cover up for them. They see nothing wrong. No action has been taken to force the banks to redress the business owners affected, nor to impose legal changes to alter the balance of power between the banks and small businesses. Meanwhile, vast bonuses continue to flow to the bankers undisturbed.

After a long period of procrastination the banks were told to compensate those businessmen to whom they had mis-sold hedging contracts. More than 30,000 such contracts were sold between 2003 and 2012. Bank customers were often forced into buying the contracts when they took out a loan, but did not properly understand what the contracts entailed and were not told that if interest rates fell then they had to compensate the bank. More than 1,000 businesses were needlessly destroyed and many others were compelled to cash assets to meet the payments. Business owners were often ruined.

The Financial Services Authority found that 90% of the hedging contracts had been mis-sold. Bully Banks demanded that there be compensation for the victims. Thus far, only £1.9billion has been paid out in compensation when the estimated liability was put at £30billion. The Financial Conduct Authority changed its compensation scheme after intensive lobbying by both the banks *and the Treasury,* and limited the scheme to exclude businesses with loans of more than £10million, denying more than 5,000 businesses compensation.[894]

A Bank of England report showed that the banks lent less to businesses every month since April 2010 and in the year to February 2014 the total lent to small firms fell by £4.3billion. It was reported in September 2014 that lending by the five major British banks fell by £365billion over the previous five years. Banking malpractice and criminality continued undisturbed by the government – be it fixing interest rates, laundering drug money, or general fraud. By August 2015, HSBC, Lloyds, Barclays and RBS had had to put aside as much as £50billion to cover fines and charges since 2008. Even so, the fantastic bonuses which the bankers awarded themselves were soon resumed. In an observation that applies to Britain's bankers today, speaking of the Wall Street Crash, Galbraith said: 'The fact was that American enterprise in the twenties had opened its hospitable arms to an exceptional number of promoters, grafters, swindlers, imposters and frauds. This in the long history of such activities, was a kind of flood tide of corporate larceny'.[895]

The cost of the banking crisis is not limited to the cost of the various bailouts. In the Spring of 2009, the British authorities had put together a rescue package of special liquidity measures, guarantees of inter-bank lending, asset protection and capital to the sum of £1trillion. Then there has been the cost of the ongoing QE. There is also the cost of the reduced interest rates to savers, who have lost £130billion, around £5,000 per household, according to research by Hargreaves Lansdown in March 2015. By May 2015, RBS had lost £50billion since being bailed out by the taxpayer. Then there is cost to borrowers as the banks have failed to fully pass on the low interest rate cuts.

The British economy is being run as a Ponzi scheme. Debts are being run up and assets sold off to pay for consumption. Living standards are falling. Ordinary people are being needlessly deprived of their inheritance, their homes, their incomes, and their country; their whole standard of living is being relentlessly eroded. GDP *per capita* was still below the 2008 level even seven years later. And still the government and the wider Ponzi class escalate the scale of the unpaid bills and debts. Meanwhile their own pet projects such as the EU and overseas aid continue to consume ever larger sums of money.

Ponzi induced investors to invest in his scheme by making glib promises of fantastically lucrative returns on the monies invested. For a very short while, he lived the high life. He continued to make his promises even when the scheme went wrong and hoped he could use new investors' capital to fund payments to existing investors. The Ponzi class treat taxpayers in the same way. They make promises of future welfare and pension provisions and then take taxpayers' monies and spend it as it suits them, blandly assuming that future taxpayers will stump up more money. Unlike Ponzi himself, the Ponzi class are able to dishonour commitments and rely upon Beveridge's maxim that the government is not subject to the same morality as ordinary people. Taxpayers' monies are taken and spent and yet the promises of services and welfare provisions made are dishonoured. Whereas an insurance company might face criminal proceedings for deciding to dishonour commitments to its customers and simply taking their monies for the management's own purposes, government, as per Beveridge, does not. The Ponzi class can choose not to make payments and can choose to leave bills unpaid. To say that public services are stretched to breaking point is merely another terminology for saying that bills are not being paid; the resources necessary to sustain a commitment made and to sustain services that were already being provided have been reallocated elsewhere.

The full cost of Ponzi economics is not merely the £1.5trillion, and rising, government debt. There is also the off balance sheet debts such as the variety of PFI contracts. Then there are the costs imposed on wider society detailed above: the cost of university tuition fees, the cost to the elderly of being in a care home, the cost of having to pay for child minders so that mother can go out to work. Then there are the incomes foregone such as the lower state pensions due to the refusal to increase them as promised, lower interest receipts on savings, and the lower wages if not unemployment due to immigration. Then there is the cost of the diminution of the quality of life such as the damage done to children by family breakdown and being brought up by state employees rather than their mothers, the deprivation of motherhood as mothers are forced out to work, the misery caused by divorce (in addition to the vast fees pocketed by lawyers), the plight of pensioners forced into care homes and forced to sell their homes to pay for care home fees, the lost inheritance, the misery caused by people not being able to afford their own homes, and the loss of social cohesion and breakdown of national community caused by mass immigration. These are all costs imposed on ordinary people by the Ponzi class.

Assets, be it pension annuities, fishing grounds, ownership of British industry, power stations, etc., are sold off, given away or simply trashed. North Sea oil has almost gone and the Royal Navy, once the largest in the world, has been run down to being little more than a fishing patrol fleet that has more recently been engaged in helping people smugglers, including IS, ship illegal immigrants across the Mediterranean.

Then there are the costs of the various pet projects pursued by the Ponzi class, whether it be the EU, overseas aid, and climate change; in addition to which there is the cost of the Ponzi class itself, be it the vast bankers' bonuses, MPs salaries and expenses, civil servant salaries, other salaries and bonuses of state sector organizations (e.g. the BBC and the NHS), the House of Lords (now stuffed with ex-MPs, chums and cronies), and a horde of lawyers, including judges, pocketing monies on an ever-increasing and damaging scale (immigration, human rights, divorce etc.).

In the 21st century, the oppression of ordinary people is not by the bourgeoisie in the pursuit of capitalism, whatever the malevolent prattle of the Communist Manifesto of 1848 might say – such prattle still being spouted by many, including many of the

Ponzi class. In fact, it is the Ponzi class that is responsible for oppression today. The Ponzi class is systematically harming the lives and livelihoods of the general public and, cocooned in political correctness, they could not care less.

As has been stated above, 'an economy has been defined as a community amongst whom resources are shared'. For List, the community is the nation state – the national community. From a globalization perspective, there is no community. There are no national boundaries. Milton Friedman once pointed out that there could either be a welfare state or open borders, but there cannot be both. The resources of the nation are insufficient to fund an international welfare state, as open borders would entail, and any attempt to ignore this can only result in the disintegration of the welfare state as the money runs out. The Ponzi class, with its Ponzi economics, political correctness and globalization policies, do attempt to ignore the need for national boundaries and are more than happy to see the national infrastructure generally, and the welfare state in particular, starved of resources and allowed to disintegrate. Conversely, however, they assume that their own incomes, pensions and pet projects should be ring-fenced and lavishly funded. The bankers were happy to pronounce the virtues of globalization until the credit crunch impacted, when suddenly, despite their supposed laissez-faire, free market, capitalist credentials, they expected to be bailed out by the national taxpayer with their own standards of living protected. The Ponzi class are all in favour of globalization etc. until it adversely affects them; they are arrogant in their willingness to sacrifice other people's money and living standards, but not their own; they have no affinity with the nation whose interests, monies and even existence they are so willing to squander.

Keynes' banana plantation parable needs to be updated with another, more fitting to the 21st century. Once there was a very prosperous place known as Gangle Land. Gangle Land became wealthy due to its advanced manufacturing techniques for the production of pins. Other lands dubbed these pins as Ganglepins as only Gangle Land could produce them. For many years Gangle Land enjoyed its monopoly on the production of Ganglepins and the wealth that was accumulated.

However, eventually other lands too wanted to produce their own pins to the same quality as Ganglepins and so share in Gangle Land's prosperity. But the dominance was such that Gangle Land was able to undercut rival producers on price and also surpass them on quality. The producers in other lands demanded that their governments should use underhand methods and impose extra changes on Gangle Land's pins. These demands were met and so rival producers gradually established themselves. In a short space of time these new rivals started to match Gangle Land's pins on price, but not on quality. However, to obtain sales, some rival producers marketed their pins as Ganglepins too and so duped unsuspecting consumers that they were buying Gangle Land's superior products when in fact they were not.

Gangle Land responded to this by forming a new trade association for all those lands which produced pins in the expectation that order could be established and unfair practices curtailed. However, this initiative failed as those who joined the trade association were keen to impose new rules but did not adhere to those rules themselves. Some lands did not even bother to join the trade association and simply carried on regardless.

Bit by bit Gangle Land's producers were driven out of not only foreign markets, but also the home market of Gangle Land itself. Workers lost their jobs and living standards fell. Tax revenues fell short of what was needed and the government sank into deficit. The ordinary people of Gangle Land became restless and demanded action. They wanted to withdraw from the trade association, the rules of which were strangling, as they saw it, their producers and burying them in red tape. They saw no reason to abide by rules which other lands ignored.

The government of Gangle Land angrily rejected these calls and denounced those making them as xenophobes. Even so, the unrest continued to grow as living standards fell. Yet the government remained firm and pointed out that if Gangle Land were to leave the trade association then it would lose all influence, and cited an example where Gangle Land had successfully insisted not only that there should be chocolate on the biscuits served during a tea break at committee meetings, but that custard creams should also be served. This just went to show the influence that Gangle Land had as a result of membership of the trade association; on leaving, this influence would be lost.

Gangle Land had a very generous pension scheme, in addition to which many had built up substantial private pension investments. The inflow of monies in the form of pension contributions to the government was very large and, contrary to what ordinary people intended, the government decided to use that inflow to solve world poverty. After many years of extravagant expenditure and as the demands for pensions increased as people retired, the pension scheme was penniless. The financial minister of Gangle Land, known to his colleagues as 'Fingers', made a big speech in which he announced that the people of Gangle Land were expecting too high a standard of living and the present pension scheme was no longer affordable. Cuts would have to be made. Privately, Fingers bewailed the size of the private pension investments. If only he could get his sticky mitts on those funds then he was convinced that he would be able to abolish world poverty.

Gangle Land also had a very well funded and successful legal assistance fund, which would finance legal action in defence of its people. However, the chief legal minister, who prided himself on being known as 'Small Print', tabled an amendment to the scheme that would enable those living in foreign lands to also be funded in legal action, even against the people of Gangle Land, despite the fact that they had made no financial contribution to the fund. Judges had agreed to this extension, saying that it was their role to defend all of those who produced pins and not just Gangle Land. They believed that they were setting a moral example to the whole world. In note 15 to paragraph 141 in section 5 of the legislation, Small Print had inserted a clause which stated that lawyers would be able to claim their fees from the Gangle Land legal assistance fund even if they were acting for those suing Gangle Land and its people and even if they lost their claim. Within two years the legal assistance fund was penniless and still more claims against Gangle Land and its people were being filed in court. Fingers arranged for a transfer of funds to bolster the scheme out of Gangle Land revenues, but this caused much resentment as it increased the size of the Gangle Land deficit.

The leader of the government of Gangle Land believed that it would make Gangle Land much more sophisticated and cosmopolitan if foreign peoples were allowed to move there. This sparked strong resentment from the ordinary people, but they were angrily accused of being racist and some even lost their jobs for holding such views. A large flow of immigrants moved to Gangle Land and the ordinary people of Gangle Land found that they could no longer get the housing, healthcare and education that they had come to expect. In addition to which many were out of work due to the immigrants being prepared to work for lower wages.

The leader of Gangle Land himself sacked his nanny to replace her with an immigrant, believing that he was enriched by having a foreign nanny for his children. The sacked employee was angry and complained that it was unfair, but was told to stop being racist and to go and stack shelves in a supermarket.

The government of Gangle Land was increasingly angry at the opposition to their immigration policy, and announced the creation of a new commission of immigrants who would prosecute anyone suspected of anti-immigration opinions. Those on this commission were very well paid and had the freedom to enrol ever more immigrants and others who considered the inhabitants of Gangle Land to be racist onto the commission and its subordinate organizations.

At one notorious court hearing, a woman was sent to prison for six months before the trial was even concluded. In sentencing her, the judge pronounced that: 'The whole basis of civilization is respect for the rule of law. We cannot and will not tolerate those who go around attacking judges. Informed opinion across the whole world would demand nothing less'. The woman's crime was that she had been overheard telling her husband outside the court that she considered the judge to be 'a pompous ass'.

The leader of Gangle Land refused to comment on this case, excusing himself that he was abroad at the time attending a conference of the trade association, which he had declared had been a great success. At the conference, to a rapturous applause, the leader had announced that in future the government of Gangle Land 'would not simply be pursuing Gangle Land's own narrow self-interest' but would govern for the benefit of the whole world. 'What is Gangle Land's is yours' proclaimed the leader as he announced a lavish aid package to solve world poverty. The leader said that Gangle Land would be an 'aid superpower'. The speech was warmly received and there were numerous pictures of the leader beaming, smiling broadly and waving in response to a standing ovation.

Meanwhile, Fingers wanted to bail out some bankers who had squandered vast sums of their customers' monies on a variety of get-rich-quick schemes. Fingers therefore had managed to change the law to allow him to tax the private pension investments and further to lure pensioners to spend the capital they had saved; in return Fingers had issued some IOUs promising a pension income from the government to those affected. Fingers booked down the extra consumption expenditure resulting from these changes as growth. Those who questioned the wisdom of spending capital as income were dismissed by Fingers as 'gloomsters' who were 'talking Gangle Land down'.

And so the once-proud, hapless people of Gangle Land sank ever deeper into poverty and servitude.

13 CONCLUSION

Keynes is to be respected as he was an imaginative economist, with a voluminous output of written items of various lengths and depths, who tried to grapple with the seemingly insuperable levels of unemployment in the inter-war years. He adopted and successfully promoted the concept of the multiplier, which expanded economic understanding at the time. His theory, that it might be possible to cut real wages and hence unemployment by reducing the value of the currency, was as bold as it was reckless.

Keynes had a point in that classical economic theory did not explain the high levels of unemployment. Why did not supply and demand come back into balance as a result of price changes? Keynes was correct to raise the question, but wrong to limit the solution to a purely economic issue when there are many social factors to consider too (for example the birth-rate of many years previously and the disruption caused by WWI).

Writing at a time when much damage was being done on the continent as a result of hyperinflation, and much damage was being done then in Britain due to the attempt to stay on the Gold Standard at pre-war parity, then Keynes should have been more cautious as to extolling the virtues of artificially trying to alter the value of the currency.

Keynes *was* an inflationist. Inflation was his solution. That solution should have been rejected and not adopted by responsible governments. While it is true that the focus on growth after WWII enabled the British economy to bounce back and reduce the burden of its debts much more successfully than after WWI, and while it is true that Keynes himself was responsible for the successful funding of WWII and some of the international structure that emerged after it, it was not necessarily Keynesianism that was responsible for the post-war boom. Germany, for example, did not embrace Keynesianism and was a highly successful economy. The contemporaneous analysis highlighted the failure of Keynesianism to control the economy as predicted and the various computer models were wrong to varying degrees.

In reading the *General Theory*, one can easily be disappointed. Keynes' supporters and devotees may well have gushed at the book's contents and conclusions, but there is no divine revelation, only bald assertions. There is no crushing intellectual argument. There is no undeniable logic previously overseen. The book is an abstract *theory* and nothing more than that. The disappointment with the book is only matched by the incredulity that so many supposedly intelligent people, economists and senior politicians, mindlessly adopted the book's theory so simplistically. That they did so reinforces the view that the better educated people are the more stupid they get. It is incredible now that so many actually believed ferociously that they could control the economy on a monthly basis by tinkering about on a monthly basis. It never, it would seem, occurred to them that the statistics they relied upon may be incomplete and/or out of date, that there were time lags between policy introduction and effect, and time lags in the money supply. Controlling the economy so precisely was not feasible.

Ultimately, Keynesianism failed. The 1970s put paid to the politicians' blind acceptance of Keynesian orthodoxy. The theory broke down and the measures the theory called for were impossible to implement. For Britain, the 1970s was a decade of economic failure and a catastrophe for manufacturing. The 1980s were more successful, courtesy of North Sea oil, denationalisation and deregulation for the economy, and yet for manufacturing the decade was far less successful; much of British industry never recovered from the recession at the start of the decade.

The credit crunch and subsequent Slump of 2008 led to a call for Keynesian type policies again; although the return to some growth after approaching six years of overall stagnation has led to talk of the success of the policy of austerity claimed by the coalition government. The existence of certain vanity projects, such as HS2, hint at a Keynesian thinking within the so-called austerity programme, which is scheduled to double the national debt from roughly £800billion in 2010 when Osborne became chancellor to roughly £1,600billion by 2020. The opposition political parties want a much more expansionist and aggressively Keynesian economic policy. The Germans dismissed the calls for crass Keynesianism. The term Quack Keynesianism would be more accurate. The banks have pocketed vast sums of various bailout monies and have happily kept the lot, lent less to business, continued their previous crooked and disreputable practices, and are unrepentant as to their continued bonuses. The government response has been to give them yet more money, very cheap, in the hope that they might lend it out again. They have not. To shower those already hoarding money with yet more money is not Keynes' thinking. Keynes was alert to the danger, as he saw it, of liquidity preference and of the desire to hoard money.

Keynes' *General Theory* was written to try and tackle an unemployment problem – not to ensure the continued enrichment of bankers. Were it not for the actions of bankers then the real economy was quite capable of continuing its then rate of growth in 2008. The bankers dragged the economy into recession, the consequences of which we are still lumbered – not least in the form of the still increasing level of government indebtedness. Much of the unemployment today is as a result of the EU, both due to the crisis of the Eurozone and the level of immigration. There is then the immigration from the rest of the world. Printing money to boost demand is not a solution to this and Keynes never advanced his theory as being such.

In the run up to the general election in 2015, Cameron announced that the Tories would create two million new jobs were they to be elected into government, and even went so far as to promise to create 'a job for everyone who wants one'. This imbecility betrays the lack of intellectual substance of the Tories. Since there are open borders, with immigrants pouring in from the EU and elsewhere across the world, then it is impossible to quantify the numbers seeking work. For Keynesianism to be applicable, the number unemployed and hence the number of jobs needed has to be quantified in order to measure the shortfall of the current number of jobs. Since the Eurozone, consisting of many countries whose standards of living and wage rates are a fraction of Britain's, is in such poor economic straits with large-scale unemployment, then the more jobs there are perceived to be in Britain, given the open borders, the greater will be the number of immigrants moving to Britain. Hence the greater the strains on Britain's public services and the more wages must be forced down. Cameron's promise is economically illiterate and would produce lower living standards for the English. The more immigrants there are, the more jobs Cameron has promised to create and hence, due to the law of supply and demand, the lower will be the wage rate and/or the higher will be the unemployment rate.

There are similarities between our current problems and those of the 1920s and 1930s; and there are lessons to be learnt from the 1920s and 1930s. Now as then, there is an attempt to fix exchange rates at an artificial level. Now as then, there is widespread unemployment. Now as then, we face competition from countries which are using protectionism to shut out our goods from their markets. The real lesson from the inter-war Depression is that it was only when Britain resorted to a more protectionist stance, using tariffs to protect British interests, that we returned to growth. Unilateral free trade was not sustainable. The policy of unilateral free trade has evolved into a policy of globalization. One major difference now compared to then, is that now the ruling class, the Ponzi class, is prepared to watch Britain's interests sacrificed. The Ponzi class is not prepared to defend the national interest; the commitment to globalization is paramount. The economic policy being pursued is not Keynesianism, but its evolution: Ponzi economics, with the costs of the Ponzi scheme being dumped on ordinary people by means of collapsing public services, higher taxes and other expenses, and lower standards of living generally. These costs are nicely hidden away without any real analysis of them and the government interest, the interest of the Ponzi class, is treated as the same as the interest of the nation. It is not.

A responsible economic policy would grasp the thorny problem of the ongoing trade deficit – currently running at around £120billion per annum. A genuinely imaginative economist today would tackle the issue as to why this deficit has continued for so long, just as unemployment continued indefinitely in the 1920s and 1930s. Some, if not most, of the reason is political and therefore beyond the scope of economics. But to bring the trade back into balance would make a dramatic difference to the British economy. £120billion worth of demand that is currently flowing out of the economy would be directed towards British goods. Then there is the multiplier effect. Then there is the increase in tax revenues given that the government is pocketing a little under 40% of economic output. Then there are the savings to be made by abandoning the Ponzi class's pet projects. Leaving the EU would not only involve the saving of our payments to that organization, and a saving in red tape, but also it would allow us to reclaim our own fishing grounds, thus creating further jobs and prosperity (as well as allowing us to properly preserve our fish stocks). Leaving the EU is a necessity in order to regain controls over immigration and control over trade policy, which is currently subcontracted to and subordinate to the EU.

The EU does not act in Britain's interests. It is a Berlin-dominated, Brussels-run bureaucracy on a mission to expand its powers and create a United States of Europe. The creation of the euro currency has been highly detrimental to British interests as it allows Germany and the other North European states to use the, for them, undervalued currency to extend their trade surpluses with Britain. For the EU, the British balance of trade deficit is of no more concern than the balance of trade between Yorkshire and Lancashire is to the British government. Leaving the EU is a prerequisite to the adoption of a strategy to bring Britain's trade with the EU back into balance. Britain needs a sovereign trade policy.

In the 19th century, Britain adopted a policy of unilateral free trade as a trade policy. Britain had entered the industrial revolution ahead of other countries and sought to persuade those countries to concentrate on non-manufacturing economic activities and to buy their manufactures from Britain. Britain's arguments were unpersuasive. However, today, free trade's latest manifestation, globalization, and membership of the EU is being presented as a replacement for the need for a trade policy. This is wrong and is akin to looking through the wrong end of a telescope. Britain should only adopt a policy of globalization and continued membership of the EU if it is in British interests. For the reasons set out above, it is not in British interests.

The ongoing balance of trade deficit is unsustainable, as is the ongoing looting of assets within Britain and the escalating levels of debts. Selling assets to pay for imported goods cannot go on forever as eventually the assets will all be sold and long before then the diminished tax revenues will have caused the disintegration of the welfare state. We should no longer allow foreigners to take us to the cleaners. A sovereign trade policy is incompatible with the policy of globalization. Globalization should be rejected just as free trade was rejected in 1932.

The real lessons of the inter-war years need to be learned and the Keynesian myths rejected. At that time Keynes was an irrelevance at best, at worst a nuisance. Keynes' criticism of government policy may have been right on many occasions, but it was also wrong on many occasions and he was on the wrong side of the argument more often than not. He was spectacularly wrong regarding free trade and the need for tariff reform. Britain's adoption of a more protectionist stance worked. Unilateral free trade was a disaster. Joseph Chamberlain was proved right. His arguments remain relevant to this day. The Unionist Party may well have lost the general election of 1906, but this did not mean that the Tariff Reformers were either beaten or wrong. They were scuppered by Balfour's inept leadership.

The inter-war years up to 1931 witnessed the hegemony of free trade economics with the failure to build upon the lessons of WWI and Britain's industrial weaknesses; instead Britain embraced unilateral free trade again and the resurrection of the Gold Standard at pre-war parity. The Free Traders had it all their own way and they were disastrously wrong. As the consequences of their policies hit home the hegemony of free trade was weakened. The humiliating ejection from the Gold Standard gave rise to a reappraisal of trade policy and, finally, Tariff Reform succeeded. The General Tariff and the Preferences agreed at the Ottawa Conference put Britain on the path to recovery. Britain enjoyed strong growth and falling unemployment. Had Balfour given support to Joseph Chamberlain's campaign of 1903 and 1904, then the cause of Tariff Reform might have triumphed so much sooner and history would have been so very different.

Post-WWII witnessed the triumph of Keynesianism and its attendant collapse in the 1970s, having failed to even address Britain's economic decline and having failed to combat rising unemployment. Free trade was once again embraced and evolved into globalization as Keynesianism evolved into Ponzi economics, with assets consumed as income, escalating debts and a much lower standard of living for ordinary people. Class oppression is not by the bourgeoisie, it is by an unrepentant Ponzi class. Via the tax system, the Ponzi class help themselves to ordinary people's monies, spend it as if it were their own and then run up debts and leave unpaid bills in addition. Ordinary people are losing a large part of their incomes, their pensions and even their homes if they need residential care in old age, assuming that they can even afford to own their own home. Business owners can be swindled by the banks and lose everything. Children lose their inheritance. Thatcher's property-owning democracy has given way to a beds in sheds lawyers' dictatorship.

The Ponzi class and its supporters should no longer be allowed to dump costs onto other people. If someone chooses to import immigrants to staff his organization then let that person pay the full cost of that immigration. This could be by imposing a charge per immigrant to meet the costs of present and future expenses to the taxpayer and to compensate those who find that they are priced out of housing. The government should consider a solidarity tax to get those who thus far have escaped the adverse consequences of the policies they loudly advocate to contribute to the costs they have caused. The government should stop hiding debts off balance sheet via PFI arrangements and the sort, or student loans. Pensions need to be ring-fenced beyond the sticky fingers of the Ponzi class with constitutional checks to prevent politicians raiding those pensions when they run out of other sources of money. The banks should no longer be allowed to operate above the law, no longer be allowed to profiteer, and no longer be allowed to act recklessly safe in the knowledge that the taxpayer will bail them out periodically; they should be taxed to repay the costs of the 2008 slump. The bonus culture for the banks and public sector must end.

The City should no longer have priority over manufacturing. The economy needs to be rebalanced with a more thriving manufacturing sector and with the balance of trade brought back into balance. Britain needs to get tough with those who are manipulating their currencies and using unfair trade practices.

These things are doable if there is the determination to do them. What is needed is a rejection of Ponzi economics, a rejection of globalization, a removal from office of the Ponzi class, and a government committed to protecting the national interest. It is time to reverse Britain's economic decline or else we face not an economic Dunkirk, but an economic Fall of Singapore.

1   John Maynard Keynes, *The General Theory of Employment, Interest, and Money*, Palgrove MacMillan, Basingstoke, 2007, page 383

2   *Keynes and the Modern World*, edited by David Worswick and James Trevithick, Cambridge University Press, Cambridge, 1983, page 2

3   *The Critics of Keynesian Economics*, edited by Henry Hazlitt, D Van Nostrand Company Ltd, Toronto, 1960, page 11

4   John Maynard Keynes, *The General Theory of Employment, Interest, and Money*, Palgrove MacMillan, Basingstoke, 2007, page 18

5   Thomas Sowell, *Say's Law: An Historical Analysis*, Princeton University Press, Princeton, 1972, pages 180 and 181

6   Thomas Sowell, *Say's Law: An Historical Analysis*, Princeton University Press, Princeton, 1972, page 5

7   Thomas Sowell, *Say's Law: An Historical Analysis*, Princeton University Press, Princeton, 1972, page 14

8   Thomas Sowell, *Say's Law: An Historical Analysis*, Princeton University Press, Princeton, 1972, page 17

9   Thomas Sowell, *Say's Law: An Historical Analysis*, Princeton University Press, Princeton, 1972, page 19

10 Thomas Sowell, *Say's Law: An Historical Analysis*, Princeton University Press, Princeton, 1972, page 20

11 Thomas Sowell, *Say's Law: An Historical Analysis*, Princeton University Press, Princeton, 1972, pages 29 and 30

12 Thomas Sowell, *Say's Law: An Historical Analysis*, Princeton University Press, Princeton, 1972, page 32

13 Thomas Sowell, *Say's Law: An Historical Analysis*, Princeton University Press, Princeton, 1972, page 50

14 Thomas Sowell, *Say's Law: An Historical Analysis*, Princeton University Press, Princeton, 1972, page 54

15 Thomas Sowell, *Say's Law: An Historical Analysis*, Princeton University Press, Princeton, 1972, page 96

16 Thomas Sowell, *Say's Law: An Historical Analysis*, Princeton University Press, Princeton, 1972, page 116

17 Thomas Sowell, *Say's Law: An Historical Analysis*, Princeton University Press, Princeton, 1972, page 117

18 Thomas Sowell, *Say's Law: An Historical Analysis*, Princeton University Press, Princeton, 1972, page 121

19 Thomas Sowell, *Say's Law: An Historical Analysis*, Princeton University Press, Princeton, 1972, page 220

20 Oswald St. Clair, *A Key to Ricardo*, Routledge & Kegan Paul Ltd, London, 1957, page 2

21 Oswald St. Clair, *A Key to Ricardo*, Routledge & Kegan Paul Ltd, London, 1957, page 46

22 Oswald St. Clair, *A Key to Ricardo*, Routledge & Kegan Paul Ltd, London, 1957, page 181

23 Oswald St. Clair, *A Key to Ricardo*, Routledge & Kegan Paul Ltd, London, 1957, page 182

24 Oswald St. Clair, *A Key to Ricardo*, Routledge & Kegan Paul Ltd, London, 1957, page 182

25 Oswald St. Clair, *A Key to Ricardo*, Routledge & Kegan Paul Ltd, London, 1957, page 187

26 Oswald St. Clair, *A Key to Ricardo*, Routledge & Kegan Paul Ltd, London, 1957, page 203

27 Oswald St. Clair, *A Key to Ricardo*, Routledge & Kegan Paul Ltd, London, 1957, page 205

28   Oswald St. Clair, *A Key to Ricardo*, Routledge & Kegan Paul Ltd, London, 1957, page 251

29   Oswald St. Clair, *A Key to Ricardo*, Routledge & Kegan Paul Ltd, London, 1957, page 252

30   Oswald St. Clair, *A Key to Ricardo*, Routledge & Kegan Paul Ltd, London, 1957, page 252

31   Oswald St. Clair, *A Key to Ricardo*, Routledge & Kegan Paul Ltd, London, 1957, page 298

32   Oswald St. Clair, *A Key to Ricardo*, Routledge & Kegan Paul Ltd, London, 1957, page 300

33   Thomas Sowell, *Say's Law: An Historical Analysis*, Princeton University Press, Princeton, 1972, page 141

34   Ha-Joon Chang, *Bad Samaritans: The Guilty Secrets of Rich Nations and the Threat to Global Prosperity*, Random House, London, 2007, page 47

35   Ha-Joon Chang, *Bad Samaritans: The Guilty Secrets of Rich Nations and the Threat to Global Prosperity*, Random House, London, 2007, page 47

36   Ha-Joon Chang, *Bad Samaritans: The Guilty Secrets of Rich Nations and the Threat to Global Prosperity*, Random House, London, 2007, page 44

37   Ha-Joon Chang, *Bad Samaritans: The Guilty Secrets of Rich Nations and the Threat to Global Prosperity*, Random House, London, 2007, pages 41 and 42

38   Julian Amery, *Joseph Chamberlain and the Tariff Reform Campaign: The Life of Joseph Chamberlain, Volume Five – 1901-1903*, MacMillan, London, 1969, page 199

39   Julian Amery, *Joseph Chamberlain and the Tariff Reform Campaign: The Life of Joseph Chamberlain, Volume Five – 1901-1903*, MacMillan, London, 1969, page 198

40   Ha-Joon Chang, *Bad Samaritans: The Guilty Secrets of Rich Nations and the Threat to Global Prosperity*, Random House, London, 2007, page 44

41   Ha-Joon Chang, *Bad Samaritans: The Guilty Secrets of Rich Nations and the Threat to Global Prosperity*, Random House, London, 2007, page 45

42   Ha-Joon Chang, *Bad Samaritans: The Guilty Secrets of Rich Nations and the Threat to Global Prosperity*, Random House, London, 2007, page 45

43   Ha-Joon Chang, *Bad Samaritans: The Guilty Secrets of Rich Nations and the Threat to Global Prosperity*, Random House, London, 2007, page 49

44   Julian Amery, *Joseph Chamberlain and the Tariff Reform Campaign: The Life of Joseph Chamberlain, Volume Five – 1901-1903*, MacMillan, London, 1969, page 199

45   Cited in Larry Elliott and Dan Atkinson, *Going South: Why Britain Will Have a Third World Economy By 2014*, Palgrave Macmillan, Great Britain, 2012, page 45

46   Larry Elliott and Dan Atkinson, *Going South: Why Britain Will Have a Third World Economy By 2014*, Palgrave Macmillan, Great Britain, 2012, page 46

47   Friedrich List, *The National System of Political Economy*, Longmans, Green and Co, London, 1885, page vi

48   Friedrich List, *The National System of Political Economy*, Longmans, Green and Co, London, 1885, page 11

49   Friedrich List, *The National System of Political Economy*, Longmans, Green and Co, London, 1885, page 16

50   Friedrich List, *The National System of Political Economy*, Longmans, Green and Co, London, 1885, page 24

51   Friedrich List, *The National System of Political Economy*, Longmans, Green and Co, London, 1885, page 26

52   Friedrich List, *The National System of Political Economy*, Longmans, Green and Co, London, 1885, page 35

53   Friedrich List, *The National System of Political Economy*, Longmans, Green and Co, London, 1885, page 37

54   Friedrich List, *The National System of Political Economy*, Longmans, Green and Co, London, 1885, page 38

55   Friedrich List, *The National System of Political Economy*, Longmans, Green and Co, London, 1885, page 39

56   Friedrich List, *The National System of Political Economy*, Longmans, Green and Co, London, 1885, page 40

57   Friedrich List, *The National System of Political Economy*, Longmans, Green and Co, London, 1885, page 40

58   Julian Amery, *Joseph Chamberlain and the Tariff Reform Campaign: The Life of Joseph Chamberlain, Volume Five – 1901-1903*, MacMillan, London, 1969, page 198

59   Friedrich List, *The National System of Political Economy*, Longmans, Green and Co, London, 1885, page 43

60   Friedrich List, *The National System of Political Economy*, Longmans, Green and Co, London, 1885, page 43

61   Friedrich List, *The National System of Political Economy*, Longmans, Green and Co, London, 1885, page 66

62   Friedrich List, *The National System of Political Economy*, Longmans, Green and Co, London, 1885, page 72

63   Friedrich List, *The National System of Political Economy*, Longmans, Green and Co, London, 1885, page 72

64   Friedrich List, *The National System of Political Economy*, Longmans, Green and Co, London, 1885, page 75

65   Friedrich List, *The National System of Political Economy*, Longmans, Green and Co, London, 1885, page 40

66   Friedrich List, *The National System of Political Economy*, Longmans, Green and Co, London, 1885, page 369

67   Friedrich List, *The National System of Political Economy*, Longmans, Green and Co, London, 1885, page 87

68   Friedrich List, *The National System of Political Economy*, Longmans, Green and Co, London, 1885, page 95

69   Friedrich List, *The National System of Political Economy*, Longmans, Green and Co, London, 1885, page 96

70   Michael Pettis, *The Great Rebalancing: Trade, Conflict, and the Perilous Road Ahead for the World Economy*, Princeton University Press, Oxford, 2013, page 8

71   Ha-Joon Chang, *Bad Samaritans: The Guilty Secrets of Rich Nations and the Threat to Global Prosperity*, Random House, London, 2007, page 50

72   Ha-Joon Chang, *Bad Samaritans: The Guilty Secrets of Rich Nations and the Threat to Global Prosperity*, Random House, London, 2007, page 50

73   Friedrich List, *The National System of Political Economy*, Longmans, Green and Co, London, 1885, page 97

74   Ha-Joon Chang, *Bad Samaritans: The Guilty Secrets of Rich Nations and the Threat to Global Prosperity*, Random House, London, 2007, page 51

75   Friedrich List, *The National System of Political Economy*, Longmans, Green and Co, London, 1885, page 98

76   Friedrich List, *The National System of Political Economy*, Longmans, Green and Co, London, 1885, page 99

77   Friedrich List, *The National System of Political Economy*, Longmans, Green and Co, London, 1885, page 100

78   Ha-Joon Chang, *Bad Samaritans: The Guilty Secrets of Rich Nations and the Threat to Global Prosperity*, Random House, London, 2007, page 53

79   Ha-Joon Chang, *Bad Samaritans: The Guilty Secrets of Rich Nations and the Threat to Global Prosperity*, Random House, London, 2007, page 54

80   Ha-Joon Chang, *Bad Samaritans: The Guilty Secrets of Rich Nations and the Threat to Global Prosperity*, Random House, London, 2007, page 93

81   Ha-Joon Chang, *Bad Samaritans: The Guilty Secrets of Rich Nations and the Threat to Global Prosperity*, Random House, London, 2007, page 54

82   Ha-Joon Chang, *Bad Samaritans: The Guilty Secrets of Rich Nations and the Threat to Global Prosperity*, Random House, London, 2007, page 55

83   Ha-Joon Chang, *Bad Samaritans: The Guilty Secrets of Rich Nations and the Threat to Global Prosperity*, Random House, London, 2007, page 55

84   James Rickards, *Currency Wars*, Penguin Books, London, 2011, page 86

85   Friedrich List, *The National System of Political Economy*, Longmans, Green and Co, London, 1885, page 181

86   Friedrich List, *The National System of Political Economy*, Longmans, Green and Co, London, 1885, page 119

87   Friedrich List, *The National System of Political Economy*, Longmans, Green and Co, London, 1885, page 120

88   Friedrich List, *The National System of Political Economy*, Longmans, Green and Co, London, 1885, page 126

89   Friedrich List, *The National System of Political Economy*, Longmans, Green and Co, London, 1885, page 126

90 Friedrich List, *The National System of Political Economy*, Longmans, Green and Co, London, 1885, page 181

91 Friedrich List, *The National System of Political Economy*, Longmans, Green and Co, London, 1885, page 133

92 Friedrich List, *The National System of Political Economy*, Longmans, Green and Co, London, 1885, page 115

93 Friedrich List, *The National System of Political Economy*, Longmans, Green and Co, London, 1885, page 217

94 Friedrich List, *The National System of Political Economy*, Longmans, Green and Co, London, 1885, page 219

95 Friedrich List, *The National System of Political Economy*, Longmans, Green and Co, London, 1885, page 226

96 Friedrich List, *The National System of Political Economy*, Longmans, Green and Co, London, 1885, page 228

97 Friedrich List, *The National System of Political Economy*, Longmans, Green and Co, London, 1885, page 318

98 Alan Sykes, *Tariff Reform In British Politics 1903-1913*, Clarendon Press, Britain, 1979, page 116

99 Larry Elliott and Dan Atkinson, *Going South: Why Britain Will Have a Third World Economy By 2014*, Palgrave Macmillan, Great Britain, 2012, page 29

100 Larry Elliott and Dan Atkinson, *Going South: Why Britain Will Have a Third World Economy By 2014*, Palgrave Macmillan, Great Britain, 2012, page 30

101 Correlli Barnett, *The Audit of War*, Macmillan London Ltd, London, 1986, page 94

102 Larry Elliott and Dan Atkinson, *Going South: Why Britain Will Have a Third World Economy By 2014*, Palgrave Macmillan, Great Britain, 2012, pages 31-38

103 Sidney Pollard, *Britain's Prime and Britain's Decline: The British Economy 1870-1914*, Edward Arnold, London, 1989, page xii

104 Forrest Copie, *Depression and Protectionism: Britain Between the Wars*, George Allen & Unwin, London, 1983, page 14

105 Forrest Copie, *Depression and Protectionism: Britain Between the Wars*, George Allen & Unwin, London, 1983, page 26

106 Sidney Pollard, *Britain's Prime and Britain's Decline: The British Economy 1870-1914*, Edward Arnold, London, 1989, page 215; Frank Trentmann, *Free Trade Nation*, Oxford University Press, New York, 2009, page 2

107 Ha-Joon Chang, *Bad Samaritans: The Guilty Secrets of Rich Nations and the Threat to Global Prosperity*, Random House, London, 2007, page 25

108 Lawrence James, *The Rise and Fall of the British Empire*, Little, Brown and Company, London, page 171

109 Lawrence James, *The Rise and Fall of the British Empire*, Little, Brown and Company, London, page 174

110 Lawrence James, *The Rise and Fall of the British Empire*, Little, Brown and Company, London, page 174

111 Lawrence James, *The Rise and Fall of the British Empire*, Little, Brown and Company, London, page 176

112 Lawrence James, *The Rise and Fall of the British Empire*, Little, Brown and Company, London, page 177

113 Tim Rooth, *British Protectionism and the International Economy: Overseas Commercial Policy in the 1930s*, Cambridge University Press, Cambridge, 1992, pages 2-5

114 Frank Trentmann, *Free Trade Nation*, Oxford University Press, New York, 2009, page 28

115 Frank Trentmann, *Free Trade Nation*, Oxford University Press, New York, 2009, page 6

116 Frank Trentmann, *Free Trade Nation*, Oxford University Press, New York, 2009, page 1

117 Forrest Copie, *Depression and Protectionism: Britain Between the Wars*, George Allen & Unwin, London, 1983, page 62

118 *Keynes and the Modern World*, edited by David Worswick and James Trevithick, Cambridge University Press, Cambridge, 1983, page 24 (quoted in GT page 334)

119 Robert K Massie, *Dreadnought: Britain, Germany, and the coming of the Great War*, Jonathan Cape, London, 1992, page 181

120 Travis Crosby, *Joseph Chamberlain*, I.B.Tauris, London, 2011, page 161

121 Thomas Pakenham, *The Scramble for Africa*, George Weidenfield & Nicolson, London, 1991, page 487

122 Robert K Massie, *Dreadnought: Britain, Germany, and the coming of the Great War*, Jonathan Cape, London, 1992, page 240

123 Robert K Massie, *Dreadnought: Britain, Germany, and the coming of the Great War*, Jonathan Cape, London, 1992, page 237

124 Frank Trentmann, *Free Trade Nation*, Oxford University Press, New York, 2009, page 60

125 Richard Rempel, *Unionists Divided: Arthur Balfour, Joseph Chamberlain and the Unionist Free Traders*, David & Charles (Publishers) Limited, Newton Abbot, 1972, page 15

126 Frank Trentmann, *Free Trade Nation*, Oxford University Press, New York, 2009, page 61

127 Martin Wiener, *English Culture and the Decline of the Industrial Spirit 1850-1980*, Penguin Books, London, 1981, page 99

128 Alan Sykes, *Tariff Reform In British Politics 1903-1913*, Clarendon Press, Britain, 1979, page 7

129 Alan Sykes, *Tariff Reform In British Politics 1903-1913*, Clarendon Press, Britain, 1979, pages 33-37

130 Frank Trentmann, *Free Trade Nation*, Oxford University Press, New York, 2009, page 44

131 Frank Trentmann, *Free Trade Nation*, Oxford University Press, New York, 2009, page 63

132 Frank Trentmann, *Free Trade Nation*, Oxford University Press, New York, 2009, page 95

133 Frank Trentmann, *Free Trade Nation*, Oxford University Press, New York, 2009, page 100

134 Frank Trentmann, *Free Trade Nation*, Oxford University Press, New York, 2009, page 56

135 Frank Trentmann, *Free Trade Nation*, Oxford University Press, New York, 2009, page 58

136 Travis Crosby, *Joseph Chamberlain*, I.B.Tauris, London, 2011, page 157

137 Julian Amery, *Joseph Chamberlain and the Tariff Reform Campaign: The Life of Joseph Chamberlain, Volume Five – 1901-1903*, MacMillan, London, 1969, page 14

138 Julian Amery, *Joseph Chamberlain and the Tariff Reform Campaign: The Life of Joseph Chamberlain, Volume Five – 1901-1903*, MacMillan, London, 1969, page 15

139 Julian Amery, *Joseph Chamberlain and the Tariff Reform Campaign: The Life of Joseph Chamberlain, Volume Five – 1901-1903*, MacMillan, London, 1969, page 17

140 Julian Amery, *Joseph Chamberlain and the Tariff Reform Campaign: The Life of Joseph Chamberlain, Volume Five – 1901-1903*, MacMillan, London, 1969, page 47

141 Julian Amery, *Joseph Chamberlain and the Tariff Reform Campaign: The Life of Joseph Chamberlain, Volume Five – 1901-1903*, MacMillan, London, 1969, page 54

142 Travis Crosby, *Joseph Chamberlain*, I.B.Tauris, London, 2011, page 154

143 Julian Amery, *Joseph Chamberlain and the Tariff Reform Campaign: The Life of Joseph Chamberlain, Volume Five – 1901-1903*, MacMillan, London, 1969, page 142

144 Julian Amery, *Joseph Chamberlain and the Tariff Reform Campaign: The Life of Joseph Chamberlain, Volume Five – 1901-1903*, MacMillan, London, 1969, page 151

145 Julian Amery, *Joseph Chamberlain and the Tariff Reform Campaign: The Life of Joseph Chamberlain, Volume Five – 1901-1903*, MacMillan, London, 1969, page 151

146 Julian Amery, *Joseph Chamberlain and the Tariff Reform Campaign: The Life of Joseph Chamberlain, Volume Five – 1901-1903*, MacMillan, London, 1969, page 144

147 Julian Amery, *Joseph Chamberlain and the Tariff Reform Campaign: The Life of Joseph Chamberlain, Volume Five – 1901-1903*, MacMillan, London, 1969, page 145

148 Mrs Chamberlain, cited in Julian Amery, *Joseph Chamberlain and the Tariff Reform Campaign: The Life of Joseph Chamberlain, Volume Five – 1901-1903*, MacMillan, London, 1969, page 145

149 Julian Amery, *Joseph Chamberlain and the Tariff Reform Campaign: The Life of Joseph Chamberlain, Volume Five – 1901-1903*, MacMillan, London, 1969, page 145

150 Julian Amery, *Joseph Chamberlain and the Tariff Reform Campaign: The Life of Joseph Chamberlain, Volume Five – 1901-1903*, MacMillan, London, 1969, page 159

151 Peter Fraser, *Joseph Chamberlain: Radicalism and Empire, 1868-1914*, Cassell & Company Ltd, London, 1966, page 235

152 Robert K Massie, *Dreadnought: Britain, Germany, and the coming of the Great War*, Jonathan Cape, London, 1992, page 328

153 Julian Amery, *Joseph Chamberlain and the Tariff Reform Campaign: The Life of Joseph Chamberlain, Volume Five – 1901-1903*, MacMillan, London, 1969, page 189

154 Julian Amery, *Joseph Chamberlain and the Tariff Reform Campaign: The Life of Joseph Chamberlain, Volume Five – 1901-1903*, MacMillan, London, 1969, page 191

155 Julian Amery, *Joseph Chamberlain and the Tariff Reform Campaign: The Life of Joseph Chamberlain, Volume Five – 1901-1903*, MacMillan, London, 1969, page 192

156 Julian Amery, *Joseph Chamberlain and the Tariff Reform Campaign: The Life of Joseph Chamberlain, Volume Five – 1901-1903*, MacMillan, London, 1969, page 194

157 Julian Amery, *Joseph Chamberlain and the Tariff Reform Campaign: The Life of Joseph Chamberlain, Volume Five – 1901-1903*, MacMillan, London, 1969, page 194

158 Julian Amery, *Joseph Chamberlain and the Tariff Reform Campaign: The Life of Joseph Chamberlain, Volume Five – 1901-1903*, MacMillan, London, 1969, page 252

159 Julian Amery, *Joseph Chamberlain and the Tariff Reform Campaign: The Life of Joseph Chamberlain, Volume Five –*

1901-1903, MacMillan, London, 1969, page 246

160 Julian Amery, *Joseph Chamberlain and the Tariff Reform Campaign: The Life of Joseph Chamberlain, Volume Five – 1901-1903*, MacMillan, London, 1969, page 301

161 Julian Amery, *Joseph Chamberlain and the Tariff Reform Campaign: The Life of Joseph Chamberlain, Volume Five – 1901-1903*, MacMillan, London, 1969, page 302

162 Robert K Massie, *Dreadnought: Britain, Germany, and the coming of the Great War*, Jonathan Cape, London, 1992, page 330

163 Julian Amery, *Joseph Chamberlain and the Tariff Reform Campaign: The Life of Joseph Chamberlain, Volume Five – 1901-1903*, MacMillan, London, 1969, page 278

164 Julian Amery, *Joseph Chamberlain and the Tariff Reform Campaign: The Life of Joseph Chamberlain, Volume Five – 1901-1903*, MacMillan, London, 1969, page 368

165 Julian Amery, *Joseph Chamberlain and the Tariff Reform Campaign: The Life of Joseph Chamberlain, Volume Five – 1901-1903*, MacMillan, London, 1969, page 374

166 Peter Fraser, *Joseph Chamberlain: Radicalism and Empire, 1868-1914*, Cassell & Company Ltd, London, 1966, page 242

167 Travis Crosby, *Joseph Chamberlain*, I.B.Tauris, London, 2011, page 168

168 Julian Amery, *Joseph Chamberlain and the Tariff Reform Campaign: The Life of Joseph Chamberlain, Volume Five – 1901-1903*, MacMillan, London, 1969, page 389

169 Julian Amery, *Joseph Chamberlain and the Tariff Reform Campaign: The Life of Joseph Chamberlain, Volume Five – 1901-1903*, MacMillan, London, 1969, page 389

170 Julian Amery, *Joseph Chamberlain and the Tariff Reform Campaign: The Life of Joseph Chamberlain, Volume Five – 1901-1903*, MacMillan, London, 1969, page 391

171 Julian Amery, *Joseph Chamberlain and the Tariff Reform Campaign: The Life of Joseph Chamberlain, Volume Five – 1901-1903*, MacMillan, London, 1969, page 406

172 Julian Amery, *Joseph Chamberlain and the Tariff Reform Campaign: The Life of Joseph Chamberlain, Volume Five – 1901-1903*, MacMillan, London, 1969, page 412

173 Julian Amery, *Joseph Chamberlain and the Tariff Reform Campaign: The Life of Joseph Chamberlain, Volume Five – 1901-1903*, MacMillan, London, 1969, page 434

174 Julian Amery, *Joseph Chamberlain and the Tariff Reform Campaign: The Life of Joseph Chamberlain, Volume Five – 1901-1903*, MacMillan, London, 1969, page 435

175 Julian Amery, *Joseph Chamberlain and the Tariff Reform Campaign: The Life of Joseph Chamberlain, Volume Five – 1901-1903*, MacMillan, London, 1969, page 445

176 Julian Amery, *Joseph Chamberlain and the Tariff Reform Campaign: The Life of Joseph Chamberlain, Volume Five – 1901-1903*, MacMillan, London, 1969, page 445

177 Julian Amery, *Joseph Chamberlain and the Tariff Reform Campaign: The Life of Joseph Chamberlain, Volume Five – 1901-1903*, MacMillan, London, 1969, page 447

178 Julian Amery, *Joseph Chamberlain and the Tariff Reform Campaign: The Life of Joseph Chamberlain, Volume Six – 1903-1968*, MacMillan, London, 1969, page 455

179 Travis Crosby, *Joseph Chamberlain*, I.B.Tauris, London, 2011, page 170

180 Julian Amery, *Joseph Chamberlain and the Tariff Reform Campaign: The Life of Joseph Chamberlain, Volume Six – 1903-*

1968, MacMillan, London, 1969, page 460

181 Julian Amery, *Joseph Chamberlain and the Tariff Reform Campaign: The Life of Joseph Chamberlain, Volume Six – 1903-1968*, MacMillan, London, 1969, page 461

182 Julian Amery, *Joseph Chamberlain and the Tariff Reform Campaign: The Life of Joseph Chamberlain, Volume Six – 1903-1968*, MacMillan, London, 1969, page 462

183 Julian Amery, *Joseph Chamberlain and the Tariff Reform Campaign: The Life of Joseph Chamberlain, Volume Six – 1903-1968*, MacMillan, London, 1969, page 463

184 Julian Amery, *Joseph Chamberlain and the Tariff Reform Campaign: The Life of Joseph Chamberlain, Volume Six – 1903-1968*, MacMillan, London, 1969, page 463

185 Julian Amery, *Joseph Chamberlain and the Tariff Reform Campaign: The Life of Joseph Chamberlain, Volume Six – 1903-1968*, MacMillan, London, 1969, page 464

186 Julian Amery, *Joseph Chamberlain and the Tariff Reform Campaign: The Life of Joseph Chamberlain, Volume Six – 1903-1968*, MacMillan, London, 1969, page 470

187 Julian Amery, *Joseph Chamberlain and the Tariff Reform Campaign: The Life of Joseph Chamberlain, Volume Six – 1903-1968*, MacMillan, London, 1969, page 470

188 Julian Amery, *Joseph Chamberlain and the Tariff Reform Campaign: The Life of Joseph Chamberlain, Volume Six – 1903-1968*, MacMillan, London, 1969, page 471

189 Julian Amery, *Joseph Chamberlain and the Tariff Reform Campaign: The Life of Joseph Chamberlain, Volume Six – 1903-1968*, MacMillan, London, 1969, page 475

190 Julian Amery, *Joseph Chamberlain and the Tariff Reform Campaign: The Life of Joseph Chamberlain, Volume Six – 1903-1968*, MacMillan, London, 1969, page 476

191 Julian Amery, *Joseph Chamberlain and the Tariff Reform Campaign: The Life of Joseph Chamberlain, Volume Six – 1903-1968*, MacMillan, London, 1969, page 476

192 Julian Amery, *Joseph Chamberlain and the Tariff Reform Campaign: The Life of Joseph Chamberlain, Volume Six – 1903-1968*, MacMillan, London, 1969, page 480

193 Julian Amery, *Joseph Chamberlain and the Tariff Reform Campaign: The Life of Joseph Chamberlain, Volume Six – 1903-1968*, MacMillan, London, 1969, page 483

194 Julian Amery, *Joseph Chamberlain and the Tariff Reform Campaign: The Life of Joseph Chamberlain, Volume Six – 1903-1968*, MacMillan, London, 1969, page 492

195 Julian Amery, *Joseph Chamberlain and the Tariff Reform Campaign: The Life of Joseph Chamberlain, Volume Six – 1903-1968*, MacMillan, London, 1969, page 492

196 Julian Amery, *Joseph Chamberlain and the Tariff Reform Campaign: The Life of Joseph Chamberlain, Volume Six – 1903-1968*, MacMillan, London, 1969, page 494

197 Julian Amery, *Joseph Chamberlain and the Tariff Reform Campaign: The Life of Joseph Chamberlain, Volume Six – 1903-1968*, MacMillan, London, 1969, page 508

198 Julian Amery, *Joseph Chamberlain and the Tariff Reform Campaign: The Life of Joseph Chamberlain, Volume Six – 1903-1968*, MacMillan, London, 1969, page 508

199 Julian Amery, *Joseph Chamberlain and the Tariff Reform Campaign: The Life of Joseph Chamberlain, Volume Six – 1903-1968*, MacMillan, London, 1969, page 514

200 Julian Amery, *Joseph Chamberlain and the Tariff Reform Campaign: The Life of Joseph Chamberlain, Volume Six – 1903-1968*, MacMillan, London, 1969, page 515

201 Julian Amery, *Joseph Chamberlain and the Tariff Reform Campaign: The Life of Joseph Chamberlain, Volume Six – 1903-1968*, MacMillan, London, 1969, page 516

202 Robert K Massie, *Dreadnought: Britain, Germany, and the coming of the Great War*, Jonathan Cape, London, 1992, page 335

203 Julian Amery, *Joseph Chamberlain and the Tariff Reform Campaign: The Life of Joseph Chamberlain, Volume Six – 1903-1968*, MacMillan, London, 1969, page 566

204 Richard Rempel, *Unionists Divided: Arthur Balfour, Joseph Chamberlain and the Unionist Free Traders*, David & Charles (Publishers) Limited, Newton Abbot, 1972, page 127

205 Richard Rempel, *Unionists Divided: Arthur Balfour, Joseph Chamberlain and the Unionist Free Traders*, David & Charles (Publishers) Limited, Newton Abbot, 1972, page 135

206 Robert K Massie, *Dreadnought: Britain, Germany, and the coming of the Great War*, Jonathan Cape, London, 1992, page 335

207 Robert K Massie, *Dreadnought: Britain, Germany, and the coming of the Great War*, Jonathan Cape, London, 1992, page 336

208 Julian Amery, *Joseph Chamberlain and the Tariff Reform Campaign: The Life of Joseph Chamberlain, Volume Six – 1903-1968*, MacMillan, London, 1969, page 614

209 Julian Amery, *Joseph Chamberlain and the Tariff Reform Campaign: The Life of Joseph Chamberlain, Volume Six – 1903-1968*, MacMillan, London, 1969, page 617

210 Julian Amery, *Joseph Chamberlain and the Tariff Reform Campaign: The Life of Joseph Chamberlain, Volume Six – 1903-1968*, MacMillan, London, 1969, page 634

211 Richard Rempel, *Unionists Divided: Arthur Balfour, Joseph Chamberlain and the Unionist Free Traders*, David & Charles (Publishers) Limited, Newton Abbot, 1972, page 124

212 Julian Amery, *Joseph Chamberlain and the Tariff Reform Campaign: The Life of Joseph Chamberlain, Volume Six – 1903-1968*, MacMillan, London, 1969, page 655

213 Julian Amery, *Joseph Chamberlain and the Tariff Reform Campaign: The Life of Joseph Chamberlain, Volume Six – 1903-1968*, MacMillan, London, 1969, page 668

214 Richard Rempel, *Unionists Divided: Arthur Balfour, Joseph Chamberlain and the Unionist Free Traders*, David & Charles (Publishers) Limited, Newton Abbot, 1972, page 127

215 Peter Fraser, *Joseph Chamberlain: Radicalism and Empire, 1868-1914*, Cassell & Company Ltd, London, 1966, page 258

216 Julian Amery, *Joseph Chamberlain and the Tariff Reform Campaign: The Life of Joseph Chamberlain, Volume Six – 1903-1968*, MacMillan, London, 1969, page 668

217 Richard Rempel, *Unionists Divided: Arthur Balfour, Joseph Chamberlain and the Unionist Free Traders*, David & Charles (Publishers) Limited, Newton Abbot, 1972, page 143

218 Julian Amery, *Joseph Chamberlain and the Tariff Reform Campaign: The Life of Joseph Chamberlain, Volume Six – 1903-1968*, MacMillan, London, 1969, page 699

219 Julian Amery, *Joseph Chamberlain and the Tariff Reform Campaign: The Life of Joseph Chamberlain, Volume Six – 1903-1968*, MacMillan, London, 1969, page 712

220 Julian Amery, *Joseph Chamberlain and the Tariff Reform Campaign: The Life of Joseph Chamberlain, Volume Six – 1903-1968*, MacMillan, London, 1969, page 718

221 Julian Amery, *Joseph Chamberlain and the Tariff Reform Campaign: The Life of Joseph Chamberlain, Volume Six – 1903-

1968, MacMillan, London, 1969, page 724

222 Julian Amery, *Joseph Chamberlain and the Tariff Reform Campaign: The Life of Joseph Chamberlain, Volume Six – 1903-1968*, MacMillan, London, 1969, page 757

223 Julian Amery, *Joseph Chamberlain and the Tariff Reform Campaign: The Life of Joseph Chamberlain, Volume Six – 1903-1968*, MacMillan, London, 1969, page 758

224 Julian Amery, *Joseph Chamberlain and the Tariff Reform Campaign: The Life of Joseph Chamberlain, Volume Six – 1903-1968*, MacMillan, London, 1969, page 767

225 Peter Fraser, *Joseph Chamberlain: Radicalism and Empire, 1868-1914*, Cassell & Company Ltd, London, 1966, page 270

226 Julian Amery, *Joseph Chamberlain and the Tariff Reform Campaign: The Life of Joseph Chamberlain, Volume Six – 1903-1968*, MacMillan, London, 1969, page 772

227 Julian Amery, *Joseph Chamberlain and the Tariff Reform Campaign: The Life of Joseph Chamberlain, Volume Six – 1903-1968*, MacMillan, London, 1969, page 789

228 Richard Rempel, *Unionists Divided: Arthur Balfour, Joseph Chamberlain and the Unionist Free Traders*, David & Charles (Publishers) Limited, Newton Abbot, 1972, page 174

229 Julian Amery, *Joseph Chamberlain and the Tariff Reform Campaign: The Life of Joseph Chamberlain, Volume Six – 1903-1968*, MacMillan, London, 1969, page 784

230 Julian Amery, *Joseph Chamberlain and the Tariff Reform Campaign: The Life of Joseph Chamberlain, Volume Six – 1903-1968*, MacMillan, London, 1969, page 786

231 Julian Amery, *Joseph Chamberlain and the Tariff Reform Campaign: The Life of Joseph Chamberlain, Volume Six – 1903-1968*, MacMillan, London, 1969, page 794

232 Frank Trentmann, *Free Trade Nation*, Oxford University Press, New York, 2009, page 101

233 Julian Amery, *Joseph Chamberlain and the Tariff Reform Campaign: The Life of Joseph Chamberlain, Volume Six – 1903-1968*, MacMillan, London, 1969, page 958

234 Richard Rempel, *Unionists Divided: Arthur Balfour, Joseph Chamberlain and the Unionist Free Traders*, David & Charles (Publishers) Limited, Newton Abbot, 1972, page 199

235 Peter Clarke, *The Keynesian Revolution*, Clarendon Press, Oxford, 1988, page 256

236 Peter Clarke, *Keynes: The Twentieth Century's Most Influential Economist*, Bloomsbury Publishing, London, 2009, page 130

237 Peter Clarke, *The Keynesian Revolution*, Clarendon Press, Oxford, 1988, page 231

238 Peter Clarke, *Keynes: The Twentieth Century's Most Influential Economist*, Bloomsbury Publishing, London, 2009, page 130

239 John Fowler, *Understanding Keynes – An Analysis of the "General Theory"*, Wheatsheaf Books, Bury, 1981, page 38

240 John Maynard Keynes, *The General Theory of Employment, Interest, and Money*, Palgrove MacMillan, Basingstoke, 2007, page 15

241 Robert Dimand, *The Origins of the Keynesian Revolution: The Development of Keynes' Theory of Employment and Output*, Edward Elgar Publishing, Aldershot, 1988, page 21

242 Peter Clarke, *The Keynesian Revolution*, Clarendon Press, Oxford, 1988, page 86

243 Peter Clarke, *The Keynesian Revolution*, Clarendon Press, Oxford, 1988, page 87

244 *Keynes and Laissez-faire*, edited by AP Thirlwall, MacMillan Press, London, 1978, page 62

245 Peter Clarke, *Keynes: The Twentieth Century's Most Influential Economist*, Bloomsbury Publishing, London, 2009, page 134

246 Peter Clarke, *Keynes: The Twentieth Century's Most Influential Economist*, Bloomsbury Publishing, London, 2009, page 136

247 Peter Clarke, *Keynes: The Twentieth Century's Most Influential Economist*, Bloomsbury Publishing, London, 2009, page 137

248 Peter Clarke, *The Keynesian Revolution*, Clarendon Press, Oxford, 1988, page 256

249 Etienne Mantoux, *The Critics of Keynesian Economics*, edited by Henry Hazlitt, D Van Nostrand Company Ltd, Toronto, 1960, page 109

250 Robert Dimand, *The Origins of the Keynesian Revolution: The Development of Keynes' Theory of Employment and Output*, Edward Elgar Publishing, Aldershot, 1988, page 105

251 Peter Clarke, *The Keynesian Revolution*, Clarendon Press, Oxford, 1988, page 242

252 Peter Clarke, *The Keynesian Revolution*, Clarendon Press, Oxford, 1988, page 247

253 Peter Clarke, *The Keynesian Revolution*, Clarendon Press, Oxford, 1988, page 184

254 Peter Clarke, *The Keynesian Revolution*, Clarendon Press, Oxford, 1988, page 197

255 Peter Clarke, *Keynes: The Twentieth Century's Most Influential Economist*, Bloomsbury Publishing, London, 2009, page 140

256 Peter Clarke, *Keynes: The Twentieth Century's Most Influential Economist*, Bloomsbury Publishing, London, 2009, page 141

257 Robert Dimand, *The Origins of the Keynesian Revolution: The Development of Keynes' Theory of Employment and Output*, Edward Elgar Publishing, Aldershot, 1988, page 15

258 Peter Clarke, *The Keynesian Revolution*, Clarendon Press, Oxford, 1988, page 225

259 Peter Clarke, *The Keynesian Revolution*, Clarendon Press, Oxford, 1988, page 230

260 Peter Clarke, *Keynes: The Twentieth Century's Most Influential Economist*, Bloomsbury Publishing, London, 2009, page 147

261 Peter Clarke, *Keynes: The Twentieth Century's Most Influential Economist*, Bloomsbury Publishing, London, 2009, page 147

262 John Maynard Keynes, *The General Theory of Employment, Interest and Money*, Palgrave Macmillan, Basingstoke, 2007, page 89

263 John Maynard Keynes, *The General Theory of Employment, Interest and Money*, Palgrave Macmillan, Basingstoke, 2007, page 379

264 Michael Stewart, *Keynes and After*, Penguin Books, 3rd Edition, Bungay, 1986, page 110

265 John Maynard Keynes, *The General Theory of Employment, Interest and Money*, Palgrave Macmillan, Basingstoke, 2007, page 268

266 John Maynard Keynes, *The General Theory of Employment, Interest, and Money*, Palgrove MacMillan, Basingstoke, 2007, page 269

267 Keynes, The Economic Consequences of Mr Churchill (1925), *Essays in Persuasion: The Collected Writings of John Maynard Keynes*, MacMillan Press Ltd, London, 1972, page 220

268 Peter Clarke, *The Keynesian Revolution*, Clarendon Press, Oxford, 1988, page 112

269 John Maynard Keynes, *The General Theory of Employment, Interest, and Money*, Palgrove MacMillan, Basingstoke, 2007, page 296

270 Michael Stewart, *Keynes and After*, Penguin Books, 3rd Edition, Bungay, 1986, page 116

271 Peter Clarke, *Keynes: The Twentieth Century's Most Influential Economist*, Bloomsbury Publishing, London, 2009, page 148

272 *Keynes and Laissez-faire*, edited by AP Thirlwall, MacMillan Press, London, 1978, page 11

273 *Keynes and the Modern World*, edited by David Worswick and James Trevithick, Cambridge University Press, Cambridge, 1983, page 39

274 Robert Dimand, *The Origins of the Keynesian Revolution: The Development of Keynes' Theory of Employment and Output*, Edward Elgar Publishing, Aldershot, 1988, page 76

275 Peter Clarke, *Keynes: The Twentieth Century's Most Influential Economist*, Bloomsbury Publishing, London, 2009, page 102

276 FA Hayek, *A Tiger by the Tail*, The Institute of Economic Affairs, Tonbridge, 1978, page 56

277 FA Hayek, *A Tiger by the Tail*, The Institute of Economic Affairs, Tonbridge, 1978, page 61

278 FA Hayek, *A Tiger by the Tail*, The Institute of Economic Affairs, Tonbridge, 1978, page 103

279 FA Hayek, *A Tiger by the Tail*, The Institute of Economic Affairs, Tonbridge, 1978, page 130

280 Ludwig von Mises, *The Critics of Keynesian Economics*, edited by Henry Hazlitt, D Van Nostrand Company Ltd, Toronto, 1960, page 313

281 *The Critics of Keynesian Economics*, edited by Henry Hazlitt, D Van Nostrand Company Ltd, Toronto, 1960, page 338

282 Ludwig von Mises, *The Critics of Keynesian Economics*, edited by Henry Hazlitt, D Van Nostrand Company Ltd, Toronto, 1960, page 317

283 Ludwig von Mises, *The Critics of Keynesian Economics*, edited by Henry Hazlitt, D Van Nostrand Company Ltd, Toronto, 1960, page 318

284 *The Critics of Keynesian Economics*, edited by Henry Hazlitt, D Van Nostrand Company Ltd, Toronto, 1960, page 416

285 Correlli Barnett, *The Collapse of British Power*, Alan Sutton Publishing Limited, Gloucester, 1984, page 113

286 Correlli Barnett, *The Collapse of British Power*, Alan Sutton Publishing Limited, Gloucester, 1984, page 113

287 Correlli Barnett, *The Collapse of British Power*, Alan Sutton Publishing Limited, Gloucester, 1984, page 114

288 Frank Trentmann, *Free Trade Nation*, Oxford University Press, New York, 2009, page 293

289 Forrest Copie, *Depression and Protectionism: Britain Between the Wars*, George Allen & Unwin, London, 1983, page 40

290 Tim Rooth, *British Protectionism and the International Economy: Overseas Commercial Policy in the 1930s*, Cambridge University Press, Cambridge, 1992, page 37

291 Forrest Copie, *Depression and Protectionism: Britain Between the Wars*, George Allen & Unwin, London, 1983, page 41

292 Forrest Copie, *Depression and Protectionism: Britain Between the Wars*, George Allen & Unwin, London, 1983, page 44

293 Tim Rooth, *British Protectionism and the International Economy: Overseas Commercial Policy in the 1930s*, Cambridge University Press, Cambridge, 1992, page 37

294 Michael Stewart, *Keynes and After*, Penguin Books, 3rd Edition, Bungay, 1986, page 47

295 Larry Elliott and Dan Atkinson, *Going South: Why Britain Will Have a Third World Economy By 2014*, Palgrave Macmillan, Great Britain, 2012, page 130

296 Peter Clarke, *Keynes: The Twentieth Century's Most Influential Economist*, Bloomsbury Publishing, London, 2009, page 107

297 James Rickards, *Currency Wars*, Penguin Books, London, 2011, page 235

298 Keynes, Social Consequences in Changes in the Value of Money (1923), *Essays in Persuasion: The Collected Writings of John Maynard Keynes*, MacMillan Press Ltd, London, 1972, page 65

299 James Rickards, *Currency Wars*, Penguin Books, London, 2011, page 44

300 Michael Stewart, *Keynes and After*, Penguin Books, 3rd Edition, Bungay, 1986, page 51

301 Michael Stewart, *Keynes and After*, Penguin Books, 3rd Edition, Bungay, 1986, page 52

302 James Rickards, *Currency Wars*, Penguin Books, London, 2011, page 65

303 James Rickards, *Currency Wars*, Penguin Books, London, 2011, page 54

304 Peter Clarke, *The Keynesian Revolution*, Clarendon Press, Oxford, 1988, page 35

305 Peter Clarke, *The Keynesian Revolution*, Clarendon Press, Oxford, 1988, page 44

306 Julian Amery, *Joseph Chamberlain and the Tariff Reform Campaign: The Life of Joseph Chamberlain, Volume Six – 1903-1968*, MacMillan, London, 1969, page 1013

307 Julian Amery, *Joseph Chamberlain and the Tariff Reform Campaign: The Life of Joseph Chamberlain, Volume Six – 1903-1968*, MacMillan, London, 1969, page 1014

308 Richard Rempel, *Unionists Divided: Arthur Balfour, Joseph Chamberlain and the Unionist Free Traders*, David & Charles (Publishers) Limited, Newton Abbot, 1972, page 67

309 Julian Amery, *Joseph Chamberlain and the Tariff Reform Campaign: The Life of Joseph Chamberlain, Volume Six – 1903-1968*, MacMillan, London, 1969, page 1016

310 Michael Stewart, *Keynes and After*, Penguin Books, 3rd Edition, Bungay, 1986, page 52

311 Peter Clarke, *The Keynesian Revolution*, Clarendon Press, Oxford, 1988, page 38

312 Michael Kitson, *End of an Epoch: Britain's Withdrawal from the Gold Standard*, Judge Business School, University of Cambridge, June 2012, page 4

313 JK Galbraith, *The Great Crash 1929*, Andre Deutsch Limited, London, 1980 page 9

314 James Rickards, *Currency Wars*, Penguin Books, London, 2011, page 66

315 Peter Clarke, *Keynes: The Twentieth Century's Most Influential Economist*, Bloomsbury Publishing, London, 2009, page 108

316 Peter Clarke, *Keynes: The Twentieth Century's Most Influential Economist*, Bloomsbury Publishing, London, 2009, page 109

317 Peter Clarke, *Keynes: The Twentieth Century's Most Influential Economist*, Bloomsbury Publishing, London, 2009, pages 118 and 119

318 Peter Clarke, *Keynes: The Twentieth Century's Most Influential Economist*, Bloomsbury Publishing, London, 2009, page 110

319 John Hicks, *The Crisis in Keynesian Economics*, Camelot Press, Southampton, 1974, pages 67 and 68

320 Peter Clarke, *The Keynesian Revolution*, Clarendon Press, Oxford, 1988, page 40

321 Robert Dimand, *The Origins of the Keynesian Revolution: The Development of Keynes' Theory of Employment and Output*, Edward Elgar Publishing, Aldershot, 1988, page 30

322 Tim Rooth, *British Protectionism and the International Economy: Overseas Commercial Policy in the 1930s*, Cambridge University Press, Cambridge, 1992, page 25

323 CorrClli Barnett, *The Audit of War*, Macmillan London Ltd, London, 1986, page 71

324 Michael Stewart, *Keynes and After*, Penguin Books, 3rd Edition, Bungay, 1986, page 53

325 Michael Stewart, *Keynes and After*, Penguin Books, 3rd Edition, Bungay, 1986, page 53

326 Tim Rooth, *British Protectionism and the International Economy: Overseas Commercial Policy in the 1930s*, Cambridge University Press, Cambridge, 1992, page 10

327 Tim Rooth, *British Protectionism and the International Economy: Overseas Commercial Policy in the 1930s*, Cambridge University Press, Cambridge, 1992, pages 26-28

328 Tim Rooth, *British Protectionism and the International Economy: Overseas Commercial Policy in the 1930s*, Cambridge University Press, Cambridge, 1992, page 41

329 Julian Amery, *Joseph Chamberlain and the Tariff Reform Campaign: The Life of Joseph Chamberlain, Volume Six – 1903-1968*, MacMillan, London, 1969, page 1016

330 Julian Amery, *Joseph Chamberlain and the Tariff Reform Campaign: The Life of Joseph Chamberlain, Volume Six – 1903-1968*, MacMillan, London, 1969, page 1018

331 Julian Amery, *Joseph Chamberlain and the Tariff Reform Campaign: The Life of Joseph Chamberlain, Volume Six – 1903-1968*, MacMillan, London, 1969, page 1019

332 Julian Amery, *Joseph Chamberlain and the Tariff Reform Campaign: The Life of Joseph Chamberlain, Volume Six – 1903-1968*, MacMillan, London, 1969, page 1021

333 Michael Stewart, *Keynes and After*, Penguin Books, 3rd Edition, Bungay, 1986, page 55

334 Stephen D King, *When the Money Runs Out: The End of Western Affluence*, Yale University Press, Padstow, 2013, page 108

335 JK Galbraith, *The Great Crash 1929*, Andre Deutsch Limited, London, 1980 page 74

336 JK Galbraith, *The Great Crash 1929*, Andre Deutsch Limited, London, 1980 page 39

337 JK Galbraith, *The Great Crash 1929*, Andre Deutsch Limited, London, 1980 page 79

338 JK Galbraith, *The Great Crash 1929*, Andre Deutsch Limited, London, 1980 page 88

339 JK Galbraith, *The Great Crash 1929*, Andre Deutsch Limited, London, 1980 page 89

340 JK Galbraith, *The Great Crash 1929*, Andre Deutsch Limited, London, 1980 page 94

341 JK Galbraith, *The Great Crash 1929*, Andre Deutsch Limited, London, 1980 page 97

342 JK Galbraith, *The Great Crash 1929*, Andre Deutsch Limited, London, 1980 page 100

343 JK Galbraith, *The Great Crash 1929*, Andre Deutsch Limited, London, 1980 page 95

344 JK Galbraith, *The Great Crash 1929*, Andre Deutsch Limited, London, 1980 page 50

345 JK Galbraith, *The Great Crash 1929*, Andre Deutsch Limited, London, 1980 page 51

346 JK Galbraith, *The Great Crash 1929*, Andre Deutsch Limited, London, 1980 page 56

347 JK Galbraith, *The Great Crash 1929*, Andre Deutsch Limited, London, 1980 page 58

348 JK Galbraith, *The Great Crash 1929*, Andre Deutsch Limited, London, 1980 page 112

349 JK Galbraith, *The Great Crash 1929*, Andre Deutsch Limited, London, 1980 pages 122-124

350 Steven Pressman, A Time to Return to Keynes, *Critical Perspectives on International Business*, Vol %, Issue 1, page 158

351 Michael Stewart, *Keynes and After*, Penguin Books, 3rd Edition, Bungay, 1986, page 55

352 Michael Stewart, *Keynes and After*, Penguin Books, 3rd Edition, Bungay, 1986, page 56

353 Michael Stewart, *Keynes and After*, Penguin Books, 3rd Edition, Bungay, 1986, page 59

354 Michael Stewart, *Keynes and After*, Penguin Books, 3rd Edition, Bungay, 1986, page 60

355 Julian Amery, *Joseph Chamberlain and the Tariff Reform Campaign: The Life of Joseph Chamberlain, Volume Six – 1903-1968*, MacMillan, London, 1969, page 1022

356 Frank Trentmann, *Free Trade Nation*, Oxford University Press, New York, 2009, page 333

357 Robert Dimand, *The Origins of the Keynesian Revolution: The Development of Keynes' Theory of Employment and Output*, Edward Elgar Publishing, Aldershot, 1988, page 61

358 James Rickards, *Currency Wars*, Penguin Books, London, 2011, page 68

359 Michael Stewart, *Keynes and After*, Penguin Books, 3rd Edition, Bungay, 1986, page 61

360 Peter Clarke, *The Keynesian Revolution*, Clarendon Press, Oxford, 1988, page 42

361 Peter Clarke, *The Keynesian Revolution*, Clarendon Press, Oxford, 1988, page 43

362 Peter Clarke, *The Keynesian Revolution*, Clarendon Press, Oxford, 1988, page 200

363 Peter Clarke, *Keynes: The Twentieth Century's Most Influential Economist*, Bloomsbury Publishing, London, 2009, page 116

364 Tim Rooth, *British Protectionism and the International Economy: Overseas Commercial Policy in the 1930s*, Cambridge University Press, Cambridge, 1992, page 59

365 Peter Clarke, *The Keynesian Revolution*, Clarendon Press, Oxford, 1988, page 115

366 *Keynes and the Modern World*, edited by David Worswick and James Trevithick, Cambridge University Press, Cambridge, 1983, page 132

367 Robert Dimand, *The Origins of the Keynesian Revolution: The Development of Keynes' Theory of Employment and Output*, Edward Elgar Publishing, Aldershot, 1988, page 41

368 Robert Dimand, *The Origins of the Keynesian Revolution: The Development of Keynes' Theory of Employment and Output*, Edward Elgar Publishing, Aldershot, 1988, page 97

369 Hansard, 14th February 1935, Cols 2208-9, cited in: Michael Stewart, *Keynes and After*, Penguin Books, 3rd Edition, Bungay, 1986, page 64

370 Forrest Copie, *Depression and Protectionism: Britain Between the Wars*, George Allen & Unwin, London, 1983, page 120

371 Forrest Copie, *Depression and Protectionism: Britain Between the Wars*, George Allen & Unwin, London, 1983, page 7

372 Frank Trentmann, *Free Trade Nation*, Oxford University Press, New York, 2009, page 344

373 Tim Rooth, *British Protectionism and the International Economy: Overseas Commercial Policy in the 1930s*, Cambridge University Press, Cambridge, 1992, page 46

374 Tim Rooth, *British Protectionism and the International Economy: Overseas Commercial Policy in the 1930s*, Cambridge University Press, Cambridge, 1992, page 72

375 Forrest Copie, *Depression and Protectionism: Britain Between the Wars*, George Allen & Unwin, London, 1983, page 41

376 Forrest Copie, *Depression and Protectionism: Britain Between the Wars*, George Allen & Unwin, London, 1983, page 42

377 Forrest Copie, *Depression and Protectionism: Britain Between the Wars*, George Allen & Unwin, London, 1983, page 63

378 Julian Amery, *Joseph Chamberlain and the Tariff Reform Campaign: The Life of Joseph Chamberlain, Volume Six – 1903-1968*, MacMillan, London, 1969, page 1028

379 Julian Amery, *Joseph Chamberlain and the Tariff Reform Campaign: The Life of Joseph Chamberlain, Volume Six – 1903-1968*, MacMillan, London, 1969, page 1028

380 Tim Rooth, *British Protectionism and the International Economy: Overseas Commercial Policy in the 1930s*, Cambridge University Press, Cambridge, 1992, page 269

381 Tim Rooth, *British Protectionism and the International Economy: Overseas Commercial Policy in the 1930s*, Cambridge University Press, Cambridge, 1992, page 269

382 Tim Rooth, *British Protectionism and the International Economy: Overseas Commercial Policy in the 1930s*, Cambridge University Press, Cambridge, 1992, page 270

383 Tim Rooth, *British Protectionism and the International Economy: Overseas Commercial Policy in the 1930s*, Cambridge University Press, Cambridge, 1992, page 271

384 Derek Aldcroft, *The Inter-War Economy: Britain 1919-1939*, Batsford, London, 1970, page 281, cited in: Forrest Copie, *Depression and Protectionism: Britain Between the Wars*, George Allen & Unwin, London, 1983, page 134

385 Tim Rooth, *British Protectionism and the International Economy: Overseas Commercial Policy in the 1930s*, Cambridge University Press, Cambridge, 1992, page 272

386 Tim Rooth, *British Protectionism and the International Economy: Overseas Commercial Policy in the 1930s*, Cambridge University Press, Cambridge, 1992, page 272

387 Tim Rooth, *British Protectionism and the International Economy: Overseas Commercial Policy in the 1930s*, Cambridge University Press, Cambridge, 1992, page 272

388 Tim Rooth, *British Protectionism and the International Economy: Overseas Commercial Policy in the 1930s*, Cambridge University Press, Cambridge, 1992, page 273

389 Tim Rooth, *British Protectionism and the International Economy: Overseas Commercial Policy in the 1930s*, Cambridge University Press, Cambridge, 1992, page 274

390 Larry Elliott and Dan Atkinson, *Going South: Why Britain Will Have a Third World Economy By 2014*, Palgrave Macmillan, Great Britain, 2012, page 136

391 Stephen D King, *When the Money Runs Out: The End of Western Affluence*, Yale University Press, Padstow, 2013, page 105

392 Stephen D King, *When the Money Runs Out: The End of Western Affluence*, Yale University Press, Padstow, 2013, page 101

393 Forrest Copie, *Depression and Protectionism: Britain Between the Wars*, George Allen & Unwin, London, 1983, page 7

394 Larry Elliott and Dan Atkinson, *Going South: Why Britain Will Have a Third World Economy By 2014*, Palgrave Macmillan, Great Britain, 2012, page 137

395 Larry Elliott and Dan Atkinson, *Going South: Why Britain Will Have a Third World Economy By 2014*, Palgrave Macmillan,

Great Britain, 2012, page 137

396 Larry Elliott and Dan Atkinson, *Going South: Why Britain Will Have a Third World Economy By 2014*, Palgrave Macmillan, Great Britain, 2012, page 137

397 Larry Elliott and Dan Atkinson, *Going South: Why Britain Will Have a Third World Economy By 2014*, Palgrave Macmillan, Great Britain, 2012, page 138

398 Julian Amery, *Joseph Chamberlain and the Tariff Reform Campaign: The Life of Joseph Chamberlain, Volume Six – 1903-1968*, MacMillan, London, 1969, page 1029

399 Julian Amery, *Joseph Chamberlain and the Tariff Reform Campaign: The Life of Joseph Chamberlain, Volume Six – 1903-1968*, MacMillan, London, 1969, page 1030

400 Peter Clarke, *Keynes: The Twentieth Century's Most Influential Economist*, Bloomsbury Publishing, London, 2009, page 6

401 *The Critics of Keynesian Economics*, edited by Henry Hazlitt, D Van Nostrand Company Ltd, Toronto, 1960, page 339

402 Peter Clarke, *Keynes: The Twentieth Century's Most Influential Economist*, Bloomsbury Publishing, London, 2009, page 7

403 *The Critics of Keynesian Economics*, edited by Henry Hazlitt, D Van Nostrand Company Ltd, Toronto, 1960, page 339

404 *Keynes and Laissez-faire*, edited by AP Thirlwall, MacMillan Press, London, 1978, page 89

405 James Rickards, *Currency Wars*, Penguin Books, London, 2011, page 71

406 James Rickards, *Currency Wars*, Penguin Books, London, 2011, page 72

407 James Rickards, *Currency Wars*, Penguin Books, London, 2011, page 73

408 Stephen D King, *When the Money Runs Out: The End of Western Affluence*, Yale University Press, Padstow, 2013, page 109

409 Stephen D King, *When the Money Runs Out: The End of Western Affluence*, Yale University Press, Padstow, 2013, page 110

410 *Keynes and Laissez-faire*, edited by AP Thirlwall, MacMillan Press, London, 1978, page 119

411 Peter Clarke, *Keynes: The Twentieth Century's Most Influential Economist*, Bloomsbury Publishing, London, 2009, page 8

412 Peter Clarke, *Keynes: The Twentieth Century's Most Influential Economist*, Bloomsbury Publishing, London, 2009, page 162

413 Correlli Barnett, *The Collapse of British Power*, Alan Sutton Publishing Limited, Gloucester, 1984, page 13

414 Correlli Barnett, *The Collapse of British Power*, Alan Sutton Publishing Limited, Gloucester, 1984, page 14

415 Correlli Barnett, *The Collapse of British Power*, Alan Sutton Publishing Limited, Gloucester, 1984, page 14

416 Larry Elliott and Dan Atkinson, *Going South: Why Britain Will Have a Third World Economy By 2014*, Palgrave Macmillan, Great Britain, 2012, page 140

417 Julian Amery, *Joseph Chamberlain and the Tariff Reform Campaign: The Life of Joseph Chamberlain, Volume Six – 1903-1968*, MacMillan, London, 1969, page 1042

418 Julian Amery, *Joseph Chamberlain and the Tariff Reform Campaign: The Life of Joseph Chamberlain, Volume Six – 1903-

1968, MacMillan, London, 1969, page 1042

419 Julian Amery, *Joseph Chamberlain and the Tariff Reform Campaign: The Life of Joseph Chamberlain, Volume Six – 1903-1968*, MacMillan, London, 1969, page 1044

420 John Eatwell, *Whatever Happened to Britain?*, Gerald Duckworth and Co Ltd, London, 1982, page 130

421 *Keynes and the Modern World*, edited by David Worswick and James Trevithick, Cambridge University Press, Cambridge, 1983, page 131

422 Julian Amery, *Joseph Chamberlain and the Tariff Reform Campaign: The Life of Joseph Chamberlain, Volume Six – 1903-1968*, MacMillan, London, 1969, page 1046

423 Larry Elliott and Dan Atkinson, *Going South: Why Britain Will Have a Third World Economy By 2014*, Palgrave Macmillan, Great Britain, 2012, page 146

424 John Eatwell, *Whatever Happened to Britain?*, Gerald Duckworth and Co Ltd, London, 1982, page 129

425 John Eatwell, *Whatever Happened to Britain?*, Gerald Duckworth and Co Ltd, London, 1982, page 132

426 Larry Elliott and Dan Atkinson, *Going South: Why Britain Will Have a Third World Economy By 2014*, Palgrave Macmillan, Great Britain, 2012, page 154

427 Garet Garrett, *The Critics of Keynesian Economics*, edited by Henry Hazlitt, D Van Nostrand Company Ltd, Toronto, 1960, page 233

428 Garet Garrett, *The Critics of Keynesian Economics*, edited by Henry Hazlitt, D Van Nostrand Company Ltd, Toronto, 1960, page 233

429 Peter Clarke, *Keynes: The Twentieth Century's Most Influential Economist*, Bloomsbury Publishing, London, 2009,

430 *Keynes and Laissez-faire*, edited by AP Thirlwall, MacMillan Press, London, 1978, page 3

431 Employment Policy White Paper, cited in: Michael Stewart, *Keynes and After*, Penguin Books, 3rd Edition, Bungay, 1986, page 142

432 *The Critics of Keynesian Economics*, edited by Henry Hazlitt, D Van Nostrand Company Ltd, Toronto, 1960, page 213

433 *The Critics of Keynesian Economics*, edited by Henry Hazlitt, D Van Nostrand Company Ltd, Toronto, 1960, page 213

434 *The Critics of Keynesian Economics*, edited by Henry Hazlitt, D Van Nostrand Company Ltd, Toronto, 1960, page 213

435 *The Critics of Keynesian Economics*, edited by Henry Hazlitt, D Van Nostrand Company Ltd, Toronto, 1960, page 214

436 *The Critics of Keynesian Economics*, edited by Henry Hazlitt, D Van Nostrand Company Ltd, Toronto, 1960, page 222

437 *The Critics of Keynesian Economics*, edited by Henry Hazlitt, D Van Nostrand Company Ltd, Toronto, 1960, page 223

438 *The Critics of Keynesian Economics*, edited by Henry Hazlitt, D Van Nostrand Company Ltd, Toronto, 1960, page 225

439 *The Critics of Keynesian Economics*, edited by Henry Hazlitt, D Van Nostrand Company Ltd, Toronto, 1960, page 226

440 *The Critics of Keynesian Economics*, edited by Henry Hazlitt, D Van Nostrand Company Ltd, Toronto, 1960, page 228

441 Larry Elliott and Dan Atkinson, *Going South: Why Britain Will Have a Third World Economy By 2014*, Palgrave Macmillan, Great Britain, 2012, page 142

442 Correlli Barnett, *The Audit of War*, Macmillan London Ltd, London, 1986, page 27

443 Nicholas Kaldor, cited in: Peter Kenway, From Keynesianism to Monetarism: The Evolution of UK Macroeconomic Models, Routledge, London 1994, page 8

444 Nicholas Kaldor, *Keynes and the Modern World*, edited by David Worswick and James Trevithick, Cambridge University Press, Cambridge, 1983, page 1

445 *Keynes and the Modern World*, edited by David Worswick and James Trevithick, Cambridge University Press, Cambridge, 1983, page 6

446 Michael Stewart, *Keynes and After*, Penguin Books, 3rd Edition, Bungay, 1986, page 142

447 Michael Stewart, *Keynes and After*, Penguin Books, 3rd Edition, Bungay, 1986, page 143

448 Thomas Sowell, *Say's Law: An Historical Analysis*, Princeton University Press, Princeton, 1972, page 218

449 Michael Stewart, *Keynes and After*, Penguin Books, 3rd Edition, Bungay, 1986, page 148

450 James Rickards, *Currency Wars*, Penguin Books, London, 2011, pages 79 and 80

451 Larry Elliott and Dan Atkinson, *Going South: Why Britain Will Have a Third World Economy By 2014*, Palgrave Macmillan, Great Britain, 2012, page 151

452 Larry Elliott and Dan Atkinson, *Going South: Why Britain Will Have a Third World Economy By 2014*, Palgrave Macmillan, Great Britain, 2012, page 149

453 James Rickards, *Currency Wars*, Penguin Books, London, 2011, page 81

454 Peter Kenway, *From Keynesianism to Monetarism: The Evolution of UK Macroeconomic Models*, Routledge, London 1994, page 86

455 Peter Kenway, *From Keynesianism to Monetarism: The Evolution of UK Macroeconomic Models*, Routledge, London 1994, page 93

456 Nicholas Comfort, *The Slow Death of British Industry*, Biteback Publishing, London, 2012, page 244

457 Michael Stewart, *Keynes and After*, Penguin Books, 3rd Edition, Bungay, 1986, page 174

458 Nicholas Comfort, *The Slow Death of British Industry*, Biteback Publishing, London, 2012, page 104

459 Will Hutton, T*he State We're In*, Jonathan Cape, London, 1995, page 59

460 Larry Elliott and Dan Atkinson, *Going South: Why Britain Will Have a Third World Economy By 2014*, Palgrave Macmillan, Great Britain, 2012, page 155

461 Peter Kenway, *From Keynesianism to Monetarism: The Evolution of UK Macroeconomic Models*, Routledge, London 1994, page 97

462 Peter Kenway, *From Keynesianism to Monetarism: The Evolution of UK Macroeconomic Models*, Routledge, London 1994, pages 98 and 99

463 Cripps, Godley and Fetherston cited in: Peter Kenway, From Keynesianism to Monetarism: The Evolution of UK Macroeconomic Models, Routledge, London 1994, page 100

464 Cripps, Godley and Fetherston cited in: Peter Kenway, From Keynesianism to Monetarism: The Evolution of UK Macroeconomic Models, Routledge, London 1994, page 101

465 Peter Kenway, From Keynesianism to Monetarism: The Evolution of UK Macroeconomic Models, Routledge, London 1994, page 101

466 Peter Kenway, From Keynesianism to Monetarism: The Evolution of UK Macroeconomic Models, Routledge, London 1994, page 102

467 Peter Kenway, From Keynesianism to Monetarism: The Evolution of UK Macroeconomic Models, Routledge, London 1994, page 107

468 Peter Kenway, From Keynesianism to Monetarism: The Evolution of UK Macroeconomic Models, Routledge, London 1994, page 112

469 Peter Kenway, From Keynesianism to Monetarism: The Evolution of UK Macroeconomic Models, Routledge, London 1994, page 113

470 Peter Kenway, From Keynesianism to Monetarism: The Evolution of UK Macroeconomic Models, Routledge, London 1994, page 119

471 Peter Kenway, From Keynesianism to Monetarism: The Evolution of UK Macroeconomic Models, Routledge, London 1994, page 126

472 Peter Kenway, From Keynesianism to Monetarism: The Evolution of UK Macroeconomic Models, Routledge, London 1994, page 132

473 Michael Stewart, *Keynes and After*, Penguin Books, 3rd Edition, Bungay, 1986, page 154

474 Michael Stewart, *Keynes and After*, Penguin Books, 3rd Edition, Bungay, 1986, page 155

475 Michael Stewart, *Keynes and After*, Penguin Books, 3rd Edition, Bungay, 1986, page 161

476 Michael Stewart, *Keynes and After*, Penguin Books, 3rd Edition, Bungay, 1986, page 161

477 Michael Stewart, *Keynes and After*, Penguin Books, 3rd Edition, Bungay, 1986, page 163

478 Cambridge Policy Group cited in: Peter Kenway, *From Keynesianism to Monetarism: The Evolution of UK Macroeconomic Models*, Routledge, London 1994, page

479 John Eatwell, *Whatever Happened to Britain?*, Gerald Duckworth and Co Ltd, London, 1982, page 59

480 John Eatwell, *Whatever Happened to Britain?*, Gerald Duckworth and Co Ltd, London, 1982, page 13.

481 Peter Clarke, *Keynes: The Twentieth Century's Most Influential Economist*, Bloomsbury Publishing, London, 2009, page 16

482 *Keynes's General Theory After Seventy Years*, edited by Robert Dimand, Robert Mundell and Alessandro Vercelli, Palgrave MacMillan, International Economic Association, London, 2010, page 12

483 Peter Clarke, *Keynes: The Twentieth Century's Most Influential Economist*, Bloomsbury Publishing, London, 2009, page 17

484 Peter Clarke, *Keynes: The Twentieth Century's Most Influential Economist*, Bloomsbury Publishing, London, 2009, page 16

485 Peter Clarke, *Keynes: The Twentieth Century's Most Influential Economist*, Bloomsbury Publishing, London, 2009, page 17

486 FA Hayek, *A Tiger by the Tail*, The Institute of Economic Affairs, Tonbridge, 1978, page 84

487 Stephen D King, *Losing Control: The Emerging Threats to Western Prosperity*, TJ International, Padstow, 2010, page 95

488 Peter Clarke, *Keynes: The Twentieth Century's Most Influential Economist*, Bloomsbury Publishing, London, 2009, page 176

489 John Hicks, *The Crisis in Keynesian Economics*, Camelot Press, Southampton, 1974, page 71

490 John Hicks, *The Crisis in Keynesian Economics*, Camelot Press, Southampton, 1974, page 71

491 John Hicks, *The Crisis in Keynesian Economics*, Camelot Press, Southampton, 1974, page 83

492 *The Critics of Keynesian Economics*, edited by Henry Hazlitt, D Van Nostrand Company Ltd, Toronto, 1960, page 427

493 Will Hutton, T*he State We're In*, Jonathan Cape, London, 1995, page 8

494 Michael Stewart, *Keynes and After*, Penguin Books, 3rd Edition, Bungay, 1986, page 180

495 John Smithin, Keynes, Chicago and Friedman: a review essay, *Journal of Economic Studies*, Vol 31, issue 1, page 83

496 John Smithin, Keynes, Chicago and Friedman: a review essay, *Journal of Economic Studies*, Vol 31, issue 1, page 83

497 Michael Stewart, *Keynes and After*, Penguin Books, 3rd Edition, Bungay, 1986, page 190

498 Peter Kenway, *From Keynesianism to Monetarism: The Evolution of UK Macroeconomic Models*, Routledge, London 1994, page 133

499 Peter Kenway, *From Keynesianism to Monetarism: The Evolution of UK Macroeconomic Models, Routledge*, London 1994, page 145

500 Peter Kenway, *From Keynesianism to Monetarism: The Evolution of UK Macroeconomic Models*, Routledge, London 1994, page 148

501 Peter Riddell, *The Thatcher Government*, Martin Robertson, Oxford, 1983, page 45

502 James Rickards, *Currency Wars*, Penguin Books, London, 2011, page 94

503 *Bank of England Quarterly Bulletin*, February 1991

504 Will Hutton, T*he State We're In*, Jonathan Cape, London, 1995, page 65

505 Will Hutton, T*he State We're In*, Jonathan Cape, London, 1995, page 72

506 Will Hutton, T*he State We're In*, Jonathan Cape, London, 1995, page 71

507 Will Hutton, T*he State We're In*, Jonathan Cape, London, 1995, page 73

508 Will Hutton, T*he State We're In*, Jonathan Cape, London, 1995, page 151

509 Michael Stewart, *Keynes and After*, Penguin Books, 3rd Edition, Bungay, 1986, page 186

510 Michael Stewart, *Keynes and After*, Penguin Books, 3rd Edition, Bungay, 1986, page 186

511 James Rickards, *Currency Wars*, Penguin Books, London, 2011, page 129

512 James Rickards, *Currency Wars*, Penguin Books, London, 2011, page 184

513 James Rickards, *Currency Wars*, Penguin Books, London, 2011, page 185

514 James Rickards, *Currency Wars*, Penguin Books, London, 2011, page 186

515 James Rickards, *Currency Wars*, Penguin Books, London, 2011, page 187

516 Larry Elliott and Dan Atkinson, *Going South: Why Britain Will Have a Third World Economy By 2014*, Palgrave Macmillan, Great Britain, 2012, page 159

517 Stephen D King, *Losing Control: The Emerging Threats to Western Prosperity*, TJ International, Padstow, 2010, page 206

518 James Rickards, *Currency Wars*, Penguin Books, London, 2011, page 8

519 James Rickards, *Currency Wars*, Penguin Books, London, 2011, page 175

520 James Rickards, *Currency Wars*, Penguin Books, London, 2011, page 176

521 James Rickards, *Currency Wars*, Penguin Books, London, 2011, page 193

522 Mitch Feierstein, Plant Ponzi, Bantum Press, London, 2012, page 239

523 Mitch Feierstein, Plant Ponzi, Bantum Press, London, 2012, page 165

524 Larry Elliott and Dan Atkinson, *Going South: Why Britain Will Have a Third World Economy By 2014*, Palgrave Macmillan, Great Britain, 2012, page 70

525 Larry Elliott and Dan Atkinson, *Going South: Why Britain Will Have a Third World Economy By 2014*, Palgrave Macmillan, Great Britain, 2012, page 71

526 Larry Elliott and Dan Atkinson, *Going South: Why Britain Will Have a Third World Economy By 2014*, Palgrave Macmillan, Great Britain, 2012, page 81

527 Larry Elliott and Dan Atkinson, *Going South: Why Britain Will Have a Third World Economy By 2014*, Palgrave Macmillan,

Great Britain, 2012, page 84

528 Larry Elliott and Dan Atkinson, *Going South: Why Britain Will Have a Third World Economy By 2014*, Palgrave Macmillan, Great Britain, 2012, page 339

529 Larry Elliott and Dan Atkinson, *Going South: Why Britain Will Have a Third World Economy By 2014*, Palgrave Macmillan, Great Britain, 2012, page 345

530 Pete Comley, *Inflation Tax: the plan to deal with the debts*, published by Pete Comley, Britain, 2013, page 176

531 Mitch Feierstein, Plant Ponzi, Bantum Press, London, 2012, page 158

532 Mitch Feierstein, Plant Ponzi, Bantum Press, London, 2012, page 158

533 Mitch Feierstein, Plant Ponzi, Bantum Press, London, 2012, page 167

534 Mitch Feierstein, Plant Ponzi, Bantum Press, London, 2012, page 172

535 Mitch Feierstein, Plant Ponzi, Bantum Press, London, 2012, page 276

536 Mitch Feierstein, Plant Ponzi, Bantum Press, London, 2012, page 289

537 Mitch Feierstein, Plant Ponzi, Bantum Press, London, 2012, page 307

538 Mitch Feierstein, Plant Ponzi, Bantum Press, London, 2012, page 306

539 Mitch Feierstein, Plant Ponzi, Bantum Press, London, 2012, page 340

540 James Rickards, *Currency Wars*, Penguin Books, London, 2011, page 179

541 Larry Elliott and Dan Atkinson, *Going South: Why Britain Will Have a Third World Economy By 2014*, Palgrave Macmillan, Great Britain, 2012, page 58

542 Mitch Feierstein, Plant Ponzi, Bantum Press, London, 2012, page 230

543 James Rickards, *Currency Wars*, Penguin Books, London, 2011, page 172

544 James Rickards, *Currency Wars*, Penguin Books, London, 2011, page 116

545 Paul Krugman, *End This Depression Now*, WW Norton & Company Ltd, London, 2012, page 168

546 Mitch Feierstein, Plant Ponzi, Bantum Press, London, 2012, page 148

547 Mitch Feierstein, Plant Ponzi, Bantum Press, London, 2012, page 265

548 James Rickards, *Currency Wars*, Penguin Books, London, 2011, page 117

549 James Rickards, *Currency Wars*, Penguin Books, London, 2011, page 117

550 Paul Krugman, *End This Depression Now*, WW Norton & Company Ltd, London, 2012, page 175

551 Michael Pettis, *The Great Rebalancing: Trade, Conflict, and the Perilous Road Ahead for the World Economy*, Princeton University Press, Oxford, 2013, page 121

552 Michael Pettis, *The Great Rebalancing: Trade, Conflict, and the Perilous Road Ahead for the World Economy*, Princeton University Press, Oxford, 2013, page 129

553 Paul Krugman, *End This Depression Now*, WW Norton & Company Ltd, London, 2012, page 179

554 Stephen D King, *When the Money Runs Out: The End of Western Affluence*, Yale University Press, Padstow, 2013, page 236

555 Stephen D King, *When the Money Runs Out: The End of Western Affluence*, Yale University Press, Padstow, 2013, page 236

556 Stephen D King, *Losing Control: The Emerging Threats to Western Prosperity*, TJ International, Padstow, 2010, page 227

557 Stephen D King, *Losing Control: The Emerging Threats to Western Prosperity*, TJ International, Padstow, 2010, page 227

558 Stephen D King, *Losing Control: The Emerging Threats to Western Prosperity*, TJ International, Padstow, 2010, page 227

559 Stephen D King, *Losing Control: The Emerging Threats to Western Prosperity*, TJ International, Padstow, 2010, page 221

560 Stephen D King, *Losing Control: The Emerging Threats to Western Prosperity*, TJ International, Padstow, 2010, page 246

561 Stephen D King, *When the Money Runs Out: The End of Western Affluence*, Yale University Press, Padstow, 2013, page 251

562 Larry Elliott and Dan Atkinson, *Going South: Why Britain Will Have a Third World Economy By 2014*, Palgrave Macmillan, Great Britain, 2012, page 20

563 Larry Elliott and Dan Atkinson, *Going South: Why Britain Will Have a Third World Economy By 2014*, Palgrave Macmillan, Great Britain, 2012, page 23

564 Nicholas Comfort, *The Slow Death of British Industry*, Biteback Publishing, London, 2012, page 24

565 Nicholas Comfort, *The Slow Death of British Industry*, Biteback Publishing, London, 2012, page 76

566 Nicholas Comfort, *The Slow Death of British Industry*, Biteback Publishing, London, 2012, page 77

567 Nicholas Comfort, *The Slow Death of British Industry*, Biteback Publishing, London, 2012, page 29

568 Nicholas Comfort, *The Slow Death of British Industry*, Biteback Publishing, London, 2012, page 69

569 Nicholas Comfort, *The Slow Death of British Industry*, Biteback Publishing, London, 2012, page 184

570 Nicholas Comfort, *The Slow Death of British Industry*, Biteback Publishing, London, 2012, page 186

571 Nicholas Comfort, *The Slow Death of British Industry*, Biteback Publishing, London, 2012, page 187

572 Nicholas Comfort, *The Slow Death of British Industry*, Biteback Publishing, London, 2012, page 45

573 Nicholas Comfort, *The Slow Death of British Industry*, Biteback Publishing, London, 2012, page 65

574 Nicholas Comfort, *The Slow Death of British Industry*, Biteback Publishing, London, 2012, pages 50 and 51

575 Larry Elliott and Dan Atkinson, *Going South: Why Britain Will Have a Third World Economy By 2014*, Palgrave Macmillan, Great Britain, 2012, page 62

576 Nicholas Comfort, *The Slow Death of British Industry*, Biteback Publishing, London, 2012, page 9

577 Nicholas Comfort, *The Slow Death of British Industry*, Biteback Publishing, London, 2012, page 56

578 Nicholas Comfort, *The Slow Death of British Industry*, Biteback Publishing, London, 2012, page 2

579 Nicholas Comfort, *The Slow Death of British Industry*, Biteback Publishing, London, 2012, page 8

580 Nicholas Comfort, *The Slow Death of British Industry*, Biteback Publishing, London, 2012, page 57

581 Nicholas Comfort, *The Slow Death of British Industry*, Biteback Publishing, London, 2012, page 173

582 Nicholas Comfort, *The Slow Death of British Industry*, Biteback Publishing, London, 2012, page 4

583 Alex Brummer, *Britain for Sale*, Random House Business Books, London, 2013, page 107

584 Nicholas Comfort, *The Slow Death of British Industry*, Biteback Publishing, London, 2012, page 315

585 Nicholas Comfort, *The Slow Death of British Industry*, Biteback Publishing, London, 2012, page 336

586 Alex Brummer, *Britain for Sale*, Random House Business Books, London, 2013, page 104

587 Nicholas Comfort, *The Slow Death of British Industry*, Biteback Publishing, London, 2012, page 240

588 Larry Elliott and Dan Atkinson, *Going South: Why Britain Will Have a Third World Economy By 2014*, Palgrave Macmillan, Great Britain, 2012, page 85

589 Larry Elliott and Dan Atkinson, *Going South: Why Britain Will Have a Third World Economy By 2014*, Palgrave Macmillan, Great Britain, 2012, page 228

590 Larry Elliott and Dan Atkinson, *Going South: Why Britain Will Have a Third World Economy By 2014*, Palgrave Macmillan, Great Britain, 2012, page 191

591 Larry Elliott and Dan Atkinson, *Going South: Why Britain Will Have a Third World Economy By 2014*, Palgrave Macmillan, Great Britain, 2012, page 74

592 Larry Elliott and Dan Atkinson, *Going South: Why Britain Will Have a Third World Economy By 2014*, Palgrave Macmillan,

Great Britain, 2012, page 74

593 Larry Elliott and Dan Atkinson, *Going South: Why Britain Will Have a Third World Economy By 2014*, Palgrave Macmillan, Great Britain, 2012, page 229

594 Larry Elliott and Dan Atkinson, *Going South: Why Britain Will Have a Third World Economy By 2014*, Palgrave Macmillan, Great Britain, 2012, page 75

595 Alex Brummer, *Britain for Sale*, Random House Business Books, London, 2013, page 192

596 Larry Elliott and Dan Atkinson, *Going South: Why Britain Will Have a Third World Economy By 2014*, Palgrave Macmillan, Great Britain, 2012, page 252

597 Stephen D King, *When the Money Runs Out: The End of Western Affluence*, Yale University Press, Padstow, 2013, page 45

598 Eamonn Butler, *The Rotten State of Britain*, Gibson Square, London, 2009, page 195

599 Stephen D King, *When the Money Runs Out: The End of Western Affluence*, Yale University Press, Padstow, 2013, page 46

600 Eamonn Butler, *The Rotten State of Britain*, Gibson Square, London, 2009, page 228

601 Eamonn Butler, *The Rotten State of Britain*, Gibson Square, London, 2009, page 207

602 Larry Elliott and Dan Atkinson, *Going South: Why Britain Will Have a Third World Economy By 2014*, Palgrave Macmillan, Great Britain, 2012, page 97

603 Larry Elliott and Dan Atkinson, *Going South: Why Britain Will Have a Third World Economy By 2014*, Palgrave Macmillan, Great Britain, 2012, page 190

604 Larry Elliott and Dan Atkinson, *Going South: Why Britain Will Have a Third World Economy By 2014*, Palgrave Macmillan, Great Britain, 2012, page 199

605 Larry Elliott and Dan Atkinson, *Going South: Why Britain Will Have a Third World Economy By 2014*, Palgrave Macmillan, Great Britain, 2012, page 189

606 Will Hutton, *How Good We Can Be*, Little, Brown, Great Britain, 2015, page 61

607 Will Hutton, *How Good We Can Be*, Little, Brown, Great Britain, 2015, page 62

608 Pete Comley, *Inflation Tax: the plan to deal with the debts*, published by Pete Comley, Britain, 2013, page 95

609 Pete Comley, *Inflation Tax: the plan to deal with the debts*, published by Pete Comley, Britain, 2013, page 97

610 Pete Comley, *Inflation Tax: the plan to deal with the debts*, published by Pete Comley, Britain, 2013, page 98

611 Larry Elliott and Dan Atkinson, *Going South: Why Britain Will Have a Third World Economy By 2014*, Palgrave Macmillan, Great Britain, 2012, page 99

612 Stephen D King, *When the Money Runs Out: The End of Western Affluence*, Yale University Press, Padstow, 2013, page 13

613 Stephen D King, *When the Money Runs Out: The End of Western Affluence*, Yale University Press, Padstow, 2013, page 19

614 Larry Elliott and Dan Atkinson, *Going South: Why Britain Will Have a Third World Economy By 2014*, Palgrave Macmillan, Great Britain, 2012, page 199

615 Larry Elliott and Dan Atkinson, *Going South: Why Britain Will Have a Third World Economy By 2014*, Palgrave Macmillan,

Great Britain, 2012, page 232

616 Larry Elliott and Dan Atkinson, *Going South: Why Britain Will Have a Third World Economy By 2014*, Palgrave Macmillan, Great Britain, 2012, page 257

617 Larry Elliott and Dan Atkinson, *Going South: Why Britain Will Have a Third World Economy By 2014*, Palgrave Macmillan, Great Britain, 2012, page 205

618 Larry Elliott and Dan Atkinson, *Going South: Why Britain Will Have a Third World Economy By 2014*, Palgrave Macmillan, Great Britain, 2012, page 209

619 Larry Elliott and Dan Atkinson, *Going South: Why Britain Will Have a Third World Economy By 2014*, Palgrave Macmillan, Great Britain, 2012, page 348

620 Stephen D King, *When the Money Runs Out: The End of Western Affluence*, Yale University Press, Padstow, 2013, page 112

621 Larry Elliott and Dan Atkinson, *Going South: Why Britain Will Have a Third World Economy By 2014*, Palgrave Macmillan, Great Britain, 2012, page 237

622 Stephen D King, *When the Money Runs Out: The End of Western Affluence*, Yale University Press, Padstow, 2013, page 32

623 Larry Elliott and Dan Atkinson, *Going South: Why Britain Will Have a Third World Economy By 2014*, Palgrave Macmillan, Great Britain, 2012, page 238

624 Stephen D King, *When the Money Runs Out: The End of Western Affluence*, Yale University Press, Padstow, 2013, page 1

625 Stephen D King, *When the Money Runs Out: The End of Western Affluence*, Yale University Press, Padstow, 2013, page 3

626 Alina Barnett, Sandra Batten, Adrian Chiu, Jeremy Franklin and María Sebastiá-Barrie, *Bank of England Quarterly Bulletin*, Q2 2014, page 115

627 James Meadway, The UK's Productivity Puzzle, New Economics Foundation, 24th January 2014

628 David Blanchflower, *The Independent*, 4th January 2015

629 Pete Comley, *Inflation Tax: the plan to deal with the debts*, published by Pete Comley, Britain, 2013, page 121

630 Larry Elliott and Dan Atkinson, *Going South: Why Britain Will Have a Third World Economy By 2014*, Palgrave Macmillan, Great Britain, 2012, page 240

631 Larry Elliott and Dan Atkinson, *Going South: Why Britain Will Have a Third World Economy By 2014*, Palgrave Macmillan, Great Britain, 2012, page 241

632 Will Hutton, *How Good We Can Be*, Little, Brown, Great Britain, 2015, page 41

633 Eamonn Butler, *The Rotten State of Britain*, Gibson Square, London, 2009, page 37

634 Eamonn Butler, *The Rotten State of Britain*, Gibson Square, London, 2009, page 241

635 Eamonn Butler, *The Rotten State of Britain*, Gibson Square, London, 2009, page 242

636 Larry Elliott and Dan Atkinson, *Going South: Why Britain Will Have a Third World Economy By 2014*, Palgrave Macmillan, Great Britain, 2012, page 248

637 Pete Comley, *Inflation Tax: the plan to deal with the debts*, published by Pete Comley, Britain, 2013, page 122

638 Larry Elliott and Dan Atkinson, *Going South: Why Britain Will Have a Third World Economy By 2014*, Palgrave Macmillan, Great Britain, 2012, page 248

639 Pete Comley, *Inflation Tax: the plan to deal with the debts*, published by Pete Comley, Britain, 2013, page 114

640 Michael Pettis, *The Great Rebalancing: Trade, Conflict, and the Perilous Road Ahead for the World Economy*, Princeton University Press, Oxford, 2013, page 3

641 Michael Pettis, *The Great Rebalancing: Trade, Conflict, and the Perilous Road Ahead for the World Economy*, Princeton University Press, Oxford, 2013, page 3

642 *Keynes and Laissez-faire*, edited by AP Thirlwall, MacMillan Press, London, 1978, page 36

643 Pete Comley, *Inflation Tax: the plan to deal with the debts*, published by Pete Comley, Britain, 2013, page 89

644 *Keynes and Laissez-faire*, edited by AP Thirlwall, MacMillan Press, London, 1978, page 36

645 The Times, 4th January, 1975 cited in FA Hayek, A Tiger by the Tail, The Institute of Economic Affairs, Tonbridge, 1978, page xi

646 Robert Dimand, *The Origins of the Keynesian Revolution: The Development of Keynes' Theory of Employment and Output*, Edward Elgar Publishing, Aldershot, 1988, page 71

647 Keynes, Inflation (1919), *Essays in Persuasion: The Collected Writings of John Maynard Keynes*, MacMillan Press Ltd, London, 1972, page 57

648 Robert Dimand, *The Origins of the Keynesian Revolution: The Development of Keynes' Theory of Employment and Output*, Edward Elgar Publishing, Aldershot, 1988, page 8

649 John Maynard Keynes cited in FA Hayek, A Tiger by the Tail, The Institute of Economic Affairs, Tonbridge, 1978, page 3

650 *Keynes and the Modern World*, edited by David Worswick and James Trevithick, Cambridge University Press, Cambridge,

1983, page 227

651 *Keynes and the Modern World*, edited by David Worswick and James Trevithick, Cambridge University Press, Cambridge, 1983, page 227

652 *Keynes and the Modern World*, edited by David Worswick and James Trevithick, Cambridge University Press, Cambridge, 1983, page 227

653 *Keynes and the Modern World*, edited by David Worswick and James Trevithick, Cambridge University Press, Cambridge, 1983, page 227

654 Robert Dimand, *The Origins of the Keynesian Revolution: The Development of Keynes' Theory of Employment and Output*, Edward Elgar Publishing, Aldershot, 1988, page 7

655 John Maynard Keynes cited in FA Hayek, A Tiger by the Tail, The Institute of Economic Affairs, Tonbridge, 1978, page 3

656 *Keynes and the Modern World*, edited by David Worswick and James Trevithick, Cambridge University Press, Cambridge, 1983, page 241

657 John Maynard Keynes, *The General Theory of Employment, Interest, and Money*, Palgrove MacMillan, Basingstoke, 2007, page 303

658 *Keynes and the Modern World*, edited by David Worswick and James Trevithick, Cambridge University Press, Cambridge, 1983, page 241

659 Robert Dimand, *The Origins of the Keynesian Revolution: The Development of Keynes' Theory of Employment and Output*, Edward Elgar Publishing, Aldershot, 1988, page 10

660 Pete Comley, *Inflation Tax: the plan to deal with the debts*, published by Pete Comley, Britain, 2013, page ix

661 Pete Comley, *Inflation Tax: the plan to deal with the debts*, published by Pete Comley, Britain, 2013, page 5

662 Pete Comley, *Inflation Tax: the plan to deal with the debts*, published by Pete Comley, Britain, 2013, page 6

663 Pete Comley, *Inflation Tax: the plan to deal with the debts*, published by Pete Comley, Britain, 2013, page 8

664 James Rickards, *Currency Wars*, Penguin Books, London, 2011, page 170

665 Pete Comley, *Inflation Tax: the plan to deal with the debts*, published by Pete Comley, Britain, 2013, page 64

666 Pete Comley, *Inflation Tax: the plan to deal with the debts*, published by Pete Comley, Britain, 2013, page 65

667 Pete Comley, *Inflation Tax: the plan to deal with the debts*, published by Pete Comley, Britain, 2013, page 72

668 Pete Comley, *Inflation Tax: the plan to deal with the debts*, published by Pete Comley, Britain, 2013, page 75

669 Pete Comley, *Inflation Tax: the plan to deal with the debts*, published by Pete Comley, Britain, 2013, page 78

670 Pete Comley, *Inflation Tax: the plan to deal with the debts*, published by Pete Comley, Britain, 2013, page 90

671 Pete Comley, *Inflation Tax: the plan to deal with the debts*, published by Pete Comley, Britain, 2013, page 91

672 Paul Krugman, *End This Depression Now*, WW Norton & Company Ltd, London, 2012, page 136

673 Paul Krugman, *End This Depression Now*, WW Norton & Company Ltd, London, 2012, page 79

674 Stephen D King, *Losing Control: The Emerging Threats to Western Prosperity*, TJ International, Padstow, 2010, page 68

675 Stephen D King, *When the Money Runs Out: The End of Western Affluence*, Yale University Press, Padstow, 2013, page 119

676 Stephen D King, *When the Money Runs Out: The End of Western Affluence*, Yale University Press, Padstow, 2013, page 119

677 Paul Krugman, *End This Depression Now*, WW Norton & Company Ltd, London, 2012, page 24

678 Paul Krugman, *End This Depression Now*, WW Norton & Company Ltd, London, 2012, page 126

679 Paul Krugman, *End This Depression Now*, WW Norton & Company Ltd, London, 2012, page 53

680 Paul Krugman, *End This Depression Now*, WW Norton & Company Ltd, London, 2012, page 146

681 Paul Krugman, *End This Depression Now*, WW Norton & Company Ltd, London, 2012, page 148

682 Paul Krugman, *End This Depression Now*, WW Norton & Company Ltd, London, 2012, page 155

683 Paul Krugman, *End This Depression Now*, WW Norton & Company Ltd, London, 2012, page 161

684 Paul Krugman, *End This Depression Now*, WW Norton & Company Ltd, London, 2012, page 161

685 Paul Krugman, *End This Depression Now*, WW Norton & Company Ltd, London, 2012, page 165

686 Paul Krugman, *End This Depression Now*, WW Norton & Company Ltd, London, 2012, page 185

687 Pete Comley, *Inflation Tax: the plan to deal with the debts*, published by Pete Comley, Britain, 2013, page 7

688 Pete Comley, *Inflation Tax: the plan to deal with the debts*, published by Pete Comley, Britain, 2013, page 33

689 Ha-Joon Chang, *Bad Samaritans: The Guilty Secrets of Rich Nations and the Threat to Global Prosperity*, Random House, London, 2007, page 30

690 Ha-Joon Chang, *Bad Samaritans: The Guilty Secrets of Rich Nations and the Threat to Global Prosperity*, Random House, London, 2007, page 30

691 James Rickards, *Currency Wars*, Penguin Books, London, 2011, page 147

692 James Rickards, *Currency Wars*, Penguin Books, London, 2011, page 149

693 James Rickards, *Currency Wars*, Penguin Books, London, 2011, page 155

694 James Rickards, *Currency Wars*, Penguin Books, London, 2011, page 157

695 Stephen D King, *Losing Control: The Emerging Threats to Western Prosperity*, TJ International, Padstow, 2010, page 163

696 Stephen D King, *Losing Control: The Emerging Threats to Western Prosperity*, TJ International, Padstow, 2010, page 164

697 Stephen D King, *Losing Control: The Emerging Threats to Western Prosperity*, TJ International, Padstow, 2010, page 165

698 Ha-Joon Chang, *Bad Samaritans: The Guilty Secrets of Rich Nations and the Threat to Global Prosperity*, Random House, London, 2007, page 58

699 Ha-Joon Chang, *Bad Samaritans: The Guilty Secrets of Rich Nations and the Threat to Global Prosperity*, Random House, London, 2007, page 59

700 Stephen D King, *Losing Control: The Emerging Threats to Western Prosperity*, TJ International, Padstow, 2010, page 163

701 John Eatwell, *Whatever Happened to Britain?*, Gerald Duckworth and Co Ltd, London, 1982, page 89

702 Paul Krugman, *The Return of Depression Economics*, Penguin Books, London, 2008, page 60

703 John Eatwell, *Whatever Happened to Britain?*, Gerald Duckworth and Co Ltd, London, 1982, page 138

704 John Eatwell, *Whatever Happened to Britain?*, Gerald Duckworth and Co Ltd, London, 1982, page 139

705 Alan Binder, There are Capitalists and Then There Are Japanese, *Business Week*, 8th October 1990, page 21

706 Chalmers Johnson, Their Behavior, Our Policy, The National Interest, 17, 1989, pages 17-27

707 William Easterly, *The White Man's Burden*, Oxford University Press, Oxford, 2007, page 302

708 Peter Drucker, cited by James Fallows, Looking at the Sun, *The Atlantic Monthly,* November 1993, page 90

709 Chalmers Johnson, Trade, Revisionism, and the Future of Japanese-American Relations.' In Kozo Yamamura (ed.), *Japan's Economic Structure: Should It Change?* Seattle, WA: Society for Japanese Studies, 1990, page 129

710 Chalmers Johnson, Trade, Revisionism, and the Future of Japanese-American Relations.' In Kozo Yamamura (ed.), *Japan's Economic Structure: Should It Change?* Seattle, WA: Society for Japanese Studies, 1990, page 135

711 Karel Van Wolferen, The Japan Problem, *Foreign Affairs*, 65,2 1986, page 302

712 Samual Huntington, Why International Primacy Matters, *The Cold War and After: Prospects for Peace,* Sean Lynn-Jones editor, Cambridge, MA: The MIT Press, pages 72 and 75

713 Samual Huntington, Why International Primacy Matters, *The Cold War and After: Prospects for Peace*, Sean Lynn-Jones editor, Cambridge, MA: The MIT Press, page76

714 Richard Gephardt, Toward a Better US-Japan Partnership in the 21st Century, Address before the Center for National Policy, 6th December 1991

715 Michael Pettis, *The Great Rebalancing: Trade, Conflict, and the Perilous Road Ahead for the World Economy*, Princeton University Press, Oxford, 2013, page 158

716 Michael Pettis, *The Great Rebalancing: Trade, Conflict, and the Perilous Road Ahead for the World Economy*, Princeton University Press, Oxford, 2013, page 158

717 Michael Pettis, *The Great Rebalancing: Trade, Conflict, and the Perilous Road Ahead for the World Economy*, Princeton University Press, Oxford, 2013, page 159

718 Stephen D King, *Losing Control: The Emerging Threats to Western Prosperity*, TJ International, Padstow, 2010, page 78

719 Paul Krugman, *The Return of Depression Economics*, Penguin Books, London, 2008, page 61

720 Paul Krugman, *The Return of Depression Economics*, Penguin Books, London, 2008, page 76

721 James Rickards, *Currency Wars*, Penguin Books, London, 2011, page 38

722 James Rickards, *Currency Wars*, Penguin Books, London, 2011, page 101

723 James Rickards, *Currency Wars*, Penguin Books, London, 2011, page 106

724 James Rickards, *Currency Wars*, Penguin Books, London, 2011, page 107

725 James Rickards, *Currency Wars*, Penguin Books, London, 2011, page 112

726 *The Economist*, 15th October 2011

727 Keith Bradsher, *New York Times*, 23rd June 2009

728 Keith Bradsher, *New York Times*, 23rd June 2009

729 James Rickards, *Currency Wars*, Penguin Books, London, 2011, page 160

730 James Rickards, *Currency Wars*, Penguin Books, London, 2011, page 42

731 James Rickards, *Currency Wars*, Penguin Books, London, 2011, page 163

732 *Financial Times*, 18th July 2015

733 Larry Elliott and Dan Atkinson, *Going South: Why Britain Will Have a Third World Economy By 2014*, Palgrave Macmillan, Great Britain, 2012, page 165

734 Stephen D King, *Losing Control: The Emerging Threats to Western Prosperity*, TJ International, Padstow, 2010, page 17

735 William Easterly, *The White Man's Burden*, Oxford University Press, Oxford, 2007, page 310

736 Stephen D King, *Losing Control: The Emerging Threats to Western Prosperity*, TJ International, Padstow, 2010, page 107

737 James Rickards, *Currency Wars*, Penguin Books, London, 2011, page 103

738 James Rickards, *Currency Wars*, Penguin Books, London, 2011, page 104

739 James Rickards, *Currency Wars*, Penguin Books, London, 2011, page 105

740 Stephen D King, *Losing Control: The Emerging Threats to Western Prosperity*, TJ International, Padstow, 2010, page 20

741 Stephen D King, *Losing Control: The Emerging Threats to Western Prosperity*, TJ International, Padstow, 2010, page 56

742 Stephen D King, *Losing Control: The Emerging Threats to Western Prosperity*, TJ International, Padstow, 2010, page 56

743 James Rickards, *Currency Wars*, Penguin Books, London, 2011, page 109

744 Stephen D King, *Losing Control: The Emerging Threats to Western Prosperity*, TJ International, Padstow, 2010, page 31

745 Stephen D King, *Losing Control: The Emerging Threats to Western Prosperity*, TJ International, Padstow, 2010, page 31

746 Stephen D King, *Losing Control: The Emerging Threats to Western Prosperity*, TJ International, Padstow, 2010, page 59

747 Stephen D King, *Losing Control: The Emerging Threats to Western Prosperity*, TJ International, Padstow, 2010, page 63

748 Stephen D King, *Losing Control: The Emerging Threats to Western Prosperity*, TJ International, Padstow, 2010, page 66

749 Stephen D King, *Losing Control: The Emerging Threats to Western Prosperity*, TJ International, Padstow, 2010, page 61

750 Michael Pettis, *The Great Rebalancing: Trade, Conflict, and the Perilous Road Ahead for the World Economy*, Princeton University Press, Oxford, 2013, page 44

751 Michael Pettis, *The Great Rebalancing: Trade, Conflict, and the Perilous Road Ahead for the World Economy*, Princeton University Press, Oxford, 2013, page 62

752 Michael Pettis, *The Great Rebalancing: Trade, Conflict, and the Perilous Road Ahead for the World Economy*, Princeton University Press, Oxford, 2013, page 10

753 Michael Pettis, *The Great Rebalancing: Trade, Conflict, and the Perilous Road Ahead for the World Economy*, Princeton University Press, Oxford, 2013, page 10

754 Michael Pettis, *The Great Rebalancing: Trade, Conflict, and the Perilous Road Ahead for the World Economy*, Princeton University Press, Oxford, 2013, page 11

755 Michael Pettis, *The Great Rebalancing: Trade, Conflict, and the Perilous Road Ahead for the World Economy*, Princeton University Press, Oxford, 2013, page 11

756 Larry Elliott and Dan Atkinson, *Going South: Why Britain Will Have a Third World Economy By 2014*, Palgrave Macmillan, Great Britain, 2012, page 267

757 Stephen D King, *Losing Control: The Emerging Threats to Western Prosperity*, TJ International, Padstow, 2010, page 105

758 Michael Pettis, *The Great Rebalancing: Trade, Conflict, and the Perilous Road Ahead for the World Economy*, Princeton University Press, Oxford, 2013, page 17

759 Paul Krugman, *The Return of Depression Economics*, Penguin Books, London, 2008, page 43

760 Michael Pettis, *The Great Rebalancing: Trade, Conflict, and the Perilous Road Ahead for the World Economy*, Princeton University Press, Oxford, 2013, page 162

761 Michael Pettis, *The Great Rebalancing: Trade, Conflict, and the Perilous Road Ahead for the World Economy*, Princeton University Press, Oxford, 2013, page 164

762 Michael Pettis, *The Great Rebalancing: Trade, Conflict, and the Perilous Road Ahead for the World Economy*, Princeton University Press, Oxford, 2013, page 17

763 Michael Pettis, *The Great Rebalancing: Trade, Conflict, and the Perilous Road Ahead for the World Economy*, Princeton University Press, Oxford, 2013, page 18

764 Michael Pettis, *The Great Rebalancing: Trade, Conflict, and the Perilous Road Ahead for the World Economy*, Princeton University Press, Oxford, 2013, page 18

765 Michael Pettis, *The Great Rebalancing: Trade, Conflict, and the Perilous Road Ahead for the World Economy*, Princeton University Press, Oxford, 2013, page 37

766 Michael Pettis, *The Great Rebalancing: Trade, Conflict, and the Perilous Road Ahead for the World Economy*, Princeton University Press, Oxford, 2013, page 47

767 Michael Pettis, *The Great Rebalancing: Trade, Conflict, and the Perilous Road Ahead for the World Economy*, Princeton University Press, Oxford, 2013, page 29

768 Michael Pettis, *The Great Rebalancing: Trade, Conflict, and the Perilous Road Ahead for the World Economy*, Princeton University Press, Oxford, 2013, page 53

769 Michael Pettis, *The Great Rebalancing: Trade, Conflict, and the Perilous Road Ahead for the World Economy*, Princeton University Press, Oxford, 2013, page 59

770 Michael Pettis, *The Great Rebalancing: Trade, Conflict, and the Perilous Road Ahead for the World Economy*, Princeton University Press, Oxford, 2013, page 68

771 Michael Pettis, *The Great Rebalancing: Trade, Conflict, and the Perilous Road Ahead for the World Economy*, Princeton University Press, Oxford, 2013, page 78

772 Michael Pettis, *The Great Rebalancing: Trade, Conflict, and the Perilous Road Ahead for the World Economy*, Princeton University Press, Oxford, 2013, page 78

773 Michael Pettis, *The Great Rebalancing: Trade, Conflict, and the Perilous Road Ahead for the World Economy*, Princeton University Press, Oxford, 2013, page 79

774 Michael Pettis, *The Great Rebalancing: Trade, Conflict, and the Perilous Road Ahead for the World Economy*, Princeton University Press, Oxford, 2013, page 80

775 Michael Pettis, *The Great Rebalancing: Trade, Conflict, and the Perilous Road Ahead for the World Economy*, Princeton University Press, Oxford, 2013, page 83

776 Michael Pettis, *The Great Rebalancing: Trade, Conflict, and the Perilous Road Ahead for the World Economy*, Princeton University Press, Oxford, 2013, page 88

777 Michael Pettis, *The Great Rebalancing: Trade, Conflict, and the Perilous Road Ahead for the World Economy*, Princeton University Press, Oxford, 2013, page 85

778 Michael Pettis, *The Great Rebalancing: Trade, Conflict, and the Perilous Road Ahead for the World Economy*, Princeton University Press, Oxford, 2013, page 86

779 Paul Krugman, *End This Depression Now*, WW Norton & Company Ltd, London, 2012, page 221

780 Ha-Joon Chang, *Bad Samaritans: The Guilty Secrets of Rich Nations and the Threat to Global Prosperity*, Random House, London, 2007, page 3

781 Ha-Joon Chang, *Bad Samaritans: The Guilty Secrets of Rich Nations and the Threat to Global Prosperity*, Random House, London, 2007, page 4

782 Ha-Joon Chang, *Bad Samaritans: The Guilty Secrets of Rich Nations and the Threat to Global Prosperity*, Random House, London, 2007, page 7

783 Paul Krugman, *The Return of Depression Economics*, Penguin Books, London, 2008, page 27

784 Ha-Joon Chang, *Bad Samaritans: The Guilty Secrets of Rich Nations and the Threat to Global Prosperity*, Random House, London, 2007, page 7

785 Ha-Joon Chang, *Bad Samaritans: The Guilty Secrets of Rich Nations and the Threat to Global Prosperity*, Random House, London, 2007, page 8

786 Ha-Joon Chang, *Bad Samaritans: The Guilty Secrets of Rich Nations and the Threat to Global Prosperity*, Random House, London, 2007, page 14

787 Ha-Joon Chang, *Bad Samaritans: The Guilty Secrets of Rich Nations and the Threat to Global Prosperity*, Random House, London, 2007, page 9

788 Ha-Joon Chang, *Bad Samaritans: The Guilty Secrets of Rich Nations and the Threat to Global Prosperity*, Random House, London, 2007, page 10

789 Ha-Joon Chang, *Bad Samaritans: The Guilty Secrets of Rich Nations and the Threat to Global Prosperity*, Random House, London, 2007, page 11

790 Ha-Joon Chang, *Bad Samaritans: The Guilty Secrets of Rich Nations and the Threat to Global Prosperity*, Random House, London, 2007, page 12

791 Ha-Joon Chang, *Bad Samaritans: The Guilty Secrets of Rich Nations and the Threat to Global Prosperity*, Random House, London, 2007, page 15

792 Ha-Joon Chang, *Bad Samaritans: The Guilty Secrets of Rich Nations and the Threat to Global Prosperity*, Random House, London, 2007, page 14

793 Ha-Joon Chang, *Bad Samaritans: The Guilty Secrets of Rich Nations and the Threat to Global Prosperity*, Random House, London, 2007, page 61

794 Larry Elliott and Dan Atkinson, *Going South: Why Britain Will Have a Third World Economy By 2014*, Palgrave Macmillan, Great Britain, 2012, page 57

795 Larry Elliott and Dan Atkinson, *Going South: Why Britain Will Have a Third World Economy By 2014*, Palgrave Macmillan, Great Britain, 2012, page 265

796 James Rickards, *Currency Wars*, Penguin Books, London, 2011, page 130

797 Stephen D King, *When the Money Runs Out: The End of Western Affluence*, Yale University Press, Padstow, 2013, page 82

798 Larry Elliott and Dan Atkinson, *Going South: Why Britain Will Have a Third World Economy By 2014*, Palgrave Macmillan, Great Britain, 2012, page 9

799 *Railnews*, 13th February 2009

800 *The Manufacturer*, 28th June 2013

801 *Derby Telegraph*, 7th February 2014

802 Nicholas Comfort, *The Slow Death of British Industry*, Biteback Publishing, London, 2012, page 213

803 *The Manufacturer*, 24th February 2012 and BBC News, 22nd February 2012

804 BBC News, 5th December 2013 and 5th February 2014

805 Will Hutton, *How Good We Can Be*, Little, Brown, Great Britain, 2015, page 55

806 Nicholas Comfort, *The Slow Death of British Industry*, Biteback Publishing, London, 2012, page 94

807 Nicholas Comfort, *The Slow Death of British Industry*, Biteback Publishing, London, 2012, page 70

808 Nicholas Comfort, *The Slow Death of British Industry*, Biteback Publishing, London, 2012, page 166

809 Nicholas Comfort, *The Slow Death of British Industry*, Biteback Publishing, London, 2012, page 218

810 Alex Brummer, *Britain for Sale*, Random House Business Books, London, 2013, page 9

811 Alex Brummer, *Britain for Sale*, Random House Business Books, London, 2013, page 20

812 Alex Brummer, *Britain for Sale*, Random House Business Books, London, 2013, page 52

813 Gwen Robinson, *Financial Times*, 25th June 2007

814 Will Hutton, *How Good We Can Be*, Little, Brown, Great Britain, 2015, page xi

815 Will Hutton, *How Good We Can Be*, Little, Brown, Great Britain, 2015, page 50

816 Will Hutton, *How Good We Can Be*, Little, Brown, Great Britain, 2015, page 53

817 Alex Brummer, *Britain for Sale*, Random House Business Books, London, 2013, page 87

818 Nicholas Comfort, *The Slow Death of British Industry*, Biteback Publishing, London, 2012, page 174

819 Nicholas Comfort, *The Slow Death of British Industry*, Biteback Publishing, London, 2012, page 225

820 Alex Brummer, *Britain for Sale*, Random House Business Books, London, 2013, page 112

821 Nicholas Comfort, *The Slow Death of British Industry*, Biteback Publishing, London, 2012, page 321

822 Alex Brummer, *Britain for Sale*, Random House Business Books, London, 2013, page 113

823 Alex Brummer, *Britain for Sale*, Random House Business Books, London, 2013, page 113

824 Alex Brummer, *Britain for Sale*, Random House Business Books, London, 2013, page 174

825 Alex Brummer, *Britain for Sale*, Random House Business Books, London, 2013, page 184

826 Nicholas Comfort, *The Slow Death of British Industry*, Biteback Publishing, London, 2012, page 128

827 Nicholas Comfort, *The Slow Death of British Industry*, Biteback Publishing, London, 2012, page 202

828 Alex Brummer, *Britain for Sale*, Random House Business Books, London, 2013, page 145

829 Alex Brummer, *Britain for Sale*, Random House Business Books, London, 2013, page 147

830 Alex Brummer, *Britain for Sale*, Random House Business Books, London, 2013, page 142

831 Alex Brummer, *Britain for Sale*, Random House Business Books, London, 2013, page 158

832 Alex Brummer, *Britain for Sale*, Random House Business Books, London, 2013, page 159

833 Alex Brummer, *Britain for Sale*, Random House Business Books, London, 2013, page 154

834 Alex Brummer, *Britain for Sale*, Random House Business Books, London, 2013, page 227

835 Nicholas Comfort, *The Slow Death of British Industry*, Biteback Publishing, London, 2012, page 132

836 Nicholas Comfort, *The Slow Death of British Industry*, Biteback Publishing, London, 2012, pages 213 and 214

837 Nicholas Comfort, *The Slow Death of British Industry*, Biteback Publishing, London, 2012, page 214

838 Nicholas Comfort, *The Slow Death of British Industry*, Biteback Publishing, London, 2012, page 215

839 Dominic Lawson, *Daily Mail*, 19 October 2015

840 Alex Brummer, *Britain for Sale*, Random House Business Books, London, 2013, page 38

841 Alex Brummer, *Britain for Sale*, Random House Business Books, London, 2013, page 70

842 Alex Brummer, *Britain for Sale*, Random House Business Books, London, 2013, page 77

843 Alex Brummer, *Britain for Sale*, Random House Business Books, London, 2013, page 45

844 Alex Brummer, *Britain for Sale*, Random House Business Books, London, 2013, page 115

845 Alex Brummer, *Britain for Sale*, Random House Business Books, London, 2013, page 86

846 ONS, AA6H, 31st March 2015

847 John Mills, Britain's Balance of Payments Disaster, *Demos Quarterly*, 24th October 2014

848 ONS, Balance of Payments, 2014 Q4

849 ONS, Pink Book 2014

850 ONS, UKTrade December 2014, page 43

851 ONS, Balance of Payments, Quarter 4 and Annual 2014, page 29

852 ONS, Balance of Payments, 2014 Q4

853 Michael Pettis, *The Great Rebalancing: Trade, Conflict, and the Perilous Road Ahead for the World Economy*, Princeton University Press, Oxford, 2013, page 162

854 Robert Scott, *Stop Currency Manipulation and Create Millions of Jobs*, Economic Policy Institute, 26th February 2014, page 11

855 Robert Scott, *Stop Currency Manipulation and Create Millions of Jobs*, Economic Policy Institute, 26th February 2014, page 8

856 Robert Scott, *Stop Currency Manipulation and Create Millions of Jobs*, Economic Policy Institute, 26th February 2014, page 12

857 Mitch Feierstein, *Plant Ponzi*, Bantum Press, London, 2012, page 16

858 Mitch Feierstein, *Plant Ponzi*, Bantum Press, London, 2012, page 16

859 Eamonn Butler, *The Rotten State of Britain*, Gibson Square, London, 2009, page 240

860 Stephen D King, *Losing Control: The Emerging Threats to Western Prosperity*, TJ International, Padstow, 2010, page 127

861 Robert Rowthorn, *Large Scale Immigration: its economic and demographic consequences for the UK*, Civitas, August 2014, page 6

862 Robert Rowthorn, *Large Scale Immigration: its economic and demographic consequences for the UK*, Civitas, August 2014, page 15

863 Will Hutton, *The State We're In*, Jonathan Cape, London, 1995, page 8

864 Will Hutton, *How Good We Can Be*, Little, Brown, Great Britain, 2015, page 41

865 Will Hutton, *How Good We Can Be*, Little, Brown, Great Britain, 2015, page 100

866 Will Hutton, *How Good We Can Be*, Little, Brown, Great Britain, 2015, page 121

867 Tim Congdon, *How Much Does The European Union Cost Britain?*, UKIP, Great Britain, September 2014, page 5

868 William Easterly, *The White Man's Burden*, Oxford University Press, Oxford, 2007, page 4

869 William Easterly, *The White Man's Burden*, Oxford University Press, Oxford, 2007, page 35

870 William Easterly, *The White Man's Burden*, Oxford University Press, Oxford, 2007, page 39

871 William Easterly, *The White Man's Burden*, Oxford University Press, Oxford, 2007, page 39

872 William Easterly, *The White Man's Burden*, Oxford University Press, Oxford, 2007, page 40

873 William Easterly, *The White Man's Burden*, Oxford University Press, Oxford, 2007, page 41

874 William Easterly, *The White Man's Burden*, Oxford University Press, Oxford, 2007, page 42

875 William Easterly, *The White Man's Burden*, Oxford University Press, Oxford, 2007, page 42

876 William Easterly, *The White Man's Burden*, Oxford University Press, Oxford, 2007, page 43

877 William Easterly, *The White Man's Burden*, Oxford University Press, Oxford, 2007, page 44

878 William Easterly, *The White Man's Burden*, Oxford University Press, Oxford, 2007, page 45

879 William Easterly, *The White Man's Burden*, Oxford University Press, Oxford, 2007, page 83

880 William Easterly, *The White Man's Burden*, Oxford University Press, Oxford, 2007, page 85

881 William Easterly, *The White Man's Burden*, Oxford University Press, Oxford, 2007, page 57

882 William Easterly, *The White Man's Burden*, Oxford University Press, Oxford, 2007, page 55

883 Thomas Piketty, *Capital in the Twenty-First Century*, TJ International Ltd, Padstow, 2014, page 538

884 Stephen D King, *When the Money Runs Out: The End of Western Affluence*, Yale University Press, Padstow, 2013, page 252

885 Thomas Piketty, *Capital in the Twenty-First Century*, TJ International Ltd, Padstow, 2014, page 539

886 Stephen Tall, The Immigration Choice for the Conservatives – pro-business, or pro-UKIP, *conservativehome.com*, 23rd September 2013

887 Stephen Tall, The Immigration Choice for the Conservatives – pro-business, or pro-UKIP, *conservativehome.com*, 23rd September 2013

888 Stephen Tall, The Immigration Choice for the Conservatives – pro-business, or pro-UKIP, *conservativehome.com*, 23rd September 2013

889 James Kirkup, UKIP vs the free market: Britain's immigration debate gets interesting, *The Daily Telegraph*, 26th September 2014

890 Adam Smith Institute, quoted by James Kirkup, UKIP vs the free market: Britain's immigration debate gets interesting, *The Daily Telegraph*, 26th September 2014

891 Chris Rhodes, Manufacturing: Statistics and Policy, *Briefing Paper Number 01942*, 6th August 2015, House of Commons Library, page 5

892 Chris Rhodes, Manufacturing: Statistics and Policy, *Briefing Paper Number 01942*, 6th August 2015, House of Commons Library, page 9

893 Chris Rhodes, Manufacturing: Statistics and Policy, *Briefing Paper Number 01942*, 6th August 2015, House of Commons Library, page 13

894 Andy Verity, *BBC*, 24th July 2015

895 JK Galbraith, The Great Crash 1929, Andre Deutsch Limited, London, 1980 page 178

Printed in Great Britain
by Amazon